# *My Innocent Absence*

MIRIAM FRANK

# *My Innocent Absence*

TALES FROM A NOMADIC LIFE

ARCADIA BOOKS

Arcadia Books Ltd
15–16 Nassau Street
London W1W 7AB

www.arcadiabooks.co.uk

First published by Arcadia Books 2010

A catalogue record for this book is available from the British Library.

ISBN 078-1-906413-67-5

Typeset in Minion by MacGuru Ltd
Printed and bound in Great Britain by CPI Mackays, Chatham

Arcadia Books gratefully acknowledges the financial support of Arts Council England.

Arcadia Books supports English PEN, the fellowship of writers who work together to promote literature and its understanding. English PEN upholds writers' freedoms in Britain and around the world, challenging political and cultural limits on free expression. To find out more, visit www.englishpen.org or contact English PEN, 6–8 Amwell Street, London EC1R 1UQ

*Arcadia Books distributors are as follows*:

*in the UK and elsewhere in Europe*:
Turnaround Publishers Services
Unit 3, Olympia Trading Estate
Coburg Road
London N22 6TZ

*in the US and Canada*:
Independent Publishers Group
814 N. Franklin Street
Chicago, IL 60610

*in Australia*:
The Scribo Group Pty Ltd
18 Rodborough Road
Frenchs Forest 2086

*in New Zealand*:
Addenda
PO Box 78224
Grey Lynn
Auckland

*in South Africa*:
Jacana Media (Pty) Ltd
PO Box 291784,
Melville 2109
Johannesburg

Arcadia Books is the *Sunday Times* Small Publisher of the Year 2002/03

# Contents

For Louis, Max and Serafim,
tomorrow's people

*One can no longer say: I'm a stranger everywhere,
only 'everywhere I am at home.'*

D.H. Lawrence

# Prologue

'She looks empty.'

Käte.

My mother.

Anna, then thirteen, had just entered the room and was looking at her grandmother from the foot of the bed. Her words rang out softly in the silence of the small bedroom.

Käte lay stretched out, serene, in her bed for one. Alone, much as she had lived her life. The timbre of her laughter, warm tones in her voice, her forceful anger, her tender empathy, all stilled. The furrows on her brow – deepened by her testing life and urgent impatience – smoothed out. Her intense, olive-green eyes, unseeing now, closed for ever.

At peace.

Yes: empty.

On my mother's desk next to Anna, yellow daffodils and Clara's photograph were bathed in the soft spring morning sunlight slanting in through the French windows which looked out onto the small, suburban, back garden – in this, her latest home – in north London. Across the years and in her various homes, she had always kept that photograph of her mother Clara close to her, on her bedside table or her desk: its handsome antique frame dating from her time in Barcelona where the news had reached her of Clara's death in Germany.

During her illness my mother had remarked, 'I've been lucky. I've had a long life. And a good one. Think of all the others ...' She was remembering her friends and family in war-torn Spain, France, Germany, in those event-filled days of her youth. Like them, she too could have had her life cut short, shared their grim fates. And I along with her: long before I understood what was going on around me.

In those times we had been inseparable: mother and child, facing together the perils that threatened everywhere to engulf us. Gone now was the tension – in that motionless face – of her courage and resolve as she faced the Nazi menace sweeping Europe and grappled for our safety. She had been the centre of my world, my everything, then. Till we became estranged ... I had escaped one of history's most infamous, widespread, methodical slaughters, to find myself cut off from my own source.

I had sat with her through the night and accompanied her in her struggle right to the end. Just the two of us, with the nurse hovering in the background. She had not given up easily. I had tried to be with her, to give her what comfort and warmth I could in those, her last moments, as I felt again our closeness from all the way back to when my life was only just starting; before our conflicts and misunderstandings soured our relationship and threw me into confusion.

And now here she lay. Empty. All she had lived through and experienced, embracing three continents and much of the seismic events of the twentieth century, surrendered. She had arrived at her final destination, while I remained cast adrift, seeking my bearings, looking for answers.

Part 1

# DISPERSAL

# From a Big House to a Mattress

*Casablanca, 1941.*

A LARGE PASSAGEWAY … Or was it a veranda? Perhaps more like a big empty hall. The floor was stone, or maybe well-worn marble. Tall, sweeping arches across the length of the wall looked over the street – or were they windows? – opposite our space on the floor against the solid wall. The mattress marked our place. The mattress and the area next to it where all our possessions – in my mother's small square trunk and our old suitcase – now stood. My mother had dug out my nightdress from among our packed clothes; she was now pulling off my dress as I stood facing her on the mattress ready for bed.

The day had been exhilarating. Never before had I seen such long white flowing robes. They glided along, swathing everyone everywhere. Even those old men sitting about on the ground in the dazzling light, by the side of the dirt road, were wrapped in them. *Ce vieux, qu'est-ce qu'il fait là-bas, Maman?* They also flapped around the lively men rushing and shouting behind their stalls in the open-air bazaar – the white canvas overhead curbed the fierce sunlight – as I tiptoed round breathlessly examining their unfamiliar wares, resisting my mother's attempts to move me on. Those crossed red and black leather sandals, Maman, please can I have them? That darling little terracotta jug! But oh, the women! Maman, why can't we see their faces? Darting dark almond eyes tantalisingly imprisoned in the narrow gap between the white veils stretched across their cheekbones and the white cloth draped over their heads to slide down into their fluid white robes. And white here was whiter, in this hot bright light. And everywhere the bustle and chatter, the earthy smells, the dusty dirt paths.

But now it was night-time and we were getting ready for bed. Our mattress. One in a long row of straw mattresses, lying side by side, heads against the wall – on and on, as far as I could see – each lodging a family in transit from Marseilles to Mexico.

'You know, Maman – first we had a big house, then we had a little house, then we had a room, and now we have a mattress.'

The memory of a memory of a memory of a memory … like an image caught on facing mirrors that goes on reverberating till it is almost lost …

∾

*Marseilles, earlier in 1941.*
OUR LAST NIGHT in Marseilles I had spent with Papa in a small hotel by the port. He had come especially to say goodbye and, my mother explained to me, he had asked to be alone with me for those last hours before our departure the next day. As we came through the door into this new room with its fresh clean smell, Papa put down his leather bag. A large bed in the middle, with its foot nearest the window, took up all the space. Papa sat down on the side of the bed, on its cream bedspread. He was strangely quiet and a little list-less, seeming not to know what to do with me now we were here with each other – unlike all our past times together when we had never run out of play and chatter.

He handed me a pair of binoculars out of his bag, and remained silently seated on the bed while I stood on a chair and leaned out of the hotel window trying out all the effects I could produce with this new gadget. It made the ships in the port, beyond our short narrow street, look huge and exceedingly close. I was astonished at the detail coming into view: that ship's bow was now *massive*. I spun the binoculars to point them at the buildings across our street, and their tall shuttered windows came within such close range that I puzzled: if I reach out my hand, I ought to be able to touch them … And yet, when I turned the binoculars round, those same houses became tiny and distant.

Though I didn't know what, there was something important about the occasion. There had been any number of goodbyes in the past, but this seemed different. For one thing, Papa had come. Other times, more often than not, we had waited and waited for him in vain. *Maman, pourquoi Papa dit toujours qu'il vient, et il ne vient pas?*

In Marseilles, my mother and I had lived in an old, run-down hotel some distance from the port. Our room was reached along a dark narrow corridor. On the first floor. As you came in, a large saggy bed with a faded cover, set against the wall on the right, filled the room. On the far wall, a bare window.

Much of our time was spent in that room. All day I could hear the coming and going of people in the corridor. Now and then, someone's footsteps would stop abruptly at our door. Then a knock. Always, they knocked … I sensed the tension roused at the unknown presence on the other side of the door. My mother would sit up, very alert, and ask, '*Qui est là?*' She *always* said that. Once they replied, '*La police,*' and a sudden panic electrified the room for several long seconds. Then relieved laughter, a touch exaggerated and hollow, when a friend walked in. His idea of a joke. The bed came into this too because, if it were the police, our new friends here in Marseilles, Harry and Willi, were supposed to dive between the mattress and the bed frame.

I remember the conversation about it.

'Why do you always ask who's there, Maman?'

'Because if it's the police, Harry and Willi have to hide.'

'Where?' I puzzled, as I looked around the small room with only the bed and a chair in it.

'Under the bed.'

'But the police will see them when they look under it!'

After a moment's thought, she suggested: 'Between the bed and the mattress.' Now, *that* made more sense …

Willi was a quiet young man with kind blue eyes and straw-coloured hair, while Harry was tall and broad-shouldered, had receding dark hair and pale blue eyes like water or the sky. He used to take me, perched high on his shoulders, to fetch oranges from the port when his friends on the ships came in with a cargo of them. Before starting back to the hotel with the small precious load, still within sight of the ships, he would sit me on a ledge and pass me one orange after another, in joyous celebration, impatient to see me feast on them.

Harry also taught me how to box. He went over the rules with me. We would stand in the opposite corners of a room facing each other, more than six feet of Harry at one end and I, four years old, at the other; take three steps towards each other as we counted out loud, 'Eins, zwei, drei', meet in the middle, shake hands, and start boxing. We would swipe at each other with our fists and at the end he lifted my arm in triumph declaring me the winner.

He would also take me to the café when he went to meet his friends. They always sat in animated conversation, around the small round table, sipping their coffee. I wanted coffee too, so Harry would pick a sugar cube from the glass bowl and dip its corner into his black coffee. I would watch, fascinated, as it slowly climbed up the cube, turning it brown, and then he would give it to me. It was *my* coffee – even if it didn't come in a cup.

The bed in the hotel room was also where I lay ill with fever one day. From the bed I could see them, my mother and her friends, talking about it. They were standing to my left, just inside the door, in the narrow space between the bed and the wall. After much discussion they decided to make me sweat out the fever, and everybody brought their blankets and bedcovers and heaped them on top of me. Even Harry's big coat was there. And there I was, in the middle of that enormous bed, my small burning body crushed under that huge weight, drenched in an ocean of sweat, crying and vainly begging to have all that stuff removed from on top of me.

My mother would tell me, years later, that I also suffered from jaundice in Marseilles. She worried I had caught it from a rotten egg. We were rationed to one each per week, and she fed me hers as well as mine, though they were not fresh and one seemed on the point of spoiling.

At mealtimes, when we emptied the plate we shared and there was no more food, I remember breaking our bread and dunking it in oil on which my mother had sprinkled salt, and feasting on this with relish.

Early one morning, I was standing naked on the bed waiting to be dressed when there was a knock on the door.

'Qui est là?'

'Lou.'

'Qui?' my mother let out incredulously.

It was Papa!

6

I was brimming over with joy at his unexpected visit. My mother, though, became very angry and was trying to make him explain himself. He seemed to have come to Marseilles on some unrelated errand and to have decided, as if quite by chance, to drop by. The tense scene turned my first moments of delight into confusion.

By contrast, my mother described another dawn visit to our hotel room of which I recall nothing. Maybe her calm and the unfamiliar visitors, on that occasion, made it unmemorable for me. Or could some dim notion of unimaginable threats looming over us have blocked it from my memory?

It was the police. They had come to arrest my mother.

'What about the girl?'

'We're not taking her. Our orders only mention you.'

'But I can't leave her here all on her own!'

'That's none of our concern. Hurry up now, and come along!'

After some discussion they finally agreed to let her take me to a distant acquaintance, for she could not lead the police to our friends. When they finally arrived at the police station, the official there apologised to my mother and said it was a mistake.

'We're rounding up the men this week,' he explained. 'Next week will be the women's turn. We'll come for you then.'

She was not at the hotel the following week.

My mother also described the time she was caught in the street inside an area cordoned off by the police for a random check of everyone's *papiers*. She had boldly walked up to the police chain, swept down her hands, palms together, to break the grasp between two astonished policemen, and stepped between them to lose herself in the crowd outside.

I remember her taking me to the cinema whenever there was a children's movie, like the newly released *Snow White and the Seven Dwarfs*. And *Tarzan* … I loved watching Tarzan swing on his rope, yodelling across the jungle, with Cheetah close behind. But before the main film, Maréchal Pétain would appear on the screen with his white walrus moustache and braided, cylindrical peaked cap. He would stand to attention saluting or talking with other important-looking men in uniform to the accompaniment of marching music and a barking commentary. I would sense my mother, sitting next to me, stiffen imperceptibly and listen intently – investing those scenes with a mysterious, weighty significance out of my reach ...

We also knew two Maxes in Marseilles. One was stout and the other slim, so I naturally called them Fat Max and Thin Max to tell them apart. Fat Max was bald and wore glasses and had a small car. He sometimes drove my mother and me to the mountains outside Marseilles for a day's outing. It was a treat for me to run about in all that space, just grassy banks and trees and birds and nothing else, without care or restraint. Further over it dipped down into a deep valley, and I remember catching my breath at the sight of the mountains beyond, rising very tall, in a blue haze.

By contrast, our meetings with Thin Max took place at the entrance to a garage-like room, packed with books, papers and a massive printing machine, which we reached through a short, narrow alleyway from the street. Thin Max had a kindly face that broke into a huge beaming smile. Every time we went to meet him, I would stand quietly by while my mother and he engaged in endless, serious-sounding discussions in German, as they faced each other on their feet, at the cobbled entrance to his workroom in a corner hidden from the street.

We also started frequenting an office in downtown Marseilles. My mother lifted me every time on to the wooden counter in front of her, while she spoke to the clerk through the window. He always had a friendly word and playful quip for me. One day, as we were walking away from one of these visits, already out in the street, my mother blurted, 'He still hasn't given me the passport!' and started sobbing uncontrollably. I became very concerned. Apart from the one time, a year earlier, when I spilt the semolina she had prepared for my supper, I had never seen my mother cry. '*Mais comment, Maman*? He's such a nice man! I'm sure he'll give it to you,' I tried to console her. And she laughed, her tears not yet dry.

I spoke French well by now – after my earlier period of *Franspañol* when we first moved to France from Barcelona. In Marseilles, people frequently remarked, '*La petite, elle parle si bien le Français!*'

We were walking down a street towards the port one day: my mother, Harry, Willi and I. Harry and Willi were like our brothers: we were all in this together, whatever it was that was going on around us, the bond unbreakable. Today the tone of their conversation that came down to me, from above my head, was distinctly more serious and animated than usual. Suddenly my mother turned to me and, with uncommon solemnity, said I should now say goodbye to Willi.

In the corner of a small garden square off the street, he squatted down to my level, looked at me closely and tenderly, put his arms around me, gave me a kiss and said goodbye.

In the midst of all the flurry around me, I may have had a glimmering notion that we were preparing for a departure more momentous and far reaching than all the others. Or that my mother had at last been given our stateless travel document. Though I remember little of any of this – maybe the adults were too busy with their fevered preparations to take much notice of me.

*Saying goodbye to Willi in Marseilles*

Harry would be on the same ship as us on our journey to Mexico through Casablanca.

But not Willi. I never saw Willi again.

∾

*Barcelona, 1936.*
PHOTOGRAPHS CAPTURING STILLS of my mother's life in the 1930s, in her native Germany, England and finally Spain, show her slim and attractive: her eyes defiant, even tiger-like, in some, tender and smiling in others, her pose often sensuous, her stance assured. Crisp cotton blouses and long linen skirts accentuate her athletic figure, and in an early movie clip shot by the Penrose family – with whom she stayed in their home in Bloomsbury and holidayed in Wales – she takes long-legged, pendular strides when she moves.

In later life my mother sometimes referred, with some apparent regret, to the many suitors of her youth. Of these, she always remembered with the greatest affection and admiration the Galician actor Alexander Granach – who wrote the book *Da geht ein Mensch* – from her time as a spirited young girl in 1920s Berlin. Though that city's heyday was then at its height, its rich cultural and liberal ambience was already clashing with the gathering, sinister political unrest, which finally led her to leave her homeland.

She chose to come and live in Barcelona, along with Seppel – a close friend since their nurse training days in Stuttgart's children's hospital. They formed a lively and captivating pair: dark-haired Käte, with her intense sparkling eyes, from a liberal Jewish background, and Seppel, with her chiselled face and cropped blonde hair, from a Roman Catholic one.

The two women soon formed part of Barcelona's bohemian scene and politically active circles. And here, amid new friendships and acquaintances, my mother met my father Lou. They were drawn to each other, started a relationship, and decided to have a child.

*Seppel and Käte in Spain, 1933–34*

Even so, theirs remained a free liaison. Lou's time was taken up with his business and other unspecified activities for which he often travelled. He was away during much of Käte's pregnancy – though he would be present at my birth and give my mother his devoted support throughout her difficult labour.

When Käte became pregnant, she and Seppel returned to the Mallorcan mountain village of Deyá, which they had grown to love on previous visits. They rented one of the last houses in Es Clot where Deyá starts petering out on the way down to the *cala:* the small secluded bay reached after walking down through the rocky olive groves to the tinkling sound of goat bells in the soft vibrant light which permeates through the Mallorcan landscape. Photographs show them stretched out on the rocks, exposed to the sun, in the empty *cala*. My mother would also wistfully recall their long walks across the hills or along the coast, and the bunches of flowers and baskets full of fruit which they found on their return, left on their kitchen table by the local people.

She would always refer to her times in Deyá as her idyll. The Deyá of the 1930s: a peaceful mountain village poised above the sea with a warm, gracious local community and a small handful of foreign artists and writers.

*Seppel in Deyá*

In March I was born. In July, the Spanish Civil War broke out. My father took a large country house in La Floresta, half-an-hour's train ride inland from Barcelona. In a photograph, it has a high slanting roof, tall windows and a spacious balustraded terrace overlooking the wooded mountains nearby. My father joined us at weekends. Some of my earliest memories are of him lifting me in the air, nibbling my toes, kissing the soles of my feet, and blowing raspberries into my soft plump belly, rubbing his face against it and making me laugh. Visiting friends also fussed around me, and the local children played with me and took me for walks. My mother told how, when bombers flew overhead, she encouraged me to clap my hands playfully.

My earliest memories converge on the sensuous: the infinite softness of my mother's earlobe which I fondled while I sucked my other thumb to go to sleep. And her attempts to persuade me to use my own, which I didn't readily agree to as it felt nowhere near as magically silken smooth as hers … I also recall her eyes, soft and tender and shining with love, as she looked down at me in her arms and sang to me:

*Lou at La Floresta, 1936*

*The house at La Floresta*

*Meine süsse, meine süsse,*
*Meine kleine, kleine süsse M ...*

They called me *mimosa*, maybe for my moody sensibility.

My mother described how, as soon as I was crawling, I went missing on several occasions. One night, on finding my cot empty, she combed every room, up and down stairs – which she didn't believe me yet capable of manoeuvring – and throughout the whole house. At last, stepping out into the garden, she found me sitting there on the ground, gazing silently, enrapt, at the full moon. My most memorable escapade was the time she discovered me, after several hours' anxious search and many enquiries, in a caravan already a long way from home, playing happily with the children of a family of gypsies who had accepted me as one of their own.

In La Floresta, I had a special Catalan friend, Lali, who taught me the sense of ownership. Up till then I had thought everything belonged to everyone. But Lali would not let go of a toy: '*Es meu*,' she would say, and I could not have it. In the photo album my mother made and saved, on the pages marked Spring 1937, one has photos showing Lali and me tumbling about in the snow in warm woolly clothes from head to foot, and in the next we are seen lying in light cotton dresses under large umbrellas sheltering from the hot sun.

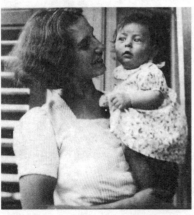

*Käte and myself, Barcelona, 1936*

I was growing in La Floresta, free and happy, surrounded by friends, affection and the countryside. My album's photos show me playing in the garden with the local children and reading books upside down on my lap. I was also speaking Spanish well by then. With so much to absorb me, and so many good neighbours to attend to me and keep me busy and entertained, I did not miss my mother on her increasingly frequent errands to Barcelona on behalf of the ongoing war efforts.

*My early life in La Floresta*

But the idyll was not to last.

As Franco's troops were closing in, my father – who never lived with us, but seemed to come to the rescue every now and then – drove us in his old Ford convertible along the path of a column of Spanish refugees to the coastal village of Collioure on the French side of the Pyrenees.

*Collioure, 1938.*

ON HIS VISITS, my father took obvious pleasure in taking a walk with me.

I remember strolling with him along the road by the sea, my hand in his, my arm held high to reach it. We were on our way back home, a small cottage further along the coast road. As a rule I tired of walking: I would start lagging behind and finally squat down, refuse to budge, and call out 'Oopah! Oopah!' till an adult turned back, lifted and carried me. This time, I was walking. There was a sense of calm and communion between us alone on that long winding road. To our right the sea stretched away to merge, far out, into the sky.

The bright light of day was fast fading into an intense blushing dusk. All around me the radiance of the evening light was dissolving into glowing corals and pinks, filling me with wonder. I threw back my head to gaze into the immense space above us, picking out the pinpoint, palpitating stars coming to life, one by one, in the soaring depths of the darkening sky. In the enveloping peace with my father by my side, the vastness of the universe suddenly struck me with breathtaking clarity, flooding me with a sense of awe I could barely contain.

The moment froze and fixed in my memory.

Our kitchen in Collioure was a simple workbench in a short passage leading to the side access to the cottage. My mother stood bent over the worktop making sandwiches, the door next to her ajar. She would go through it with the food she had prepared, along the side of the cottage to the front gate, and back to the kitchen for more, to distribute it among the people walking past our house in an interminable slow column. She always threw herself into this activity with an intense sense of purpose, lending it a peculiar importance.

This time, as I stood watching her at work, she handed me a jug of milk and said to take it out while she buttered more bread. A flush of excitement gripped me as I stepped up from mere observer in these events to active participant, and a tremendous sense of my usefulness, small as I was, swept through me. I went to the gate holding the jug of milk very tightly in front of me, as though it was the most precious thing in the world, and lifted it towards them. Someone took it from me and passed it to a gaunt-looking man with dark burning eyes who pressed it against his lips and took two feverish gulps. He then lifted it high to pass it over their heads to someone else. This person did the same. I watched, puzzled, as the jug passed from one to another, each time to someone pointed out by those who were nearest as being in particular need, yet even so no one taking more than one or two mouthfuls. I wondered: why don't they drink it all up if they are so thirsty?

I didn't know who they were, where they came from or were going to – only that these were the people my mother was feeding with so much resolve. They appeared to have been walking a long time; they looked tired, sweaty, unshaven, hungry and thirsty. They were heading up the coast. Away from Spain and into France.

The sand on the beach in Collioure was grainy and silvery. I busied myself digging, heaping and shaping it, in sight of the old stone

*The exodus from Franco's Spain passing through Collioure*

church by the lighthouse. Walking along the water's edge, I loved to examine the clear, smoothly rounded wobbly jellyfish washed up along the shoreline, their rims overhung with delicate frills and an intricate radial pattern inside their transparent flesh. I played and splashed in the water too, but when my mother went in the sea and swam out of sight, my usual pluck abandoned me and I cried desperately for her to come back – *Mami! Mami! Mami!* – for the water out there became a vast silent mass stretching away into a disquieting unknown.

In another part, the shoreline was rocky. There I liked scrambling up the warm craggy rocks on my bare feet till I reached the highest point. I stand – in one photograph – with a spotted kerchief around my head, my arms outstretched, naked, on the rocky summit.

A carousel came to town. I loved riding on its bobbing horses and waving to Mami every time it came round to where she stood. She always waved back with her handkerchief and a bright, loving smile. My father visited us again around this time. Wishing to give me a treat, he took me to the carousel. He fondly lifted me onto a bobbing horse, but when the carousel turned to where I had left him and I waved excitedly at him – Papá's place was empty …

My mother and I, instead, spent all our time in each other's company. I now see how important I must have been to her too, in her increasing isolation. I can still hear her tender voice, as she delved into her fond memories of happier times and summoned up lively Spanish folk and children's songs to share with me.

'La cucaracha, la cucaracha ...'

∽

FROM LA FLORESTA to Collioure had been a gentle change for me. My mother was always there for me and I relished the closeness of the sea. Aged two, I was already very articulate, and – my mother's friends being mostly from Spain – we continued to speak Spanish here though French was seeping into my consciousness too. My father didn't live with us any more than he had in La Floresta, but I loved his sporadic visits. In a letter to her sister, Lotte, my mother wrote, 'I haven't heard from Lou for a month, I have no idea where he is, and he hasn't sent any money. We have nothing to eat ...'

*My mother with me in Collioure, 1938*

Even so, she would have said that the greatest suffering was borne by all those refugees, fleeing from Franco's Spain, who streamed past our house. In later years, my mother spoke of her visits to the concentration camp at nearby Argeles, where many were interned. She went to see one of her friends, Ortega, who was ill, and she took him food and warm clothes. At the end of one of her visits, she went up to a guard:

'Would you allow Ortega to come as far as the gate with me, please? I need some help with this large package!'

The guard waved his assent.

Reaching the gate, she grabbed Ortega's hand. 'Come on, let's run!' she urged him, and dragged the feverish man across a field and over a fence until they were out of the camp's view.

They managed to get away.

∽

IN A BUNDLE of German letters my mother wrote to Lotte in 1939 and '40, the earliest is from Collioure, dated 3 February 1939. Her sister had suggested my mother should leave France for her own safety and join her. I have translated Käte's reply here:

'... if everything before me did not appear so black and grim and deso-late, I would do everything in my power to join you and see how we can go on. I fully sympathise with your frame of mind ... But Lotte, think of it as a temporary refuge. What I have lived through these last few days here, has been maybe even worse than everything I expe-rienced in the war in Spain itself. Thousands of people fleeing with nothing other than what they can carry on their bodies, the poorest of the poor, workers, university professors, children, in small rowing boats or on foot, chased by planes that keep spraying their wretched paths with machine-gun fire, in snow and in rain, at night, almost starved, that is how they arrive here. I have seen things which I can never forget, that will weigh on me for ever, I no longer know what to think or feel any more. Dead children in bundles, dying soldiers far from their army hospitals. I have the house full of people. We feel a common bond, we understand each other as though we had always known one another. I couldn't leave here now, I couldn't even think of it. I must stay here, till we all know where we can go, I would not wish to abandon my friends ...'

Yet we left Collioure not long after. I shall never know what prompted our move to the small, unknown village of Foëcy in the centre of France.

*Foëcy, 1939.*
I WAS UNDRESSED and put into a big bed in the far corner of the back room. From my new position, I could hear them in the front room still chattering animatedly around the table, which – when I had left it a short while ago – was strewn untidily with the remains of the dinner they had shared with us. We had had a leisurely meal of several courses amid much talking between the family of the house and my mother. It was very late, well past my usual bedtime. On our arrival earlier that evening, the family had sat my mother

and me down at their table and treated us like old friends, though we were meeting for the first time.

I was soon joined in bed by an older girl and a young woman: all three of us tucked in together. I lay in the middle. Feeling warm and cosy between my two new friends, and perhaps as a mark of my command of the situation, I rested one leg across each of my bed companions' warm soft tummies and promptly fell asleep.

This family shared everything with us. The older couple became Yaya and Yayo: the Catalan terms for grandma and granddad which my mother gave them, maybe to compensate for the absence of my own. There were also two girls older than me, Claude and Michèle, and two young women, Jeanne and Marguerite. The two-bedroomed cottage had a small front garden where flowers grew and a larger backyard with rabbits, chickens, the coalhouse and latrine: a shed containing a wooden bench with a hole in the middle. I always hung on tightly to the edge of the bench and leant well forwards, as the hole seemed alarmingly large for my small rump and I feared falling into the cesspit below. The railway ran right next to the house and across the street. Every now and then a loud bell announced the next train followed by a lot of noise and shaking as it rattled past.

Living closely with this family in Foëcy, my speech was now a melange of French and Spanish.

I enjoyed playing with Claude and Michèle. Sometimes we picnicked all together on a sandy bank of the River Cher. Another member of the family, André, treated me to cycling jaunts along the small country roads. He sat me on the back of his bicycle and I clung to him, my legs raised high from the turning wheels.

*Yayo, with me on his shoulders, and Yaya in Foëcy in 1939*

We were cycling one mild peaceful day beside the Cher as it flowed lazily through the countryside with rows of leafy trees along its borders, when I momentarily forgot or grew tired and my left heel became caught in the revolving wheel. At the sight of my torn shoe and bleeding heel, I took fright and started crying. Young André lifted me in his arms and carried me through the trees and down the steep bank to the river's edge where he held me on his lap and bathed my foot – ever so gently – in the cool flowing water. The bleeding stopped and I calmed down. Years later my mother would tell me the local people believed the waters of the Cher had healing powers – but the way I remember it, it was André's tenderness and caring concern that brought me relief.

I also made friends with a little boy in the village. One day he showed

*Michèle, Claude and myself in the River Cher*

me his beautiful new, bright red tricycle. Next time Papa came to visit us I told him that what I wanted more than anything else in the world was a bright red tricycle. When, on his next visit, he produced a brand new, shiny, bright red tricycle for me, I was beside myself with joy.

A few days later, after he had left again, my mother set off with me and the tricycle for a picnic. We came upon a green field, with a large spreading tree in the middle, where the path reached the river. This was a good spot to try out my new tricycle, my mother said. We were settling down at the foot of the tree for a bite to eat first, when a bull suddenly appeared and came towards us. My mother grabbed my hand and started running round and round the tree, with the bull close behind. After circling the tree for what to me seemed an eternity, the bull finally gave up its chase, ambled slowly to the foot of the tree, examined the red tricycle with interest, bashed it with its horns into a useless piece of twisted metal, and walked away ... My mix of emotions here turns into a blur in my memory: I may have been in too much shock, or too relieved, at having escaped the bull's wrath, to give vent to my dismay at the mauling of my cherished tricycle. Or maybe my distress, like Munch's silent scream, was unable to break free, for by now the loss of something recently gained was so commonplace an occurrence that I had learned to expect it. 'Aguántate!', the word I remember hearing most often from my mother – Spanish for something between 'restrain yourself', 'bottle it up', 'choke it back' – was becoming deeply embedded in my psyche.

Yayo had an orchard outside the village where he grew tomatoes. My mother sometimes walked with me down the long dirt road to the orchard where she would chat with Yayo while he tended the plants. Once, as we stood among the tomato plants watching him at work, he told my mother the news of a bridge breaking with a train on it, and a large number of people drowning at sea. The horror of the scene was conveyed to me through my mother's shocked response.

One day Yayo's old father died. It was my first encounter with death. I became very troubled by this new idea that there is an end to life. *Everyone's*, including my mother's and my own. My mother was the most important person in the world. We were one: indivisible. She never left my thoughts. She was my guardian, provider and protector. And I, in turn, suffered when I saw her sad and laughed when she was happy. I would have done anything for her. I couldn't imagine a world without my mother. Anything else was dispensable, but not her. And now she was telling me that there would, one day, be an end to her life ...

My mother and I moved to the old man's now empty room. Its one door and window looked out onto a bleak concrete courtyard round the back of the building. It was dark inside. There were a bed, a table, and a small cooking stove. One evening my mother was dishing out some semolina she had just finished cooking. As she passed it to me, the pot fell and it spilt. My mother suddenly broke into uncontrollable sobbing. I had never before seen her cry. What's more, I thought only children cried: that mothers could cry had never even entered my head. I was very upset. I thought it was because I had spilt the semolina, but she said no.

'Why are you crying?' I insisted.

'I'll tell you some day. When you're older.'

I never forgot and, one day – many years later, when I decided I must now be old enough to know – I asked my mother why she had cried that night in Foëcy when I spilt the semolina.

'I can't remember,' she said.

The following is an excerpt from a letter my mother wrote to Lotte at around this time, which describes her situation.

19.10.39

*My dear Lotte,*

*I turn to you for refuge, for life is difficult to bear, lonely as I am. It is midnight. One of those nights one doesn't forget in a lifetime, so sad are they. Even little Miri is not here with me, she is with a good elderly lady who looks after her while I am at work. Every morning at seven o'clock I ride my bicycle across country for one hour in cold, rainy weather to work at a farmer's. Ten hours a day for 25 francs. Now is the vine harvest, then the sugar beet, then I must see how to go on. At seven every evening, I return dead tired, hardly able to stand upright, into this cold room. There is no one waiting for me, no warm soup, the bed still unmade. The mice in the cupboard have been eating the bread and cheese. I take off my wet clothes, wash myself and go to Miri, who is well looked after but says she is very sad on my account. I give her some food and put her to bed and go home and am too tired to light a fire and eat nothing and get undressed and lie down in my bed and knit till my lids drop. Only today I can't, for I am too wretched ... And tomorrow morning when it is still dark, I'll put on my clothes which are still wet, sit on my borrowed bicycle and go back to work ten hours, bent double or squatting. Lou is in Paris and I have no idea what he does there. He sends very little money very irregularly, not even enough for Miri alone.*

The knitting mentioned in the letter refers to clothes she knitted for soldiers to earn some extra francs: worth one centime in today's currency. Though my father appears to have contributed little towards our upkeep, he writes in his autobiographical notes that he amassed a fortune in Spain, and friends he knew in Paris during the war said he was well off at the time.

All this may account for her distress that night.

Though she also writes, in another letter, of her tormented love for a Spaniard who had been obliged to leave her without explanation ...

On the brief occasions when I saw my mother during this period, I felt sad at her sadness without understanding it – though she tried her best to shield me from it, having placed me in Yayo and Yaya's care. I had taken no time to settle in to my new circumstances in Foëcy, and my life had acquired a certain rhythm of its own with that warm generous family who had adopted us in this small French village and its peaceful rural surroundings.

But that was to be short-lived and, once again, come to an abrupt end.

SITTING ON MY MOTHER'S LAP, on the front aisle seat near the driver, we were hemmed in by people standing pressed against us with their various pieces of luggage. Ours too was on the floor, at my mother's feet. It had long turned dark, and I kept dozing off and vaguely waking again with the interruption of the movement and the noise each time the bus stopped, dimly aware of my body's total floppiness, my closed lax eyelids, the unbroken rhythm of my breathing, the warmth of my mother's body against mine and her strong arms firmly clasped around me while voices and shuffling resumed as people brushed past to get off the bus and others climbed on and squeezed into the crowd with the humid smell of old worn overcoats. Then the rickety bus would lurch forward as the engine noise picked up again and my body once more would start shaking monotonously against my mother's while the bus rattled along the road and changed pitch in a sequence I had learned by now. In my suspended state between sleep and waking, I was surprised to still find ourselves in this bus well into the night – for, as a rule, night-time meant bedtime. But I trusted implicitly that my mother would know when and where we were to get off, and accepted our situation in that old bus in the middle of the night as a matter of course.

~

IT WAS LATE AFTERNOON when we walked up a garden path to an isolated country house. My mother knocked at the front door. It opened cautiously and a woman hastily and silently bade us enter. Inside, everything was crisp and clean, warm and welcoming. The woman barely talked, and then only in a low, quiet voice, yet she was unusually attentive to our every need. She led us upstairs to a small attic room with two freshly made beds and a view out over the fields. We left our suitcase there.

Back downstairs, she sat us down at a table in a small alcove in the far corner of the main room. It was covered with a clean, checked tablecloth and napkins, and our places were laid with care. The woman served us a hot country soup and fresh bread and butter. I hadn't had food as sublimely delicious as far back as I could remember. Before going to bed, I asked to go out into the garden. After marked hesitation, my mother finally relented and accompanied me outside, but with a disquiet that puzzled me. As we stood on the garden path looking out towards the yellow fields gently swaying under a light wind in the late evening sun-light, I became aware of a sweet, insistent, silvery sound which surged forth in strong regular bursts from the whole countryside and invaded my head.

'What's that noise, Maman?'

'The crickets. They're singing.'

'What's that? Crickets?'

'Small insects that make music in the evenings ...'

The next morning the woman served us a homely breakfast with the same care and attention.

I was happy. I liked it here.

But the moment we finished our meal, my mother hurriedly collected our suitcase, took me by the hand, said goodbye to the woman, and started back to the road.

'Where are we going, Maman? *C'est bien ici!*'

'We have to catch the bus.'

'*Non, Maman! Non*! I don't want to go! I want to stay here!' I insisted, distraught, while my mother forcibly dragged me, crying noisily, past the lovely flowers along the garden border I had enjoyed the previous evening, back to the road to wait for another bus.

∾

AN OLD POSTCARD from Chemnitz, Germany, yellowed with age, dated 14 November 1940, is addressed to a Mlle Jacqueline Maurice at an address in Montauban, to thank her profusely and with great courtesy for her news of the wellbeing of the sender's daughter, Käte, and the child, about whom he had not heard anything in a long time. It is signed Oscar Lichtenstein. Another card, sent on 17 September 1941, to the same recipient and address, is from the Red Cross in Geneva. It relays Monsieur Oscar Lichtenstein's thanks and joy at receiving further news of his daughter and grandchild.

∾

MY MOTHER, in later years, said we had left Foëcy in a rush when she heard the motorcycles of German troops entering the village. She had climbed out of the window with me and a few possessions – might they have been packed already in anticipation? – avoiding the door in case the Germans had already come for her, and we walked across the fields to the next village to continue by bus towards the free, unoccupied zone.

My father spoke on another occasion of taking us in his old Ford convertible, along a road full of fleeing refugees, to Biarritz.

I never worked out how these accounts fitted together, or with my memories of the long bus journeys and the isolated country house, or with my grandfather's postcards.

Once or twice I stayed with my father at the home for Spanish children refugees, which he ran for the Quakers, in Biarritz.

Small, square tables, with four children at each, filled the dining room. My father – the only adult among all those children in the room – always sat me at his table next to him. Our meal was likely to consist of a thin soup into which we broke pieces of bread, followed by a glass of water and more bread (*'Qu'est-ce que tu as mangé?'* my mother asked me once when she came to see me. *'De l'eau avec du pain.' 'Et après?' 'Du pain avec de l'eau,'* I remember replying after a moment's thought, noting the pattern with interest.) The usual dessert was a pudding with raisins. My father would carefully pick out all his raisins and pass them on to my plate, and I dutifully ate up both our portions. One day, faced with yet another heap of them on my plate, I finally asked him:

'Why do you always give me your raisins, Papa?'

'Because I don't like them.'

'I don't either.'

*'Et alors!* Why didn't you say so?'

He sometimes sang to me in his deep, relaxed, bass voice, which gave me a sense of peace and calm, an old Spanish song that he was clearly fond of:

*Ya se van los pastores, a la Extremadura ...*
*y se queda la tierra triste y oscura ...*

I also stayed sometimes with my mother in Anglet, near Biarritz. I remember standing with her on the platform of its small railway station. If we took the train going down the line, we were on our way to Biarritz to see Papa. If we took the train up the line, we were going to Bayonne for my mother's shopping.

∾

THE CAPRICIOUS NATURE of memory ... It guards an indelible record of the small heaps of raisins my father always passed on to me at the children's home, and my restraint of my dislike of them so as not to let him down in his belief that he was pleasing me, yet not a trace of the emotional reunion with my mother on the day she appeared heavily escorted by armed German military officials.

My mother, though, never forgot it. She gave her account of that event on several occasions, and it was remarkably consistent down to the last detail.

The Germans had taken Biarritz and it was no longer safe for her to stay in the area. My father, however, as an American citizen, was quite safe and could move about freely. My mother left me with him in Biarritz while she went to Marseilles, in the free zone under the Vichy government, to check the situation and find somewhere for us to live, relying on his word to return me to her a week later. But he didn't. After another week, she decided to go and fetch me herself. To get back to Biarritz she needed a special permit, a *laissez-passer*. A friend, Nina, who had cultivated an official so as to aid her friends in trouble, managed to procure one for her, and she set off.

When the train arrived at the border with the occupied zone, it ground to a halt. The German military police, the feared *Feldgendarmerie*, rifles slung over their shoulders and their conspicuous identifying metal plaques swinging from their necks, came on board and proceeded to check everybody's papers. My mother watched them calmly as they made their way to where she was sitting.

'Your *laissez-passer*?' one of them requested on reaching her.

She dug into her handbag and passed it to him. He examined it with interest and called the others over to take a look.

'Where did you obtain this permit?'

'It's written there. It has the officer's signature,' she pointed out nonchalantly.

They scrutinised it further and exchanged some words with each other before turning to her again.

'This permit is not satisfactory. Not even the *Führer* himself would have the right to sign this paper. You must get off the train and come with us.'

It was early evening. They escorted her through the gathering twilight to a large country house appropriated from its French owners and turned into their quarters. Once there, she was taken to an upstairs room completely emptied of its contents apart from one large table. They stood her in front of the bare table – the only object on it a prominently placed pistol pointing in her direction – and proceeded to interrogate her. One officer sat behind the table while the others stood or stalked about the room in their polished leather boots.

She assumed the role of a naive young German girl uninterested in politics or the current situation.

'Where are you from?'

'Chemnitz.'

'What's your father's name?'

'Oscar Lichtenstein.'

'Isn't that a Jewish name?'

'Oh, no! I don't think so!' with a devil-may-care voice and gesture.

'What's his job?'

Here she had to navigate carefully around the facts, as referring to him as a *manager* might rouse further suspicion.

'He's the foreman at the Chemnitz Strumpf und Handschuh factory.'

'The factory's address?'

'*Wiesenstrasse* 56.'

'What was your last job before you left Germany?'

Here again she had to come up with an answer in character with the part she was playing.

'I was a factory worker at Sigmund Goeritz's' – a textile factory, owned by one of her father's business associates, where her brother Fritz had been apprenticed with a view to becoming assistant manager.

'Its address?'

'It's on the corner of *Zwickauerstrasse* and *Ulmenstrasse.*'

'Why are you crossing into the occupied zone?'

'I'm on my way to pick up my small daughter in Biarritz.'

'Where is your husband? What's his name?'

Another tricky question. Lou, with his soulful look, dark hair and aquiline nose, would in all likelihood be recognised as a Jew, though his American citizenship gave him immunity from Nazi persecution, given America's non-intervention policy in 1940. But she, passing herself off as a gentile German, would have been forbidden to marry a Jew. On the other hand, a Spanish friend who had recently gone to Mexico was working for a jewellery firm with a Nazi connection that might be looked upon favourably by her interrogators.

'A Spaniard by the name of Farés. He emigrated to Mexico and I'm planning to join him.'

'What's his work?'

'He works for a jewellery firm.'

'Its address?'

From some remote corner of her mind the name and address of the jewellery business came to her rescue.

They nodded their approval.

And so on, relentlessly, till the early hours of the morning. She was finally shown into a bedroom on the upper floor of the house where she was told she could sleep for what remained of the night. In the meantime, they were going to contact headquarters and check out all her answers. Before allowing her to retire, they gave her two bowls of a watery soup to take down to the cellar where they were holding two men in an iron-grilled cage. As she passed them their supper, they looked at each other silently ... not a whisper exchanged between them. She hastily returned upstairs.

My mother lay on the bed, wide awake, pretending to sleep. In the morning, the young German officers greeted her cheerfully. They had checked it all out. It was all true. The factories she had named in Chemnitz *did* exist. The addresses *were* correct. And so on. They were satisfied. So far. They would drive her to Biarritz to fetch her daughter.

'You can't imagine how marvellous it feels to be with a *real* young German woman again!' one of them enthused as they all sat down to breakfast.

On their way, the German driver kept looking at her suspiciously.

'You wouldn't have got away with it if the boss had been here,' he would jeer at her, full of hostility, when they were alone for a moment. 'He's away for a few days. You don't know how lucky you are.'

When they arrived in Biarritz, my mother led them, not to the children's home where my father was, but to another where María, Ortega's wife, was also helping look after child refugees from the Spanish Civil War. She knew María would understand the situation and handle it with the necessary delicacy. As María saw her coming up the path escorted by the German military officials, she knew instantly my mother was in trouble.

'Hello María! I've come for Miri.' And when they were out of earshot from the Germans: 'Tell Lou not to show himself.'

María managed to get word to my father who was traced to the local cinema with me. A short while later, my mother and María froze when they saw his old Ford approach. Lou was in the driver's seat, staring straight ahead, his face pale and stony, with me sitting next to him. The car stopped, we stepped out and walked across to the waiting group. My father handed me over to my mother without a word.

'I shall be eternally grateful to you for this,' she whispered to him under her breath.

And – as she started walking away with me ...

'Au revoir, Papa!' I called out.

The Germans looked at each other, and then at my mother.

'The children at the home are mostly orphans. They all call him Papa!' she said quickly.

They escorted my mother and me to the railway station and watched us board the train to Marseilles.

∾

OF THE OLD SPANISH SONGS my mother used to sing to me during our later time in France, the one I remember hearing most often – her voice ringing softly with a melancholic tenderness, barely concealing a deeper anguish – went like this:

*Donde estás corazón?*
*No te oigo palpitar.*
*Es tan grande el dolor*
*que no puedo llorar.*
*Yo quisiera llorar*
*y no tengo mas llanto ...*

∾

IN MARSEILLES, it had taken a year before my mother succeeded in getting our travel documents. We finally boarded a ship full of refugees on its way to North Africa – the first leg of our voyage to Mexico.

We were standing on the deck one day, when she excitedly pointed to a strip of land that appeared in the distance.

'Look! That's Spain over there!' she exclaimed, her voice laden with emotion.

Our first port of call was Oran, from where we went on to Casablanca to wait two more weeks for our next ship, the Portuguese vessel *Serpa Pinto*.

During the early stage of our journey we slept on straw mattresses on the floor in the hold of the ship along with the other refugees, everyone's belongings by their mattress, one family crowded next to another. The ship heaved and rolled continually. My mother was very seasick and stayed below. Mollie, a petite young woman with a mane of curly brown hair and a joyful smile, looked after me. Mollie and Senya had fled Russia, known my father in Paris, and became our friends.

*Our travel document*
*photograph*

Harry was also on the *Serpa Pinto*. I later learned from my mother that a few years earlier he had jumped off his German cargo vessel when she had changed course for repairs to Hamburg: the city of his birth where he was now sought for his anti-fascist activities. He was picked up in the Channel by an English ship, the news of his heroism splashed across British newspapers, and then promptly expelled from the country – having been plucked from the water without an entry visa.

When my mother had gained her sea legs, we would sit together in the dining room at the long communal table. Here I worked out right from left, one day, as I was registering the hand I used to hold my fork. I also tended absent-mindedly to lean my elbow against the dining table, much to my mother's annoyance, until the day she lost all patience and slammed it very hard against the table … Maybe my tired misplaced elbow had triggered her frustrations at what life had been dealing her. Or maybe, too, I was beginning not always to fit in with her desired, cherished image of me.

She soon managed to get us a small cabin with bunk beds next to the engine room. I loved sleeping on the top berth. One night I was woken abruptly from my deep sleep by a sheet of cold water that left me drenched and shivering. My mother switched on the light, lifted me down, took off my wet nightdress and rubbed me dry with a towel. She closed the porthole through which the water had come in, and settled me now dry and warm on the lower

*With Mollie on the* Serpa Pinto

bunk, which had escaped the wave, while she arranged herself on the wet and cold top one.

And so, the days and weeks went by on the *Serpa Pinto* with nothing to see but the ship and the sea. And I began to long for dry land again.

1941 was drawing to a close.

As the *Serpa Pinto* sailed westwards through Atlantic waters leading us to our New World, the evacuation eastwards of those left behind in Europe was under way. In Marseilles, they were being tracked down by the French police, parents and children pulled apart and sent to separate camps. Until the day they were reloaded into trucks, by German officials this time, and taken to the railway station on the next step of their journey. In most cases, the final one.

*Our* fate had been deflected.

But I didn't know.

My innocent absence from the tangled pyramids of naked men women and children mixed with urine shit blood and vomit in the midst of grisly screams choking gasps invocations to God and a string quartet the children crushed underfoot in the scramble for air …

# Life Before

*Chemnitz, 1907.*

MY MOTHER, KÄTE, was born the fourth child of Oscar and Clara Lichtenstein.

Oscar was an amiable, kindly looking man, a little shorter when he stood – for a photograph – next to the more delicate, cultivated Clara with her gentle elegance. He grew up in the Baltic city of Königsberg, in East Prussia, later to become Kaliningrad under Soviet rule. After a business apprenticeship in Breslau, he established a textile firm of gloves and stockings in the industrial town of Chemnitz, then in Saxony, later renamed Karl Marx Stadt under East Germany, and now back to Chemnitz in integrated Germany.

*Oscar, Chemnitz, 1893*

Clara was born in Posen, in Central Prussia, which reverts to Poznań in Poland every time a war shifts back the border. She trained as a teacher, married Oscar and bore their children. The family lived in a spacious, eight-roomed apartment, the rooms on the street side separated by an L-shaped corridor from the inner, glass-roofed veranda and a small enclosed garden, with its central bed of rose bushes and a large rhubarb plant, where the children played in summer among the berries and the fruit trees.

My mother was looked after by her nanny while Clara was busy planning the family meals, organising the household, going to town to do the shopping and, once a week, to an afternoon outing at her

*Kränzchen* – a group of lady friends who would meet to exchange news over coffee and their home-baked cakes at each other's homes. The one moment my mother looked forward to every day was when, already tucked in bed by her nanny, her mother would come to kiss her goodnight. Her older sister, Lotte, was born at the turn of the century, followed by the two boys, Fritz and Hans. Lotte and Hans were pale-skinned and red-haired, while Fritz and my mother had olive skin and dark hair. At times, Clara would treat one or other of her children to an outing in town. She would take them to a *Konditorei* where they were served hot chocolate and a delicious pastry of

*Lotte, Hans, Käte and Fritz, Chemnitz, 1910*

their choice: the boys in their sailor suits and the girls in pretty lacy dresses, their long hair – Lotte's lightly waved and my mother's thick and curly – tied back from their faces with a trailing, shiny ribbon. Clara always sat very upright in a high collar up to her chin of white lace or black velvet, her prematurely white hair swept back into a knot under her large fashionable hat.

They led a German way of life within their Jewish circle of friends and business associates. They were part of that group of assimilated, German-speaking Jews that was growing in the liberal climate of the German states, although a social divide still existed between Jews and gentiles. At school, my mother and her Jewish classmates didn't mix with the oddly dressed, Yiddish-speaking girl, with her different ways, recently arrived with her family from Poland. '*Ostjuden*', Eastern Jews. The family didn't attend synagogue or observe Jewish customs. On the other hand, they followed the German traditions of

*Käte*

hiding chocolate eggs at Easter and decorating a tree on Christmas Eve. Yet my mother was sent as a matter of course to Hebrew School every Sabbath, until the day she refused to attend again, following a disagreement with the rabbi.

During a lesson, he had asked her to name the two most important attributes we should strive for.

'Health and happiness,' she had replied.

'No! Patience and piety!' the rabbi corrected her. She refused to agree, stuck to health and happiness, and ended her religious education.

As the youngest, she felt rather isolated. Her sister, Lotte, was seven years older and had other interests, and her brothers often teased and played pranks on her. Once they hid her dolls – all eight of them, that she was closely devoted to and she adored – and she ended up in bitter tears. Her distress still lingered when she recalled the event, even in adult life. Her most treasured moments appear to have been those she spent with her mother in a stately country guesthouse, where they sometimes went for a long weekend – just the two of them – during her school holidays.

They led an orderly life: everything in its right place and at the right time. Fritz's best remembered game was playing under Lotte's leadership at 'being obedient' to please their parents. The cook prepared their meals and a maid came twice a week to do the washing and ironing. Oscar was a good German patriot, and was frequently away on business fulfilling his role as the family provider, while Clara followed her more genteel domestic and social pursuits, always demure and kind in her manner.

As they grew up, all four children broke away from that constrained lifestyle. 'Claustrophobic' as Peter – Lotte's son – would later remember it, 'in keeping somehow with the peculiarly tall, narrow windows which characterised Chemnitz architecture'.

Lotte was known as wilful, sensitive and flamboyant. She interrupted her studies to marry a doctor eighteen years her senior who, contrary to her parents, had liberal and socialist views. She bore two children, Peter and Eve, and was widowed a few years later when her husband died of an infection – meticulous as he was in his attention to hygiene in his ophthalmic practice – one year before the discovery of penicillin.

Peter remembers his grandmother, Clara, at dinner.

'The only thing you may eat with your fingers is asparagus,' she used to say to him when she served that vegetable.

'Why asparagus?'

'Because if even the Kaiser himself can use his fingers to eat it, so can you.'

He also remembers walking with Clara and one of her lady-friends along the street, when Clara's youngest, his aunt – my mother – rode past on her bicycle.

'What a striking beauty she is, your Käte!' he overheard Clara's friend enthuse.

'Yes, but so irresponsible,' came Clara's unruffled reply.

Lotte began to spend the winters with her children at the Swiss lake, Lugano. As life became increasingly difficult in Germany's emerging political, racist climate, she finally settled with Peter and Eve in her beloved Italian city of Florence.

Fritz, the eldest son, was lined up to inherit his father's firm. He was an athletic, sports-loving youngster who excelled in his favourite subjects of history and geography. He was fervently patriotic, trusted in the Kaiser and admired his namesake, Frederick the Great of Prussia. Yet he began to see discrepancies between his parents' attitudes and ways of life, and what he witnessed in the aftermath of the 1914–18 war. He watched the growing social upheaval and political extremism around him and, while training in the running of a textile factory, he listened and sympathised with views of individuals he befriended in the workforce. In the end, though, none of this seemed to throw light on his position. Unlike the rest of the family, he started exploring his Jewish roots and to share ideas with other

Jews who talked of forming a new community – based on socialist principles and more attuned to their culture – in their ancestral home in Palestine. He renounced his apprenticeship at the prosperous Sigmund Goeritz textile firm to study agriculture in preparation for his new life in a small community of like-minded Jews, with whom he cleared malarial infested swamps and tilled the earth in a kibbutz precursor in northern Palestine.

Hans, to Clara's delight, sang and played the piano from an early age. He studied music in Leipzig, became the youngest orchestral conductor in Germany and faced a promising future as a musician – a life his father thought ill-advised. 'Good for a break, but not for bread,' Oscar would say, even though the family had a tradition of musicians, and his great-uncle, a chief cantor of Berlin's great synagogue, had inspired one of Max Bruch's compositions with his melodies. Hans was appointed conductor of the Hamburg State Opera and gave a concert tour in Holland, and later in London, with Richard Tauber. On his return to Hamburg, the opera's director informed Hans regretfully that he could no longer employ him, for fear of the Brownshirts' reprisals. Hans's musical career in Germany thus came to an abrupt end. He left to start a new life in Holland.

Käte, my mother and the last of the four, trained in Stuttgart as a children's nurse. In the hospital her duties were strict and demanding, yet she loved her work and became closely involved with every one of her small charges. Here she met and formed an enduring friendship with another student nurse, Seppel. Käte enjoyed cross-country skiing expeditions in Switzerland and nature holidays on the Baltic coast. She spent time in Berlin where she was drawn into an exciting liberal world of theatre, cabaret, freethinking and free love, a desire for social justice and a defiant stand against the rising fascist movement. In the growing climate of intolerance and

*Käte and Lotte in 1920s Berlin*

*Käte and Hans in 1920s Berlin*

ultra-nationalism, she joined the German Communist Party. She followed Seppel to London and, as Hitler gained power in Germany, the two of them went to Barcelona. Here Käte was seduced by the dizzy mix of idealism, enthusiasm and firm friendships in recently democratised Spain. She travelled to New York with the family of a child she was minding, but returned to be at Seppel's side upon the tragic death of her new husband, a renowned and much admired Catalan politician, Rafael Campalans, whom Seppel had married barely a year earlier.

Soon after, Käte visited her sister Lotte in Italy and talked of her attachment to the child she had left in New York and her heartbreak at having to leave him.

'I want to have a child of my own,' she said. One she could keep, from whom she wouldn't have to part.

And she returned to her life in Barcelona.

∽

LITHUANIA, UNDER TSARIST RULE, around 1896.

My father was born in a small rural Jewish community under the Russian Empire towards the end of the nineteenth century.

His earliest memory was of rolling off his mother's lap during a struggle with some drunks who had attacked her with a knife while she milked the cow. He was the youngest of her brood of eight: all under her sole charge since her husband, a musician in the Russian army band, died of typhoid. On market days, she would be seen walking with her kerchief round her head and a live calf across her shoulders to the nearby village of Prenn: which consisted of a few streets, a small square and the schoolhouse. She also sold vodka clandestinely, which she hid in my father's cot.

When he was a boy, my father walked every day two to three kilometres to the village school. The teacher was a Jew with pockmarks on his forehead, which – my father was told – were dents from a hammer to activate his brain. On his way to school, he stole fruit from the trees to supplement the bread he bought with the kopeck his mother gave him every morning for his lunch.

His older brothers started immigrating to America to seek a better life. Jewish life was difficult under Russia's discriminatory laws; there were also sporadic pogroms in the area. My father was left behind with his mother and one sister. As the only male in the household now, in accordance with Jewish law, he became its head, led the family prayers and made the decisions. When he was nine, his older brothers sent for the three of them.

The year was 1905. They travelled by train from Kaunas in Lithuania to north Germany, where they boarded a ship and travelled third class, crowded together with many other emigrating families. Food was scarce, and one day he ventured up the forbidden steps to the first class area to steal an apple for his mother. In his rush to run back and give it to her, he fell and injured himself.

They arrived in New York and started a new life. They lived in a small room behind his brothers' grocery store on the West Side of Manhattan and he was put to work in the store and sent to school. His rural rustic environment had been replaced by a crowded vertical city, and his presiding position over the family by a lowly subordinate one. He attended school with his sidelocks and skullcap as his religious upbringing demanded and had been the custom in Prenn. Here, the boys called him 'Sheeny' and chanted:

*'Greenhorn, popcorn,*
*Five cents a bag,*
*July, July,*
*Go to hell and die.'*

They made him fight inside a disused railway carriage and gave him a black eye. Once, in a park by the Hudson River, they also forced him to drink urine. Having stood up to their tests, he gained their respect and they took him along on their escapades to steal fruit, which they shared out with him in the school playground.

The family changed their names, my father from Ruven-Leiba to Louis, according to archives dug out by a Mexican film producer researching his life – for he never disclosed his original name, not even on being pressed to reveal it. An older surviving sister told the film producer, Marcela Arteaga, that, on the first leg of their journey from Lithuania to New York, the bible in which all their names, birthdays and other details of their identity and origins had been written and kept, fell from the boat into the river they were crossing and was never retrieved ...

Louis rapidly mastered English, his new language.

The brothers sold the store, and my father moved with his mother and sister to a ghetto of immigrant Jews and Italians on the Lower East Side. Here they lived in a room on the second floor of a tenement house on Madison Avenue. They had cold running water but no electricity, and shared the single lavatory on their floor with all the other tenants.

He liked his new school and teachers. He was introduced to literature, carpentry and gymnastics, and became actively involved in the after-school social activities. He went on to Dewitt Clinton High School, with 5,000 black-and-white pupils, at the corner of 59th Street and Tenth Avenue. He plunged eagerly into his studies and added French and Spanish to his knowledge of American and Yiddish, and more than likely some Russian and Lithuanian. He enjoyed taking part in student life which included a zealous support of American football. At inter high school matches he joined in the chanting, spurring on his school team:

*'Give 'em the axe, give 'em the axe, give 'em the axe.*
*The axe, the axe, the axe.*
*Where?*
*Right in the neck, the neck, right in the neck.*
*There!'*

In his last year of high school he was chosen for the Dotey Squad which policed the students and kept them in order. He was also elected president and gave the farewell speech before an enormous audience of parents and students who clapped enthusiastically.

Young Louis said his prayers every day and went to synagogue every Friday and Saturday with his older brothers, but he began to reflect that the behaviour of his Jewish elders at work during the week was at odds with their pious prayers and rituals on the Sabbath. Following his Bar Mitzvah, at which he earned his place among adults along with the responsibility and right to choose, he decided to break away from the traditions of his race. He himself resolved to lead a pure life, to remain chaste until marriage, and to fight against the ills of the world – according to the autobiographical notes he left behind.

He won a scholarship to attend Cornell University where he studied humanities. He remembered the professor of philosophy who used to say, 'The important thing is to *live*. Anyone can "make a living", which is secondary!'

The First World War interrupted his studies. He was chosen to go with a French-speaking unit intended to coordinate the French and American armies but, on reaching France, ended assisting with the sick and injured in a hospital in the south of France. One day a colonel from the intelligence service arrived and recruited the young Louis to serve in the counter-intelligence section. He was given the task to survey the various movements and activities at the Spanish border: Spain being in sympathy with the German cause. As a 'civilian', he freely crossed the frontier to Fuenterrabía and the casino at San Sebastián where he met many colourful characters. In his new lifestyle, he

*Lou in the American army, 1917*

came across German agents, the French intelligence, high-ranking army personnel, petty criminals and aristocrats. Young women too, who initiated him into the games of love and sex.

When the war ended, he spent six months in Paris and resumed his studies at the Sorbonne while waiting to return to the United States. He also visited London, flying across the channel in some of the earliest aeroplanes. He described how, during one such flight, the pilot encountered technical problems and walked out onto the wing of the plane to fix it. He returned to New York and, finding himself penniless again, joined a business that imported leather from Spain, with the aim of going back to university. But he fell in love with his senior partner's wife and started a liaison with her during her husband's absence on business. On his return, Louis was dismissed.

By now he had learned a great deal about the leather trade and made contacts with buyers from as far afield as China, Switzerland and Buenos Aires. He moved to Spain where he set up his own business. He travelled extensively throughout the country and met people from all levels of life. He found that, unlike his experiences in America, there was a general absence of racial prejudice here and an open and easy mixing between people. In this ambience there was no need for pretence, he felt free to act and be himself and enjoyed his new life. He became enamoured of the country and its people and chose to stay.

Over the next twelve years he gathered a large network of new friends and acquaintances and his business grew and flourished. He had a number of love affairs, including a long-standing relationship with a cheerful young woman from Valencia of Berber descent, with whom he had a daughter and twins – all of whom died in infancy. The little girl choked on a plum stone and could not be revived, and the twins were born premature and did not survive. In his intense grief, Lou found himself reverting to the rites of his discarded Jewish tradition. He tore his clothes, beat his head, recited his prayers, and refrained from shaving or grooming himself for seven days.

Then Lou met Käte in Barcelona. They became romantically involved.

On a visit to Italy where Käte introduced Lou to Lotte, her son

Peter tells me that Lou was utterly enamoured with Käte. Yet in later years my father insisted he had never loved her: such is the capacity for memory to go into denial – maybe in the face of hurt, misunderstanding, guilt, disillusion ... There is much to suggest that Käte, in her own way, was also drawn to Lou: her voice betrayed her fondness – cutting through her decades of bitterness – on the rare transatlantic telephone calls between them I overheard.

Back to the lovers in Barcelona: their bond was deepened by their mutual desire to have a child, which would soon be fulfilled. Though their free liaison was readily acceptable in their progressive, nonconformist circles, Käte began to worry about the distress her pregnancy would cause her conservative parents in Chemnitz. Her wish to legalise their union led to Lou and Käte's first serious clash of wills, and the start of their fraught and uneasy relationship ...

# An Earth That Shakes

*The Atlantic Ocean, 1941.*

THE SERPA PINTO was delivering us to our New World and a new start.

After many days at sea, we finally sighted land.

It was Cuba.

The ship entered the harbour and docked. I was surrounded by much bustle and movement as people prepared to leave the ship. I too was excited at the thought of stepping on land again and looking at all the new things here. After all those unrelieved weeks, of one dreary day after another of the same and more of the same, hemmed into our confined space by the ship's perimeter, I was yearning to walk on firm land again. I was impatient to explore the new sights this place promised as I caught whiffs of land smells rising up to meet us and glimpses of the busy port far below. The gangway finally in place, people started disembarking, but when our turn came the man guarding the gangway barred our way.

'Your disembarkation papers,' he requested.

'We're not staying in Havana. We're going on to Mexico,' my mother told him.

'You can't get off here. Only those who're staying.'

'We'll only take a walk around the port. The girl's longing to be on land again after being cooped up in the ship for so long!'

'Not possible,' the man said dryly and firmly.

Seeing my face start to contort with disappointment, my mother promised him we would be back on board in ten minutes.

'No way. You can't get off. Those are the rules.'

Back at sea, not long after, we watched as the ship approached another strip of land.

Mexico!

As we came closer, the details emerged more distinctly. Now I could make out a large flag fluttering in the port, and I started to cry.

'What's the matter?' asked my mother surprised.

'That's not Mexico! It's France! We're back in France!' I blurted between sobs.

'Why … Whatever makes you think that?'

'That's the French flag over there!' I pointed.

Blue, white and red. In the distance, the Mexican flag's green stripe looked blue …

The first night we stayed in a small hotel, not far from the port, in Veracruz.

The following morning, as we trudged along the dirt road carting our baggage on our way to the bus that was to take us to Mexico City, I suddenly remembered my pillow. It was still on the bed in the hotel room.

'We must go back for it!' I desperately urged my mother in a flood of tears.

'We can't, we have to catch the bus.'

It was a small, semicircular, flat pillow, its soft, fine cotton case delicately hand-embroidered, white on white, and bordered by a pretty flounce all the way round its crescent edge. It had been my one familiar, constant piece of bedding on which I had laid my head to go to sleep every night, all the way from Barcelona. Everything else from our diverse 'homes' had disappeared or been left behind or replaced. The pillow had been mine like other people have a house, a street. My portable home, like the shell of a snail. And now it lay on a bed in a hotel room in Veracruz to which we would never return.

I was disconsolate …

*Aguántate!*

And so, I set off to face my new life in this new country with no mementos from the old. Just my mother and my memories.

*Mexico City, end of 1941.*

OUR FIRST HOME in Mexico City was on the top floor of a yellow, five-storey, corner building in Calle Michoacán. We shared the small apartment with Helene, who had also sailed on the *Serpa Pinto* and spoke German with my mother. Her hair was the colour of corn and fell softly to her shoulders. I was in awe of her gentle beauty. She was mostly out and I rarely saw her, which added to her air of mystery.

Soon after our arrival, my mother came home early one evening and said I should wait in the bathroom while she prepared a surprise for me. I stood by the bathtub in the narrow, white-tiled room, feeling very curious. I could hear my mother's footsteps and unusual rustling sounds on the other side of the door. After a while, bored and impatient, I went up to the door and peered through the keyhole. To my astonishment, almost the full length of the mirror in the hallway came into view with the gleaming reflection of a tree dripping with colourful tinsel and other curious objects. I caught glimpses of my mother standing next to it teasing wisps of cotton wool and draping them on its branches, making it appear as though it had been in a fresh snowfall.

'You can come out now!' my mother finally called out.

I stood, utterly speechless, before the scene that met me, taking in its every small detail the like of which I had never seen before in our life in France. As I lowered my gaze, I saw a pile of toys under the tree with two celluloid dolls sitting on top.

'Who are they for?' I asked bewildered when I found my voice again.

'For you!' My mother was brimming with delight at my surprise.

Helene was also there to share the occasion with us that evening, making it even more special.

It was our first Christmas Eve in Mexico.

I started going to school, El Colegio Hispano Mexicano, and was relearning the Spanish I first spoke back in Barcelona and forgot in France. I was retrieving something which by then had grown distant and remote. Yet I was so taken up with meeting all the immediate demands and necessary readjustments of my new life, that these language changes went unremarked.

Being a new girl, the children were curious about me.

'Are you Catholic?'

'No.' (What might that be?)

'Do you believe in God?'

'No, but I believe in Santa Claus.' In Marseilles my mother had given me some chocolates from *Père Noël* unlike any chocolates I had ever seen before, which proved his existence to me.

'Where are you from?'

'I was born in Spain. In Barcelona.'

'And your father?'

'He's in France. He didn't come to Mexico with us.'

'And your mother? Where's she from?'

'Germany.'

So from then on they called me *la alemana*, the German girl, and considered me to be on the enemy side of the ongoing war they had heard about. Which puzzled me for, as I understood it, from what I picked up from my mother's talk with her friends, the Germans were *our* enemies ... But notwithstanding their nickname for me, we played together and generally paid little attention to it.

One day, not long after our arrival, I found Helene in a distraught state. Her eyes were red and swollen and my mother was trying to comfort her. She explained to me that a burglar had made his way from the roof into Helene's room and had stolen everything she possessed. All of her clothes – she had always dressed with charm and care – and, among the rest of her things, all gone now, an old gramophone and collection of records that she had treasured and managed to bring with her when she fled Europe. I always found Helene in tears from then on. She left soon afterwards.

My mother was out every day until late and I looked after myself until she came in. I was six by now. She taught me how to fry an egg so I could have a bite to eat when I came home from school. As I let myself into the flat, I looked forward to going into the kitchen and practising my new skill. I followed my mother's instructions to the letter, taking care not to spill things or burn myself. I liked best the trickiest part of cracking the eggshell on the rim of the pan and dropping its contents into the hot oil. I would watch with fascination how the clear mucus turned white around the rich plump orange yolk in the middle, and then carefully slide it onto my plate. I finally buttered a piece of bread and sat down to my snack with relish. Eggs had always been a favourite.

I was carelessly gazing, from the lavatory, at the shiny, white tiles on the bathroom walls and the tub before me. Above it, a small window overlooked the inner courtyard of the building. It had turned dark outside, but my mother wouldn't be home for some time yet. I was absent-mindedly dangling my legs, which hung short from the floor, and lifting my gaze when – to my surprise – I saw the light bulb swinging widely from the middle of the ceiling. Back and forth. I noted the window was closed and there was no draught. I looked back at the light, but it was still swinging. Maybe I had disturbed something when I switched it on? I let myself down from the lavatory and tried turning the switch on and off, but the light kept swinging. I left the bathroom to see if anything else in the flat was moving or out of place, and waited uneasily for my mother.

'Mami! The light was swinging in the bathroom!'

'Yes, that was an earthquake,' she told me. And she explained: 'In Mexico, sometimes the ground shakes and makes things move.'

Another evening after dark, around eight o'clock, my mother had just come home, drawn and tired, and was preparing our meal when she noticed we were out of butter. She asked me to slip down to the grocery store across the street to get some. As I stepped out of the building onto the pavement and stood waiting to cross the road, the entire scene before me became suddenly flooded in brilliant light, etching out every detail of the street with unnatural clarity as though the night had been interrupted by broad daylight. Moments later, back in the dark, a thunder rumbled and roared. My first Mexican electric storm.

One morning I woke very early, my mother still asleep, and stood by the window of my room watching the sun, a huge glowing orange ball, slowly rise above the city skyline. And as I raised my gaze and scanned the pale dawn sky, myriads of colourful suns – blue, green, yellow, red, orange, purple – flashed and bounced in rapid succession across it in every direction in a frenzied display …

At school, my teacher came up to me one day in the playground and asked why I wasn't playing.

'Because I have no one to play with.'

At that moment, another girl, with lively dark eyes and long graceful limbs, walked past also on her own. The teacher asked her the same question.

'Because I have no one to play with.'

The teacher suggested we play together.

We took each other's hands and started walking together.

'What's your name?'

'Lucía. What's yours?'

'Miriam.'

'What shall we play?'

'I don't know … What would you like to play?'

'I don't know.'

The end of playtime found us still hesitant and undecided. From that moment we became firm friends.

My mother would take me on her visits to her old friends from Spain. They formed part of our life here in Mexico and, at the same time, gave a sense of continuity with our pre-Mexican past and my mother's fervent stance in the world I had experienced so far. We were all refugees from some fearsome iniquity which I could see they all felt very strongly about.

There was Viadiu, a Catalan man with a wild head of white hair and a kindly face whom we would find at his small bookshop, more a cubicle crammed with books, to one side of the entrance of an arched passageway beyond the Zócalo in the city centre. My mother would stand in the passageway next to the books and periodicals and become absorbed in lengthy discussions with him – reminiscent of her conversations with Thin Max by the garage with the printing press in Marseilles.

Then there were the Riojas who lived in a pleasant apartment in a block approached from the street through a side courtyard. Enrique was a university professor. He had a large body with a small head, while his wife had a slim body with a large head.

'Did you ever see a hippopotamus?' Enrique would ask me.

'Yes. They're next to the elephants in the zoo.'

'I keep one on the roof,' he used to tell me every time we visited them.

'It's impossible. I don't believe you.'

'Ah, yes!' he insisted, and he would show me a picture of it.

'So how did you get it up there?'

'By the back stairs,' he would try to convince me.

'You couldn't have. It wouldn't fit.'

I knew he was teasing, but was intrigued that his conversation with me always turned to hippopotami when he looked so much like one himself.

The Riojas were related to the Santalós, whom my mother knew from Barcelona. One of the Santaló brothers had been the Republican Spanish Consul in Collioure and my mother had assisted him with his dedicated work aiding refugees from Franco's Spain. Another Santaló brother now in Mexico, lived with his family in a small flat several floors up a high-rise building in a humble suburb of the city. They had a seven-year-old son, Miguelito. He was tall, slim and beautiful, and though only a year or two older, I felt uncharacteristically timid in his presence. This was intensified by his charm and close attention to me when we played together. On top of that, one day I suddenly noticed his enchanting smile. At the end of our visit, as my mother and I reached the bottom of the concrete stairwell and started walking down the street, I was still reeling from the effect of Miguelito's smile.

'When I grow up, I shall marry Miguelito,' I declared out loud. My mother laughed – though to me it seemed a serious decision.

This fierce passion was to be the first of many that followed, with barely a rest between them, in our barren, continually shifting world.

Among my mother's German friends were Gustav Regler and his wife, Marie Louise, who lived in a spacious house in Villa Álvaro Obregón in the Spanish colonial district of San Ángel. Gustav had fought in the International Brigade in Spain. On our visits to the Reglers, we would sit around the table in the shade of a large spreading tree in their garden, the adults drinking coffee and talking. Gustav was always affectionately playful with me. On an especially hot afternoon, while Marie Louise prepared the coffee, he was watering the garden in a pair of shorts, stripped to the waist. Every now and then he squirted a little water at me in playful mood. In the spirit of his teasing, I picked the hose while he was busy fixing something in the flower bed, waited for him to turn, and aimed it at his bare chest. Regler jerked wildly and screamed at me, enraged. He remained highly disturbed and unable to settle back to his relaxed, cheerful self for the rest of that afternoon. I was bewildered and frightened. My mother was trying to calm him down, without effect. I didn't understand what was going on ...

For I didn't yet know of the tensions and fears which had sprung from the events we had left behind in Europe, of Regler's and my mother's support of a cause they had believed in during the rise of fascism in their country and abandoned when faced with its own ruthlessness in Spain. Or of the price many were paying for their misplaced ideals, the loss of trust in friends, and the paranoia grown out of the collapse of their initial hopes and convictions as they witnessed the disappearance and executions, by their own party, of many of their companions. I could not have imagined Regler's fear for his life after renouncing the Party – as my mother had also done – following his high command in the Spanish Republican forces. Or that, when the cold water hit his chest, he thought my mother had shot him.

Trotsky's murder by a trusted acquaintance had taken place not long before, not far from where we stood.

My mother divided her days in Mexico between work, seeing old friends and looking after my basic needs: ours was an austere life, without luxuries or indulgences. Yet I occasionally came across some small, cherished leftover my mother still kept from a less frugal past, such as the handsome little bottle of Chanel No. 5 that she kept among her personal things. On rare occasions, my mother would dab a touch of the perfume behind her ears with the rod on the glass stopper, and I smelt the pleasing sweet scent mingled with my mother's own smell.

I was so engaged in absorbing the ever-changing life situations I found myself in, that I don't remember questioning our immediate past or thinking anymore of the friends we had left behind in Marseilles and Foëcy, or of their possible fates. But then, I had not yet become aware of the danger we had faced. I understood by then that Franco had caused much suffering to our friends and that my mother felt passionately about the injustices she had witnessed. I also knew a war was raging in Europe and soldiers were killing each other the way I must have seen in the cinema. I remember fearing 'Nazis', whom I sensed could harm me, with the same aversion I felt for snakes, and when I was alone in the apartment I sometimes had an irrational fear of being suddenly confronted with them. All these realisations emerged insidiously – much like the appearance of a pattern when weaving a fabric … And each friend, each encounter, each situation added yet another piece to the growing mosaic.

I was deciphering my surroundings on my own. My mother was rarely at home, and even then she was tired and our exchanges were erratic. I realise now she must have been working, though she never spoke to me about her day's activities or herself.

We soon shifted to a new apartment that went with a café frequented by Austrian and German refugees recently arrived in Mexico like ourselves, and my mother now looked after the café in addition to some regular night-nursing work in a nearby hospital.

I would peer from the street into the small dark room of the Café Viena trying to make out the clientele – many of them friends and acquaintances – eating and chatting at the small tables, while in the background my mother was busy preparing and serving the evening meal. Her work in the café demanded her full attention and she had made it strictly out of bounds for me. So I, instead, would amuse myself in the park, Parque México, across the street, with its rich variety of trees, shrubs and small ponds. There was one particular secluded spot with a circle of grassy bushes, like giant upside-down mops, where I liked playing out my world of make-believe. I would make a private place for myself inside one of these bushes, hiding behind its green curtain of blades, and here I would sit and think and dream without interruption. Or I rented a bicycle from the shop at the far end of the park to ride along the park's footpaths and across the raised wooden bridges over the water channels that fed the ponds. I soon got to know other children in the street and played outside with them every afternoon till dusk, when my mother called me in for dinner.

Our new street, Calle México, came alive with the violet-blue and flaming orange of the flowering jacaranda and *tabachín* trees that lined its length facing the park. Our flat above the café was reached from the street through a large iron gate that led into a side courtyard with a staircase up to our balcony and entrance. It had three rooms: the living-dining room, which doubled as my mother's bedroom, my own miniscule bedroom, and the kitchen.

Among my mother's acquaintances that frequented the café was a tall young woman called Ilse. She had straight, light brown hair, sky-blue eyes, and dressed in smart suits and leather gloves. She became my mother's friend and I saw her often. She came to play an important part in our later life.

At school, a boy in the next class by the name of Aldama captured my attention and took over my waking and sleeping thoughts. I remember waking from a dream one night calling out his name – such was my passion.

My first school friend, Lucía, lived around the corner in Calle Amsterdam. Though Lucía was seldom allowed out, we sometimes met and played together. I felt close to her and confided everything to her. Once or twice Lucía invited me to her apartment: a dark, heavily curtained place, crowded in an orderly manner with antique furniture, books and other valued objects, where people dared not raise their voices. Her father, a doctor and émigré from Spain by the name of Segovia, appeared a remote and awesome figure.

One day when we had arranged to meet, Lucía arrived and looked at me with her large dark eyes.

'I'm not allowed to be your friend anymore,' she said steadily and calmly.

'Why not?' I asked her, stunned.

Some childish indiscretion, which her father disapproved of …

'I can't play with you anymore.'

'What, *never*?' I stared at her in disbelief, holding back the terrible pain which started gnawing at my insides.

'Never,' Lucía said quietly and firmly.

And she kept her word.

My mother was busy attending to the café, working somewhere else until late afternoon and doing night shifts in a hospital. Now Lupe, a young Mexican girl with long black plaits from a village in the outskirts of the city, started helping with the household and looked after me.

I was in the kitchen watching Lupe at work one afternoon when the floor suddenly started jerking. Everything was moving every which way and chairs and other objects were falling over. Lupe, her face struck with terror, started yelling urgently at me to go outside. Holding on to whatever I could along the way to help me stay upright, I finally caught up with her already on the balcony. She made me kneel next to her, facing the courtyard below, and told me to press my hands together, point them at my chin as she was doing, and repeat each phrase after her: '*Padre nuestro, que estás en el cielo, santificado sea tu nombre ...*'

Lupe went through all these motions with such panic-stricken fervour that each detail became engraved in my mind as the procedure to be followed at all future earthquakes. The shaking finally stopped and Lupe looked very relieved. I had not had time to digest what was going on or feel frightened, but now that it was over I began to realise something of its potential danger. I hurried to the bus stop by the park to wait for my mother, concerned for her safety. Until I saw her, safe and well, getting off the bus back from work.

One late Sunday afternoon, Lupe came back from her regular weekend visits to her family in her village all dressed in black, her eyes red and swollen. She was crying.

'What's the matter? Why are you crying?' I asked her anxiously.

'They've killed my brother. He's dead.' Lupe said between sobs.

'What happened to him?' I asked astonished.

'Another man knifed him.'

'Why?'

Lupe was distraught and I was trying to understand. I was visualising a young man, dark and strong like Lupe, one moment full of life, the next dead. There seemed to be no sense in it. That was my first confrontation with death in Mexico. Violent and mysterious. I wanted to comfort Lupe but realised my helplessness in the face of her grief.

In contrast, there was a sense of pleasure and peace in the rare walks with my mother and her friends, when we used to follow a path next to a cool stream on the mountainside outside the city.

Outings and sights in the city proper filled me with a different kind of wonder. Close to the centre, the market, Mercado de San Juan, spread across several blocks. Full of bustle, jumbled voices, sweet and pungent smells, bright colours. As we approached it, the beggars on the footpath became more numerous. Legless men shuffling on their thigh stumps asking for a few *centavos*, blind children with dishevelled blank faces and snotty noses, old women hiding behind dark, hand-woven cotton shawls, their *rebozos*, holding up their cupped hand in supplication.

'What's she asking for, Mamita?'

'She wants a *centavo*.'

'Why?'

'Because she's poor.'

'Can I give her one, please?'

My mother reached into her handbag and handed me a coin. I held it towards the deeply wrinkled, old woman sitting hunched up in her *rebozo* on the dirty footpath, her glazed, clouded eyes staring vaguely in my direction.

'Here you are!' I called out with the intention of pleasing her.

'She can't see you. She's blind. Go over and drop it in her hand.'

Inside the market, the world came alive. Row after row of stands with woollen *sarapes*, ponchos and rugs, hand-woven tablecloths, leather thong *huarache* sandals, brightly glazed pottery, mountains of chillies, sacks full of countless varieties of beans, fruit stands heaped with sweet oranges, pineapples, mangoes, papayas, green and black zapotillas, *jícamas*, and much more beyond. It was a few blocks past the Zócalo: the large central square overlooked by the baroque Hispano-Mexican cathedral, with the rust-red government buildings on one side, and the arched colonnades crowded with silver jewellery shops and newspaper stands on the other.

When Lupe took me on her errands to the centre of town, we would never go past the cathedral in the Zócalo without entering it. Lupe would lift her *rebozo* from her shoulders to cover her head, and place a handkerchief over mine. Inside the entrance, she dipped her fingers in the water in the massive stone bowl and reverently crossed herself. Then we stood, side by side, in silence, in the back of the cathedral's vast shadowy interior – young Lupe, maybe fifteen or sixteen years old, dark eyed and dark skinned, her *rebozo* over her head, next to me, aged seven, my green, almond eyes wide open in my freckly face, with a small white handkerchief on top of mine – while Lupe quietly prayed for her brother's soul.

I sat motionless in the dark, next to my mother – spellbound by the mounting stillness and peace in a forest clearing after the last gasps of a wild, raging storm had shaken me to my depths with the ominous rumblings of cellos and the thundering of drums – listening attentively to every change of mood in Beethoven's Pastoral Symphony from the back of the large auditorium. Other nights I was held entranced by the beauty and delicacy of movement of the Russian Ballet dancers, marvelling at their individual precision and the group's perfect synchronisation. And in the spacious foyer of Bellas Artes, I gazed excitedly at Senya's photographs on the walls: close-up portraits of the Ballets Russes dancers.

Mollie and Senya – our friends from our *Serpa Pinto* days – lived a few streets beyond La Alameda, by the massive monument to the revolution, near the busy intersection with Cuauhtémoc's statue, which marks the start of the tree-lined Avenida de la Reforma. Their apartment and photographic studio was on the seventh floor. A small notice next to the doorbell announced

*Self-portrait Senya Flechine. Photo: SEMO*

*Senya's studio photo of me, Mexico, 1942.*
Photo: SEMO

them: *Foto Semo*: a fusion of Senya and Mollie. Mollie always welcomed us with a warm smile as she sat us at the small table in their minimal kitchen, wedged in the space between Senya's darkroom on the other side of the wall and the long, brightly lit corridor lined with Senya's photographic studies – Cantinflas, María Félix, Alicia Markova and Anton Dolin in a ballet pose, Mexican woman and daughter, dancers' hands, a cob of corn, a ripple of shadows – leading to his studio. Mollie would serve us her special Russian tea with a sliver of lemon, and we would sit around the table, the adults exchanging news. Their friend and assistant Raúl would also be there, and they would talk about their hopes for a better world where people would live in harmony and care for each other. Mollie did most of the talking, forever smiling and bubbling over with love, while Senya, hardly bigger than the tiny Mollie, would sit quietly next to her, a sad smile lighting up his gaunt face, the odd strand of dark hair straying over his forehead matched by his black-rimmed glasses. Raúl never spoke at all, a furtive silent figure around whom Mollie would put her arm and declare, 'This is our great friend Raúl.' Then he would disappear to the mysterious world of Senya's darkroom …

Senya – noting my passion for the ballet – used to give me glossy prints of the Russian dancers that I kept among my treasures.

Facing the leafy Alameda Park was a row of Mexican shops of arts and crafts and silver jewellery in between elegant, high-rise hotels in Avenida Juárez. Sometimes my mother left me for an hour or two in one of these jewellery shops. With Harry. He worked in the shop.

He showed me how to shine the silver and put me to work cleaning and polishing rings, brooches, bracelets, earrings. I enjoyed being with Harry. We understood each other. I liked helping him. And he would always find something to give me: a silver ring with a turquoise flower, a silver brooch of a donkey or a Mexican man with his sombrero. Once he gave me a gold ring with a small ruby set in a circle of hearts, and another time a heavy silver ring with my initials he had made especially for me.

My life had acquired a certain flow and rhythm in my Mexican surroundings. I was beginning to feel part of everyday Mexican life – the sun, the language, my friends. The street smells of exotic flowers mingled with spicy food and poverty no longer surprised me. The noisy beeping and tooting of cars in busy streets; the cries of the newspaper boys, hardly older than myself, from every street corner; the rich deep voices of the mariachis accompanied by their strings and trumpets as they sang lustily about their death-defying pride of being Mexican. They were all my world too now.

I remember suddenly bursting into song one day with all the patriotic ardour I could muster – as I had heard the great charro actor, Jorge Negrete, do – much to my mother's amusement:

'Hay, Jalisco no te rajes!
me sale del alma
gritar con calor.'

But, in addition to my growing sense of 'Mexican-ness', I also felt 'Spanish' in the ambience of our Spanish refugee friends who, in their turn, zealously held on to their own identity. I witnessed their love and longing for all that was Spanish and that they had left behind. They regarded Mexico as a temporary home while they marked time and waited for the end of Franco's regime so they could return to their true home. They firmly retained the Spanish way of speaking, carefully lisping their 'c's and 'z's, and correcting me or anyone else who might lapse into the Mexican 's' pronunciation. And I would switch with ease between the Mexican and Spanish ways of speaking the language – and with it, my 'identities' – depending on the company.

And all our friends here in Mexico, as various as they were, and whether Spanish, German or Russian, were all linked to each other and our past, and shared with my mother what I sensed to be her passionate views and sentiments.

Among my mother's friends were an earthy, Spanish anarchist couple and their adopted daughter, Libertad – Spanish for Liberty – whose father had been executed in the aftermath of the Spanish Civil War. Libertad and I became good friends and I entreated my mother to let me attend her school, the Spanish Republican Colegio Madrid, in my third year of primary school.

Here, I loved my new teacher and her classes, especially history which covered the life and trials of the local indigenous peoples before the Spanish 'discovered' these lands. I sat transfixed as I listened to the story of the young prince, Netzahualcóyotl, who watched some men from a neighbouring hostile tribe kill his father, from behind a bush where his father had hidden him on being sur-prised by their enemies on their journey. He returned to his people alone and grew up to be their king.

On special commemorative days, the school defiantly sang the Spanish Republican Anthem and raised the purple, yellow and red flag of pre-Franco's Spain.

I soon made friends with the other children, and they posed the same old questions.

'Are you Catholic?'

'No.'

'Are you Protestant?' derisively.

'No.'

'What are you then?'

'I don't know. Nothing.'

At home after school, I asked my mother, 'What's "Catholic"? And "Protestant"? What is "God", which the children at school keep talking about?'

My mother saw I was troubled and puzzled.

'We are something too,' she told me.

'Ah, yes? Does it have a name?'

'Yes. We are Jews.'

'Oh!' I exclaimed with delight at this new information.

The next day, at the start of playtime, I went up to my friend Niobe. She had clear blue eyes and thick blonde plaits neatly looped around her head.

'I am a Jew!' I told her proudly.

'Really!' Niobe looked impressed. She was especially friendly towards me that morning and played with me with a new respect.

The next day Niobe came up to me in the playground.

'I *hate* Jews,' she announced, spitting out the words at me.

Though she soon forgot the whole thing and we continued to be friends.

Playing on the roof, running in and out of the washing hanging on the lines. Row after row of white billowing sheets in the bright sunshine. Beyond the lines, stone sinks stood side by side for the use of the tenants. I was playing with Libertad in front of her rooftop home, high above the busy main road, San Antonio Abad. Another of her friends had joined us in our play, a boy called Volney. He was full of life, ideas and laughter, and every time his bright smile lit his face, it sent my heart spinning.

'Will you marry me when we grow up?' I asked him on a sudden impulse in the middle of our play – and he pretended to go into a faint among the washing.

Some weekends my mother took me to a palatial villa in the outlying Spanish colonial district of San Ángel, where she was minding Léonide Massine's small daughter. And here, at the entrance to a large pavilion in the flower-filled gardens, I would flatten myself against the wall, hardly daring to breathe, to watch the nimble figure of Massine in his black figure-hugging outfit – utterly focused – taking the Ballets Russes group of dancers through their steps in rehearsal. My mother had impressed on me to make myself practically invisible so as not to disturb Massine.

I found it thrilling. Dancing was my passion. I loved the body's motion and rhythm in time to the changing beats and nuances of the music, the transformation of every shade of emotion the music evoked into movement. I too wanted to dance, and started attending classes in classical ballet and flamenco. I got pink ballet shoes for one and wooden castanets for the other. I learned to move on the points of my toes and arch my arms over my head, and to click simultaneously different rhythms with my fingers while I stamped my heels. And I would look forward to my dance classes after school.

My mother was nursing an abstract painter, from her circle of friends, who was ill with tuberculosis. While she disappeared to Paalen's sickroom at the back of the house, I stayed with his young wife in their Mexican garden, earthenware pottery and archaeological figures scattered among the tropical plants, watching her prized marten which was tied to the trunk of an ancient tree. I was not allowed near the sick man's area, though once or twice I got as far as the landing from where I strained to see into that mysterious room with everything white and a strong smell of antiseptic. My mother explained his illness was contagious, and even *she* had to wear a special mask to enter his room.

She was with Paalen when he died. I overheard her describing to a friend how he had tried to hang on to life till the very last.

Paalen published a Mexican art magazine, *Dyn*, from the early 1940s, which my mother collected and kept – a then avant-garde magazine with articles on political, philosophical and archaeological topics, poems, black-and-white photographs of Mexican subjects, and colour prints of paintings, with a wide range of international and Mexican contributors including Anaïs Nin, Henry Miller, Alexander Calder, Henry Moore, Braque, Valentine Penrose and César Moro. There are several articles by Gustav Regler and drawings by Marie Louise. Diego Rivera and Frida Kahlo's Coyoacán home, now turned museum, bears an uncanny likeness to my memory of Paalen's house and garden. It is only a few streets from Trotsky's house, also turned museum, where he was killed shortly before our arrival in Mexico. My mother mentioned how she had come across the assassin, Ramón Mercader, at political meetings back in Barcelona, where he seemed a timid young man.

I stretched my legs to reach up the steep steps of the massive Pyramid of the Sun in Teotihuacán, the ancient City of the Gods, as I trod the path of the ancient Mexicans leading their victims to sacrifice. At the top of the pyramid, the priests cut open their chests with their obsidian blades, tore out their beating hearts and lifted them towards the sun in offering – that it might rise again to light and warm the land another day – while the now lifeless body was flung down the steps to the watching multitudes below. I paused to rest at the first terrace breaking the ascent, before starting on the next stretch to reach the wider one halfway up this monument to the sun, which was beating down on me, intensifying the challenge. When I finally reached the square platform on the summit, the whole countryside lay before me. To my right, the Pyramid of the Moon rose at the end of the broad avenue which swept past below me to peter out on the other side of the archaeological area. There, set further back, the temple of Quetzalcóatl: that mysterious figure portrayed as a plumed serpent and referred to as prince, prophet, god and the morning star, who was to return from the East across the sea as a white God – though some suggest this idea was used by the conquistadors to persuade the natives into venerating them. From the stepped friezes of the temple of Quetzalcóatl protruded alternating heads of the plumed serpent and the god of corn.

On the ruined walls of a palace next to the Pyramid of the Moon, the faint remains of what were once brilliant murals in red, black, yellow and turquoise were still waiting to be studied. Geometric patterns and stylised depictions of jaguars, snakes, owls and butterflies, of gods and priests, and of the religious practices and everyday life of the ancient peoples from this place.

Little was known of the origins of Teotihuacán. Tunnels bored through the centre of the Pyramid of the Sun revealed many layers of cultures which go back to the first century and very likely beyond – a telescoping of history the further back we search. Like memory ...

Drifting through a thick carpet of water lilies, the sturdy young punter navigated the flower boat through the canal while we lazily glided along. Flowers everywhere. More flower boats passed by with families and friends floating through the waterways of Xochimilco. The flat-bottomed barges that crowded the canal were decorated with brightly coloured flowers spelling the boat's name across the arch framing the prow – *Margarita, Josefina, Mirella*. Flowers floated on the water, and some flower boats carried bunches of them to give away or offer for sale to passing boats. A group of mariachis were singing lustily to the accompaniment of their strings and trumpets as they moved past in their flower boat. Then the heady smells of Mexican cooking wafted in our direction as a kitchen flower boat approached and offered us tacos, tamales, iced fruit drinks and other delicious snacks. The sun glinted through the tall poplars lining the banks of the canal; the sky beyond bright blue. All around us was the sound of chatter and laughter and music as people enjoyed their day's outing along the canals of Xochimilco – a leftover of the lake on which the city of Mexico, Tenochtitlán, was built by the wandering Aztecs.

Back to our life in the city: we moved again. This time to an apartment in a large block in the centre near Bellas Artes.

Lying in bed in my room in the dark every night, I listened to the ceaseless cacophony of tooting and beeping which rose to my window from the traffic on San Juan de Letrán. I would watch a series of lights move across the wall near the ceiling every time I heard the sound of a car approaching from what I imagined must have been a certain angle in the street below. The lights would follow each other like soldiers marching in file, one behind the other. I could tell when the next soldiers' march was due from the sound of the approaching car. And I passed the time watching the lights and shadows move across the white wall to the accompaniment of the racket, like a cat's choir, until I fell asleep.

Sitting in the dark next to my mother in a cinema on our street, San Juan de Letrán, a story was unfolding on the screen of courage and resistance in the face of menacing soldiers careering on their motorbikes through the streets of a village. Maybe in France. There was a great deal of action and suspense. One man in particular, who had done some heroic deed and was trying to evade capture, is chased and finally caught on a bridge. At that point, I felt my mother's great emotion. Maybe her breathing had altered. Or she was crying silently. In the darkness of the cinema, I sensed – as if by osmosis – the distress the scene appeared to have unleashed in my mother, without yet comprehending it …

It was 1944. The war in Europe was coming to an end.

It was around this time that my father came into our lives again. He told us that he had been interned in Baden Baden, in Germany, when the Americans joined the war, and freed as part of a prisoners' exchange deal. He had been held at the Brenner Park Hotel, along with many other privileged and interesting prisoners, and been well treated: the only hardship, his enforced confinement within the hotel's grounds which he described as vast and pleasant.

He moved in with us in the apartment in San Juan de Letrán. I was very happy to have my father back. In the mornings I would get into bed and play with him till it was time to get up. We had never before actually lived, the three of us together, in one home – this was a novel experience.

One day he came home curiously pleased.

'My wallet was stolen on the bus!'

The buses in the city were generally crammed full. People stood so tightly packed together, that those who didn't fit inside the bus held on by the handle at the back entrance with a foothold on the steps. Pickpockets abounded and it became a natural habit to watch one's things.

'That's terrible! Did you catch the thief?' I asked.

'No!' he replied. 'It was amazing! He was so skilful! He managed to slide his hand into my pocket and pull out the wallet with barely a flicker of his fingers! I only felt the lightest brush as he withdrew it. I decided he deserved to keep it.'

After maybe a month or two, my mother packed our things again. My father had found a place for her and me to live on the outskirts of Cuernavaca.

*Acapantzingo, 1944.*

THE OLD TAXI drove us down a bumpy dirt road full of potholes and puddles and finally came to a stop. As I stepped out into my new surroundings, a large sow surrounded by her squadron of piglets came trotting down the middle of the mud road grunting loudly.

Carrying our suitcases, my father walked through a wooden gate that led into a small house and garden, followed by my mother and me. That was to be our temporary new home; my father would live in the city and visit us at the weekends.

I stopped attending school. I missed my friends and my teacher, whose lessons I had found inspiring and with whom I had got on especially well. Now my mother sat with me every day at the dining table and went over my schoolwork with me. But her teaching was different.

'It's not like that. My teacher explained it another way.'

'Don't be naughty and get on with your work. This is right, I'm telling you.'

'No. It's not.'

A terrible tug-of-war would follow, and I would walk out of the room following these disagreements bursting with resentment. My mother was fighting for her now failing authority over me on matters she believed she knew best. And I was fighting for my passionately felt right to my own judgement, which I believed deserved respect. The first serious cracks, in what had been such a close relationship between mother and daughter – even though we had seen little of each other in the city, she with her long hours at work and I at school – were appearing.

She seemed tense and irritable much of the time.

The odd moment, we still connected.

One morning, before breakfast, she said to me: 'Come! I want to show you something.'

She led me out into the garden. The sun was barely out and the dew-soaked leaves and grass shone in the early morning light. She took me to a corner of the garden by the side of the house and pointed. There, a partly finished, perfectly formed spiderweb stretched across from the wooden fence to some tree branches, while a small green spider with an intricate pattern on the back of its body was skilfully weaving the final strands into the web. When it was completed, the spider made its way to the centre and remained there motionless – the web glinting in the soft, slanting sunlight.

'I come out and watch it every morning,' she told me. 'The spider starts weaving its web at exactly the same time every day. Seven o'clock. Then it sits there completely still for two hours, and finally unweaves it again and goes away. Until the same time the next morning.'

'Where does it go in between?'

'I don't know. It's a mystery.'

Around this time, my mother told me she was expecting a child. I was thrilled. At long last I would have company.

In the meantime, as the house had been rented for two months only, we had to move again.

# A Mexican Village

*Acapantzingo, 1945.*

THE DUSTY DIRT ROAD scorched my bare feet. The brilliant green foliage of the mango trees sparkled in the blazing sun. The heavy sweet scent of guavas mingled with the faint stench from the *apantle* flowing along the verge of the road. Out of the corner cantina with the bright red Coca-Cola sign on its turquoise façade, the jukebox was blasting a mariachi song about a certain Juan Charrasqueado's drunkenness, sexual allure and violent death. The powdery earth's soft caress outdone by its fierce heat quickened my pace. I decided to take a short cut across the empty field facing the cantina, so my feet might tread on cool grass. It grew tall and wild here and I instinctively scanned it for snakes. Back onto the road around the corner, the penitentiary appeared before me. A large building with a tall lookout tower surrounded by a high wall topped with barbed wire – from where, on odd occasions, all hell broke out as the inmates tried to escape. Past the penitentiary, I turned into the shady lane with the villa where I always stopped to gaze, from the fence, at its airy veranda, fresh green lawn and cool blue swimming pool.

Our new home was a short stretch down the road from the corner cantina. Bougainvillea grew in a luscious tangled mass of cherry red around the tall iron garden gate, matched by more scrambling up the front of the house to disappear over the flat roof above and frame the tiled veranda below. Masses of yellow, red and white gladioli grew for the market in an empty plot next to the house, while another *apantle* trickled past behind it. At the *apantles,* native women knelt to scrub their pots and pans, rub and squeeze their laundry, wash their long black hair, and splash their wholesome brown faces in the clear flowing water. Further up stream, I had seen little boys pee into them. My mother once saw someone throwing the excrement of a man dying from typhoid into the one at the back of our house. Birth and death were everywhere in evidence here. In the street, in front of our house, girls barely into their teens walked past with their bulging, pregnant stomachs on their way to their chores, and small boys ran about in short shirts without buttons exposing their taut balloon bellies above their skinny legs. Left largely to myself here again, I would pass the time standing at the gate, or swinging myself on its railing, watching the boys at play from the adobe shacks across the street, and the girls plaiting their jet-black hair into thick braids, working woollen cords of many colours into them. In the evening, young men hosed down the street transforming the hot dusty atmosphere into cool moist freshness, inundating the senses with the earth's peppery scent. On Saturdays, pay day, the sound of loud voices and drunken brawls from the corner cantina reached our gate, and by late afternoon the men wove their way down the road, singing and cursing loudly.

One such Saturday, as the evening drew close, I looked on from the gate as two men shouted and rushed at each other with knives while the local people gathered to watch the unfolding drama in the street. From fragments of conversations I gleaned that the aggressor had turned up after a long absence and found his abandoned woman now settled with the other in one of the adobe shacks. My mother would call a doctor who tended the injuries and illnesses of the families across the street without charge. He was also a refugee. Austrian, I think. Every now and then, a procession passed our gate on the way to the cemetery on the edge of Acapantzingo. At the head: a tiny coffin held high, followed by the family and a long line of local villagers, the women enveloped head and shoulders in their *rebozos* and the men pressing their sombreros against their chest, their looks solemn and resigned. I once caught a glimpse of two little hands folded, pale and still, with a bunch of flowers peeping over the open coffin. The older women would admit to having had some fourteen to twenty children of which two, or at most four, survived. Then, on the 2nd of November, the Day of the Dead, they all went to the cemetery with food and shoes and other presents to place on their relatives' graves, followed by feasting. Small sugar skulls appeared everywhere, in the market, on street stands, in shops, each bearing a Christian name written in pink, red, violet, green or blue icing, and there were flowers, music and dance.

I sometimes joined the procession of mourners behind the small coffin and walked with them part of the way. I knew every detail of the route to the cemetery, starting with the long walk down our street. On our side, the colonial-style villas with their well-tended, tropical gardens: weekend homes of families from Mexico City. Across the street, the jumbled group of adobe dwellings ended at the broad track to Conchita's ranch, followed by more villas, their gardens on this side gently sloping away until, beyond reach and out of view, the ground dropped abruptly into the mysterious depths of the ravine that cuts through Acapantzingo and Cuernavaca – the bottom of which, rumour went, no one had ever reached alive. Vultures were often seen circling over it.

Halfway down the road, I turned left, past the local school, then right again. Here the vegetation became wilder and more luxuriant and the homes sparser and more primitive as the dirt road reached the neglected, overgrown remnant of Maximilian's house and garden: the Austrian archduke's retreat during his brief Mexican reign the previous century. Facing it, a bare patch of ground with an ancient ceiba tree formed the forecourt of a simple, baroque church. On a saint's day, the local people took their cattle covered with yellow flowers into the church to have them blessed. From here on, the road narrowed to a path flanked by dense, tropical vegetation. Discrete clouds of tiny flying insects would appear near ground level and flit upwards, stop still in front of me for a few seconds and move on in unison to a new space. I was mindful of my mother's warning about mosquitoes here, as there was talk of malaria in these parts. Now the growing silence was broken only by distant dogs barking and the occasional birdcall. Here I could be myself, without reproof or demands, in this tangled buzzing natural world that felt in full harmony with me, and I immersed myself in its beauty and my serenity. Then, finally, the view suddenly opened before me. On my left, the small cemetery appeared crowded with wooden crosses, painted turquoise, pink and white, stuck at various angles into the ground. Among them, a few neglected ancient graves with headstones. Fresh mounds of earth marked the latest arrivals. I would pick my way with difficulty between the graves, many so small that there was almost no space between one cross and the next. And I felt a peculiar closeness to all those dead babies and children in the hushed peace that enveloped us.

Across the open countryside, in the far distance, the two snow-capped volcanoes, Popocatépetl and Ixtaccíhuatl, stood out against the azure sky. Ixtaccíhuatl stretched out in the form of a sleeping woman, the snow spread over her like a flimsy white mantle glinting in the sun, while Popocatépetl crouched, his domed summit a thick crown of snow, watching over his beloved for eternity. They rose mistily, in all their radiance, out of the flat landscape, much as they must have appeared before the gaze of the local Tlahuicas and Mexicas who wove their legendary tales about them before the Spanish arrived.

This, now, was my world.

⁓

AFTER OUR INITIAL STAY in the house further down our street, my father had decided we should remain here. That had spelled the end of my schooling in the city and I missed my lessons and friends in Colegio Madrid. Even more, I regretted the loss of my dance lessons.

I started going to school in Cuernavaca. Escuela Pestalozzi was on the other side of town. Every day, I walked to the centre of Cuernavaca and on past the ancient Hispanic cathedral and Borda Gardens to reach the school – a rust-red building in the busy main street through which the traffic from Mexico City entered Cuernavaca.

The children at this school, mostly mestizo, were disarmingly friendly. Here I faced no questions about my religious, national or other group affiliations and was instantly accepted without preconditions. On the other hand, the classes were lax and undemanding – though I happily pursued my interests through my own reading at home.

Soon after I arrived, the school started preparing for a special commemorative day in Cuernavaca. The girls in my class were to march in a procession behind the brass band through the main streets of the town, wearing a military-style, light blue, cotton blouse and skirt, a forage cap to match, and white socks and sandals. We were each asked to bring a pineapple to school and had to slice from it long twisting peels, which were left to ferment in large earthen-ware vats. On the day of the fiesta, the resulting mildly alcoholic *tepache* was offered to parents and friends following the triumphant procession through town.

My father came to Acapantzingo from the city at weekends to tend his tomato plants in the back garden. He talked a lot about his tomato plants. He liked looking after them and watching them grow. The large spacious room to one side of the front veranda – some-what remote from the rest of the household – was kept for him. He was, in fact, becoming a more distant figure, and my initial excite-ment at our reunion in Mexico City was fading …

The bougainvillea-bordered veranda led straight into my moth-er's room, her bed to the right and her desk, with Clara's photograph, in the far corner. Behind it, my bedroom overlooked the back garden through two large windows with the customary mosquito netting. Every night before bed my mother would scan the ceiling for scorpi-ons between the black wooden beams, brush them off with a broom and stamp on them. Between my mother's room and the dining room was a small basic bathroom, where a centipede once surprised me by climbing out of the drain hole while I washed my hands.

The dining room looked out onto the field of gladioli, and black wooden shelves along its walls displayed the brightly glazed crockery my mother bought from the native potters in the market. Behind the dining room was a large kitchen, which overlooked my father's tomato plants in the back garden. The food was prepared on a table, beside which a swinging rack with a large bottle of drink-ing water stood on the floor – the tap water not being fit to drink. These bottles were delivered regularly, though my mother once saw the driver, having run out of them, fill an empty one from a tap by the side of the road. Food was fresh from the market. That which needed storing was kept in a small refrigerator with a shelf for the ice block that was delivered daily by a small truck and left on the front garden path. The dishes were washed under cold running water with a soaped loofah, while the laundry was soaped, rubbed and slapped repeatedly against the ridged stone surface of a shallow sink in the garden, rinsed copiously under the cold tap, and hung on the lines in the burning heat of the day.

A cat and dog were added to the household. The dog was a friendly Alsatian which my father named Lloveta, Catalan for young she-wolf. The cat soon had one litter after another, ending in a large number of wild cats running in and out of the house.

At the back of the garden were two small service rooms. My mother offered them to a woman and her children from the adobe shacks across the street. They had been left homeless when the father had abandoned them. Josefina was a thin, wry woman with two long plaits and who had three children, aged nine, eleven and fourteen: the older two already at work. They all slept together in one room and used the other for cooking, eating and living in. Josefina would squat near the entrance of this room, her skirt neatly caught under her knees, turning back and forth between her pestle and mortar – where she mixed and ground her chillies and other spices – and her flat *metate* and grinding bar, all of the same black volcanic stone. The coal brazier was also within reach on the ground.

I used to sit with Josefina for hours on end, watching her at work. I was determined to learn how to make tortillas. She started by kneading the maize dough on her *metate* with the grinding bar, frequently splashing a little water onto it. When it was ready, she would pinch off a piece, enough to fit into the palm of her hand, roll it between her hands and start patting and shaping it with her fingers until it was flat and round. She then clapped it back and forth, from one hand to the other, turning it flatter and larger. She gave it a final touch balancing it to and fro between her hands and, finally, holding it by the edge – the tortilla by now very fine and perfectly round – spread it on the *comal,* a large griddle on top of the brazier. When small bubbles appeared in the tortilla, Josefina would gently press her index and middle fingers on its edge to pick it up and turn it over. After a few moments it puffed up – and it was ready. She took it off the *comal* and added it to the others in a basket inside a cloth, which she folded over them to keep them warm.

Tortillas were an essential part of every meal, either neat or with food wrapped inside them. They became tacos, rolled up with chicken or mashed potatoes and fried till crackly, with strips of lettuce, sliced onion, chilli, fresh coriander, a bit of sour cream and some cheese crumbled on top.

---

I used to squat next to Josefina, carefully tuck my skirt under my knees too, and try to make tortillas.

'Would you let me have a go?'

'Help yourself to the dough. I'll make room on the *comal*.'

But the tortillas would break halfway through my endeavours, or wouldn't turn out as fine as Josefina's, or as evenly rounded. Dumpy little tortillas that nowhere near matched hers.

Next door, on the other side of the house from the plot with the gladioli, lived a lively elderly lady whom my mother encouraged me to call *abuelita*, or granny. Her house was set well back from the street behind an extensive lawn, in the middle of which was an amputated tree trunk with a monkey tied to it. The droll creature would pass the time playfully romping on the lawn and up and down the tree trunk within the radius its rope allowed.

Abuelita often invited me to her elegant home and sat me down to tell me stories.

'One day, a small girl was kidnapped,' she told me, her look benign and gentle behind her glasses, her grey hair collected in a bun at the back of her head. 'The kidnappers locked her in a dark room and came back to torture her every day. They did dreadful things to her and finally killed her. Her father and mother were desperate to find her, and the kidnappers phoned them and told them to wait on a particular street corner at five o'clock. They stuck all the pieces of the girl together with wire and drove past very fast with her sitting in the front seat, allowing the parents to get a glimpse of her.' She would go into the bloodthirsty details of the story with a quiet relish, assuring me it was all true. She also told me of the time she left half a dozen eggs in the fridge and forgot about them. After a week or two, she opened the fridge to find small chicks had emerged out of three eggs, while the others had borne scorpions.

One day, abuelita's household was enveloped in doom. The wife of one of her two sons, who regularly came with their families at the weekends from Mexico City, had committed suicide. But, to my astonishment, it was not her loss they mourned, but the unforgivable sin of her missing the last rites and confession.

Friends from Mexico City often came to visit us. The house in

Acapantzingo was generally full of children. Libertad came too, and we would play at being mothers, pushing our toy prams with our dolls to a quiet passage behind the house where we would sit and have coffee out of little Mexican pottery cups and saucers, and gossip together the way grown-ups did.

I also missed Volney with whom I had played on the rooftop among the washing. I remembered his heart-stopping smile and would walk dreamily from room to room thinking of him, unable to dismiss him from my thoughts. This must be what love, *amor*, is, as in the movies. I sat down and composed a poem declaring my love and how much I missed him. Then I carefully folded the sheet of paper with the poem and walked towards my mother's desk, opened the drawer, placed it inside, hiding it under some papers, and walked away again, mixing my intense sentiments with some imagined melodramatic scene in a film. I forgot all about it until a few weeks later, when my mother came across it.

'Did you write this poem?' she asked me.

I was too tongue-tied with embarrassment to reply.

But she laughed.

'It's lovely!' she exclaimed.

I played marbles on the dirt road with the boys from the adobe shacks across the street. In our front garden, I climbed the guava trees and bit into their fragrant, fleshy fruit. Banana trees grew among them, and tall hibiscus bushes with scarlet flowers and lush pink ones, their petals all tousled and ruffled. Tiny, brightly coloured humming birds swooped down to point their long slender beaks into them, their fast fluttering wings a colourful blur about their motionless bodies while

*On our roof, Acapantzingo, 1945*

73

they gathered the nectar. In the side garden, next to *abuelita's*, there were several lemon trees, under which I once saw a black snake, and a tall papaya tree next to a silvery *guamúchitl,* its branches spread over our flat roof where I would climb to eat the sweetish acrid flesh in its curly brown pods.

Past the plot with the gladioli, the spicy treacly smell of *piloncillo* – a brown cone of unrefined sugar chipped off for cooking – announced Don José's general store where I went for my chewing gum and Orange Crush. Further on, a left turn by the cantina brought me to the penitentiary on my way to Cuernavaca.

The dirt road took up a winding course until it reached the bridge over the ravine. Here Acapantzingo ended and Cuernavaca started. The fresh aroma of maize dough wafted from the mill by the bridge where a continuous stream of women wrapped in their *rebozos* came and went to buy the dough for their tortillas. Across the bridge, the dirt road became cobbled and rose steeply to the crenellated Palacio de Cortés and three central squares at the top. The thick green foliage of the ancient Indian laurel trees in the middle square blotted out the sky, and one could hardly hear oneself speak above the deafening din from the birds' peeps and twitters. Men sat on benches with old typewriters typing and reading letters for the illiterate native men and women, many of whom came from distant villages to have their documents read to them. Overlooking the square was a colonial hotel with a wide veranda where smartly dressed people sat and chatted with their friends over leisurely drinks. The next square was full of newspaper and magazine stalls and a stand with bottles of red, green and yellow syrups that were poured into glasses with crushed ice, for those who needed to quench their thirst in the heat and were indifferent to their parasitic complement. From here, a narrow street lined with shops selling local silver jewellery, clothes, shoes, and other goods climbed to a small square with a church on one side and the entrance to the market on the other.

First the indoor part with the meat, poultry and fish. A vast hall with a high, glass ceiling, granite floor, and the reverberating echos of people's bustle and chatter as they sought their cuts from the hanging carcasses. The rancid smell of raw meat and blood. Scrawny, hungry dogs making their way in and out between stands and people's legs. In the central area, cows' and pigs' heads with glazed, lifeless eyes and buzzing flies. Intestines spread out fan-like from their mesentery. Lungs and hearts hung from large hooks still joined together. One or other sturdy young man at these stands would be blowing into a pair of cow's lungs, trying to fill them with air to make them pink and spongy. I used to stand and watch his extreme efforts, cheeks taut and puffed out, face flushed and tense, eyes wide open. And I marked the ease with which I filled my own lungs as I breathed, and that of cows' breathing in the fields too, and would be mystified by the resistance of the animal's lungs to inflation outside the body.

Beyond the meat hall started the open market. On stepping out, I always came across the same old woman sitting on her haunches guarding a tin half full of insects crawling over each other, which she kept poking back with a stick.

'What are those for, Mami?'

'I don't know. Ask her, *la viejita*.'

'What do you do with those insects?' I asked her.

'*Se comen, m'hijita*.' You eat them.

'What ... like that?'

'*Sí. Así nomás*.'

Then, stand after stand of frijoles, brown, beige, black, speckled, in large heaps on a cloth or straw *petate* on the ground and in jute sacks standing alongside. Chillies, red, green, maroon, fat, thin, long, round. More stands with vegetables stacked into piles, maize, onions, red and green tomatoes, large bunches of fresh coriander, pyramids of avocados. Then the fruit stands, a profusion of watermelons, papayas, mangoes, guavas, zapotillas, mameys, mountains of oranges, limes and lemons. My mother always bought a large bagful for our breakfast orange juice; the lemons were pressed into our drinking water to make a delicious refreshing drink.

During one of our first trips to the market, at the start of our life in Acapantzingo, my mother and I became separated. I didn't find her again in the bustling crowd, so I walked on, absorbed in the stands and the scenes around me, making my way down the market until it petered out in a side street that ended at the bridge over the ravine. Once there, I took the road back to Acapantzingo, ambling along and looking at everything on the way. There was the ancient woman who always sat on a chair by the side of the road where it dipped into a hollow towards the ravine. A blacksmith worked in the open down there. I would watch him pick out glowing chunks of red-hot iron from the furnace with his tongs, hammer at them, and shape them into horseshoes. That thin, deeply wrinkled woman, sitting very straight and still, her gaze dead – how old might she be? A hundred? More? I exchanged a greeting with her and she faintly nodded in my direction, her milky eyes staring at nothing. From below, the regular metallic thuds of the hammer against the horseshoe. When the shape was right, the blacksmith dropped it into a tank of cold water and a loud sizzle reached me in the street above. Was she his mother? A neighbour? After several more bends in the road, I reached the penitentiary. Then: round the corner, and I was home.

My mother arrived two hours later in a distraught state. She had looked *everywhere* for me. It had not occurred to her that I knew my way home.

My mother's birthday was approaching and I wanted to buy her a present. In past years I had maybe drawn a picture for her, but never before had I *bought* her something. So I set off to the market on my own, with some change I had saved up. After wandering among the various stands, I came across a woman, wrapped in her *rebozo,* sitting on the ground with bunches of bright orange flowers neatly laid out on a cloth in front of her. Their trumpet-like petals were fine and delicate. They were especially lovely. My mother would surely like them. I bought a bunch and happily took them home.

'*¡Feliz cumpleaños!* I got you a present!' I told my mother on the day, as I stretched my small fist with the bright orange flowers towards her.

My mother burst out laughing.

'They're beautiful! Thank you! But you *eat* those! They're cour-gette flowers!'

To one side of the adobe dwellings across the street, a path led to Conchita's ranch on the open land behind them. A large terrace on the first floor of her residence overlooked the back courtyard and garden, the stables further back, and the land beyond disappearing precipitously into the ravine. The terrace led into Conchita's main living room with its Spanish colonial furniture and ornately framed oil paintings. Family heirlooms. The one Conchita delighted in most, and never tired of pointing out, was prominently placed above her elegant settee, facing the terrace. The Virgin Mary stood on a cumulus cloud in Heaven surrounded by playful cherubs flying in and out of the clouds. Conchita would stand there with her mischievous smile, pointing her finger at one of the little angels who had been given her great-aunt's face and wavy black hair.

She would also bring out a glamorous close-up photograph of the Hollywood actress, Kathryn Grayson, with an affectionate dedication to Conchita written diagonally across the lower corner in lavish handwriting.

When Conchita became melancholic, maybe after an evening of playing cards with my mother and one or two other friends – she taught me her expert card-shuffling technique – she would put on her record of 'Un viejo amor' or 'Solamente una vez'.

*Solamente una vez amé en la vida*
*solamente una vez y nada más …*

Conchita belonged to a wealthy *hacendado* or land-owning family. Lean and tanned from her outdoor life, her hair short, straight and brown with a grey streak in front, always in trousers, she would stand leaning slightly back, her hands in her pockets, her head a little to one side, and a brazen smile which hid who knows what mysterious pains and loves from her past. Her brother, Antonio Algara, was the Director General of the Mexican Bullring and to all accounts immensely wealthy, while Conchita seemed to be always broke.

After her milk round to her clients in Cuernavaca, Conchita would often meet my mother and give her a lift home from the market. We would all sit squeezed together in the cab of her milk truck. Her friend Kitty was a frequent visitor to the hacienda: a pretty young woman with a mass of curly brown hair and the great-granddaughter of Porfirio Díaz – the general whose thirty-year rule had led to the Mexican Revolution.

'What are those funny green leaves?' Kitty asked my mother once, pointing to her basket bursting with shopping, as she joined them in the cab.

'That's spinach!'

'No! *Really?* The kind we *eat*? Is *that* what it looks like before it's cooked?'

At certain times of the year, Conchita drove out to her sugar cane plantation outside Cuernavaca. I loved these trips, sitting next to her in the cab. Manuel, the peon, travelled in the back. Once there, he would load the truck with the cane other workers had cut with their scythes and collected together, or with fodder for the cows. I would watch Manuel's strong, graceful movements as he lifted the heavy bundles and arranged them neatly onto the back of the truck. He was maybe sixteen, humble, hardworking, appealingly gentle, and I was a little in love with him.

∽

DURING THE RAINY SEASON, as the skies released their torrential load every night, I would lie in bed and listen to the rain pelting the ground in a mad dance. Thunders cracked and roared and lightning flashes streaked across the sky or flooded it in bright light. Back in the darkness, the rain went on splashing noisily into its own puddles and making streams that ran every which way. The next morning I would wake up to a fine, clear day with the sun shining out of a blue sky. By early afternoon small clouds would appear and slowly start to grow, darken and coalesce until, towards evening, the sky was laden again with threatening storm clouds. Then the rain would break and the cycle repeat itself.

The dry season was unrelentingly hot and swimming became my most sought after pursuit. I got to know and show up at every hotel with a swimming pool in Cuernavaca.

∽

NOW AND THEN, shots would ring out from the penitentiary. The noisy exchange would be heard for hours all the way down the street. I would take cover behind the house hoping no stray bullets would find their way there …

One day, on my way home from school, just before reaching the spot with the ancient woman and the blacksmith, I came across a crowd of people gathered around a small, two-storey building under construction. A group of men were lowering a stretcher from the first-floor balcony down to the street. A young man, his black curly hair lying loosely about his head and shining in the sun, lay motionless on the stretcher. During the shift, his arm slipped lifelessly sideways. I heard talk of an electric shock. The crowd blocked my view so I continued on my way feeling shaken, the image of the young man still vivid in my mind. Was that what death looked like? The suddenness with which it could strike? And yet the blazing sun's sparkle was undiminished, the Mexican colours dazzled as vibrantly as before, the rhythm, breath and clatter of the living all around me continued unabated.

Every once in a while, on that same road, I would come across a rattlesnake lying in the middle of it, twisted, mangled and still, stoned to death by the local people. And I would give it a wide berth as I walked round it.

Irene came to help with the household. She was a girl of sixteen with smiling eyes and thick plaits looped behind her neck. She was being courted by Gumesindo, our neighbour from our first house further down the street.

Courting couples would meet in the street in the early evening when their day's work was done. The girls stood inside the iron gates waiting for their young men. When they showed up, the couples would stand on either side of the gate, their fingers intertwined around the vertical railings, chattering softly tête-à-tête until dark. Gumesindo worked till late, Irene already in bed by then in my father's front room where she slept during the week. Before retiring, she would pass a long piece of thread through the window, leaving one end by the gate and tying the other around her finger. On his way home after his day's work, Gumesindo tugged his end of the thread to wake Irene, and she went to the gate for their love talk. One evening, one of the local boys snipped the thread: that night Gumesindo gathered a long piece of thread, but no Irene.

In the meantime my mother was getting bigger and was pleased to find cotton skirts with elasticised waistbands in the market for her growing stomach. She spent her time looking after the household and friends from Mexico City when they came to visit, or with Conchita and her circle.

We saw little of each other apart from mealtimes, and spoke nothing of great significance. The one thing she did one day for me,

Photo of my mother with her dolls on the wall by my bed

with a sense of purpose, was to frame an enlarged photograph of herself, aged seven, posing with all her beautifully groomed dolls in her garden in Chemnitz, and hang it next to my bed – so it was the first thing I saw when I woke in the morning and the last when I went to sleep at night. She attached a peculiar importance to this photograph, though I never understood what she was trying to tell me with it. Was I one of her dolls she feared losing? Or was she, in some way, implying the reverse: there's a little girl in me that needs caring for in my present straits ... A combination of both? Or neither ... Whatever she meant by it, she continued to leave me largely to my own devices. My father's visits, meantime, had become scarcer, and he too less communicative. Left to myself as I was, I became increasingly absorbed in the lush Mexican wilderness of my surroundings, where all those stressful pressures and complicating factors became irrelevant and melted away.

As the birth drew near, my mother went to Mexico City. After a long and painful labour with my father by her side, a baby girl was born. My mother brought her back to Acapantzingo. I thought she looked beautiful. They called her Evelyn.

My mother now became fully occupied with the new child, while

I – aged nine and approaching puberty, and as though in parallel – became more involved and maternal in my games with my dolls.

*With my new sister, Atlacomulco, 1945*

Doña Elodia, from across the street, started coming to help with the new baby.

Doña Elodia's Saint's Day was approaching and she invited me to the big fiesta. There, everyone was helping with the preparations. Doña Elodia was cooking the *mole* in the open. She was stirring the thick dark sauce, to which she now added a turkey, in a huge earthenware pot over the fire. The aroma from the *mole* revealed its rich mixture of spices, chillies, peanuts and chocolate. And there were fresh tortillas, frijoles and tacos – though I forewent the risky lettuce piled on the tacos. Everyone from the adobe huts, from the youngest baby to the oldest resident, was at the fiesta. The children ran in and out among the adults, noses snuffling, shouting and laughing, helping themselves to the hot food, unperturbed by the fiery chillies. As the afternoon advanced they began to sing and dance into the night – but I returned home on my mother's firm bidding.

There was great excitement across the street on another day when a family won the lottery. I watched from the gate as a large van arrived and unloaded a brand new bed, refrigerator, radio, and many other luxury items. They moved everything into their one-roomed adobe shack. After a day or two, they moved everything out again. For one thing, they had no electricity. It seems they had also found sleeping on a bed uncomfortable. So they leaned all their purchases against the wall outside their hut, and the whole family went back to sleeping on their straw *petate* on the mud floor.

Pieces of my mother's silver cutlery started to vanish. The silverware engraved with her initials was a treasured present from her parents when she was a young girl in Germany, and which she had managed to save during her many moves in war-torn Europe. There was one particular spoon with a pretty scalloped edge around its handle, on which her name had been carefully engraved:

*Käte*

This spoon had been a special present from her mother.

The timing of their disappearance coincided with Doña Elodia's service. So one day my mother went to Doña Elodia's adobe hut, chatted with her for a while, and there, among *la doña's* spoons and forks, she spotted her cutlery. My mother asked politely if she could have her pieces back, but Doña Elodia insisted they were hers. My mother showed her the spoon with her name engraved on it.

'That's mine too!' Doña Elodia told her indignantly. 'Do you think that's the only spoon like that in the world?' For she couldn't read.

My mother didn't wish to upset her, and left.

After some thought, she approached a policeman at the penitentiary and asked if there was a way of getting her cutlery back without pressing charges against Doña Elodia. The policeman went with my mother to Doña Elodia's hut and agreed with *la doña* that the cutlery was hers.

So the silver spoon with her name that had come all the way from Chemnitz, through Spain, across France, and over the Atlantic, ended up in Doña Elodia's mud shack in Acapantzingo.

∾

THE WIDE TERRACE at the back of the Cortés Palace overlooked the bus terminal below and a vast panorama towards Acapantzingo and beyond, while its walls covered with Diego Rivera murals depicted the life of the native people before and after the conquest. Humble, barefooted Indians would come into the palace in their white shirts and white, cross-over, cotton trousers – the same as those in the murals' post-conquest scenes – and stand, hat in hand, silently looking for long periods at a time at every detail in Diego Rivera's paintings.

∾

IT WAS 1945. The war in Europe ended.

My mother started receiving a regular periodical with long lists of the dead in the concentration camps. She knew her sister Lotte was alive and well in New Zealand and her brother Fritz in Palestine. But she had heard nothing from her brother Hans whose last contact had been from Holland before the war. Nor had she had news of her father who had stayed in Chemnitz. Her own mother had died from an illness barely a month after my birth.

Every time the lists arrived, she scanned page upon page of names searching for those of her father and brother, yet dreading she might find them. She sometimes came across the name of someone else she had known, and became dispirited for days on end. She was going through a new set of lists one day and became especially upset. She started weeping. Conchita came over and was trying to comfort her. It emerged she had seen Hans's name. All day she wept inconsolably. A few days later, though, it turned into joy and relief when she found there had been some mistake and he was alive. She received news that he was in Holland, where he had survived the war hiding in the home of a Dutch family. But her father had not escaped. He had died in the concentration camp in Theresienstadt – the significance of which would emerge more fully in my later life. For now, I watched my mother's emotional turmoil and grief during those days; her anxious concern for family members, whom I knew only as names and from old photographs – my memory of our brief meetings when I was a small child in Europe long faded.

Soon afterwards, my mother decided to leave Mexico and join her sister Lotte in New Zealand. Lotte encouraged her with letters full of glowing praise for her adopted country and its education and health systems. The relations between my mother and father had reached rock bottom once again. I caught vague references to my father and Ilse Altmann, my mother's close friend from our Café Viena days. Though I had seen little of my father in my life, and he was something of a stranger to me, I had felt a deep affection for him. Now I began to feel let down by him, betrayed, and my trust would be forever marred. Though my relations with my mother had become strained, I felt I could rely on her. But I wasn't given time to think much about all this. In preparation for our new life in New

Zealand, it was decided I should be moved back to Mexico City to attend the English, Windsor School. I was to stay with my father in the city during the week and return at weekends to my mother in Acapantzingo.

*Mexico City, 1947.*
MY FATHER'S SHORT STREET was off the tree-lined avenue, Paseo de La Reforma, near the traffic island with Diana's fountain: its brilliant display of widely arcing jets of water lit up nightly in every colour of the rainbow.

In Windsor School, the English classes were taught by a young American teacher who expressed herself in a heavy colloquial American with a Southern drawl. And that was how I learned English in anticipation of our move to New Zealand.

I soon made new friends.

'Are you Catholic?'

'No.'

'Protestant?'

'No.'

'Do you believe in God?'

'No.'

'Where are you from?'

'I was born in Spain.'

'You're Spanish! Like the Conquistadors who took over our *patria* and oppressed our people!' the mestizo girls, who were descended from the Spanish colonialists and practised the Conquistadors' religion, accused me: the offspring of a German Jewish mother who chanced to be in Spain when I emerged into this world. And, though I got on well with them, they never quite forgave me for being 'Spanish', and therefore their enemy.

In the early mornings, waiting on the broad, leafy sidewalk of La Reforma for the orange school bus, I would button up my navy blue, Windsor School cardigan against the cold and watch the steam I blew into the icy morning air with each breath. By midday the cardigan was off and I was too hot even in the short-sleeved, white cotton shirt of my uniform, as I played punchball with my classmates in the playground, or hopscotch with strings of tiny beads we threaded together in the prettiest patterns. In class, we studied the history and geography of the Latin American continent in this, the fifth year of primary school, and in biology, the cellular structure of tissues such as muscle, skin and nerves. We were taught the theory of the beginning of the universe and the origins of the solar system and planet Earth, and drew a picture of the planets being flung out and whirled away from the central star, the Sun – and I was fascinated. I enjoyed my new friendships too. One of my classmates, Rosita, invited me to her beautiful large home in the leafy district of Las Lomas.

'I'll tell you a secret, if you promise not to tell the others!' she said when we were alone in her room.

'Yes?' I replied expectantly.

'You must promise!' she urged me.

'I promise.'

After a significant pause, preparing herself for the shattering news she was about to disclose, Rosita – with her long thick braids, the colour of golden corn – almost whispered with great emotion, 'I'm not *really* Catholic. We're *Protestants*!'

'Why do you keep it a secret from the others?' I asked in astonishment.

Rosita, her voice trembling, was trying to make me understand: 'They wouldn't like me anymore if I told them! They'd stop being my friends and never play with me again!'

Which explanation confused me still further. But I kept my friend's secret.

Mabel Duarte was flaxen-haired and olive-skinned with turquoise blue eyes and a singular charm and grace. She had recently moved with her family to Mexico from Brazil and spoke Spanish with a slight lilt. She was different, yet confident with it. I found myself often thinking of her in Acapantzingo. Which puzzled me. How could a *girl* intrude in my thoughts as Miguelito, Aldama and Volney had?

Diana Villaseñor, a pretty girl with lively dark eyes and a cascade of brown curly hair, became one of my best friends, even though she was the one who objected most to my 'Spanish' origins. She invited me to her birthday party: a huge fiesta in her palatial home, one of several the family owned across the country, her father being the director of the Bank of Mexico. All afternoon, we were shunted en masse from one organised event to the next, including hired clown shows and Disney home movies, and finally to the birthday feast and cake, while I waited for the spontaneous play to start.

In my father's small apartment, I was looked after by Marina: a pale, drawn woman, with thick glasses, from Mérida, Yucatán. Although I was now, for the first time, living with my father, he had become an even more shadowy figure than before: a vague personage, enveloped in the agreeable aroma of Havana cigars, who came and went with minimal conversation. I saw little of him in the apartment aside from the rare occasions in which he brought home a business acquaintance, when I would be sent to bed early– a screened couch in the far corner of the L-shaped living room – so they could talk about their grown-up matters over supper.

My eleventh birthday arrived. That evening, both my mother and father were there, in my father's apartment. The baby was asleep in his bedroom.

As I went to join them for supper, I was first led to the low table by the sofa where a present for me had been placed. It was a round, prettily lined, lidded basket, with an assortment of coloured cotton yarns, needles, pins, scissors, pieces of material and a thimble, each held in place in its own loop. I stood there, silently, examining it.

'Don't you like it?' asked my father who had bought it for me, it would seem on my mother's suggestion. I had recently been doing some embroidery in Acapantzingo.

'Oh, yes!'

'She's like that,' my mother explained. 'She doesn't say much when she's moved.'

I wasn't sure that I was moved … perplexed, maybe.

∾

MY BREASTS were starting to grow. First on one side: a small tender lump under my nipple slowly swelling in size. Then on the other. And the source of my emotions was also shifting from a vague general location to those sensitive budding lumps.

∾

ONE AFTERNOON AFTER SCHOOL, I was getting off the school bus at the spot where a man stood every day playing the same tune on his street organ hoping for a few *centavos*, and as I stepped down, all my books fell to the ground. They ended up all over the place. And as the bus pulled out and I was bending down to recover them, I suddenly broke into uncontrollable sobbing. I started shaking and straining and gasping and tears were dripping off my wet face and an overwhelming sense of desperation blew up inside me – as if out of nowhere. I knew it wasn't just the books. Their fall was a trivial thing really, yet it had triggered a whole, pent-up accumulation of hurt and frustration that up till that moment I hadn't even known existed inside me. And I was still sobbing and shaking convulsively as I picked up the last of the books from the pavement.

I took stock of myself, walked into my father's building, up the stairs and into his flat – composed now and back to my impassive self. My mother's repeated instruction, *'aguántate'*, all the way back to my early childhood, must have been firmly rooted by now. My stresses, hurts and disappointments had become so well guarded, that to this day – though I might stab an intelligent guess at what underlay this sudden, unannounced eruption of anguish and despair – I cannot actually dig out its sources.

As our impending move to New Zealand took shape, talk about my father became more disturbing. It seemed Ilse wanted to have his child. My father was also trying to keep my baby sister. When that failed, he approached me.

'Wouldn't you like to stay here with me when your mother goes to New Zealand?' he asked me, one day. 'I would send you to a good boarding school in the States, and when you turn fifteen you'll be eligible for American citizenship. You would be an American!'

Not only was I taken aback at the idea of a remote American boarding school, I also had no interest whatsoever in becoming a *gringa*, the official advantages of which were lost on me. But what perplexed me most of all was that he should want to keep me in order to send me away. This aside, I felt closer to my mother and her sister and brothers, whose memory she had kept alive by her frequent reference to them, giving me an impression of a closely-knit family even though we were dispersed across four continents.

I went back to my ballet and flamenco classes in Mexico City. At the end of a flamenco lesson, in conversation with another pupil, I mentioned I was born in Barcelona. I felt that here, at the Spanish flamenco classes, this would not be held against me. It might even be seen in a good light.

'No, you weren't!' disagreed my friend.

'Yes,' I confirmed. 'I'm from Spain. I was born in Barcelona.'

'You were *not*,' she retorted firmly. 'You're *Mexican*. The same as me and everybody else.'

So here I was being taken for a native – and my foreign status denied! – just as I was facing my next move to a new continent, culture and language ...

My year in Windsor School came to an end and it was decided I should return to Acapantzingo for the remaining months before leaving for New Zealand.

*Back to Acapantzingo, later in 1947.*

I STARTED GOING to Nancy's school. Nancy was Irish, kept horses, and ran a small school for children of mostly American families in Cuernavaca.

Six children, aged seven to eleven, sat around the table in Nancy's veranda, under a pergola dripping with flowers, while Nancy skilfully managed our different grades with an assortment of American schoolbooks. Before our play-break she read us, from a thick book, vivid descriptions of space journeys to the moon, sun and planets, based on the scientific knowledge to date. I found it so inspiring that I decided, if it became a reality in my lifetime, I would love to go to the moon ...

I lost no time in picking up my new friends' American slang. At playtime, we crossed the road into the wild uncultivated land in front of Nancy's house and switched into our fantasy world. We climbed the tree across a pond of muddy water to see if friend or foe was in sight, or how best to negotiate the land that lay ahead. We attempted to cross the pond on stones and branches we threw in to bridge it, and once the 'bridge' came apart and we all fell into the muddy water and got soaked. Nancy cleaned us up, wrapped us in towels and hung our clothes to dry. Some days we wandered further out, investigating rocks, plants and animals in our path, weaving them into our quixotic play, and would come across the decaying carcass of a horse: already mostly cleaned of its flesh by the vultures, the ribcage spread out in the sun and the skull lying nearby. And the dead horse would find its way into our games too. Then back to sit in Nancy's veranda for more absorbing lessons.

I was back in my element here, close to the wildlife and nature of Acapantzingo and Cuernavaca, and to peers and even adults – Nancy – with whom there was goodwill and understanding. There was nothing here to make me sob or despair ...

I enjoyed my long, daily walk from Acapantzingo to Nancy's. Past the penitentiary, I turned into the leafy lane with the villa and swimming pool and continued down the middle of the empty road, under the lush foliage of the tall mango trees, singing my latest favourite Mexican song. The route took me through the next village onto the long stretch of woods near the old railway line. Here I liked clambering up and walking on the rails, where I came across a snake once, but never a train. I finally came out onto the main road, by the *Casino de la Selva*, from where I reached Nancy's house opposite the wild open ground with the muddy pool, the tree and the horse's carcass.

Back home, I used to sit with my fine, cross-stitch embroidery, which my mother had decided I should do for my aunt Lotte. My mother had chosen the most intricate pattern in the embroidery book. I had made some mats following some of the simpler patterns, stitching the tiny crosses with different coloured yarns on a material with small gaps in the weave as a guideline. The one for Lotte's mat was of roses, branches and leaves in a system of loops.

'It gives me a terrible headache!' I would complain to my mother.

'You must go on with it,' she always insisted. 'Think of the great pleasure it will give Lotte when you give it to her in New Zealand!'

I would spend hour after hour, painstakingly following the elaborate pattern with a fine needle and various coloured cotton threads. After several weeks of work and many splitting headaches, the mat was finally finished and ready to give to Lotte. My mother was pleased with it and folded it away.

I still have it. Though my mother never told me, Lotte can't have liked it. I found it carefully hidden among my mother's things after her death.

My mother looked after children as paying guests, since my father's allowance had become increasingly frugal the more strained their relations became. An older girl came to stay and attended Nancy's school with me. Her main love was the piano. So every day, after Nancy's lessons, I accompanied her to a house with a piano for her practice.

As we slowly ambled along the dirt road in the advancing afternoon, I loved watching our lengthening shadows and the fluttering clouds of white and yellow butterflies, forming and unforming again, all around us. Every once in a while, as though responding to an invisible signal, the butterflies would all, to the last one, descend in unison, separating off white from yellow as they alighted on the ground to settle in their respective patches – a yellow here, there a white – turning the road into a white and yellow patchwork. And not a single butterfly ever strayed into the wrong patch.

Unlike me ...

Conchita was often in and out of the house now, helping my mother with her final chores. She would also combine her milk round with my mother's various errands in Cuernavaca. My mother had always praised Conchita's excellent driving. Yet, it would be during one of these last trips that I discovered Conchita's secret, so zealously guarded till now, behind her cushions on her driving seat. A pocket-sized bottle of tequila. And Conchita's permanently flushed face and the fine tremor of her hands ...

Finally, everything was packed and we were ready to leave. The cats had become completely wild and procured their own food, so they could be left alone. But Lloveta needed a home. One of the last things we did before our departure was to drive Lloveta in the back of Conchita's milk truck to one of her clients who had a large home and garden in a well-to-do suburb near the entrance of Cuernavaca.

Lloveta was led into the tall fenced garden, tied down, and left there. As we drove away, she was whining desperately as she tried to break away from her tie and leap over the high fence to get back to us.

And that was the last I saw of Lloveta.

# At the Other End of the World

*Christchurch, 1948.*
AN AMERICAN ONCE SAID OF CHRISTCHURCH, New Zealand, that it is half the size of the Boston cemetery and twice as dead.

When I first arrived, I was struck by its orderliness. Box-like family homes with corrugated tin roofs, neatly lined regular streets, their well-kept lawns scattered with shrubs and bushes and bordered with pretty flowers. Gardening was the family man's weekend occupation, and Christchurch was proudly known as the Garden City.

The Square with its neo-Gothic cathedral marked the centre of Christchurch. The Avon River wound its way through the nearby Botanic Gardens and Hagley Park, weeping willows along its banks dripping their slender branches into its shallow crystalline waters, then followed on its course through the town. A few short blocks further on, Papanui Road cut obliquely across the rectangular arrangement of streets to reach the pleasant garden suburb of Merivale. Bicycles were ridden everywhere, carefully, close to the curb. Branching off to the left here was quiet, leafy Rugby Street. Lotte's road. This was where my mother's many letters from Acapantzingo to her sister were addressed: 69 Rugby Street. A large wooden house with a corridor down the middle leading to various rooms on either side and ending at the back veranda, which overlooked the garden. Lotte was especially fond of her large cherry tree. There were also a spreading oak, several apple, pear and plum trees, redcurrant and gooseberry bushes along the fence, and flowers on the grass border: red and purple fuchsia, yellow snapdragons and red-hot pokers being among her favourites. She had prepared the front bedroom for us, with three beds.

As soon as we arrived, my mother was out of the house from early morning working at a hospital or convalescent home. As in Mexico, she didn't speak to me about her activities and it was only through fragments of her conversations with others that I became vaguely aware of her movements. Maybe she thought children oughtn't, or were not interested, to know. Or she was simply too busy and tired to think of it.

My mother's carefully chosen Mexican presents did not fit Lotte's taste here in New Zealand. My attention was also drawn to the absence of American slang in this country.

'We don't say "okay" here! We say "all right",' my aunt pointed out to me, a little testily. Or, again, 'We don't use expressions like "great"! We say things are "nice".'

So I set to work to relearn English the way it was spoken here, with a different vocabulary, a crisper pronunciation and faster tempo than that which I had picked up from my American teacher and others in Mexico.

At lunch we sat around the table on the veranda overlooking the back garden. My aunt was particularly fond of this spot. I asked my mother to pass me the butter in Spanish, which I was still accustomed to using in my communication with her.

'It's very rude to speak Spanish in my presence. I don't understand a word of it,' Lotte angrily told my mother in German, who in turn translated it for me. Lotte had taken to her life in her adoptive country with great enthusiasm, transplanting the orderly existence she grew up with in Germany to this peaceful corner of the world, and was finding me, with my American slang and foreign manners, somewhat taxing. Following her husband's untimely death and initial moves with her young children to Lugano and Florence, and then the turmoil of their further displacement at the outbreak of the war, first to Palestine and finally New Zealand, she had adapted to her new life here with a kind of staunch devotion. Though she spoke fluent Italian and French, and slipped back into German – the language of their childhood together – when she talked with my mother, she was adamant that even in the privacy of one's own home, one must speak English in New Zealand.

'If you want to live with me, you'll have to speak English. I never want to hear Spanish spoken in my house again,' she told me sternly. So I never again spoke Spanish – the language of my origins which, even if somewhat broken up by our French interlude, had by then become part of me – for the length of time I lived in New Zealand.

One bright spring morning, my mother already at work, I got out of bed and put on my red cotton dress with tiny white dots and

flounces for sleeves. I greeted Lotte happily and sat down to join her
for breakfast.

'You can't have breakfast in that dress,' was her response.

'Why not? What's wrong with it?' It was a style commonly worn
in Mexico, and in Colegio Madrid we wore it as a pinafore over a
white blouse as an optional uniform.

'We don't wear dresses like that in New Zealand. Take it off and
put on something sensible.'

'What do you mean? Why isn't it sensible?'

'It's too bright. We don't wear red in New Zealand.'

'So what colours do people wear here?'

'We wear pastel shades. Go and change into something in a pastel
shade. And with proper sleeves.'

'I only wanted to have some Corn Flakes.'

'You can't have any till you put on another dress.'

So I went into my mother's room, lay on my bed by the window,
wept my eyes out, and skipped breakfast.

We had arrived on the ship, *Marine Phoenix*, from San Francisco,
and met Lotte – tallish, straight and ginger-haired – on disembarking in Auckland. She had come all the way from Christchurch to
meet us, and seemed both pleased and somewhat strained – a very
Lotte combination as I soon learned. On landing in New Zealand –
*Aotearoa*, the Land of the Long White Cloud, as the Maoris named
it on their first sighting of these beautiful isles from their boats – my
first impression was of a turning back in time. The cars were small,
upright, old models, and the women's clothes, dull and dowdy. The
New Look at the time of widely flared, ankle-length skirts, all the
rage in Mexico and the Western world, had not yet reached New
Zealand. The houses were made of wood, giving a sense of improvised construction and impermanence. And corrugated tin roofs. As
we climbed the higher end of Auckland's main street, Queen Street,
a stale, unpleasant odour wafted out of doorways. Mutton lard.

We picked up my aunt's bags from one of these wooden houses
towards the top of Queen Street, where she had stayed overnight in
a rented, dark room cluttered with old furniture, and took a train to
Wellington. We were looking forward to meeting my cousin Eve and

her New Zealander husband, Tom, there. My other cousin, Peter, was in England reading history at Cambridge.

Eve and Tom were a friendly, bright, happy young couple. We all crossed the straits from Wellington to Picton, on the northern coast of New Zealand's South Island, to spend a few days in Tom's family's holiday 'bach' – both to get our first taste of New Zealand life and to get to know each other. Some of us, again after years of separation, while others for the first time.

'Would you like some juice, Tom?' Lotte asked the next morning as she was preparing breakfast, eager to please him. Her voice softened whenever she spoke to him.

'No thanks! I've already got enough of those around me!' came his jovial reply.

Eve was dark-haired and attractive and had an appealing smile. Tom, an electrical engineer, was tall and strong, with an irreverent sense of humour. And while they were all busy with each other – Lotte and my mother had not seen each other since before the war and it was an emotional reunion for the two sisters with much catching up to do – I quietly hung back on the sidelines, outside the family circle, watching. I was feeling awkward and isolated in the face of yet another convulsive change in my surroundings, at a time when I was trying also to deal with my own difficult inner changes, as my childhood was slipping away from me and a new alien self emerging. I had by now lost my innocent ready confidence and felt clumsy and self-conscious. Tom – the only one present who wasn't a blood relative – was ever kind and attentive towards me. Which touched me. I even became a little enamoured of him.

On the other hand, Lotte – cheerfully oblivious to all this – insisted on teaching us an old English song she clearly thought fitted the occasion, getting us, estranged newcomers to her adopted land, to sing it all together in an atmosphere of New Zealand *Gemütlichkeit*:

> Row, row, row your boat,
> Gently down the stream.
> Merrily, merrily, merrily, merrily,
> Life is but a dream.

… its incongruity serving only to alienate me even further …

One afternoon I was sitting at the bay window in the front room watching Tom and Eve playing quoits outside on the lawn. They laughed a great deal. They were happy and radiant.

After a while, Eve put down the quoit and went up to Tom.

'Kiss me,' she said, when she was right up close to him.

He whispered in her ear and she looked up and saw me, and greeted me with a happy smile and a wave.

Later that afternoon, Tom was trying out some acrobatics with me on the lawn.

'When I say jump, take a leap and I'll catch you,' he told me.

And so I did – but I came down too heavily, he lost his grip, and I fell down. As I tried to break the fall, I damaged my wrist. They organised a car to take me to the hospital.

It was a late Saturday evening. We made our way down the empty corridor of the small country hospital, breaking its silence. An X-ray confirmed a fracture and a doctor was called in. As I lay on the trolley in theatre waiting to be anaesthetised, I watched all the goings-on as the doctors and nurses bustled around me getting things ready to mend my arm.

'An' wheh d'ye come from?' asked the surgeon with friendly curiosity.

'From Mexico.'

'Mexico! D'ye have any fleeahs theh?'

'Any what?'

'Fleeahs. You know, fleeahs.'

'What's "fleeahs"?'

'You know: fleeahs! Those pink and rid things that grow in the gardin?'

'Ah!' I exclaimed with a sudden flash of recognition. '*Flowers!* Yes, there are flowers in Mexico.'

They put a mask of gamgee on my face, started trickling ether onto it and told me to start counting. I got up to maybe nine or ten … and my voice stopped working. I felt my head flop. My body had slumped, I could no longer move or command it, but I could hear them talking and made sense of what they said. Then I lost consciousness.

I would be back in Picton, half a century hence, to a reunion of my medical class. As an anaesthetist.

Elmwood Primary School was three short blocks from Rugby Street.

The teachers couldn't decide into what grade to place me. I had just turned twelve, but had not gone through the New Zealand school system. They decided to start me off in the fourth grade and see how I got on. The first thing the teacher set out to do was to change my handwriting. Mine was small, rounded and vertical. The teacher told me this was definitely unacceptable here. So I practised every night at home to write narrow, elongated, steeply slanting letters, close to horizontal, with long gaps between them, not lifting the pen off the paper till the end of each word. The longer the gap between the letters, the more satisfied the teacher became until I could only fit two or three words to each line. When I had exaggerated her instructions to the point that I thought it was getting ridiculous, and worried she might think I was making fun of her, I found instead that she was really pleased.

'That's it. You've got it right. Very good,' the teacher said.

Having mastered the handwriting, it was decided that I should go on to the sixth grade, the last in primary school.

My new teacher, her white hair piled on top of her head and her glasses sitting low on her nose, had a nasal voice and a kindly smile. She offered to help me after school to catch up with work I hadn't encountered in my Mexican curriculum. So I stayed in to learn how to do sums with 'pounds, shillings and pence': twenty shillings to a pound and twelve pence to a shilling. A strange notion, I thought, of a system of money. Yet decimals, which I found simple and straightforward, were a mystery to children in New Zealand. I mastered my '£, s & d' sums after two evenings' hard work – at the end of which the teacher looked at me, an expression of puzzlement on her kindly face.

'What queer people you are!' she told me across the empty classroom.

In my new class, as soon as we were let out into the playground at my first morning break, a girl with straight fair hair cut short, in a pastel dress, came up to me.

'May I play with you?' she asked me, with great courtesy and a gentle eagerness to make contact with me.

'Yes,' I answered, baffled. I expected, as the new girl, it would have been *my* privilege to play with *her*. And before we could take the next step, another girl came and asked if she might join us, and then another, and still another. They all crowded around me, competing with each other to be my friend. They were all very well mannered and made me feel welcome. Which confused me.

I got on well with my classmates. They wrote their names on the plaster of my broken arm, which ended up covered with signatures, little poems and funny drawings by the time it was removed after six weeks.

My new friends all lived within a small radius of my aunt's house, and we started meeting after school. We rode on our bicycles to each other's houses along the quiet, tree-lined streets, and played as safely outdoors as inside. My friends' homes proudly displayed a framed portrait of the English King and Queen or the young Princess Elizabeth with her new husband – they were all unquestionably respectful of their English Royals. And here, they were all Protestants …

In class, we spent the time learning to recite, by heart and in unison, the long poem of *Hiawatha*, with the teacher leading us.

The whole class also had to repeat, with one voice, after the teacher: '*I, said the fly, with my little eye, I saw him die.*' To help break the habit of saying 'doy'. And:

'*Mr Brown, Mr Brown,*
*Are you going down to town,*
*Would you stop and take me down.*
*Thank you kindly, Mr Brown.*'

To help stop saying 'breeahn'.

Otherwise, I learned little. Serious study seemed to start at secondary school here.

The children's politeness was in great contrast to the more aggressive behaviour I was used to from Mexico. I was faced with rudeness only once, when a small child from the lower school, whom I had never seen before, ran up to me in the playground and yelled, 'You dirty Mexican girl!'

Halfway through the year, the class photograph was taken. We were arranged in three, neat, ascending rows. I was in the front, and when the photograph came out my friends pointed disapprovingly at my feet. I was the only girl whose feet were not aligned, with my toes slightly parted. And my hands on my lap were partly upturned, instead of facing down like the rest of them. I had broken the class photograph's uniformity.

Everybody had a bicycle. They were ridden everywhere with their baskets hanging from the handlebars stacked with shopping, school-bags, dogs or any other thing. Bicycles were left leaning against the wall or a fence, unguarded and unlocked, while people did their shopping. And – to my surprise – the bicycles were still there when they came out.

And here, everybody drank tea. No one drank coffee. There was no place in town where one could sit with a friend and have a cup of coffee. And when the shops closed every one went home and the place became empty, deserted. Here there were pubs, where men drank beer and no woman ever ventured, which closed sharply at six o'clock. At six every evening, men poured out of the pubs into the streets swaggering and zigzagging along the footpaths on their way home; you gave them a wide berth if you were on the same footpath. Wine, like coffee, was unknown. And cheese – apart from cheddar. An evening meal was typically roast mutton, boiled pota-toes and mushy cabbage. And lots of salt. Mint was the only herb used, and though onions might be added to the cooking, garlic was definitely not. Meat was plentiful, and butter. Frying was generally done with beef or mutton lard; olive oil was another unknown ingre-dient here. A common snack was baked beans on toast or spaghetti sandwiches. And though I sorely missed the rich variety of fruit in Mexico, here I came across new ones. Such as the egg shaped tree-tomatoes, which we cut in half, added a little sugar, and scooped out the dark red, fleshy pulp. Chinese gooseberries – years later to be known throughout the world as Kiwi fruit – were also new to me and delicious.

Washing dishes was different here too. My aunt filled the sink with hot, soapy water, placed all the dishes inside it, wiped them with a mop and stacked them next to the sink without rinsing them. By the end of the wash the water was dark and murky. It was my chore to dry them. Different from Irene's and Josefina's way of scrubbing plates and pots and cutlery with a soapy loofah under cold running water until they sparkled in the sun of Acapantzingo.

And in this country people didn't touch each other. Not only did they never hug or kiss as a form of greeting between friends or relations, but they didn't even shake hands. When someone arrived or left or was meeting another person, their arms hung limply close to their body. At most they would give a nod. 'Goo'dye,' they might say, or 'Heahd'yedo,' if they were being introduced – with never a sign of human contact in public.

And just as the brilliant sun, intense skies, blinding lightning and crackling thunders, the vibrant pinks, purples and oranges, just as spicy food, lively songs and rhythmic dancing didn't exist here, so also extravagant wealth and undue poverty were unknown.

The seasons – unlike Mexico's dry and wet periods – were exactly as they appeared in Grimm's and Anderson's fairy tales which I had read and enjoyed in Mexico. The fresh, delicate greens of spring, the bright flowers and ripening fruit in summer, followed by the golds and rusts of autumn, turning finally bare and bleak in winter. And I was amazed to see in nature all around me what had been a fairy tale fantasy.

The first year in New Zealand, I cried. I would disappear into the room I shared with my mother and sister in my aunt's house, and sit alone on my bed and cry. I missed the music and the colour, the sun, food and smells of Mexico. I couldn't connect with the people here. They were *nice*. They were friendly and hospitable. But there was no real meeting point with them. And my mother, who was the only thread of continuity in all these changes, was too busy. Busy at work, or when she was home, with the others. She had a lot to talk about with her sister – though by the sound of their exchanges in German they were not happy conversations, each trying to correct the other about one thing or another. My mother had other things on her mind. Our communication had, in fact, already broken down some time before, back in Mexico. I remembered our first clashes when I started asserting my separate will, when I was seven, and the final rupture when she tried to take over my schooling in Acapantzingo. From my viewpoint, my warm, loving mother had turned into an angry, distant person. There was so much vexation on her side, hurt on mine, and an irreconcilable division. And worse than my geographical rootlessness was the human desolation I found myself in.

I had, as well, been cut off from my own language, that which represented the world around me and which I used to express myself and connect with others. And as I struggled to adjust to my new surroundings, all my new experiences and sense of alienation were in English. So, for me, English became a cold language, a language inextricably linked with the repression of all I felt and mustn't express. My passion, my self, were on the way to becoming the casualties.

Around this time too, I had my first period. My mother gave me a belt, some cloth towels and two large safety pins, and showed me how to use and wash them each time I changed – disposable consumerism being still some way off – resulting in my increased use of the bathroom to my aunt's exasperation.

One evening, as I entered our room to retire for the night, I stopped by my small sister's bed which was nearest the door. I stood and watched the sleeping child, her head turned towards the wall. I found a pencil and piece of paper and drew the line of her forehead down to the eyebrow, her eyelashes below, and then her soft, rounded cheek. A short space across, the wavy lines of her hair which fell loosely away from her face with a small earlobe peeping under them. I was surprised that such a simple sketch could capture such a tender image.

I had, ever since her birth, felt a deep fondness for the child and lamented that she too was kept from me. I saved that drawing for a long time.

We received a letter, one day, from friends in Mexico. It said, 'Lou and Ilse have had a small son whom they have named Joey ...'

The news also reached us of Conchita's sad and terrible death in Acapantzingo. She was said to have died of rabies from a dog bite, though this conflicted with another story that she had died in a fire, in the middle of the night, started by a cigarette she had been smoking in bed. The manner of her death has remained forever a mystery ...

Acapantzingo was becoming a distant, almost unreal memory, and our friends too, fading now, even dying. It bore echoes of Marseilles, and Willi and the two Maxes, all of whose memories had dimmed in my child's mind, though by no means *ever* forgotten, and who had had their lives tragically taken from them after our departure ...

～

CHRISTCHURCH GIRLS' HIGH SCHOOL was a neo-Gothic building facing leafy Cranmer Square, two or three blocks from Hagley Park, close to the town centre. Around the corner were Christ College, Canterbury University, the museum and the Botanic Gardens.

The entrance exam placed me in the top academic stream, which included Latin, French, maths, science, history and geography, preparing us for the national examinations of School Certificate and University Entrance. The streams moved right across to the home science class, where the subjects of cooking and sewing predominated to prepare the girls for a domestic life.

The uniform consisted of a navy blue tunic, a long-sleeved white blouse, a striped red and blue tie, brown lisle stockings and brown lace-up shoes. Hair had to be either plaited, tied back, or if worn loose at least one inch above the shoulders. When outside the school grounds, we had to wear a navy blue hat with the school badge on its band, navy blue gloves, and navy blue blazer with the badge on its pocket. In summer, we wore a short-sleeved, navy blue, cotton dress buttoned up the front, white socks, and a panama hat with the same band and badge. If we were seen with any part of the uniform missing or deviating from regulations – including, for instance, walking in single file and in silence, at *all* times, along the school's long cold corridors and staircases – we were given a detention. Three detentions resulted in the dreaded conduct mark, and after three of these the girl was expelled from school.

Lessons at the start of school were preceded by assembly, where the school sang hymns, prayed and heard the day's announcements.

One morning, as Miss Stewart, the headmistress, and the teachers approached the assembly hall in their gowns, I stood up with the rest of the girls as usual from the floor – where we always waited in complete silence – briefly wiping the floor dust off my tunic as I did so, and stood to attention. The teachers were still some way off and the whole school waited with the customary, absolute stillness and silence. Not the rustle of a leaf would have dared intrude. Miss Stewart finally reached the hall and came up to me and stopped. The long trail of gowned teachers behind her also came to a sudden halt. Miss Stewart stood before me and glared at me, through her glasses, in complete silence for several long seconds, and then walked on and up the platform as usual. After the hymns and prayers, she announced to the whole school that I was to go to her room after assembly. So I excused myself from my next teacher, regretting I would miss some of her lesson, and went to Miss Stewart's office wondering what it was all about.

'When I walk into assembly, I expect you to stand to attention. You don't brush your dress when you stand up from the floor,' she told me severely. 'I'll let you off this time, but next time you'll get a conduct mark. You can go to your class, now.'

And I was surprised and bewildered about the ways of this country and its people's priorities in matters of human behaviour.

I cycled to school every day. I would wake up in the mornings to a stiff white frost over the whole world outside: gardens, fences, pavements ... And as I cycled along the path that cut diagonally across the white frosted expanse of Hagley Park, my breath steamed the crisp icy air. As I cycled back again through the park in the late afternoons, I would watch the naked branches on the trees stretch out, finger-like, carbon-black against the clear pallid sky, which shaded – as I lowered my gaze – from palest blue to a tinge of green through light yellow into a clear then dusky orange culminating in a fiery scarlet above the horizon. And I would look up again at the thick velvet blackness of the branches against the pale sky. And I never tired of looking at this scene. I felt serene, uplifted, in my element. I was comfortable with myself and my surroundings here, in the middle of Hagley Park, far from the oppressive, rule-laden atmosphere of the school I had left behind, and still some distance from home where my mother's relentless scolding so diminished me. And as I pedalled nearer home, I was filled with dread at the thought of having to face her again: the same mother to whom I had once felt so close and who had meant the world to me, and who I was now fervently wishing would disappear out of my life forever.

We had by now moved from my aunt's home to a flat in the house of a pianist, his wife and two children, known to Lotte. Our new home consisted of two studios, one above the other, facing the back garden. My mother turned a curtained corner downstairs into her bedroom and used the rest of the space as a workroom for her dressmaking, which she had taken up to earn a living, while the upstairs was divided by a partition into my sister's and my bedrooms. In the evenings, I often stood on my side of the partition and looked out onto the view of our back garden and others beyond as the gathering darkness enveloped the whole scene – a moment of peace amidst all my struggles.

The pianist practised for his forthcoming concerts in the front room of the house and I loved listening to the crisp rhythmic notes of his Bach partitas. I started having lessons from him and always looked forward to his teaching in his peaceful, spacious music room. He was a slight, neat man with alert eyes and a roguish smile,

and he would sit next to me and listen quietly and attentively to my playing. Always gentle and softly spoken, I came to idolise him.

On my way to bed, I would stand and watch my small sister sleeping peacefully in her bed at the top of the stairs as I went through her room to reach mine. One evening I got into her bed for a few moments to cuddle up close to her and feel her warmth. She woke up and, afraid my mother would get angry for my having disturbed her, I asked her not to tell her.

*Practising the piano, Christchurch, 1949*

The next morning I heard her talking to my mother downstairs.

'She told me not to tell you that she climbed into my bed.'

My mother was extremely angry.

'You must never go anywhere near her again,' she impressed firmly on the small child.

My previous attempts to get close to my small sister, whom I had looked upon as a potential friend and ally, had been frustrated by my mother's dividing influence. And now she didn't come anywhere near me any more, completing my isolation at home.

One night, everyone already in bed and asleep, my mother started crying out. She had woken from a nightmare and not found him. The pianist. I had guessed by now they were lovers. She sounded very distressed. So she too was going through a difficult time. Maybe all the changes and lonesomeness were taking their toll on her as well. We each seemed to be going through our own hell of disappointment and heartache, with no point of contact.

I was in my second year of high school.

In the classroom, I sat next to a new friend, Jennifer, and we amused ourselves in our algebra lessons having races at solving the long lists of equations in our maths books, leaving the rest of the class far behind. Sometimes Jennifer won, and others I did, but never by more than one or two equations.

Jennifer sometimes invited me to her house. Her family were Christadelphians and believed that the Jews were the Chosen People of God. I never understood the logic of it, but Jennifer explained that it was written in the Bible which she believed to the letter.

I never said I was Jewish, but Jennifer must have known.

One day we were eating our ham sandwiches in the playground and the conversation turned to pork being a banned food for Jews. I was thinking I liked pork and would be sorry not to eat it.

'I'd *hate* to be a Jew,' I heard myself saying, to my astonishment and immediate regret. I think I meant to say, I hate the endless pains and complexities of being Jewish.

At home I spent my time reading. I went through each author in turn, starting with Dickens, then Jane Austen, George Eliot, Thomas Hardy ... I thoroughly immersed myself in the worlds evoked by each writer, eclipsing everything else around me. I was getting to know my new English milieu, perspective and way of thinking, and loving it. My next author, D.H. Lawrence, resonated – in contrast to my surroundings – with my own forceful sensuous stirrings and discordance, and his books heartened me.

At school I loved playing netball and enjoyed athletics. Sport was an intensive activity and fertile ground for 'pashes'. Everyone had a pash on the tall, golden-haired, athletic champion, Margaret Spencer, with her magnetic smile and winning ways. I not least ... She must have noticed my interest and, with typical generosity, invited me once to go horse riding at her family farm near Kaiapoi: a delightful, mind-blowing treat for me.

I also loved swimming, which I would do at every opportunity. I trained in life-saving: learning how to break the grasp of a drown-ing person, rescue them, swim six lengths of an Olympic-sized pool in breaststroke, crawl and backstroke, and hold my breath under water for twenty seconds. I gained a Bronze Medal to hang from a ribbon – pinned by my School House badge on my tunic – on which were also a row of metal stripes with the subjects I had excelled in engraved on them: Latin, French and Mathematics.

An international tennis team came to Christchurch with a Mexican player, Pancho Segura. I went to see them play, so I could exchange a few words again with a Mexican when I asked for his autograph. He was the only Mexican I ever saw in New Zealand.

A group of flamenco dancers came to Christchurch too. I came alive again as I watched them, arched back, head high, stamping their heels to their complicated rhythms, their powerful emotions woven into their every movement. And I felt transported back to the world I had left behind. Another time, the Ballet Rambert came to that remote land and I watched the dancers express with movement all that which would defy words. Subtle sensibilities in place of argu-mentation. And I wanted to ask them to take me away with them, to train me to dance like that, that I might escape this cold country where feelings were kept under lock and key and out of sight and life seemed reduced to a system of rules of behaviour.

At home, the angry remonstrations continued.

'Don't leave your coat lying about!' were my mother's first words when I came in from school. Never a gentle word or, 'How was school today?' The weekends were one long struggle. It wasn't so much what the arguments were about, as the animosity and denigration that attended them. Her grim intolerance, the insufferable anger on her face.

I had just finished washing my hair in the shower of the small windowless bathroom next to my mother's screened-off bedroom, and I was back upstairs, combing it back in front of the mirror. It was black and wet, and stuck flat against my head. I stared at me. I looked ugly. Exceptionally ugly. I took a pair of scissors and cut my hair very short.

I began reading books about adolescence and psychiatry to try and understand what was happening to me, and I became absorbed in the subject. I thought I should like to devote my life to helping people solve their problems and find happiness – that which seemed to be eluding me so. But to understand psychiatry in depth, I would have to study medicine. That was when I decided to be a doctor. Turning my attention to healing rather than the hurting.

In my third year of secondary school, I dropped languages – which I had excelled at, and won first prize at every intercollegiate competition – and chose science subjects in preparation for my School Certificate exams, with my medical studies in view.

We were now taught ballroom dancing every Thursday after classes. We would all congregate in the school gymnasium, and go round and round the room, en masse, anti-clockwise, practising our quick-step and foxtrot, 'turn back, short-short-long, now sideways, two-quick-steps, slide your foot, then forward, one-two-three, turn again …' Without music. Eventually, boys from Christ's College, in their striped black-and-white blazers and grey flannel trousers, came to try it out. Now both boys and girls, still separately, continued practising the steps anti-clockwise around the room. And finally, together. Very timidly, at arm's length from each other, and clumsily. I started noticing one boy. He was tall and fair and had a vaguely sulky expression on his face. Perhaps it was his somewhat unkempt appearance and unpolished shoes, along with a certain shyness, that appealed to me. A sign of some rebellious spirit in him, of not easily falling in and conforming, maybe. But apart from one brief greeting, when I saw him one day sitting on his bicycle on the bridge over the Avon River at the entrance into Hagley Park, one foot on the ground and the other on the pedal, with his panama hat on, we never exchanged a word.

I sometimes went with my friends to the 'church socials'. These evenings were organised by the church and held in the church hall. Here, the girls sat on hard-backed, wooden chairs against the wall, all around the hall, while the boys stood in a tight group close to the door – as though ready for a quick getaway. When the music started, the boys would come towards us, pick someone to dance with and then shuffle around the room, unsure of their footwork and shy of conversing. For refreshment we drank orangeade and there might be some sandwiches. At the end of the 'social', around eleven, we all joined hands, sang 'Auld Lang Syne' and went home.

Otherwise, there was little else in my after-school life in Christchurch.

I was thirteen now, and I started earning some pocket money by taking an elderly lady, who had suffered a stroke, for her walk every Saturday afternoon. On arriving at her home in the pleasant leafy suburb of Fendalton, I would make her a pot of tea which we drank out of her special china cups while we chatted together. The stroke had slurred Mrs Turner's speech, but I managed to understand her. When we finished, I wiped her mouth and chin, as she dribbled on her paralysed side. Then I would hold her firmly under her arm, lift her from her chair and help her across to her wheelchair, as she took one step at a time, dragging her paralysed leg in calliper and built-up shoe behind her. Once settled in her wheelchair, we would set off along the tranquil, tree-lined streets chattering happily together in the sunshine. Mrs Turner was always very courteous, and I loved helping her and taking her for her walk which gave her such obvious pleasure.

Then I would return home, back to my rows with my mother, her coldness and distance, our irrevocable estrangement, the oppressive atmosphere …

During my next school holidays, I worked as a nurse aide in a small cottage maternity hospital in the countryside. I helped with general chores as well as giving a hand with the women who were admitted in labour. The smells of freshly laundered linen and strong antiseptic mixed with those of the countryside from the open windows. At each new admission, I ran the hospital bath, testing its temperature with my elbow, assisted the woman to the bathroom, and helped her unclothe and get into the water. After soaking for some time, I helped her into the delivery room from which I was sent out during the birth. There were four beds and only two women at any one time in the little hospital. I found it awesome and satisfying.

On a following school-break I went to Hanmer Springs, where there was a large convalescent hospital in a leafy valley encircled by a chain of snow-capped mountains. Hanmer was famous for its thermal waters. Here again I had found a holiday job as a nurse aide. I rose every morning before dawn and walked across from the staff quarters to the main building in my light blue cotton uniform and a little white cap on my head. It was late autumn and the smooth mantle of snow on the mountain peaks blushed a delicate pink as the first rays of the sun fell upon it, the valley below still plunged in dark shadow. At six o'clock I set to work polishing the medical superintendent's mahogany desk and dusting his room, before going on to the matron's. Two or three other schoolgirls were also working as nurse aides here over their holidays. We used to go through mountains of dishes together laughing at each other's comic remarks. At night we headed for the women's hot pool, which was round and deep and full of hot spring water. We stripped off our clothes and immersed ourselves in the piping hot water, holding onto the rope strung across the bottomless pool as we watched the steam rise into the black, icy, night sky cluttered with bright, twinkling stars above.

I returned to Hanmer several times. I received my first romantic kiss here after an evening of square-dancing: an American country-dance that was popular at the time. The engaging young man had danced with me all night: he had a lovely sense of rhythm and we danced well together. He accompanied me through the grounds back to my quarters, stopped in a clearing among the trees, and kissed me long and sweet. I had just turned sixteen.

Another time, my mother was there too. I had been told at the last moment that she was going to Hanmer Springs for treatment and convalescence. She appeared to be going through some kind of crisis. I visited her in her ward, taking time off my work within the patients' strict visiting hours, and tried to give her what support and comfort I could – though I remained as much in the dark as before, learning nothing from her about what she was going through. Maybe her own pain was too great: she was clearly no longer coping. And she didn't know how to communicate it. Or her stoicism was in the way of it. Perhaps our constant moves in the uncertain world we had lived in, which had at first held us so close together, was now pulling us apart and isolating us one from the other – each feeling let down by the other. And the gulf had become insuperable.

I had by now completed my School Certificate examinations. Though it was usual to spend two more years at school to prepare for university, I decided, against my teacher's advice, that one more year of Christchurch Girls High School – the minimum to qualify for university – was enough. I was impatient to move on to freer surroundings.

As a senior girl now, I had privileged access to Cranmer Square during our morning break between lessons. I would take a walk on its ample lawn or around its leafy perimeter, trying to look into the future. I looked forward to being at university and meeting other students in a new atmosphere. The first year, Medical Intermediate, which consisted of the basic sciences underlying medicine, I would do in Canterbury University in Christchurch. Competition for entrance into the only medical school in New Zealand, situated in Dunedin, was very stiff. Only the top 120 students from the whole of New Zealand were accepted every year. Although this intimidated many, I would not be put off. And I would turn over in my mind the likely impact of my decision on my life before me. I felt, for the first time, in control of my destiny. I thought too of the friendships that lay ahead, the sharing of thoughts and ideas, and the companionship. Maybe even someone to be truly close to … And I tried to imagine my life as a student and beyond, with renewed optimism.

At home I was preparing for my advanced level piano examinations. I was perfecting a Bach piece I especially liked. I also loved listening to the piano teacher practising his part of the César Franck violin sonata for an approaching concert. My next time in Hanmer, the rich autumnal scenery had brought back the music to me: the intensely lyrical dialogue between violin and piano blending perfectly with the bursting golds and russets of the forests, the glinting snow draped peaks, and pale sky beyond.

I also visited my cousins in Wellington during my school holidays: Eve and Tom, or Peter and his new wife, Anne. Peter had returned from his studies in Cambridge and was now teaching history at Victoria University. We spent happy, relaxed days together, discussing everything from everyday issues to philosophical questions and sex, talking over a late breakfast in our dressing gowns in the kitchen, or lounging in the living room surrounded by exotic Indian objects and artwork which they brought back from their frequent visits to Benares in India.

Lotte had moved to Wellington. I met her new Czech friends, the Steiners – also refugees from Nazi Europe – in their beautiful home overlooking Oriental Bay. Helli was warm and vivacious with intensely brown eyes, and George was more relaxed and full of humour. The boys appeared to have settled well into their New Zealand life. Johnny, the older one, took me for a walk along the shore one day. As we scrambled out here among the rocks surrounded by sea and sky, thinking we might have some common ground, I would have welcomed a point of contact between us, a real dialogue. But though attentive towards me, he kept an almost studied detachment, skimming over the surface of things and talking of his mates in true New Zealand form. He would become a leading Kleinian psychoanalyst. Other common friends were the Hirshfelds, whose red-haired daughter, Nomi, showed me her lovely room and wardrobe full of gorgeous clothes. Nomi was eighteen. I made a pledge with myself that when I turned eighteen, I too would find happiness and leave behind all my present troubles. From then on, to help me through the present, I kept my sights on that target.

While still in Christchurch, Lotte had introduced us to the small refugee community that had escaped from Hitler's Europe. Dr Kral, from Vienna, had three daughters who encouraged me to join them at the summer camps they frequented. The Jewish Habonim camp was intended to give Jewish boys and girls a chance to get together and consider life in Israel. I had never thought about this but was willing to learn, and I liked the sound of outdoor camp life.

My first was near Wellington. We slept in tents and ate in a large marquee. It was the first time I found myself in a large Jewish group, and I made new friends and enjoyed the camping way of life: walking on soil and turf under sky and sun all day, eating and sleeping under canvas, washing my body in the clear icy river every morning. We sang Hava Nagila and many other, to me, new songs with lovely Eastern European melodies, and danced the Hora. I met my first cockney here, a good-looking boy with very brown eyes who said things like 'Core blimey' and 'Cop my form'. The Friedlanders were tall, blond and blue-eyed. The oldest, Gerry, was studying dentistry, and we became good friends and would see each other in Dunedin. Nomi from Wellington was also there. The leaders held meetings and discussions and I heard once again the concept of the Jews as the Chosen People of God. I had always thought of us as human beings like everybody else and, in my view, the justification for Israel's existence was the need for a piece of land where Jews would feel safe in a world where we could be threatened or expelled or worse from our adoptive countries. Not an inalienable religious right.

❧

A NEW FILM by a Swedish film director, Ingmar Bergman, came to Christchurch and everybody was talking about it: *One Summer of Happiness*. It portrayed the love of a young girl and boy in a puritanical Protestant village and, in a tender scene by a lake, a long shot shows them undressing and taking a swim together. Nakedness captured by the camera, however distant, and the poetic depiction of love expressed out of wedlock, took New Zealand by storm. Angry letters from church ministers describing the offending scene filled the Christchurch newspapers. And again, I felt no common ground with the prevalent attitudes here, in God's Own Country – as New Zealanders liked to refer to it – being far more in tune with D.H. Lawrence's freer, sensuous voice.

∾

MY MOTHER MOVED to a new house.

The new house had two storeys and a garden. I slept in an upstairs room with a high dormer window that had a deep sill on which my mother placed a potted begonia. My sister slept in the porch through my room.

At bedtime, I would lie for hours tossing and turning in bed, chasing my thoughts away, unable to sleep. Then, just as sleep would finally overtake me, my mother would come through the room to go into the porch and look at my sister who was fast asleep and tuck her in, and then, on her way back, she would drag a chair across my room and stand on it to water the begonia on the high windowsill. I would be wide awake once more.

'I wish you wouldn't come into my room at night! I'd just fallen asleep, and it takes me ages to go back to sleep again. Couldn't you water the plant during the day?' I would implore her.

'It's the best time for me to do it. And I want to see that your sister's all right. You'll go to sleep again.'

And she would come back the following night. I came to hate begonias for the rest of my life.

Our arguments and fights continued. I would say something, and she would pick it up as something else. And when I tried to put my case forward, she interpreted it as malicious. I was deeply hurt at the image of me my mother's angry words projected, and so it would go on in an undiminishing circle. And I would feel alone, under-valued and rejected. I sometimes felt drawn like a magnet to jump out of the window to put an end to my misery. But I would resist it, reminding myself of my pledge to wait till I turned eighteen and be free of all this.

One day, we had another row. On this occasion, at the end of the violent argument, I went to my room, sat on my bed, and carefully thought out the whole situation. I then returned downstairs to my mother.

'I'd like to do my Medical Intermediate year in Dunedin, I don't want to stay in Christchurch anymore. It's no good my living in this household like this.'

'All right,' my mother replied. 'If you think that's best.'

So I sent my application form to Otago University in Dunedin, and prepared to do my first year of university away from home.

I was just sixteen. Up till now I had experienced, on the one hand, the most searing attachment and love for my mother – the one and only constant in the continuously changing world of my early years, when we had supported and stood by each other for our physical survival – and, on the other, our growing hostility and tearing apart in step with my evolving individuality, leaving me bewildered and isolated and fighting this time for the survival of my emerging self.

I was now breaking free, embarking on my own new journey ...

# Medical School

*Dunedin, 1955.*

A BUZZ OF PREDOMINANTLY MALE VOICES and the pungent, pithy odour of carbolic acid filled the room as we busied ourselves, scalpel in hand, with our dissection. The bodies were stretched out on wooden tables, a short distance apart, in two rows of fifteen. Four students were working on each body, two on either side. I had been assigned to the fourth on the left as one entered through the great central door into the dissection room. I was busy exposing the ulnar nerve at the wrist, carefully separating the tissues around it and examining its relationship to the adjacent structures, while my partner, a fresh-faced young man with a ready smile, read out the description of today's dissection from *Gowland and Cairney.* Our anatomy bible: its pages brown and smelling strongly of carbolic acid too from their continuous handling next to the bodies by generations of students, who had covered them with handwritten mnemonics and other scribbles.

I shall always remember my first peep into the dissection room through a chink in the great, central, double door, which I had timidly nudged ajar, after asking the janitor if he might unlock it. Breathless with wonder, I was looking around the empty medical school before the start of term, opening doors and glancing at lecture theatres and laboratories that would open greater vistas unravelling the workings of the human body and mind. 'The proper study of mankind is man,' Alexander Pope was quoted as saying on the first page of some book of mine. I felt on the brink of a new turning point in my life.

Dunedin was a university town with a strong Scottish tradition and the site of the only medical and dental schools in New Zealand. It sprawled prettily across gentle hills overlooking a deep bay and a long peninsula.

I was not yet seventeen when I arrived and settled myself, as a result of my late application, in the tiny annex room at the back of St Margaret's College: an all-women's residential college facing the leafy neo-Gothic university across the street. A path bordered with shrubs climbed up a wide lawn to the front entrance on the left of the three-storey building. The best rooms faced the front off a long corridor that ran the width of the college. On the second floor, the corridor followed the side of the building to make a U-turn at the back. My room was right at its far end, at the top of the back stairs. It barely fitted a narrow bed under the window and a small desk against the inner wall. But that was all I needed. And I was happy. I borrowed from the library a framed print of a buxom gypsy girl with a vivacious smile by the Spanish painter Murillo – its vitality echoing something of a past world I would not let slip into forgetfulness – and hung it over my desk. Next to my room, off the corridor, was a dark damp bathroom with two showers separated by a plastic curtain, where thin jets of warm water from the old nozzles sprinkled erratically on my body as I soaped myself every morning to emerge feeling fresh and clean and ready for another day of lectures at the university across the street.

Next to the back stairs landing lived another student who owned a powerful radio with shortwave reception. We would sit huddled around her radio late into the night, when the reception was at its best, listening to the scratchy, distant noises of exotic languages and music from a world which still existed somewhere out there.

At St Margaret's, I was blending in, getting into the spirit of my new friends and surroundings. The Freshers' Hop, held in a large hall near the university complex, introduced us to the social life of the university. I put on a pretty dress, painted my lips bright red, powdered my face, and set off to the dance with another Medical Intermediate student from a small town on the North Island. I danced all night with shy young men, who were unsure where to put their feet or what to talk about, except for one with a more commanding manner who was a bit drunk and his straight black hair kept flopping over his forehead.

'What are you studying?'

'I'm doing Medical Intermediate. And you?'

'I'm in medical school. My last year. What's your name?'

I told him. 'What's yours?'

'Ian McDonald.' Many years would elapse before I would come across him again in London, by then Professor of Neurology at the National Hospital in Queen Square.

My friend from the North Island was dancing with an engaging young man who walked us back to St Margaret's. He was friendly and attentive as he chattered with us all the way. Neil Perret was a second-year medical student who was staying in Selwyn, the male equivalent of St Margaret's, three or four blocks further out from the university.

Following the Freshers' Hop, frequent dances were held at the university. Among the tight knot of young men who stood between dances near the dancehall entrance, there was one who kept a little apart from the rest. He would stand aloof, very straight, forever an earnest expression on his face: a divinity student by the name of Paul Oestreicher. Might he too be a European refugee, I wondered? Maybe Jewish, albeit his Christian studies? He would become a renowned world peace worker in years to come.

At university I liked best our physics lectures which spread before us insights into the workings of the world around us, unfolding the mysteries of mechanics, light, sound and electricity. Zoology studies were also a source of inspiration, throwing light on the structures and functions in common in the animal kingdom and their divergent adaptations, and showing that it is the emerging patterns that hold the key to understanding. Organic chemistry was logical, like algebra. This whole science seemed to depend on the carbon atom's outer orbit's potential for eight electrons being only half-filled with four, resulting in its unique combining properties with other elements, chiefly oxygen, hydrogen and nitrogen – which forms the basis for life.

I would think about all these new revelations and puzzle over what seemed to be the common underlying determinant: the atom's 'negative' and 'positive' charges. What was known about the physical world, even life itself – then, in 1953 – appeared to depend largely, even if not exclusively, on those opposing charges, with like repelling and unlike attracting. Their unexplained difference seemed to underlie all function. And in some mysterious, metaphorical way, they reflected too the 'male' and 'female' of living creatures, and, by inference, the creation of new life. Might those forces, I wondered, lie at the heart of the universal all-powerful creator we call God?

Conversely, I also dwelt on the unreliability of our impressions of the world around us, making everything – other than our instant awareness – uncertain. Since all we perceive is filtered through our senses and processed in our brain, how can we prove the reality of our external world when our measurements, and our evaluations of our measurements, are made with those same biological sensors of which we cannot make an independent assessment? Making the distinction between imagination and reality impossible – I thought. The only thing we know for certain, I decided, is our own *awareness*, *now* – for memory too is as intangible as dreams.

I used to turn over these thoughts in my mind.

One day I mentioned them in conversation with a young philosophy student I had met at one of those university dances, while we were taking a walk along the university grounds.

'Perhaps nothing exists as we perceive it. There is no way of proving the existence of the world outside ourselves. The only thing I can be sure of is my own awareness at this moment.'

'That is what Descartes said!' he exclaimed.

'Oh?' I had not yet heard of Descartes.

'"I think, therefore I am."' Well, sort of …

The university complex was an easy walk from Dunedin's central shopping area. I liked browsing in shops, looking for new fabrics and dress patterns. I had started making my own clothes, while still in high school, with my mother's sewing machine. I would seek out prints in earthy shades, or in bright colours like red, blue and turquoise. For patterns I chose classic styles with simple lines: fitted cotton dresses or maybe a top with a swirling skirt for summer, and for winter a belted Scottish tweed suit with colourful hand-knitted jumpers.

St Margaret's had strict rules. The front door was locked at ten o'clock every night. We were allowed one late night a week, for which we had to write our name and the event in The Book, and sign it on our return by eleven, when the warden's assistant unlocked the door to let us in. Anyone caught arriving after that hour had to explain herself before the college warden: an elderly lady with a bland, kindly smile that concealed an icy severity. Only Zeppy, her sausage dog, seemed to appeal to her gentler nature.

The whole college was served with one telephone, located in a small room near its entrance, minded by us in rotation. 'St Margaret's Presbyterian College for Young and Unmarried Women,' we would say when we picked up the phone to take messages for the rest of the 135 of us.

In the meantime, at university, I was attracted to one young man after another. I would be drawn to that student by his lively, carefree smile, or the next by his shyness, or to him by his commanding manner. I read sensitivities into young men I had never spoken to, and imagined all kinds of appealing attributes. One might wear a snug, woolly jumper that suggested informality, comfort and protection ... But none would ever reach a dialogue, some common ground.

At St Margaret's, a young, Swedish physiotherapy student stood out from all these New Zealanders. As different as we were from each other, we shared in common our foreign background and became friends. Beatrice was tall and willowy and she had a way of observing the world around her with a *laissez-faire* expression. She had been a fashion model in Sweden and been through a mysteriously difficult time. Her frankness appealed to me, and she seemed to have reached a certain wisdom about the world which I wished to learn. Small and dark, tense and troubled, I sometimes felt ungainly next to her composure. 'You look like an Egyptian princess,' she would say to me whenever she sensed my insecurity.

Beatrice wore svelte, classic clothes from Sweden and used a most delicate French cream on her face. She gave me a light red, angora sweater with a soft turn-over collar, and a powder blue woollen dress, which she claimed she didn't wear anymore, from her wardrobe.

One evening, fooling around, I tried a song and dance routine in the style of Hollywood musicals. Taste and attitudes were instilled by Hollywood even here, at the far end of the world. The seductive romance that emanated from the screen as stars glided down wide central staircases in high heels and flowing frilly gowns to the background of symphonic music inevitably left an impression.

So I sang in front of Beatrice, imagining an elusive, debonair hero emerging from the clouds as I strode across the room:

*I was walking along, minding my business,*
*when out of the orange-coloured sky:*
*Whizz-bang! Ali-kazan!*
*wonderful you came by.*

Reluctantly, on being pressed for her reaction, Beatrice whispered, 'It's vulgar.'

I suddenly came to realise the fatuity of my efforts at blending into surroundings I wasn't part of. Of trying to convince myself of being something I wasn't. The façade I was erecting in search of approbation. The falsehood of it all. I needed some fresh air. It was not yet ten o'clock when the college doors closed, so I went for a walk. The night was dark. I followed the empty road along the waterfront. There was no one else about. I was glad to be alone. My sense of dislocation came tumbling out again. The confusing demands from the long array of alien homes and countries. And, to crown it, my mother's endless censure. My vain search for an acceptable image ... its sham, its shallowness. Its incongruity. A truck was approaching. It was large and heavy. I felt almost irresistibly drawn towards it. It would be so easy to step in front of it. And to end all my struggles with myself, all the pain and disappointment. It would be such relief.

But I didn't.

I turned round and went back to St Margaret's.

At university, a senior psychology student was working on the growing problem of juvenile delinquency. He started a club in a rough, underprivileged area – called, of all things, Kensington – on the other side of Dunedin, and recruited girls from university to join and mingle with the local youth. I was one of a small group from St Margaret's who regularly attended the Kensington Youth Club and jived to rock'n'roll records of Bill Haley's 'Rock Around the Clock' and 'See You Later, Alligator', Elvis Presley's 'Blue Suede Shoes' and 'Don't be Cruel' among other numbers. We would mix and chat with the boys who had been in trouble with the law for stealing motorbikes or joyriding. The rock'n'roll and friendly atmosphere helped to build confidence with the 'delinquents', and the breaking down of barriers allowed new perspectives to take hold as an alternative to the boys' rebellious ways

As I set out every week from St Margaret's to the club looking forward to that evening's intermingling and activities, I once tried to imagine my reaction should the club close down. And I was alarmed to realise my dependence on it: my reversed role as healer was maybe helping to heal me too.

The following year I moved to a room on the ground floor of St Margaret's facing the front. From here I looked out onto the university across the street, and heard its clock's quarterly tunes and hourly chimes – after Big Ben – which helped me get to lectures on time. Here I made lasting friendships with Anne Wills, a physical education student, and Liz, training as a teacher.

I was now seventeen and had lived for a full five years in New Zealand.

'You can't call me a "bloody foreigner" anymore!' I exclaimed jubilantly to my friends one day. Not that they had, but it was a common term of reference.

I had just received a certificate stating that I was now a Registered British Subject and a Citizen of New Zealand. My first nationality.

And just as I had come into this country saying everything was 'great', and 'okay', a habit my aunt had broken, I had now incorporated into my vocabulary this, my adoptive, country's linguistic expressions. 'That's beaut', 'Fair dinkum', 'You're a silly coot', 'Hell's bells and bloody cockleshells'.

A weekend hike along the coast was organised by the University

Tramping Club, of which I was a member. We walked across long stretches of sandy beach and clambered across rocky coves while the sea pounded the shoreline that stretched northwards ahead of us. By evening, we reached a long straight beach with a group of caves set back into the rockface and decided to make a log fire, have our supper and settle for the night in the largest one. During the night, in the pitch darkness and confined space of the cave, the crashing of the waves against the beach was greatly magnified. As my consciousness was beginning to flag, tucked inside my snug sleeping bag on the soft sandy ground, the sea's rolling ebb and flow started coming closer and still closer and now the water was forcing its way into the cave and I became concerned for the others too as the pounding and roaring rose to a thunderous crescendo and I was engulfed from all sides by the rushing rising water inside the dark cave without escape and I suddenly woke up, my heart thumping in my chest. We were safe and dry, and the others all fast asleep. The rhythmic beating of the waves against the shoreline could be heard outside in the distance. I turned over and went back to sleep.

St Margaret's institutional atmosphere was beginning to stifle me. A bedsit in a house further down the street became vacant, and I moved in.

The house was set back from the street on higher ground and was approached along a narrow path between the house in front of it and a fence. The room had its own entrance next to some steps that led to a higher paved area behind it. To get to the bathroom, I had to walk up these steps round to the back of the house, in the early morning or late at night, through sun, drizzle, the cold of winter or in the light of the moon. The outdoor lavatory was at the far corner of the raised backyard. On moonless nights I felt my way through the darkness and, once there, would sit and watch from my dark corner the lights of Dunedin at my feet and above the night sky full of stars. For a male, though, the absence of a light complicated matters.

'It's a case of hit and miss out there!' Barry remarked with his characteristic cascading laugh – his usual stiffer self momentarily relaxed – on his return from relieving himself on the night I invited him to sample frogs' legs for dinner. He had brought several pairs of them from the laboratory where he was doing some research for his B. Med. Sc., having opted to take an academic year off his medical course. I had fried the frogs' legs in butter on my small, single-ring, electric cooker, served them with asparagus and potatoes, and we had sat down at my table to try out our 'French' meal. The flesh on the frogs' legs was spare and tasted like fishy chicken – a change at least from roast mutton and boiled cabbage in this southern outpost of New Zealand.

The room, once a workshop at the back of the house, was long and narrow with a low ceiling which could be reached with an out-stretched arm. In the short outer wall, the entrance door was flanked by two windows. At the inner end of the room were the bed and a curtained-off area for my clothes. Along one wall, some wooden apple boxes served as bookshelf and stand for my radio and gramo-phone, and nearer the door were a table and chair at which I ate and studied. Against the facing wall were a dressing table with a mirror and another stack of apple boxes for my pots and pans and the cooker. A light bulb hung from the centre of the ceiling.

Sleeping in the innermost corner of the room, I felt cosy and secure. Womb-like. Myself. In this room, there was no need to modify thoughts or behaviour according to outside pressures from people with different habits, expectations, priorities. I felt content and self-sufficient. I covered the apple boxes with a native island print fabric and hung on the wall a picture of Van Gogh's *Le Café, Le Soir* – a flood of orange light, illuminating people at coffee tables on a French cobbled street, against the deep blue, star studded sky. And two smaller, Klee prints: one of little yellow birds, and the other an abstract house in the ghostly light of a bright round moon. All this, to the sounds from my gramophone of Bach's Suites or Dixie-land jazz rhythms. Or Eartha Kitt singing 'I Want to be Evil' in her quavering voice.

In the morning, I would switch on the radio and listen to the BBC World Service news while I dressed and prepared my coffee. There was another war, out there in the bigger world. In Indochina this time. By now I was in medical school and our first lecture of the day was biochemistry. I would sit in the front of the great, ascending lecture room, listening to Professor Edson's gentle, even intonation as he stood by the blackboard taking us through his travels of the biochemical structures and functions of the human body. Professor McIntyre taught us physiology. Of the body's various systems, I found neurophysiology the most captivating and closest to the greatest mystery of all: the link between our physical bodies, which can be measured, and the 'mind', which can't.

At the start of the year I had bought second-hand, from other students, my text books, microscope and a set of human bones, with the funds my father had agreed to send me from Mexico for my studies: £75 a term for rent, food and expenses to spare.

The mornings were filled with lectures and laboratory work, while the afternoons were spent in the dissection room: three hours every day, five days a week, over twenty months. The vast room stretched across from the front to the back of the building, its large double door at the top of the central staircase always locked except when the room was in use. An unbroken row of windows ran the length of the side and back walls, and a story used to get around about a window cleaner who was busy at work one day on his ladder outside the dissection room.

'Want a hand?' a student called out to him.

'Yes!' answered the cleaner.

And the student passed him one.

I vivdly remember the first time I walked into the dissection room with my new class. There was a hushed reverential silence as we each stood before our allocated, still intact, body. After a short introductory talk, we put aside what qualms we felt and set about our first dissection, starting at the armpit.

And I would become totally absorbed in the spatial relationships of the various anatomical structures.

'You're a wag,' one of the students dissecting the opposite arm would lean across the body and tell me. Or, sometimes, teasingly, 'You're a square peg in a round hole,' I would also be described as a 'dark horse', reflecting the native students' friendly puzzlement about me: not born and bred in New Zealand like the rest. Yet, notwithstanding my difference, here I felt comfortable and fully accepted as we all shared our studies and followed our common medical interests.

The first term, we worked our way down the arm from the armpit to the hand, the second, we dissected the lower limb, and the third, the trunk. The following year, we went over the head and neck. In that time we had dissected the whole body and were expected to know the entire human anatomy in minute detail.

The unnatural, tanned appearance and leathery consistency of the bodies from their preservation with carbolic acid made it easy to forget that they had once belonged to real people. Those that had not been donated to the medical school voluntarily by their owner while still alive, were unclaimed bodies from mental hospitals. The body I was working on had marks of arsenic injections: once the only treatment for syphilis.

Our embryology studies gave an insight into how the final structures we were looking at in anatomy came to be. Professor Adams would stand by the blackboard, his sturdy figure leaning against the tall wooden pointer held firmly in his fist, as he looked up at the class from the semicircular lecture theatre's stage below and described the development of the human embryo. He spoke with a clear resounding voice while he held the class under his powerful gaze. And I took detailed notes which I later read, as exams approached, moulding a piece of plasticine through the changes described to capture a clear, three-dimensional, moving image of the development of, for instance, the heart. In the dissection room, lecturers would walk from body to body, going over the anatomy with us. Once in a while, Professor Adams would stride into the room in his white coat, his large eyes blazing, his voice booming, his greying hair swept back from his commanding face, and the class would tremble – though his eyes were half-laughing at the frightened students. He would threaten to pull out one of the women, usually the shyest – there were twelve of us in the class of 120 – and use her to

*With Professor Adams at welcome party for women medical students*

demonstrate to the class the surface anatomy of pectoralis major, the muscle that stretches across the front of the ribcage. And the young women students would become huffed and embarrassed and the men would laugh and enjoy their discomfort, while I looked on all that theatrical machismo with amusement.

After five every evening, at the end of a day of lectures and dissection, I would return, past the university and across the Leith River, back to my room. I would put on a record while I cooked and settled down to my meal. Later, friends from St Margaret's or medical school might drop in for a chat. Or I might go out for a walk and amble along leafy Leith Street and watch the moonlight drenching Dunedin's sleepy roofs and bouncing off the leaves of the trees as they gently stirred on their branches, or sparkling its shattered reflection on the river's rippling waters. Its myriad silvery fragments bobbing and tossing on the Leith below; one full radiant moon poised in the sky above. I too, like the moon, filled the whole of me, felt my oneness – the divisions were illusionary, the shards restored – in this illumined stillness. I felt most wide-awake at this hour, my head clear and my perception at its most acute. Back in my room, as I got undressed for bed, supple and sensuous, I would move to the beat of the late-night jazz playing on the radio, and I realised I wasn't willing the dancing so much as it was being driven by the rhythm of the music. And I delighted in the sheer sensation of being alive.

Once or twice, while out walking, I knocked at the door of a classmate who lived nearby and stopped and chatted for a few minutes. As I was leaving, a book on the table caught my attention and I picked it up and opened it at random. I read: 'It is not enough for me to *read* that the sand in the seashore is soft, my bare feet must feel it.' Yes! I thought. The book was André Gide's *The Fruits of the Earth*. I bought my own copy the next day at the University Book Shop. Emerging from a close shave with death, Gide expressed his acute sense of life in these notes written during his travels in North Africa. 'At every moment of my life, I have felt within me all my richness ... *Let every moment renew your vision.'* It brought me in touch with a world, lucid and untainted, free from preconceptions. I followed with Camus and Sartre – starting with *The Age of Reason*, which took me back to occupied France, and again the sense of *being* rather than *judging*, and many more concepts to think about. My discovery of these contemporary French writers opened my mind wider again and helped me with my quest for my own bearings.

After our day's work at medical school, I often spent time with my classmates and friends, Pat and Rachel. Sometimes we joined others from our class and our meetings turned into all-night parties. An older student, who was shyer and more reticent than the rest of us, suddenly came to life one night when Jews were mentioned.

'There is a World Jewish Conspiracy,' he informed us very seriously. 'The Jews are planning to take over the world.'

I was astounded.

'If that is so, I would surely know about it, seeing I'm Jewish,' I pointed out.

'I don't care what you are!' our usually mild-mannered friend pronounced with passion. 'It *is* true! It's all been written down in "The Protocols of the Learned Elders of Zion"!' and he went on to quote his source in more detail.

Out here, in remote New Zealand, his was a lonely voice. The subject was dropped and the party continued till it was time to go home and change back into day clothes, drink a cup of strong coffee and arrive in time for the first morning lecture at medical school.

A visiting lecturer from France passed through Dunedin. A Frenchman in Dunedin seemed as likely as a green man from Mars. I met him and invited him for coffee at my place, and – as we sat and talked – he put me back in touch with my own past and origins. He spoke about things that were happening in that other world, stating candidly what he thought and felt – something I had grown unaccustomed to in this country. He spoke about a recent trip through Spain on his motorbike, and the wretchedness he had come across. It was at the height of Franco's reign.

'I arrived in a small village and found a place to stay overnight. The woman cooked me a meal and brought it to my room. As I was eating it, I began to hear strange scratching noises at the door. I sat very still and the noises stopped, but every time I returned to my meal they started again. I thought maybe I was being followed and watched: I am no admirer of the Franco regime and I had to be careful. I finally got up, walked quietly to the door and flung it open. Imagine my surprise when I found two small emaciated children, terrified out of their wits at the sight of me. They were waiting for me to finish eating so they could clean up any crumbs I had left on my plate.'

My mother came to see me once and stayed overnight. I cleaned and tidied my room, prepared my bed for my mother and cooked her a meal. When she arrived, she looked about her at the way I had set myself up in my Dunedin bedsit.

'I'm very happy to see how you live,' she said, when she looked around in my room here in Dunedin, evidently moved. 'To me, this is more important than your studies.'

I was surprised. It had been a long time since I had experienced my mother's approval.

Capping Week arrived. Dunedin filled with students in a carnival atmosphere. They strutted singly or in the Capping Procession through the main streets past the town's population. The Capping Concert was a vaudeville of farces and reworded songs.

Every night the students turned up to the Wool Store Hops at a large warehouse heaped with mountains of wool bales, which were shifted to the periphery of the huge hall to clear the central area for dancing. Students would come in droves and drink beer and dance all night. Groups of friends would sit and drink on top of the wool bales, while behind them couples were smooching or the odd drunk student would be sick or lie in a coma.

The band played jazzy numbers and the men went up to the women and asked them to dance or jive.

One evening, Dick – whom I had met through Johnny Steiner in the neurophysiology lab, where they were doing research for their B. Med. Sc. degree – came up to me.

'Would you dance?' He had a quiet way of talking and was economical with words. I liked him.

'Where were you born?' he asked me while he led me round the floor.

'In Barcelona.'

'*Everyone* should be born in Barcelona,' he said – with emphasis.

And, a few moments later:

'What made you decide to study medicine?'

'I'm interested in people.'

'*I'm* not,' he said laughing and without further elaboration.

He danced with me for the rest of the evening.

At the end of the hop, we piled into the back of a van with other students, set off to some party which didn't exist, and then back to his place, a flat he shared with Neil Perret whom I knew from the Freshers' Hop. We went upstairs to his room. He picked up his violin from the bed, scratched a few sounds on it with the bow, put it down again, and stretched his arms towards me. I went to him and he wrapped them around me and kissed me tightly and warmly for a moment. Then he took me home.

The next night we danced together again all night at the Wool Store Hop.

He talked of a small new café, a block from the university, where they played music. Things like Bach. He suggested we have coffee there. Yes, I said.

He invited me to a dance – one of those college dances, maybe Selwyn. It was in a softly lit hall, overlooked by a balcony where we sat at small tables between dances. Neil Perret was in our group.

As Dick and I danced together around the floor, I would glance up at his face above me, almost touching. And I felt too stirred to speak. So we danced mostly in silence.

Back on the balcony, the music was playing '*Some enchanted evening …*'

'"Calamity",' Neil said, naming the next number.

'Where?' his partner asked, as she scanned the room in mild concern from the balcony.

Dick started coming to see me. I would know it was he from the slow, heavy, muted steps up the side path to my room and by the height of his shadow through the frosted glass in the door as he knocked. He used to wear a thick woollen blue coat which he distractedly slipped off where he stood and I would pick up and fold over a chair. Sometimes we went for a walk along the botanical gardens, half a block down the road from my room. There was a small clearing with a seesaw and two swings at the start of the path, which then followed alongside the Leith River bordered by trees and undergrowth till it reached a cultivated area on hilly ground. In spring, a whole section was ablaze with azaleas and rhododendrons.

We were walking together in the gardens late one afternoon. I was looking at the trees.

'Some trees look plonked. They are not as nice as the ones that grow wild,' I remarked.

'Trees,' he said, as though delivering a lecture, 'are classified into the plonked and non-plonked varieties,' and he laughed.

'Don't you think?' I insisted.

'I don't like to be told what to believe. But I like to hear what you think,' he said matter-of-factly and affectionately.

During one of our walks, we had reached the higher area and started to come down across a gentle grassy slope. We stopped by a bench halfway down and stood next to it. It was drizzling. Or rather, the air was impregnated with a suspension of fine droplets turning everything into an even, translucent grey, as though seen through a veil of muslin.

Dick had his arm around me, and his hair and face and coat were all covered with a fine white layer of tiny droplets, like thick dew.

'I went to see the play they're showing over at varsity. About tigers. It was really good,' I was telling him, outlining the details of the plot and its meaning.

When my voice stopped, I heard the silence that enveloped us. There was a tremendous calm. The moisture-laden atmosphere seemed to cut us off from the world and create a beautiful strange stillness.

'Isn't it quiet. Sometimes I feel as though I merge and become one with my surroundings. Like this drizzle and the silence. And the extraordinary tranquillity. And then thinking stops. It becomes irrelevant.' I heard my voice had dropped to a lower key and was slow and even.

'That's what I've been doing. I've been listening to your voice, but I didn't hear the meaning of the words.'

On moonlit nights, I would stand outside my room and look

across at the scattered woodland and houses on the opposite hill bathed in moonlight. Sometimes I would stroll down to the Leith River in the university grounds across the street, and listen to the water trickling over the stones and watch the moon splintering on the ripples. One night, I wanted to share this with him. I walked across to his flat and called him softly from under his bedroom window. He came to the window. He had already gone to bed.

'Come for a walk! It's beautiful outside.'

So he slipped on his clothes and came out.

We walked up a winding road along the side of a hill over-looking the town. As we started coming down again, we stopped and looked across Dunedin cradled between the hills and the bay beyond. Up above, the moon – a glistening disc of burning platinum suspended in the clear night sky – shone down full force on the sleeping town. After a few moments we continued on our way down, barely breaking the silence. He left me at my doorstep and returned to his flat.

St Margaret's Ball was approaching, and I asked if he would go with me.

'Yes,' he said.

The day arrived. I put on a long dress I had made of a red nylon fabric covered in tiny white dots: a fitted halter top with a circular skirt. I slipped on a white, furry, waist-length jacket with a silky lining I had also sewn. I painted my eyes, put on lipstick and combed my hair. And then I waited for him.

The time passed and it was getting late; I decided to walk down and meet him. I went past the university, through the green with the zoology department, and across the road to his flat. I rang the bell. After a moment, he opened it in his casual clothes looking somewhat surprised.

'Sorry! I'd forgotten all about it! I'll dress and come over.'

He turned up shortly after in his black suit and bow tie, and we went off to St Margaret's.

The large dining hall had been cleared for the occasion and was crowded with St Margaret's girls in their long ball dresses and their boyfriends in their monkey suits. I still felt a little piqued that he had forgotten. He wasn't bothered at all.

'Sometimes you look beautiful,' he said in his quiet voice, after looking at me for a moment. 'And tonight you're beautiful.'

At the end of that term, he came over to see me on the last night. We drank coffee and kissed and talked. We stood by the door as he was leaving and he fastened his eyes on me for a few moments.

'I'll come back to see you next term,' he said, his voice firm, his mind made up.

So he went off to his parental home in Tauranga, on the north-eastern coast of the North Island. While I went to mine in Christchurch to count the days, the hours and the minutes till I would see him again.

He came to see me at the start of the following term. He kissed me as we stood inside the entrance of my room, and then suggested we go for a walk. Not the gardens this time, he said as I started in that direction, but just along the streets. As we were walking along the last stretch of street that led back to my place, he turned towards me.

'Would you mind if I take out someone else?' he asked.

'You are free to do as you like,' I told him quietly, firmly holding back the tearing pain – *aguántate!* – that was suddenly trying to well up inside me.

'You're being very kind,' he said.

I remained silent while I turned over in my mind this news.

'Does that mean you won't come to see me anymore?' I asked him.

'Yes. It's better not to.'

Now I was too upset to say anything more. We reached my door and he left.

Back in my room on my own, I sat on my bed and wept freely. This had been the first time I had felt so strongly and deeply for someone who had, in turn, seemed to care for me too. And now this, without warning, without explanation …

I would sit in my room after my day's lectures trying to come to terms with this new and latest disappointment. I wrote a letter to my mother. 'I have always had a great struggle between my brain and my heart. My brain tries to tame my heart – with the consequence that my heart always loses, becomes crushed, pushed aside, and I am in so much pain …' I expect she must have felt for me – she had after all had her own share of heartache – but she couldn't put it into words.

My friends came to visit me and tried to console me. One day, one of them suddenly mentioned who that 'someone else' was.

'She's been very jealous of you,' she told me. 'Her friend used to come to St Margaret's to try and find out from us what you and Dick had been up to, to go back and report it to her. She wanted to know *everything*, to the last detail. Dick had danced with her in the Wool Store Hop the night before he danced with you, and she went back the next night with great expectations. Instead, she sat and watched you dance together all night, and she's been dying to get him back for herself ever since. So she made a plan to go to Tauranga during the term holidays, and look him up and entice him back.'

'Really?' I was astonished.

I had never felt drawn to her. She too, it seemed, had come to New Zealand as the daughter of Jewish refugees, though at a much younger age, and the family had turned Anglican. Perhaps – I had tried to imagine – that was one way of forgetting a difficult past and blending more easily into one's new surroundings; even so, it was not a path I could identify with.

I missed Dick. I would remember our brief romance for a long time. I would be haunted for years to come by his memory, and the illusion that the happiness I had been looking for had once been almost within reach.

The end-of-year exams were drawing close. I read through my lecture notes and leafed through *Gowland and Cairney*. My anatomy exam paper came back with a lovely comment from Professor Adams: 'Very competently answered and satisfyingly devoid of errors and ambiguities. Very good indeed!' Considering his exceptionally high demands, his praise delighted me. On many other students' papers he had written 'ROT' across the pages!

The anatomy oral exams were held in the pathology museum, its shelves lined with various diseased and abnormal parts of the human body displayed like bottled pickles: a man's yellowed head with his eyes half open and the characteristic squashed syphilitic nose, or the grotesquely pinched liver from a woman who had followed the tightly laced bodice fashion of the previous century. Suits were worn to orals: I bought a charcoal grey flannel suit, formal and classic, and resolved to face the examiners at ease and with a clear head.

A story circulated about a student asked what is the foramen magnum (the orifice at the base of the skull through which the spinal cord leaves the brain).

'The opening at the bottom of the oesophagus which leads to the stomach.'

'Mm,' reflected Professor Adams, '*there*'s food for thought.'

Many students took a job during their holidays to pay for their year's expenses at university. The men would do well at the woolsheds or freezing works. I took on a variety of holiday jobs, from selling tickets at the Cathedral Square cinema in Christchurch, to packing cigarette papers and making ice cream.

On my mother's birthday, I bought her with my savings a beautiful set of silver-plated teaspoons. She was my mother, I thought, and whatever our differences, I wished to give her something special that would give her pleasure. When she unwrapped her present she looked both moved and puzzled. She glanced at me uncertainly, as though trying to understand ... But her hesitation didn't last and our estrangement was restored.

In the third year, the First Professional exams tested in detail our knowledge of the normal structure and function of the whole of the human body, paving the way for the start of our clinical studies in the hospital 'across the road'.

I was dissecting part of the head in the dissection room when I overheard a student saying, 'I've gone over *Gray's Anatomy* seven times and I still haven't managed to memorise it!'

This shook me up. I hadn't even started my own revision yet. I made a rapid calculation of the time left before the exams. Six weeks in which to revise *everything*. That evening I sat down in my room and made a plan of the entire revision. I could just about fit it in if I worked day and night without interruption. I pinned the plan on my wall above my table and started straight away.

From that day, I spent all my spare time in front of my books.

As exams approached, lectures at medical school stopped. I started going to bed early and rising before dawn when silence reigned and all of Dunedin was still asleep. I would make myself a cup of strong ground coffee and a piece of toast with strawberry jam. I was the only person up and stirring, and mine the only light on, in the whole sleepy town. I would wedge myself into a corner of my room, jamming the table against me and wrapping my sleeping bag firmly around me which, apart from keeping me warm – it was July and mid-winter – also helped to hold me in place and overcome my restlessness. And while I studied, enveloped in the silence and stillness of the night, the faintest glimmer of dawn would start breaking through the darkness outside, and a bird would venture its first hesitant chirrup, followed soon after by another's tentative melodic reply, and then a few more would join in, until the sweetest symphony of chirps, gurglings and twitters filled the dying night's air while I visualised the citric acid cycle against this delightful pot-pourri of birdsong: the acetate molecules in the final pathway of carbohydrate breakdown interacting with the enzymes in the cell, the whole reaction moving dynamically like clockwork, picking up and dropping parts of molecules as the cycle progressed to finally combine with oxygen and liberate the energy that maintains life. Then the manner in which nerves exchanged ions through their membranes and relayed their impulses to produce muscle move-ment and deliver sensations to the brain, controlling and coordi-nating the body and a gateway to our minds. And I found it all amazing.

The exams came. Finally, the last paper and oral were over. I returned to my bedsit, had my evening meal, and then played a record. It was Schubert's String Quintet in C major. I lay across the bed with my legs raised, leaning against the wall and my head hanging over the side surveying the room upside down. The music wove in and out in strange, intense, unexpected patterns as the strings interacted and built up, held, and released tensions with a nervous, excited poignancy and energy which invaded my senses, completely taking over. A tear started rolling down my temple upside down into my hair, followed by another, until a flood of them were spilling over with the music into streams soaking my face and hair right up to the last agitated note. And I felt released of all tension and fresh and new again, after all my disciplined study and exams.

Rachel, Pat and I moved into a flat in Queen Street, a few minutes' walk from medical school. It occupied the top floor of a two-storey house perched over the steep, rocky garden. Pat moved a piano into her room and Rachel hung a Matisse print of a woman in a billowing blouse with a scarlet background. My own room looked out onto the side garden, and I placed a lithograph of three, long-plaited Mexican girls on my wall. From the semicircular porch at the front of the flat, a panoramic view stretched across the whole of Dunedin with the harbour and peninsula beyond.

At medical school, we now embarked on our clinical studies.

We crossed the street in our short white coats and went into the hospital to listen in on ward rounds, examine our allocated patients, and sit in the observers' gallery in the operating theatre to watch surgeons at work while they gave a running commentary for the students' education.

I would never forget my first post-mortem. The room's steeply ascending rows faced a white ceramic sink slab in the centre stage below. We entered the room, and there, on the slab, was a man, maybe in his fifties, lying stretched out, naked, looking like any other man except for his pallor and total stillness.

'This man was driving his car at five o'clock yesterday afternoon,' Professor D'Ath – yes, that was his name – started telling us, in his deep mellow voice, when we had all settled down on the benches and our attention was glued to the figure lying before us, 'when suddenly,' here he paused for a moment, 'he was struck by a severe pain in his chest.' And he stopped and looked up benevolently through his spectacles at the class, his thick, white hair framing his rosy face. In the meantime, the morgue technician was busy with his knife, having made a long incision all the way down from the base of the neck to the crutch, and was starting to excise the long loop of intestines and other organs with practised skill, allowing the growing roll of ash at the end of the cigarette butt hanging from the side of his mouth to drop into the open abdominal cavity. I noticed the heaviness of the dead man's arms when they were lifted, now at the sole mercy of gravity and the other man's will, since the last flicker of life – the tone of the muscles and the lightness of movement when willed by their owner, as these limbs had been only a few hours ago – had left them. 'At five o'clock yesterday evening.' And I saw my own image lying in like manner some day. In the front row sat a group of students who chattered and laughed at their jokes – the noisiest eventually becoming a pathologist himself – without apparent reflection on the man lying little more than an arm's length from them.

Back walking along the main street, full of shops and people and the bustle of life, I felt better again. These people's scalps were in place, where they should be, not cut back and pulled over their faces to remove their brains. And I delighted in feeling alive, sensing the warm sunshine on my skin, watching the windswept, ruffled clouds in the blue sky, and feeling part of this busy, moving, happy chunk of living humanity all around me.

At the hospital, the importance of *observation* was drilled into us. As you approach a new patient, you start looking for clinical signs already from the foot of the bed, and the vigilance is maintained throughout the history-taking and detailed medical examination. One of the patients I was allocated had testicular cancer. He was a fit young man in his prime. The prognosis was bad, yet I had to conceal it from him: patients were kept ignorant of a life-threatening diagnosis then, in the 1950s. This troubled me. Were there not circumstances in which they had a right to know? And then, how would one break the news? And I would weigh up the distress from disclosure against the deception …

Our introduction to hospital practices required that we learn some of the nursing skills too. We were taught how to make a bed, tucking in the corners of the sheets and blankets neatly like an envelope. And we practised how to give intramuscular injections using a syringe and needle on a raw potato before sticking them into patients. During my first attempt at catheterising a male patient, I forgot to lubricate the catheter and wondered why I was having such difficulty – the young man, very kind and patient, didn't even flinch, though he must have had reason to.

In our Queen Street flat, Pat disappeared into her room after our evening meal to play the piano and study, while Rachel and I would sit by the gas fire in my room, deep in talk. Back in my Leith Street bedsit, we had exchanged ideas on whether neurophysiology could explain consciousness. I had tried to express the difference of our experience of, for instance, *redness*, against the measurable events that accompany our vision of it. 'You can describe how the light waves in the red end of the spectrum travel to your eye, cross the eye's medium, interact with the receptors in the retina and are transmitted along the optic nerve to reach the occipital lobe of the brain, firing further pathways to other areas of the brain – the entire network of which might even, in theory, be traced some day. But none of this describes or explains our *experience* of redness. Or of our imagination and thoughts. You can't pick those up and measure them. They may be inextricably bound to measurable physical changes, but their quality is of another dimension and remains a mystery.' But Rachel didn't see it that way.

And now, here in Queen Street, we discussed roofs.

'In Mexico, the roofs of houses are *beautiful*. They're *tiled*. While here in New Zealand, they're all made of tin! Corrugated tin! And they're green instead of red!'

'Green corrugated tin roofs are *nice*. The houses up north where I grew up have green corrugated tin roofs, and they've always been special to me. I remember them from my childhood, they are part of my life,' Rachel argued in her quiet, forceful way.

'They don't have any character, like the red-tiled roofs have.'

'It's the other way round. The green tin roofs have a lot more character!'

And none of these problems were ever resolved.

We would listen to The Goons on the radio singing 'Ying Tong Yiddle Eye Po' and 'I'm Walking Backwards for Christmas across the Irish Sea', or to Blue Bottle's abrupt change of voice, up several octaves, following an explosion. We had parties in our flat and danced to our rock'n'roll records – I loved moving to the slow rhythm of Gene Vincent's 'Be Bop O Lula' or Elvis Presley's 'Heartbreak Hotel', or jiving to Little Richard's fast and frantic 'Tutti Frutti', or stepping and swirling in time to Johnny Ray's 'Yes, Tonight Josephine'. The smooth swing of Glenn Miller was Rachel's favourite. Or we listened late into the night to traditional Dixieland jazz and blues or the more chaotic, syncopated sounds of the then modern Dave Brubeck. I made myself a short, strapless dress from a piece of Swiss draping material, scarlet with shiny black and gold circles and dots, apparently admired by Professor Adams from his house across the street, though he didn't recognise the wearer as one of his students.

Barry Cant, with whom I had eaten frogs' legs back in the days of my bedsit, would take me to university dances, or the pictures, or for a drive in his antique, upright, yellow Austin to the peninsula across the other side of the harbour. Once we went to see a Hollywood film about the Second World War. Both the British and German military commanders were very gentlemanly in this film, and I felt it had missed the war's horror.

'This culture doesn't understand the Nazis' inhuman cruelty!' I was telling Barry on our way home.

'Germans are just as human as anybody else,' Barry tried to reason. 'They fought on their side of the war with the same spirit as the British.' But my image of German army officials was a sinister one of clicking heels and hands shooting up to 'Heil Hitler' while rounding up innocent civilians to shoot them against the wall or send them to their deaths in some concentration camp with merciless efficiency – and Barry's attempt to humanise them made me feel more alone than ever in this country. Our evening ended in fierce disagreement. Though we would be of one mind, years later, at our meetings again in Europe.

Other films which came to New Zealand gave me glimpses of a world I had lost and missed. Such as *I am a Camera*, after Christopher Isherwood's novel about Berlin in the thirties, as my mother must have known it. Or Alain Renais's *Hiroshima Mon Amour*, displaying both the intensity and transience of an unexpected love against background memories of fried, radioactive Hiroshima and a forbidden young passion which breached war's artificial barriers in a French town. This was at the start of Cinéma Verité and both films reflected on the horror of the human war machine and the mysterious and unpredictable nature of sex and relationships.

Once again I was going through an unsettled period. I didn't know where to begin to conquer my maladjustment. In spite of my efforts, I didn't fit into the ways of life around me, and my human contact was uneasy. I felt cut off, in spite of my friends. Barry was totally honest with me, which I deeply appreciated. He would say to me, more than once, 'I like you, but I don't understand you,' and he was probably one of the most perceptive of those around me. I came to the conclusion that here in New Zealand I would not find someone to share the love and deep friendship I longed for, or have a child on whom to lavish my love and attention to make up for what I had missed.

The obstetrics professor was a man of charm and ready humour. At the start of lectures, Professor Wright would stand at the bottom of the lecture theatre facing us.

'Well chaps,' he always started, his gaze skipping the front row, where most of the women sat, to address the rest of the class beyond.

We each had to deliver twenty babies. We resided for a fortnight in the obstetric hospital, and the chief midwife assisted us through the required training. The labouring women were turned into the 'left lateral position', the right leg held up in the air by a nurse, while we stood behind, arms around the thigh, controlling the emerging head so as to allow it out gently. My first sight of a baby's birth left me breathless with emotion. I was more excited than the mother at the end of her unplanned pregnancy. Freshly born, all pink, tiny fingers and toes, dazed, blinking eyes taking in the first blur of meaningless dancing lights and colours, all the parts in miniature. And I thought of how it would soon lose that initial purity and inno-cence, be moulded, hurt and restrained as it grew into an adult. Like a first fall of snow, smooth and untouched, will inevitably become crushed and marked – so it would be with that brand new creature barely out from its dark, warm, watery enclosure.

New Zealand was proud of its tradition of Plunket babies. It had greatly reduced infant mortality, but it also ignored bonding. Careful attention to sterility meant minimum touching, wearing of masks, fathers looking at their offspring through a glass divide, and babies removed to nurseries where they lay in long rows in aseptic sur-roundings, to receive their feed and be returned to their cots every four hours by the clock.

The second baby I delivered was called after me – it was the mother's fifth and she had run out of names. 'What's your name, doctor?' she asked me, and, 'That's a nice name, I'll call her that.'

We sat our pathology, pharmacology and microbiology exams at the end of our fourth year. Then came fifth year: the easiest, most relaxed of the course after

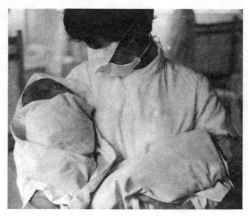

*My first two deliveries*

the grind of the previous ones. It covered the subjects of public health and medical jurisprudence. We had to learn the detailed stages of putrefaction of the human body after death, as well as the various clues that indicated the medium in which it had lain and the time and cause of death – all illustrated with florid photographs in our textbook. Then, more close-ups of the bodies of rape victims, violent suicides, homicides, the habitually buggered, and such subjects we might be called upon to assist with the law. I found it disturbing and depressing. I failed my fifth year exams and wondered whether to continue with my medical studies. I went to see the new dean, Edward Sayers.

'Where do you come from? Originally?'

'I was born in Spain.'

'And your parents, are they Spanish?'

'No. My mother's German. My father American.'

'Did your family leave Europe as a result of the war?'

'Yes. My mother and I.' I was surprised he had worked that out.

'Where did you go?'

'Mexico.'

'So how old were you when you came to New Zealand?'

'Eleven.'

'It must have been hard for you, with all those changes,' he remarked.

I was dumbfounded. Never before, in all my years in New Zealand, had anyone made such an observation.

'Don't give up your medical studies,' he told me kindly. 'You've done very well in all your other subjects and you've nearly completed the course. These exams are the least important: they're a bit of a break in a tough course. You can go ahead with your final hospital year, and sit them again early next year without interrupting your studies.'

I went to Auckland – in the north, where it was warmer and livelier – to do my final year of medicine.

# My Hospital Residency

ONE O'CLOCK in the morning. The night was dark and cold and a fine mist hung in the air as I hurried down the path in my long white coat towards the separate building, at the back of the main hospital, with the children's surgical ward. The ringing of the telephone by my bedside, in my room at the doctors' residence, had woken me a few moments earlier.

'Hello?'

'There's an admission, doctor. A seven year-old boy with suspected appendicitis.'

'I'll be right down.'

I had slept barely half an hour, the same as the previous two nights when I had also been woken to admit my small surgical patients and kept busy till four or five in the morning. Even so, every day I had to rise again in time for my morning ward round and an uninterrupted day's work, other than a hurried cup of tea snatched, mid-morning and afternoon, in the ward's side room.

Tonight, as I walked down the dark path which cut diagonally across the grounds of Auckland Hospital – my footsteps intruding into the silence of the night – my nose suddenly started streaming. I reached for a tissue to wipe it, but it wouldn't stop. I marvelled at the pinpoint onset of the flu: witness to the plunging effect of sleep deprivation on our resistance to infection. Once in the ward, I took the history of the child's complaint from the mother and further details from the little boy himself. On examining the small tender abdomen I found the specific signs of appendicitis. I sent blood and urine samples to the lab to confirm it, organised the time for surgery with the theatre sister, and woke the surgical registrar and anaesthetist to prepare for the appendicectomy. Trevor, the registrar, was very neat and fast. He was known to take out a child's appendix in five minutes, 'skin to skin'. Twice he had passed me the scalpel and guided me through the whole operation: the small incision, blunt separation of the muscles with the gloved fingers, opening the lining of the abdominal cavity, identifying and freeing the inflamed little tail hanging from the bulbous start of the large intestine, crushing and tying its base, then – with a meticulous procedure to avoid contamination from the gut – slicing it off and burying the stump into a purse-string suture, rechecking, and finally closing the abdomen each layer in turn. I now felt confident that, should I ever find myself stranded on a desert island with someone suffering from appendicitis, I would manage. In the meantime, more problems arose in the ward that needed sorting after the surgery: the replacement of an intravenous drip, a urinary catheter to be cleared, and a new admission waiting to be seen.

After a busy night I found myself going through the following day's work as if in slow motion. Yet I was always conscious of a permanent watchdog in a corner of my mind maintaining an unflagging vigilance over everything, as there was no margin for error. We did a one-in-two rota, and could catch up with our sleep on alternate nights and weekends. But if one of us went off sick or was on annual leave, the remaining resident was on permanent call for both firms, day and night, in addition to their own daily routine. I had been in that position for a week now, sleeping on average three hours a night and working more than 100 hours. My flu got worse, but I couldn't stop working till my opposite number was back, and then *he* had to do every night on call till I was well enough to return to the wards.

∾

A YEAR HAD PASSED since I came to Auckland during my last holidays as a medical student to do my first hospital job-in-training: the 'student elective' before the start of my final year of medical studies. In keeping with my interest in psychiatry, I had chosen to work at Avondale Mental Hospital, New Zealand's largest psychiatric hospital.

Avondale Hospital was spread across several buildings. At the entrance were the doctors' and administration offices, with the separate male and female admission wards beyond them. The buildings further back maintained the same left-right gender separation all the way down the hospital's vast grounds. I worked mainly in the female wards, being sent into the male areas only on exceptional emergencies for – I was told – the men sometimes turned violent in the presence of female staff.

Three doctors looked after some 3,000 patients: the medical superintendent; an English Jewish psychiatrist who emigrated to New Zealand and took up psychiatry because, he said, he couldn't stand the sight of blood; and a third, laid-back character from Ireland. My duties consisted of the admission of all new female patients with a detailed psychiatric and physical examination; the ECTs or electro-convulsive therapy prescribed by the consultants which I was to do single-handedly – not something that would be left to a fifth-year medical student today, but done jointly by a qualified anaesthetist and a psychiatrist; and the six-monthly follow-up of chronic patients. I was presented with a new set of files every morning and went round the wards to interview and examine the patients and write my findings in their files. Between these checks they were not seen by a doctor except in the case of a physical ailment. In other words, they had become permanent inmates of the mental institution with no redress to speak of.

My first day at work, I was given a bundle of enormous keys attached to a long heavy chain – the kind seen in museums or films on medieval subjects – which I had to carry with me at all times. After closing behind me the back door of the relatively civilised acute ward, I walked through the grounds to the next brick building which housed the chronic psychotic female patients. There I would stand in front of the heavy door, pick out the largest iron key of the bunch, and unlock it. I would never forget the scene that met me here on my first day. A senior sister was showing me round the hospital: after that, I would be on my own. As the door swung open that first time, I caught my breath and stood rooted to the spot for some time as I took in the vast hall full of women, each standing still, variably dressed or undressed, in her chosen place in the room, seemingly oblivious of all the rest. The hall reverberated with the sound of disjointed voices, each woman chattering away, lost in her own, monotonous, incomprehensive monologue – as I would later hear at closer quarters from those in my path when crossing the room to reach the door on the other side. A strong smell of cheap disinfectant laced with stale urine and a dash of faeces reached my nostrils. The nursing sister was trying to reassure me.

'Don't worry. They won't harm you. But do be careful. You're a new face to them, so it's best not to draw attention to yourself. Always make sure to lock the door behind you again after you've entered, and walk swiftly across to that door on the other side which leads to the corridor and the single cells, where they sleep. The dangerous ones are locked in their cells and aren't allowed out. If they're violent, they are kept in straitjackets until they settle down. It's bathtime now: that nurse over there is getting them ready.' And sure enough, a young nurse was struggling with the women nearer the door on the other side of the huge communal hall, making them take off their clothes and then follow her naked out of the room.

I would subsequently find each woman always standing in her same spot repeating the same phrase over and over, every time I walked across that room. Hair straggling, their faces blank, inward-looking, arms hung loosely by their sides or lifted to clasp their hands under their chins. One was forever twirling the same small rag, all day, every day. I came to recognise those that stood in my path as I crossed the room; those further out, I never came in contact with.

There was a separate smaller ward for the congenitally retarded suffering from cretinism, Down's syndrome and other anomalies. I was given the task of supervising the weekly bath of a girl in her teens whose grotesquely large head was too heavy for her to lift: it took four nurses to move her, cradled in her sheet, from her cot to the bath. Her brain largely destroyed by the pressure of the blocked fluid in her head, she was grossly retarded and only grunted, yet her eyes would silently cry out in terror of the water, should the weight of her head pull her under.

I applied myself to my duties at this hospital, determined to do my best for the patients and learn as much as possible. I did a daily round of the wards with the nursing sisters who knew the patients well. I was also given each day a pile of files for the patients' six monthly 'follow-ups', and during my assessments I tried to understand why they were there and something about their condition. Above the acute admission ward, were the chronic 'neurotic' and 'paranoid' groups of patients.

'How have you been since you were last seen by a doctor?'

'Just the same,' a patient hospitalised some twenty years would answer.

'What's been your problem? Why are you in hospital?'

'My granddad died and the family didn't want me to get the inheritance he left me, so they had me certified,' one said. Another: 'I got pregnant when I was sixteen and my parents made out I was mad to get rid of me.' And yet another: 'Because I masturbated.'

The stories were often entirely plausible, and I felt frustrated at not being able to distinguish between reality and artful delusion or paranoia.

My entry in a file would typically read as follows:

25/1/1959. Patient's condition appears not to have changed since the last entry. She claims that her relatives manipulated her certification so they could receive her inheritance. She said nothing during the interview which appeared irrational or delusional.

I also discussed these questions with the consultants in their office in the administration building – which to my knowledge they never left. They would listen politely and suggest I should not get too involved.

There was a memorable admission of a young Maori girl who had become acutely paranoid. She yelled and cursed using the most obscene language, and physically attacked all who came within range, nurses included. I went into her room in some trepidation accompanied by a male nurse for protection, but managed to assess and examine the patient without arousing her anger. I was astounded to see her dramatic transformation, after two ECTs, into a rational, polite, quietly spoken, delightful young girl – apparently her 'normal' self. And I learned to respect the complexity of these conditions and their treatment and to realise that there were no ready explanations or solutions, contrary to much I had come across in my psychoanalytic reading.

With the chronic ward's frankly psychotic patients, on the other hand, there was no communication. They lived in an inner world of their own I could not prise open. One woman in her fifties had not spoken since her wedding day thirty years earlier. Her story intrigued me, and I would sit and talk to her, trying to coax her into saying something, every time I passed through the ward. And she – normally stony and expressionless – would smile at me warmly, hugely enjoying the attention she was receiving. Once in a while, she would bend forward and part her lips as though about to speak, and I listened expectantly for her first words … but then she closed them again and smiled secretively at me once more. She never, in the end, broke her silence. I was saddened the day she was transferred to the Auckland Hospital with jaundice: a serious complication of the massive doses of largactil given to most of the patients in that ward.

One day I was sent to do a follow-up of an especially dangerous patient in the high security block. This one was male, and he was a murderer. I walked maybe a mile through the hospital grounds before I reached this last block. It had thick concrete walls and an extra heavy door with many locks. After opening it, the male nurse delegated to accompany me for my protection, led me into a short, bare corridor with more heavy doors. We reached the murderer's cell and the nurse took some time to undo all the locks and double-locks. I took courage and walked in. And there, in a corner of the quite pleasantly fitted out room with thick metal grilles in the windows, sat a mild little old man painting a picture. He looked up and smiled at me.

'How have you been?' I asked him after introducing myself and explaining the purpose of my visit.

'Fine, thanks!' He had stood up to greet me and was obviously pleased to have company. He then showed me his meticulously detailed landscape paintings: hills, trees, flowers, autumn scenes – and talked to me about them with timid enthusiasm. He insisted he had been perfectly content ever since he had taken up painting some years earlier, and he enjoyed spending his days in this activity. He had no complaints.

'Why is he locked up?' I asked the nurse as we walked back.

'He killed someone when he was twenty.'

'But he doesn't seem dangerous anymore. Surely he doesn't
need all those locks?'

'That's true ...'

∾

AT THE TIME, I had met
again a past friend who lived in
Auckland. And I thought I was
in love. In those days, in New
Zealand, men divided women
into the 'nice' ones you marry,

*Photo: Marti Friedlander*

and the 'naughty' ones you have a good time with. I was decidedly
neither: I was *me*, whole and passionate, and fully ready to make
love with someone I loved. But it felt equally wrong to 'have sex'
with someone in that 'naughty-nice' mindset. Lovemaking was
what it said – making love, intimately, fully, sublimely, with your
love. Apart from my great love Dick in Dunedin who, though I had
secretly so longed for him, had firmly restrained himself because I
suspect he had bracketed me into the 'nice' camp, I had not found
that reciprocal love I yearned for. And now, this friend with whom I
thought I was in love took me out of the cold into his warm bed one
night and made love to me, innocently and naturally – and I felt this
strange, new, tender intimacy.

But we were absorbed in different pursuits and it was not to last.

∾

THREE IN THE MORNING, in the children's surgical ward. Struggling to pass a fine needle into a tiny vein buried in baby fat in the
back of a small hand ... I had been called out of bed, 'the intravenous drip has fallen out, doctor,' and now, here I was, making my
first ever attempt to cannulate a baby's vein ... essential to succeed
... the baby needs the fluid ... Half an hour later, I phoned Trevor,
the registrar, to ask for his more expert assistance. He broke off at
mid-sentence, followed by silence ... I rang again ... his phone was

engaged … must have dropped back to sleep holding the phone, collapsed, unrousable. I went back to the baby and tried again. Total concentration … grim determination … delicate, resolute aim … a drop of blood finally started flushing back … *very* slowly … the needle was in … strapped with care. Fluid flowed again into the baby. And Trevor got his sleep.

We were thrown in the deep end. It was a period of intensive training and hard work. Some memories stand out. Like that of the little boy, four years old, lively and delightful, who greeted me with a bright smile every morning as I walked early into the ward to reassess the small patients before the ward round. As the time for the round approached, the little boy would run up the corridor to catch up with me: 'Doctor Fwenk!' he would call out, eagerly trying to manoeuvre his child's tongue around my name, and announce, 'The other doctors are here!' He died two months later of his kidney tumour.

The stench around the sluice room from the eleven-year-old girl's black bloody stools, and the ease with which offensive smells and sights are overcome in the face of the underlying suffering and tragedies: a girl barely half my age covered with bruises and bleeding to death from every orifice, from her then incurable bleeding condition.

One day I noticed by the date I was writing on a patient's laboratory form that it was my birthday. I had now turned twenty-three. Otherwise the day passed off as any other.

In the ear, nose and throat department, I learned to look up noses and down throats by the light reflected from the concave mirror strapped to my forehead. Once I pulled out a fish's eye lodged up the nostril of a small albino Maori boy, and wondered whether such a combination of events had ever happened before. Another time I reassured an elderly lady, after an examination and an X-ray, that she had *not* swallowed her lower set of dentures which she claimed disappeared while she was eating a piece of Madeira cake.

In an Auckland Hospital surgical firm, my responsibilities included all the ward work, updating the consultant on each patient at the daily ward rounds, carrying out his instructions on their further management, and organising and assisting at operations. On my nights and weekends on call, I also looked after the infectious ward in another building, where a long-standing polio patient in a side room was being ventilated on an iron lung. I slept in the ward's on-call room to be immediately available in case of a respiratory emergency. One night, on my way to a patient a nurse had woken me to attend, I collapsed with the pain from an abscess that had formed in the sole of my foot. The nurse who had fetched me to deal with the emergency, now called another doctor on duty to deal with *me*. He gave me pethidine, lanced the abscess without anaesthetic, and excused me from work for the remainder of that night.

'Medicine is like the military, there are no excuses,' was a commonly quoted remark by a rather dour consultant physician.

Then I worked at the geriatric run. It was in converted wooden barracks next to Green Lane Hospital and part of the Auckland Hospital group. Here I would walk down interminably long narrow corridors in faint yellow lighting to the sound of my footsteps in the middle of the night. Not another being in sight. Relieved to be back with people again on reaching the wards, I would brace myself at the entrance of the side room where the latest death was waiting to be confirmed. On entering the room, one or two nurses were still tidying up, sheets in disarray, the pillow placed under the chin to support the lower jaw. I shone a torch into the dilated, motionless eyes to confirm there was no reflex, listened for the non-existent heartbeat, felt for the absent pulse. The skin pale, still warmish to the touch, starting already to lose its resilience ... I signed the death certificate. From the door, before leaving, I would take one more look at death: its stillness, its pallor, its acid smell, staring eyes that don't see. The immobility, the silence. The irrevocable end. And, *'That will be me one day,'* would cross my mind. The next night, I would be called to certify another. And I faced the barracks' long, empty, corridors again ...

The old German sailor in the geriatric ward who lay dying with his head turned to the wall. He stubbornly refused to acknowledge the tearful, plump elderly woman sitting by his side, desperately trying to get him to speak to her. By 'Next of kin', he had written 'None'. And he died lucid but with his lips tightly sealed and his eyes turned away from his unwelcome visitor. Stretched out in the post-mortem room waiting for the pathologist's incision, his long, thin naked body was covered, from neck to toes, in an intricate tattoo of a military uniform, colourful fringed epaulettes adorning his shoulders. What life experiences at sea and around the world, what mysteries, I wondered, might have died with him?

In Green Lane Hospital, I briefly assisted Barrett Boyes, New Zealand's pioneer in cardiac surgery, in his cardiac firm. This was before the days of cardio-pulmonary bypass surgery, and, for a heart valve repair, access into the heart was provided by an attached tent-like funnel, which acted as a blood reservoir with each pump of the heart. I remember my gloved fingers entering inside the beating heart to help with the suturing.

It was all a very hands-on experience of life and death. And of helping and healing.

*My graduation*

We were climbing up a mountain, Judy and myself, near Queenstown. We had just finished our final medical exams in Dunedin and gained our M.B.Ch.B. degree: Bachelor of Medicine and Bachelor of Surgery. Some way up, we paused to gaze at the valley below stretching out towards the great sweep of snow-peaked mountains beyond. By afternoon we had reached a bare patch below the ridge covered with loose, slippery slates, which we scampered across to reach the safety on the other side. As evening drew near, we found the trampers' hut marked on the map. Here we unloaded our packs, ate before a wood fire and slept soundly on the straw bunks. The next morning we reached the mountain ridge and started climbing down on the other side, facing a gorge below. The path in the now vertical rockface became so narrow that we could no longer get through. We threw our packs down the mountain and negotiated the steep descent, one at a time, to rejoin our packs further down. We came across a cool, bubbly stream and sat on the boulders next to it to tuck into our sandwiches for lunch. On reaching the gorge below, we walked through a wooded area to reach the road at the base of the range we had been climbing, and arrived at the bus stop, where we had started off two days earlier – only just five minutes before the weekly bus came along and took us back to Dunedin.

Two days of just ourselves and the mountains: a fitting celebration at the successful end of our long years of medical studies.

At a party, back in Dunedin, I met a new medical tutor from England, Eric Geiringer, whose unconventional methods and ideas, and transgression of medical establishment traditions, everyone was talking about – and whom I would meet again.

Back in Auckland now fully qualified, I worked at Middlemore Orthopaedic Hospital's casualty department, alternating with Elaine from my class in medical school. I diagnosed fractures, deciphered

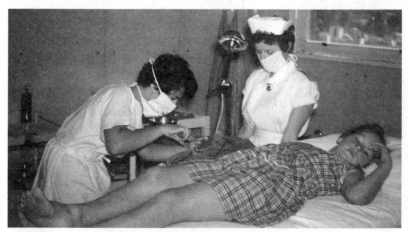

*Working at A&E, Auckland, 1961*

X-rays, realigned broken bones, moulded plaster of Paris around repaired limbs, and referred them to the consultant for a final check. One night, a truck driver and his mate were brought in with horrific injuries after a head-on collision: Elaine had to excuse herself while she was sick in the bathroom. Another time, a train had crashed into a young couple in their car at an unmanned railway crossing. None of these survived in spite of our heroic attempts. It was a demanding, steeling time. Off duty, Elaine and I relaxed chatting in each other's rooms or sunbathing on the roof; she brought me back a delicious bottle of Dior's *Fraîche* eau de cologne from a week's break in Noumea.

I continued my work at Green Lane Hospital, at the foot of One Tree Hill with its commanding view of the city's undulating hills, the harbour beyond, and the island volcano Rangitoto. At the end of my surgical run, the consultant, in keeping with his courteous tradition with his residents, invited me to dine with him at his club. The established New Zealand surgeon, renowned for his excellence, and his young female houseman still somewhat out of step with New Zealand custom, we made an awkward pair as we sat tête-à-tête: he in his good suit and I in my loosely fitting, turquoise silk dress and fashionable stiletto shoes – in the all male club's dining room.

In my medical run I looked after some fifty beds in an open ward. One night, when I suddenly realised it wouldn't stretch long enough for the work still waiting to be done, I called the registrar. Late into the night, I was still admitting patients who had arrived that morning, and other emergencies kept springing up.

'I won't be able to get through all the admissions by tomorrow morning's ward round,' I was telling him in tears. 'I've just been called to a patient who's developed pulmonary oedema and there are other problems needing attending to.'

'You go and take care of him,' he said. 'I'm on my way. I'll give you a hand.'

The patient was sitting up, drowning in his own fluid. I diluted the antidote, injected it into a vein – very, *very* slowly, over ten minutes, musn't let the finger on the plunger slip even the *tiniest* bit … His breathing easier again, he was out of danger. By then, the registrar had arrived and was waiting for me in the X-ray department where another patient's films needed checking. 'Don't worry,' he said kindly. 'You're doing a great job. It's because you're so conscientious, you're feeling upset.' *'Conscientious? Me?'* 'Yes. Others would be less thorough, cut a few corners ...' And he sorted out the remaining work between us. This registrar, who was always harping on his stretch 'back home' in London with the renowned liver specialist, Sheila Sherlock, of whom his most memorable impression appeared to be her short, tight skirts, and who would delight in embarrassing females taking part in the clinical round with his sexist remarks, was now giving me his full support and kindly encouragement. Maybe – it now occurred to me – his sexism was simply part of his cultural heritage here, a misguided show of little significance. When challenged, his care would surface ...

The nurses invited me to their non-medical parties outside the hospital – which was refreshing. Here, I met a tall, lovely, young bass singer full of charm and grace. His group of friends invited me to join them to listen to jazz records at a friend's house in the Waitakares.

The Waitakares hills are covered in native New Zealand vegetation. They lie on a narrow strip between Auckland Harbour on the Pacific side, and Manukau Harbour in the Tasman Sea; in some places both seas are seen from the same spot. Bill Haresnape's house was perched high above Manukau Harbour and surrounded by native bush. The house, built by Bill, an architect, was open-plan and multi-levelled following the mountainous terrain. Large windows along one side of the house looked down on the wild remote bay, a steep drop from Bill's land, while here a tall narrow window framed a native tree, and there a high horizontal slit captured a cluster of lush green ferns and another view of the bay. The spacious living area was separated from the lower kitchen by a long breakfast bar, and a central fireplace screened off an intimate corner lined with cushioned seating where we listened to Bill's collection of blues and jazz: a rich selection of rhythms, instruments and voices through his sensational hi-fi system.

'Would you like to come to Bill's again?' Donald, the bass singer, asked me at the end of that first evening as they dropped me off at Green Lane Hospital. 'May I take you next time?'

'Yes,' I said. Delighted.

He started phoning me at the hospital every day and taking me out when I was free. He had a rich deep voice – which he proudly pointed out reached the lowest note, managed by few bass singers – and he performed operatic arias and lieder. At his flat, we listened to records of Mahalia Jackson, Fats Waller, Dinah Washington. We cooked and dined and spent quiet evenings together, and made love with the moon streaming through his window onto our bodies.

Back at Green Lane Hospital, I found myself going about my work with a light heart, overflowing with love and warmth, enough for every human being on earth, feeling well disposed towards the whole world. No problem was too great suddenly; no patient too much trouble.

Donald made a special ceramic button for me, which he left behind to cool after glazing it, at a pottery workshop. I looked forward to seeing it. I would make myself a dress especially for it.

But he kept forgetting to fetch it. In the end, I never received it.

He left a few months later to further his singing career in Australia.

Swimming in Auckland's transparent waters, a shaft of light filtered through the surface across the watery medium down to the seabed, where delicate shadows from the bobbing waves, ten metres above me, hovered and rippled across the sandy clearing I had discovered. I was sitting weightlessly on the soft white sand surrounded by waving seaweed and plant life, sharing my aqueous surroundings with a variety of fish darting all around me, far from the human turmoil above. Bubbles escaped and rose towards the surface, as I breathed out the air I sucked from the compressed air cylinder strapped to my back, which Buzz – a friend of an old acquaintance from my Habonim days – had lent me, while his yacht swayed above us. Meanwhile, he was looking for crayfish nearby, rummaging around the cracks in the rocks with his gloved hands.

The crayfish was cooked on the small stove inside the yacht's cabin entrance, and a few minutes later, Rachel, Pat, Buzz and I tucked into its delicious flesh. We also ate oysters off the rocks, prising them open with a stone and slurping the soft, delicate contents with the fresh taste of the sea. We sailed into isolated coves in small remote islands where we dropped anchor and, after a night's sleep in the compact, narrow cabin, dived from the side of the boat into the crystalline water for a pre-breakfast swim. Weekends in our bikinis, the sun shining down from an unbroken blue sky and bouncing off its reflection from the sea all around. At night: taking turns at the rudder under the billowing sail and watching the moon light up the waves while I sang with abandon into the night Pete Seeger's ethnic music: *Back to back and belly to belly, I don't care a damn, for it doesn't matter rehlly …*

Back in Auckland, a passer-by in Queen Street exclaimed, 'Look! She must be an Aborigine!'

I had now completed my hospital year and obtained my full medical registration. I planned to return to Europe. While I waited for my passage, I did a short locum in Wellington where I stayed with my cousin Peter to say goodbye, and another in a country practice in Wellsford, north of Auckland, which looked after a whole community within a thirty-mile radius. There, I found myself doing minor surgery, taking X-rays and setting fractures, dealing with obstetric emergencies in the local cottage maternity hospital, and taking care of the medical needs of the surrounding countryside's population. I was driving the GP's car along difficult country lanes to reach emergency calls day and night, and got to know many local families including those from a small Maori community in the area.

*Peter at his home in Wellington, 1962*

The work was satisfyingly varied and challenging and I enjoyed the close relationship with the community.

While in the practice, I received a telephone call from Pat.

'Elaine was killed in a car crash,' she said.

*Elaine's wedding: Rachel, Pat, Elaine and myself, Auckland, 1962*

Only three weeks earlier, I had gone to Auckland to attend Elaine's wedding. She had looked radiant in her long, lacy white dress. She had been taken to the same casualty department in Middlemore Hospital where we had been working together a year earlier, and the neurosurgeons had worked all night trying to save her. She had been driving to a medical call for a locum she and her new husband were doing before going to England for his further studies, and a car had crashed into her.

I watched the flower-decked coffin bearing Elaine make its way down the same aisle along which she had walked, covered with flowers and smiling with joy, three weeks earlier.

I was finally ready to leave New Zealand.

I had been afforded refuge, given a nationality and trained in a profession in this country with its tradition of hospitality and a just social order. Yet I was still riddled with uncertainties and incongruities. I needed to find out who I was.

Below the surface, the conflicts with my mother had not shifted, but we had developed our own separate and different lives – she dedicating herself to my sister's music studies, and I to my medical profession and growing freedom of action. I was now turning my attention to my early life and geographical roots.

For that, I had to go in search of what I had left behind.

I might return some day to live in the Waitakares and work in Auckland.

Torrential rain was pouring and streaming down Queen Street the day I met Anne Wills – my friend from our St Margaret's days – on her stopover in Auckland on her way to Europe. We kept running down the steep pavement holding our sandals in our hands and slopping our bare feet in the water. A policeman stopped to look at us and stood there with a bewildered expression on his face, while Anne's infectious, happy, carefree laughter rubbed off on me and we both giggled and enjoyed the deluge of water drenching our bare heads and flimsy, cotton summer dresses.

Part 2

# CONVERGENCE

# Ships and Oceans

*The Indian Ocean, 1962.*

THE WAVES KEPT PEAKING and falling then sweeping along to
collide with the next set of waves and leap up once more into countless new crests, over and over. The bow of the ship cut through the
water lifting it into a long curling strip of thick white foam that
slowly spread over the ink-blue expanse to join in the pattern of
motion, bobbing up and down, in apparent randomness. Gentle
lazy splashes. Whiffs of moist salty air. Beyond: the horizon – dead
straight and steady – divided blue sea from blue sky. The only point
of reference against a restless, watery world. Not unlike the constant
thread that runs through life's flow and flux in its unpredictable trail.
Or memory's jostling currents obscuring sunken scapes beneath the
agitated surface. I leant against the ship's rail and watched the foam
make and unmake itself, froth up into a trail of white bubbles and
melt away, on and on, forever ...

The sea had grown calmer after the ship's wild heaving and plunging during the first days of my journey. The *Fairsea* had been buf-
feted every which way as it crossed the Tasman Sea, obliging me
to hold on to chairs and rails as I walked on the empty deck. Then
it would lurch steeply upwards, ride along for a few moments, followed by a deep rolling dive. A shudder, a few violent shakes, and it
would start again. Not another passenger in sight. For my part, I had
managed to ward off the seasickness, which on previous journeys
had turned me into a helpless heap, thanks to the cocktail of drugs I
thought to bring with me. The Tasman Sea's notoriety had prompted
me to search my pharmacology books for the most effective anti-
dotes, and now here I was blithely yielding to the ship's tossing and
rolling, and mealtimes found me tucking into my food in the empty
dining room.

After Sydney, where the Australian passengers came on board,
the sea had settled and the decks filled with people and bustle. As we

followed the Great Barrier Reef, the *Fairsea* made its way through the crystalline Coral Sea of turquoise, purples and blues towards the northern tip of Australia. Once around it, not a day went by without sighting land as the ship wove its way through the archipelago of islands here. The sun shone down on deck from the clear sky, and the waters below bucked into the air like cut glass with here and there fish leaping over the waves in twos and threes or more.

I was making my way from New Zealand to Europe, completing the circle around the world that began with our first sailing twenty years earlier, when I was five, from the Port of Marseilles. I remembered those weeks at sea, nothing but sea, and still more sea, and my frustrated impatience to step on land once again when the ship docked in Havana – thwarted by the official – and finally reaching the port of Veracruz. I had no inkling of what had prompted our voyage, but had witnessed my mother's concerted efforts to leave France, her many trips to the small office for those all important papers she was desperate to obtain, and her excitement at the promise of reaching Mexico. And, upon our arrival: our uncertain beginning in Mexico City as I tagged along with her, just the two of us walking up the dirt road in Veracruz with our luggage minus my pillow to catch a bus to the capital.

This time, the whole world seemed to lie open before me. By contrast, that first trip across the Atlantic had been one of survival. Our ship then, the *Serpa Pinto*, was tracing the same path as all those other Portuguese vessels which, from the time of Christopher Columbus, had crossed that ocean between the Old World and the New, distancing people from a collection of atrocities, from the Spanish Inquisition to Hitler's Final Solution. My father, with *his* mother and sister, had followed the same route before us to start a new life in New York, safe from the harsh life and pogroms in Russia. I imagined the hold of the ship, in 1905, crowded with Eastern European Jews, their trunks crammed with all they could carry from the life left behind for ever, men and women, youngsters, old people, babies and children, all making their way together. Thirty-six years later, my mother and I had followed the same path to escape the systematic extermination that awaited us in Hitler's camps – the fate our friends in Marseilles fell victim to – to turn me into one small corpse among several million. A tiny, infinitesimal statistic. My mother's fate, with her youth, vigour and good looks, might have been worse. Instead, we had reached the welcoming shores of our New World in the American continent.

Games of tennis quoits on deck, diving and swirling in the ship's pool, long hours in the sun with Durrell's *Justine* – in which an oriental Jewess, misplaced Englishmen, strewn camel body parts, clandestine adultery, mysterious deals and stealthy spying become entangled in Alexandria. Or with my Italian grammar book, learning vocabulary, prepositions and verb endings in preparation for my disembarkation in Italy. Dancing the warm nights away to the ship's band playing cha-chas and Italian rhythms.

*'Cuando calienta el sol sobre la playa ...'*

A fine brush dipped in black liquid eyeliner carefully accentuated my olive-green eyes, and I painted the nails of my fingers and toes with a layer of pearl over gold simulating pale iridescent shells. Then back to the ship's deck to lie in my bikini in the sun's warming rays while I turned the pages of my book.

Our second sea journey, when I was eleven, had taken us across the Pacific Ocean. We were setting out on yet another fresh start, with an aunt in New Zealand, after our final family break-up in Mexico. My first views of the Pacific were flashing glimpses from the train of a spectacular peacock-blue as we travelled to San Francisco to board the *Marine Phoenix*. On the ship, I made friends with a group of American children who taught me my first song in English.

*You are my sunshine, my only sunshine,*
*You make me happy, when skies are grey ...*

The *Marine Phoenix* docked in Fiji and Samoa before finally sailing past the low-lying hills, with the morning sun picking out the small, box-like houses scattered along them, into Auckland's harbour.

For fourteen years I had tried to adjust to life in New Zealand, a country renowned for its hospitality and friendliness, but a world in the end too far removed from my earlier experiences – one and two oceans away – for me to find my niche. I had lost one language here and gained a new one, battled against my sense of dislocation and isolation aggravated by my mother's estrangement, and finally started the process of my liberation with my medical studies: dedicating myself to heal others seemed in itself a healing experience. On the day of my departure, I watched from deck the crowd below come to see off friends and relatives. Colourful streamers dangled down the side of the ship, joining the travellers on deck with those being left behind on the quay, until we were pulled apart as the *Fairsea* sailed away.

Singapore: balmy and muggy. Body heat. Human sweat mingled with spicy smells. Pavements crowded with people: Malayan, Chinese, Indian. Foreign cries and chatter mixed with the clamour of tooting cars, bicycles, trams and rickshaws in the streets. Earthen colours tangled with bright ones. Dark, turbaned men in doorways absorbed in games with wooden counters. The warm, heady smells of throbbing life. After my years in New Zealand, I found this bustle and pulse of life exciting and intoxicating.

We left behind the chain of islands as the *Fairsea* emerged through the Malacca Strait into the Indian Ocean and started cruising along the calm lazuli waters that spat out, here and there, myriads of flying fish.

I watched the breaking of a shimmering dawn as the ship sailed early one morning into Colombo's harbour. The sleeping city's skyline slowly materialised through the haze, as the huge orange disc of the sun rose above the silver urban spread. As we got off the ship, we were mobbed by a crowd of street sellers of 'precious stones'. Crippled beggars, bedraggled children, the scent of tropical flowers, cobras dancing to their masters' flutes, Buddhist temples hidden in luxuriant vegetation, entered barefoot.

Back on board the *Fairsea*, we continued on our way through the Indian Ocean. The murky green waters here were said to abound with snakes. Standing on the bridge of the ship one night, I watched and listened to the eternal play of the waves. The sky receded into a deepest blue translucency as a large round moon drenched the sea in brilliant phosphorescence all the way to the horizon. The nearer waves caught the odd glint from the lights of the ship. Where I was standing, it was dark and quiet. No one else in view. I enjoyed my communion with the elements in this undisturbed calm.

Our next stop was Aden: a barren hillside covered with huge oil tanks glinting in the sun. I got off the ship with two Jewish dentists from Australia and we took a taxi to the Crater district on the other side of the hill. While driving along the port, the taxi driver pointed out various landmarks.

'Don't go there!' he firmly advised us pointing at a street. 'It's full of Jews,' he explained confidingly. 'You can tell those sons-of-bitches anywhere!' he added, with a knowing nod to warn us, as he turned his head and looked us – three Jews sitting in the back of his taxi – full in the face.

The Crater was the duty-free shopping area. Through the main dirt street, the petite local women walked in pairs entirely covered in black. Black gloves and black slippers darted out of their black drapes, and a black veil hung over their faces, as they stumbled on their way hugging the side of the road under the hot sun. The row of shops in this street was full of radios, cameras, watches and other goods. Inside one of them, a salesman came towards me in his swaying Arab clothes. I thought he meant to help me with my purchase, but he shamelessly pinched my breast through my dress.

On our way back to the port, the taxi stopped in the middle of the bare rolling landscape and waited while a shepherd moved his flock of goats out of our way in his own time.

We now left the Indian Ocean behind to find ourselves cruising along the still, slate-blue waters of the Red Sea. The air was warm and laden with moisture: smudgy sea blended with sky in a dense impenetrable haze. In the eerie calm, the atmosphere deadened sound as well as shortened vision.

On reaching Suez I disembarked with a group of passengers and we were ushered into a bus to Cairo and then on to Ismailia to meet the ship again after making its way through the Suez Canal. We saw the great pyramids and the sphinx rising immutable and eternal above a sea of sand this time. In Cairo: the large decaying necropolis; the archaeological museum by the Nile with its rich collection from the Pharaohs' tombs; the bustling bazaar with shop after shop of oriental essences; a black robed woman on the pavement covered with flies ... And finally the great mosque. I remembered my father's story of his obliging North African guide telling him proudly, as they were taking off their shoes to enter a mosque he was keen to show him, that not a single Jew had ever set foot inside it ... The bus took us again through the desert until the *Fairsea* suddenly rose before us drifting through the vast sandy landscape. As we reached it, the narrow canal came to view and we climbed on board again.

At last the ship emerged into the Mediterranean. I was filled with a sense of excited anticipation as I gazed at the indigo waters that washed along the shores of Barcelona, the city of my birth, and the port of Marseilles, the point of our departure. West of us was *Justine's* Alexandria and to the east lay the land of my long-distant ancestors and source of three world religions, while along the north-eastern shores, the ancient Greeks and Romans once fashioned our civilisation. I was back in the area of my deeply buried, almost forgotten, past and ante-past. I had come full circle and reached again the point where I started life and of my first parting. My Old World.

And yet ... as we sailed through the Sicilian strait at dawn and prepared to disembark at Naples, I suddenly felt a certain apprehension: I was leaving my dependable, familiar, floating home to be cast out, once again, into another unpredictable world.

# Back in Europe and America

BACK ON FIRM LAND again after four weeks in a swaying vessel, I watched the Mediterranean landscape of green hills and fertile valleys flashing past the train that took me to Rome with my suit-case by my side.

*Rome, 1962.*

I WOULD REMEMBER ROME as a brown city. The soft sunlight brushing the brown rusts, ochres, violets, honeys. Massive stone doorways and arched marble entrances, with maybe a glimpse of an ivy-covered courtyard and potted palms inside. Twisting alleys running into unexpected intimate *piazzas* with a small Renaissance church on one side and a niche with a Madonna and a bunch of flowers in the next, the residents' assorted washing hanging outside their shuttered windows above. Suddenly a large square with ancient columns; a splash of bright green from a roof garden above; the remnants of a great palace jutting violet into a blue sky.

I spent a day walking through the Forum Romanum, restoring the ruins in my mind to their original splendour of large columned marble courtyards, temples and halls with men in white togas walking about with a sense of purpose. And now: this was all that was left … decaying ruins examined curiously by tourists in jeans holding on to their guidebooks and cameras.

In St Peter's Basilica, I walked through spacious rooms and long corridors looking at the art collection. After my long years in the Antipodes, this was a revelation. I stood in front of a small, early *Madonna and Child*, and I was struck by the thought of how that same painting, now before me, must have moved countless others as it now moved me, across generations over close to two thousand years, through different cultures, languages and social customs. And I thought about the power of such an image. The person who had painted that picture, long since dead, his bones crumbled by now, had lived in a world so utterly removed from mine and yet, through this painting, differences and centuries had been swept aside and a universal value of humankind communicated. This must be what *art* is, I decided ...

There are certain moments in one's life in which perception, suddenly and without warning, attains an unalloyed crystal clarity, and a new meaning or understanding is revealed and becomes etched into one's being – like my sudden awareness when I was two in Collioure of the immensity of the universe. This vision now of the distillation in art of human experience and insight across time and borders, would prove another momentous one for me.

Anne Wills had come to Rome to meet me.

'I've met a *gorgeous* guy!' she giggled infectiously, her eyes narrowing with delight above her broad cheekbones. 'He's arranged to take us to a dance with a friend of his.'

He picked us up in his small Fiat and drove on to collect his friend. There was something immediately appealing about the young man who climbed into the back seat beside me. He was wearing beige and brown, his eyes – which looked at me with polite interest – were deep brown, and his hair, which he would flick off his forehead between his index and middle finger, was light brown. His name was Mauro, which means brown. We arrived somewhere on the outskirts of Rome and walked into a large dance hall.

Mauro held me closely and silently as we moved together around the floor with the music. The moment the band stopped, he would let go and utter a polite, *'Grazie'* and wait quietly for the next piece to start. His combination of closeness and shyness, a sort of restrained intensity, appealed to me.

I was putting into practice the Italian I learned on the sundeck of the *Fairsea*. I filled the gaps in my vocabulary with frequent consultations of the Collins pocket dictionary I bought on my first day in Rome and always carried in my handbag. The very procedure of searching for words, and the urgency my determined efforts conveyed, livened communication and, one way or another, I managed every kind of conversation. Here, there was a ready contact between people, even at the cobbler's where I took my shoes to be heeled.

The streets were full of life, there was a warmth and immediacy in the way people interacted with each other – and I started making up for all those lean years of isolation from which I was now emerging.

Mauro shared a work studio in central Rome with three other final-year architect students like him, in *Via di Montoro* – a small street behind *Campo di Fiori*. Tall Renaissance buildings, once ducal palaces, faced each other across the narrow street. The young men were busy at work there every day, concentrating on their architectural drawings in the light, spacious studio, taking only short breaks to run down to the *piazza* for a coffee at a stand-up espresso bar, or a meal of *fagioli* in a small *trattoria* nearby. I liked their unpretentious lifestyle, direct talk and comradely attention. They spent much of their time in animated and heated, but friendly, discussions about politics, Mauro mostly disagreeing with the communist arguments of the other three. I learnt that forty per cent of the Italian population was communist, and was intrigued to see enormous, bright red, Communist Party election campaign posters blatantly displayed in the streets of a city in the West, and the democratic freedom it reflected.

Mauro, in his odd free moments, would give me an architectural tour of some part of Rome. His comments, though economical, were always amusing. He had a way of making me see the comic side of things. He would make even an unhappy turn of events, particularly his own, appear funny without trivialising it. I felt light and buoyant at his side and the world seemed a less complicated place.

Around the corner from *Via di Montoro,* a bustling flower and vegetable market filled the long *piazza, Campo di Fiori.* People milled around and chattered loudly, the place stirring with life, while, in the centre, the tall, motionless, bronze figure of Giordano Bruno in his monk's habit, the hood lifted over his head, stood on a stone platform high above the bustle around him, holding a book in his hands: symbol maybe of the knowledge he refused to surrender for which he was burnt at the stake. In the sixteenth century he was considered a heretic, Mauro said, for insisting that God is everywhere. And now: there stood his image – the only still object in the middle of the flower market that pivoted around him with life. Like the eye of a storm, or an anchor in a turbulent sea.

I also walked in the Italian sunshine with my cousin Reni and her small son Massimo. It was our first meeting. Reni was the daughter of a cousin of my mother. Our mothers had seen much of each other in Berlin before the war. Then Reni and her parents had spent the war years in Holland, where they stayed and became Dutch.

We went into a park and sat on a bench.

'I met Renzo when my work brought me to Italy. I loved Rome and I decided to stay,' Reni was telling me, looking fondly at Massimo playing near us, his head a mass of curls, his huge eyes seeking everything out and finding it *'buffo'* – which I added to my Italian vocabulary.

Back in Reni's apartment, I sat with them to an Italian lunch she had prepared, while Renzo was asking me about my journey from New Zealand.

'How did you come to Italy?'

'By boat,' I answered.

Renzo looked disapprovingly at me.

'In English one says *bote,*' he corrected sternly in his slightly broken English, rounding the 'o' with emphasis, 'Not *beowt.*'

Renzo was also a doctor and had a flourishing paediatric practice in Rome. He had grown up in Livorno where his Sephardic Jewish family had settled, following its exodus from Portugal at the time of the Inquisition, and built up and practised its trade in a triangle between Tunis, Livorno and Amsterdam. Apart from his native Italian, he had been brought up speaking French by his Tunisian-reared mother, and also spoke English and some Arabic. Reni's childhood languages were German and Dutch, she had studied French and English, and now spoke fluent Italian too.

In my brief stay in Rome, I had begun to recapture something close and familiar to me from my earliest years in Mediterranean Europe. I had also found part of my dispersed family, and made friendships that would last a lifetime.

My mother had also come to Europe with my sister to further her flute studies, and we felt driven to retrace, however cursorily at first, the places and people with whom we had formed such strong bonds – back in those difficult times – and not seen since.

We met in Paris and went to Foëcy to look up the Grandjean family again after twenty-two years. We heard Yaya's description of Yayo's capture by the Germans and his transport to a labour camp from which he never returned, and of the Germans' search for my mother, on the village policeman's tip-off, when they entered Foëcy. All this seemed at the same time too remote and too raw for me to digest, to begin to experience its significance.

We went on to Barcelona where my mother looked up old friends. She found Duran San Pere, curator of Catalonia's historical archives, and they sat together – a singular warmth in their exchanges, and they had so much to say to each other – in *Plaza Cataluña* watching the Sardanas: the dancers' dainty footwork to the complicated rhythm of the ancient plaintive music as they followed their wide, hand-held circles. Then our reunion with Juanita Santalo and her mother, and their welcoming banquet in their modest fifth-floor apartment where they served a special new wine in renewed celebration with each of the seven, lovingly prepared courses. Later that night I was sick – maybe both that sumptuous meal and all those jostling impressions were too much to digest.

We looked for our house in the wooded village of La Floresta, where my mother had more emotional reunions with old friends, and made our way also to Mallorca's Deyá which my mother had so often recalled as her idyll from her subsequent homes. More recollections over paella in Lluch Alcari down the coast, overlooking the sapphire sea. On the other side of Deyá, La Foradada, its long rocky outline pierced by a perfect hole, still stretched serenely into the sea, altered neither by time nor all the intervening human events which had left their mark on, and scarred, so much else.

My memory of that first return visit is vague and dreamlike: we were treading in my mother's more accessible past: she was doing the retracing while I was by her side, attempting to capture something unclear and elusive.

∿

*London, winter of 1962.*
CRYSTAL FILIGREE FRAGMENTS glinted in the faint street lighting

as they emerged, one after the other, out of the dense mist. As they floated towards me their contours sharpened to reveal their breathtaking delicacy. Now and then a vague shape materialised on the pavement before me and approached with muffled footsteps to take on human form, a handkerchief held close to its lowered face, and walked past to get swallowed back into the congealed darkness. The intense cold penetrated down to the bones, and the world beyond arm's reach receded into thick nothingness.

It was the winter of 1962, reported as the coldest in London in eighty years. As I inched my way along the suburban street to my bedsit in Putney, on this dark foggy night, I watched in wonder the ice-sculpted fragments of shrubs, trees and railing become glittering gossamer phantoms: a magical crystal world hidden in the mist. Once inside my room, I found even here the view from one end to the other was fogged. And as it started to lift a week or so later, a black layer of grime was left behind on the windowsill and panes, the shelves, the table. On everything.

This was smoggy London.

On my arrival I had stayed in Bloomsbury while I explored this city about which I had heard so much and knew so little. The first time I walked down Regent Street and Piccadilly Circus came to view, I was faced by a very different scene from the large permanent circus with elephants and acrobats I had imagined. 'You're always sure to bump into another New Zealander in Piccadilly Circus,' I remembered hearing 'back home', and, in my mind's eye, I would see one walking down a broad, leafy sidewalk alongside the great canvas tent of Piccadilly Circus, the whole scene bathed in soft sunlight percolating through the trees, meeting another coming in the other direction. 'G'dye, mate! Wot you doing here?' Instead, I saw before me a small, circular, busy traffic intersection with a little bronze statue in the middle and a large spread of neon advertisements up one side. Though I did meet, a few days later, an acquaintance from New Zealand there, the Bank of New Zealand being near that corner then.

I gradually came to know London as a series of islands, with the Underground station from which I emerged to the surface at the centre of each. I met up with friends from Dunedin. Neil Perret

– whom I had first met at the Fresher's Hop, and by now settled in London and working in a medical practice – invited me to a party in his Chelsea flat in Cheyne Walk. He was leading a lively life, drawn into London's bohemian art scene and working at his painting – which he had already started doing during his medical studies in New Zealand.

One of his favourite haunts was the York Minster in Soho, known as the French Pub for its role, during the war, as a meeting place for French Resistance members with their British counterparts. It was run by friendly, moustachioed Gaston, and was always crowded with a great cross-section of humanity, from painters and poets to singers and retired boxers, its walls covered with old photographs of its renowned clientele over the years. There he would hang out with Francis Bacon and his friends, and at eleven, when the pub closed, they would go on to a club round the corner and continue their drinking and whatever else till the early hours.

I also met Eric Geiringer: the physician who started tutoring in Dunedin when I graduated. He was staying at a friend's flat in Notting Hill Gate – a part of London I found pleasing with its mix of very English and cosmopolitan, the lively markets, its elegant rows of white Regency houses and abundant greenery.

'I'm trying to decide where to settle down, now I'm back in Europe,' I told him over a light lunch at a café in Notting Hill Gate. 'I was thinking of looking into what work Paris or Rome might offer me. It's too cold in London! I can't see myself staying here with this climate – in a country too stuck in its traditions to have central heating!' There was, in fact, none to speak of, then.

'There's nothing as cosy as a good log fire.'

'It warms you up in front, but leaves your back freezing cold!' I disagreed. 'My uncle in Israel has suggested I go there. Maybe I will. I'm curious to see what it's like.'

'That's a place I've never had any desire to go to,' Eric stated emphatically.

'Why not?'

'Well, you see,' he started typically as though embarking into a scholarly explanation. 'Jews are a bit like garlic. A little of it added to your food is tasty, it improves the flavour, but too much definitely spoils it, in fact: makes it inedible. Jews, in a small dose, are good company, they liven things up, stimulate your thinking. But a whole country of them! That's too much,' he said – distancing himself from his own heritage with his reference to 'them'.

I laughed at his simile, thinking it somewhat exaggerated.

'When you laugh you sound like a gurgling brook,' he observed in the way he might describe an anatomical curiosity.

He chatted to me about his complicated love life (I couldn't quite keep track of all the women) and said he had practically decided to return to New Zealand, marry Carol – who studied medicine with the oldest Kral girl, my friend from my Christchurch days – set up a joint medical practice with her, and fight the New Zealand medical establishment which he considered too stuffy and set in its ways of thinking.

'Could you really live so far from the rest of the world? Don't you feel too isolated there?'

'No. I like it in New Zealand. I'd rather be a big fish in a small pond than the other way round,' he said. 'Here, I would be swallowed up in the crowd, I wouldn't be able to put my ideas into practice, while there, I can get things done. I have many plans; there are a lot of things I want to try out. For instance, I have a theory about hypertension and coronary artery disease, and how to prevent it …' And he went on to describe his study and ideas which I had already heard from him on previous occasions.

He planned to settle down in Wellington with Carol.

'I'll give you my cousin's phone number in Wellington. His name's Peter Munz. He is Professor of History at Victoria University. He was a student of Popper and is still in touch with him, and he knew Wittgenstein at Cambridge. You might enjoy each other's company,' I suggested. And, indeed, Peter and Eric became the best of friends for the rest of their lives.

I went back to the Underground, when we parted, to catch my train across London.

I liked travelling in the London Underground. I felt a sense of abandon in these underground tunnels with their vaguely pungent smells: a mixture of fumes and machinery, people's humid overcoats and the trains' old upholstery. The whole character of London and its people, residents and visitors alike, seemed to acquire a larger than life, almost surreal, dimension in the confined space of these artificially lit, concave passages. People converged from all areas of London and all walks of life and sat side by side in the carriages as they whizzed through the narrow tunnels, bonded together for a brief moment in time, until they emerged on the other side and lost themselves in the overground city again to go their separate ways. I was watching the people sitting on the facing lengthwise bench at our end of the carriage, and I dug into my handbag for a pencil and small pad to sketch them on my lap, trying to capture that man's earnest expression under his dark felt hat, that lady's careworn face, that child's quizzical expression, that Asian girl's dark vacant stare and pretty hairstyle.

I was working as a locum in a number of London hospitals. During this unusually icy stretch, I filled the post of casualty officer in a south London hospital. The young casualty sister and I made a good team as we attended to the various emergencies together in our daily work. She and her husband invited me out one evening to see the sights of old London. They introduced me to historical pubs in the City crowded with talk and customers and the ambient smell of ale in their dark timbered interiors crammed with old relics. Then, London Bridge: the site of the first bridge over the Thames River – her husband explained – built by the Romans at its most fordable point around London's earliest communities which settled here and grew to what is now London: with its Lyons Corner Houses and their menu of meat and two veg, the customary colonial Indian curry eating places, and where at night the Underground ran to a standstill at ten-thirty … It was all a strange, new world.

In my free evenings I frequented The Marquee, at Soho's Wardour Street, which was dark and crowded with young Londoners jiving and rock 'n' rolling to great, live jazz bands, and I danced the hours away till the last Underground train took me back to my Putney bedsit.

Then, from one day to the next, radio bulletins and headlines in every newspaper were announcing news of Khrushchev's missile construction sites in Cuba, facing the United States. Within hours, the tension became palpable, electric. In the streets, I saw people going about their business like robots: their impotence in the face of the threat of unprecedented doom showing in their drab, expressionless faces. At the height of the crisis, I found myself walking down Lower Regent Street with a leaden acceptance of the possible imminent annihilation of everything, while the two men, Khrushchev and Kennedy, exercised their ultimate power on whether or not to turn this planet's most populated cities into so many more Hiroshimas. And I thought, had Kennedy by some quirk of fate been born and nurtured in Russia and Khrushchev in the United States, would they not be doing the same for their 'countries' and 'ideologies' in their reversed roles? Making a nonsense of the destruction of the world … Here I was, finally getting a taste of the *real* world I had been seeking – maybe my last – while New Zealand which I left behind was still blissfully remote from it all, possibly fated to survive as the last link to a future world after the end of this one as we know it. Maybe, after all, the only sane place left on this planet. Then: profound relief when, just as suddenly as it appeared, the danger lifted again. Khrushchev agreed to dismantle and remove his weapons. The Cuban Missile Crisis, reported as an exercise on brinkmanship with the world at ransom, was over. And it rapidly began to recede into history.

Around this time, I received a letter from my father inviting me to come to Mexico. The idea of blue skies and hot sunshine, of seeing again missed friends and places after fifteen years' absence, excited me. 'Yes,' I wrote back. 'I'd love to come.'

I bought a passage on the *Queen Mary* which sailed from Southampton to New York, and from there I would make my way to Mexico City.

∾

As I STEPPED onto the quay from RMS *Queen Mary*'s gangway, on landing in New York, a tall young woman in a casual coat and high heels was pacing up and down calling my name in her strong American accent. I was mystified.

'Yes! That's me!' I called out.

'Thank Gahd I've found you! I've been looking all over for you.

An officer informed me that all passengers had already left the ship by now.'

'I had trouble finding my suitcase, the one stored in the luggage room,' I explained, puzzling over her connection with me.

'Here, let me help you with your baggage. I've got the car waiting. Your uncle Izzy asked me to come and collect you. He said to tell you he's sorry he couldn't come himself.'

'My uncle Izzy?' I had no idea I had an uncle called Izzy.

'Yes. We're to go to his office on Broadway where he's waiting for you.'

I now recalled my father vaguely mentioning relatives in New York, so I warily decided to follow her. She hustled me into a large shiny Cadillac and drove off through the traffic into central Manhattan. It was early evening, and the sky's luminosity in the gathering twilight matched the fluorescent lighting beginning to appear through the rows of windows in the skyscrapers silhouetted against the fading sky, giving them a curiously translucent appearance. I began to make out that the driver must be 'Izzy's' secretary.

I was led into a pair of somewhat cluttered offices in a high building in the middle of Broadway. Izzy, a trim, vigorous man, maybe in his mid-forties, was packing a bundle of papers into a briefcase and giving out last-minute instructions, while his wife, Elly, who had only just arrived too, was standing inside the entrance: a vivacious, dark-eyed woman with a rich tumble of chestnut coloured hair, hugging a thick, luscious fur coat around her.

'Hello!' they greeted me warmly and in a hurry. 'Your father phoned us from Mexico this morning to tell us you were arriving today! It's the first time he's told us about you! We had no idea he had a grown-up daughter!' they laughed unbelievingly. 'We'd already bought tickets for a concert tonight in the Metropolitan Museum Auditorium – Rudolf Serkin is playing! – and we managed to get another ticket for you.' Izzy was now finally putting on his scarf and dark woollen overcoat. 'We've just got time to take a quick snack before the concert, and we'll take you home after it. Hope these arrangements are okay with you. That's the best we could do at such short notice!'

The 'snack' turned out to consist of a serving each of a dozen large oysters followed by an enormous, thick fillet steak in a kind of elegant American snack bar. Rudolf Serkin's playing was beautiful, and their home, in the outlying district of New Rochelle, full of warmth and Elly's tasteful, creative touches. Izzy turned out to be the son of an older brother of my father, so my first cousin and also the first relative I met on my father's side. He was an estate agent with left-wing sympathies and a passion for music. He and his son David, who was wearing a T-shirt with a huge head of Beethoven on his chest, proudly played a piece of music for me on the piano and cello, while Elly overwhelmed me with her charm and generosity. She beckoned me to come and see a corner of the house that she had recently transformed into a small studio. 'I can now practise my painting here, undisturbed, when I have some time to myself,' she told me with a small, delighted shrug of her shoulders and a conspiratorial wink.

I walked down Fifth Avenue and into Central Park to get the feel of central Manhattan, and at the steps of a theatre in Broadway I met another cousin, this time on my mother's side, Verena. Her father, Erich Lichtenstein – a publisher of leather-bound classics, in Weimar, before the war – was my mother's cousin. Verena – tall, slim and good looking – was wearing a tomato-red suit and hat. She worked in an office on Broadway but had once been an acrobat in a circus and married the Greek clown, Michael, who was now a chef in a restaurant in Manhattan. They invited me to stay overnight in their cottage on Staten Island and we celebrated our meeting.

∾

*Mexico, end of 1962.*
MY FATHER WAS WAITING for me as I got off the plane. He was standing there, a small, still figure, his trousers a touch too long on his slight bow legs, his dark hair combed back from his receding temples, his pale green eyes under folding lids – maybe some distant Mongolian ancestry from the time of the Tatars? – barely revealing his quiet excitement on seeing me. He came over to meet me at the queue waiting for customs clearance – evidently not restricted to passengers here in Mexico – and gave me a warm embrace.

If anyone had asked what *I* felt, I wouldn't have known what to say. My feelings for my father – so rich and fond and warm when I had been little: I still remember my excitement on the rare occasions he came to see us at La Floresta and our various makeshift abodes in Vichy France, as well as my disappointment the times he didn't turn up, *Maman, pourquoi Papa dit toujours qu'il vient, et il ne vient pas?* – had long blunted. Even my resentment – when, after joining us in Mexico at the end of the war, he left us to start a new family with Ilse, leading to our move to New Zealand – had dissipated, or rather been replaced with a conflicting and confusing impassivity.

He proceeded to help me through customs.

'Where's your passport?' he asked me in his calm, bass voice.

'Here,' I said pulling it out of my handbag.

He took it from me, placed a new ten-peso bill inside it, closed it again and passed it to the Mexican custom's officer in front of my suitcase. The officer opened the passport, took out the bill, placed it in his pocket, stamped the custom's clearance for the suitcase, and gestured with a friendly movement of his head that we were free to move on.

My father's house, in the outlying suburb of Las Lomas de Chapultepec, was a large, two-storey, concrete building raised high above street level on hilly ground overlooking a steep ravine across the street. Tall eucalyptus, pines and jacarandas, with here and there an ancient rubber tree, a cluster of palms and a bright splash of bougainvillea, grew in abundance and blocked the view between neighbouring houses. We had driven some distance up the long, broad, tree-lined avenue, La Reforma – which I was so excited to see once again – past Diana's multicoloured fountain, along the length of the zoological gardens with Maximilian's castle poised above, till we finally reached Las Lomas. Here, large homesteads were surrounded by well-tended, tropical gardens, heavily protected with tall iron gates and ferocious dogs that barked at every passer-by. In the late evening, when night descended into velvet blackness outside people's drawn curtains, loud fluty whistles would break the silence at regular intervals, sometimes close by, others more distant. The night watchmen, my father told me, were doing their rounds and announcing that all is well to their fellow guards, whose answering whistles would follow moments later, more faintly, from somewhere out there in the darkness. Occasionally the odd gunshot would be heard from the direction of the ravine: a night watchman warning off intending thieves, or maybe aiming at a small wild animal, or breaking the boredom.

'Welcome,' Ilse said as I stepped into the house. Tall and thin as I remembered her, her face now becoming lined, her keen blue eyes looked somewhat uncertainly at me with a benevolence I was unable to trust. 'This is Joey, your brother,' she said turning towards a small, freckly boy of fourteen looking at me wide-eyed, from behind his square, black-rimmed glasses, with a deadpan expression. 'And that's your sister Susie,' gesturing towards a smaller girl of about seven, with light reddish hair, smiling at me from a carefully kept distance. It was evident that we knew little about each other.

My father – Don Luis, as he was respectfully addressed here – was driven around in his rather dilapidated Buick, for which he had a particular fondness, by Enrique, a lively, unservile, Mexican character in his thirties. Lidia, a good-looking woman with bright eyes and black hair, and small plump Amparito, who lived in a room behind the kitchen, looked after the household. Everybody rose, breakfasted, and came and went at different times, according to

*Susie, Ilse, Joey, my father and myself, Mexico, 1962*

their individual, daily demands. My father went to his office early in the morning, Ilse went to her workshop a little later and met up with her friends at various times in the day, and the children went to their schools. Two large, noisy dogs and a small fat one divided their time and energy between the house and the large garden. The main meal of the day, at around three in the afternoon, was the one time when we all met. We would sit around the large dining-room table where Lidia would serve the European dishes and Viennese cakes Ilse had taught her to make. This, Lidia did to gourmet perfection with the fresh food brought home every day from the market in quantities large enough to go round also for Enrique, Lidia and Amparito, who ate in the kitchen, as well as various friends and acquaintances who were continually dropping by. But when I, Don Luis's older daughter, suddenly turned up in their midst and began to reminisce nostalgically about the various Mexican dishes I had missed since my abrupt departure fifteen years earlier, Lidia started making them especially for me. *Huevos rancheros* for breakfast, and for supper *frijoles refritos*, *mole*, *tacos*, *tamales*, *chilaquiles*, and much else besides – with warm tortillas fresh from the market. And all those Mexican flavours would reawaken long-buried treasured memories and draw them tumbling back to me, retrieving them from some mysterious hidden dimension inside me teeming with lost tastes, smells, images and sensations stretching back to the dawn of my being ...

Every morning I would accompany my father in the old Buick, driven by Enrique, to his office in Isabel la Católica in the city centre: from where I walked again in that complex of streets taking in the heady Mexican smells and sounds, sights and ambience. The Zócalo, Bellas Artes, Alameda Park, the Mexican crafts and silver jewellery shops, in one of which I had helped Harry polish the silver ... The elegant high-rise hotels and the newspaper boys on the street corners. They were all still there. Ripping into my memories, which for so long had been held back and suppressed.

I saw again the great Hispano-Mexican baroque cathedral in the Zócalo into which Lupe had taken me to pray for her brother's soul, the great bustling market a few blocks beyond it with the brightly coloured pottery, *zarapes*, *piñatas* and endless variety of fruits and vegetables, the busy street of San Juan de Letrán with its many cinemas, Parque México and the bicycle rent shop in the corner, I found the building in Calle Michoacán where we first lived on our arrival from Marseilles, smelt the *quesadillas, tacos,* steaming cobs of corn rubbed with chilli, in the streets. In a restaurant, I asked a group of mariachis in their silver embroidered, black *charro* suits and sombreros to sing many of my old songs, starting with 'Juan Charrasqueado'. 'It's a long time since anyone's asked us to sing those!' they said. I was attempting to recapture all that which had been so suddenly interrupted, cut off midstream. Fervently striving to retrieve something ... some bit of myself which appeared to have been broken off, lost, left behind here. Trying maybe to join the various pieces of my being together, and become whole once again.

I looked up old friends, from my time here as a child with my mother. Molly and Senya, the Santalos and many others. The passage of time and divergent experiences had opened a gap with some, while with others time and separation had made no difference. All these friends had remained loyal to my mother, adding one more dimension to the sharp division between my parents for me to consider and digest. I myself had also always taken my mother's side, regardless of the chasm and differences between us. But my view was decidedly influenced by her expectation of it from me – rightly or wrongly – and the idea of making up my own independent mind on the matter seemed to bristle with danger.

Cuernavaca – guarded near its entrance by the dark Virgin of Guadalupe, near my old school, Pestalozzi. The Cortés Palace with the Diego Rivera murals. The brilliant bougainvillea against white-washed walls bordered with lapis blue. The central squares – the ancient trees, home to a million twittering birds, cut down now, gone. The old market, which unleashed another wave of vivid memories, still there, unchanged. As were also the bridge at the bottom of the steep street on my way to Acapantzingo, and the blacksmith's workshop in the hollow towards the ravine. Here I instinctively looked for the ancient woman sitting on her chair by the side of the road, but her place was empty.

Further on, La Peni was still there and the same, as was also the turquoise corner cantina with the red Coca-Cola sign and, beyond it, the road with our house and the heavy, sweet scent of guavas. Don

José's shop was there, but he had died from a rare illness, his sister told me. I dug out Irene, now married and with a brood of children, from a village further out. And I walked down to the bottom of Acapantzingo, past Maximilian's overgrown tropical garden, the small bare church where the cattle were blessed once a year, along the solitary dirt path even now bordered by the same wild lush tangle of local vegetation, as far as the little cemetery with its crooked turquoise, pink and white wooden crosses, from where I gazed beyond the open plain at the distant snow-capped volcanoes, Popocatépetl and Ixtacihuatl, their undiminished beauty sparkling in the bright sunshine.

Here in Acapantzingo, time had stood still. Frozen. I had leapt back fifteen years: I was the same eleven-year-old girl once again, and at the same time, myself, now. The intervening years had suddenly melted away. For a moment I had captured myself, felt what I was, what I had been and lost, the tattered remains momentarily retrieved, myself simply and clearly, nakedly, close to the intensity of nature and the pulsation of life, its profound harmony, overwhelming beauty and terrible violence. All I had been before the mental and emotional turmoil and acrobatics to which I had subjected myself in my attempt to fit that other unfamiliar order at the opposite end of the world.

I was facing the small cemetery and the two volcanoes, alone. I savoured my exquisite solitude in that intimate landscape and hushed stillness, intruded on only by the erratic flight of a dragonfly and distant barking. I stepped on the shallow irregular furrows between the crowded tombs, unnamed and undated, surrounded by the brightly coloured crosses stuck into the earth and inclined with time, trying to guess the age of those under them by the tiny gaps between one cross and the next. And I felt at the same time the poignancy of all those dead children's desolate fates and the silent peace all about me.

My father had a fishery in Ciudad del Carmen, in the Mexican Gulf. He had recently acquired two more fishing boats for Salina Cruz on the Pacific side.

'A man who works for me, Cantarel, is going to Salina Cruz to check my boats – he has one of his own there too. He's a bit of a scoundrel, but quite charming in his own way. I asked him to drive you down there and take you to Carmen after that. I may join you later. It'll be carnival time and you might amuse yourself. You can take a friend along too, if you like,' he said, eager to please me and with all the arrangements at his usual, easy command.

Salina Cruz was a sleepy flat town with a small, austere, open market in the port, in keeping with its mainly indigenous populace. We arrived after a thousand-kilometre drive, broken by a couple of days' stopover in the market town of Oaxaca, with Cantarel speeding and overtaking at almost every bend in the narrow mountain road during the second half of the journey. I was accompanied by my old friend Libertad, with whom I had kept in touch, and my father's new secretary who was going to take charge of the office in Carmen. In Salina Cruz we stayed at the home of another young girl who worked at my father's fisheries. Cantarel took time to look after us in between his chores. He drove us to the nearby town of Tehuantepec, which consisted of a small central square and a few dirt roads and adobe huts. Some of these were scattered up a hill where a mother was washing her small child outside her shack under the hot sun. She was scooping the cold water out of a tank on the hillside with an empty tin, pouring it over his naked little body, soaping him with her hands and rinsing him with the tin again, while he wriggled with delight at the soaping, splashing and coolness. The townswomen, *tehuanas,* went about their work under the scorching sun dressed in their long, black velvet skirts and blouses richly embroidered with brightly coloured flowers, balancing everything – from a pitcher full of water to a sack of potatoes – on their heads, tall and erect. Their menfolk instead sprawled lazily on the ground in the dusty streets flicking the flies off the snotty children playing around them. The town was having a party the following evening and we were invited to join them.

The party was held in the largest adobe house on the central square. The women, brightly dressed, their shiny black hair freshly plaited and adorned with a large flower, were handing out food and attending to everything as well as enjoying themselves, some of them dancing in pairs. The men sat about drinking and chattering, a small band of them playing some lively music in a corner with the odd one trying out some dance steps on his own. Cantarel and we three women were warmly welcomed. We were given flowers for our hair, passed food and drink, and generally absorbed into their midst with no fuss or sense of division.

Later that night, after returning to Salina Cruz and retiring to bed, ready for a good night's sleep before the next day's journey to Carmen, the small town's thick silence was suddenly interrupted by a cheerful mariachi band close by. We got up and leaned out of the first-floor balcony to investigate and, right there, in the street below us, the mariachi group – their faces under their wide sombreros upturned towards us – were singing and playing their instruments.

'They are serenading you!' my father's secretary exclaimed laughing. 'Cantarel must have put them up to it!'

And I too laughed with delight and surprise, and we stayed up and listened to them into the early hours of the morning.

All this, which I was enjoying, had been orchestrated by my father – was he maybe trying to charm me into staying with him in Mexico? Yet my mother's pull was so strong, I could never even have started to consider it.

Another long drive, across Mexico's southern waist this time, took us to Villa Hermosa on the gulf for a night's stopover, and then on to Frontera – a coastal town full of shifty characters and shops crammed with every kind of stuffed reptile: lizards, iguanas, coiled snakes, small crocodiles and others unfamiliar to me. Here we waited for the ferry to take us across the mouth of the Grijalva River, drove another stretch along the gulf's coastline, and took the last ferry across to Ciudad del Carmen: a narrow strip of land, cut off from the mainland, wedged between the still waters of the inner lagoon and the gulf's restless currents.

A cool, turquoise-blue, tiled veranda framed with a rich tangle of flowering creepers stretched across the front of my father's house in Carmen. It opened directly into the main room with its large dining table and two low windows covered with mosquito netting looking out onto the veranda. On either side were a bedroom with en-suite bathroom and, behind it, a tiled kitchen with a big wooden table where Viviana cooked local Mexican dishes for Don Luis, members of his immediate and more peripheral family, close and distant friends, business connections and occasional acquaintances, all of whom used the house when they came to Carmen. Two huge mango trees dwarfed the house and garden, their inclined trunks clambered over by iguanas, elbows pointed outwards as they stepped clumsily around the branches like small, lime-green dinosaurs. At night, the lively music from the local brothel would waft across from somewhere beyond the back of the house, and loud reports – rather like rifle shots at point blank range – interrupted my sleep at regular intervals. It was not until morning that I realised the noise came from the mangoes falling on the tin roof.

Viviana kept a large sturdy pig in the bit of garden behind the kitchen. It was attached to a tree stump by a piece of rope that allowed it some freedom of movement.

'You musn't tell Don Luis about the pig,' she confided. 'He doesn't know about it.'

'Why not?'

'He doesn't like pigs. Whenever I cook pork, *la señora* Ilse asks me to tell him it's veal. And he always replies, "Ah, yes. This meat's good. It's pork I don't like."'

Maybe, I wondered, it was the one custom that had stayed with him from his religious upbringing in that small community in some forgotten corner of the Lithuanian countryside.

Viviana told me how she would buy the small piglet, feed it all the leftovers from the household, and when it was big and fat, kill it and carve it into its various edible cuts and organs which she sold, and then start again with another piglet.

'The day of the slaughter is very strenuous,' she explained. 'I get up at dawn and it takes me right through till night-time before all the parts are prepared and ready to sell.'

She came from a humble indigenous family in a distant village and was clever and enterprising, though she had on occasion paid dearly for her independence of mind and adventurous spirit. Rumour had it that the barber's wife and her friends had dampened Viviana's pleasure with the barber by the use of a very hot chilli forced into an intimate part of her anatomy: an apparently effective local cure against adultery.

We spent the days in Bajamita, a long golden beach bathed by the gulf's pristine blue waters and backed by coconut palm trees. In the late afternoon, we would take a walk in Carmen's central square where the townspeople promenaded at that hour, freshly preened and in their best clothes. Young girls walked clockwise in twos and threes, arm-in-arm, on the broad path around the square, while young men followed the opposite course eyeing them furtively as they chatted and laughed good-naturedly among themselves – a custom apparently carried over from Carmen's Spanish colonial past. Or we went a few streets further out to explore the fishing port where circling vultures waited for the discarded leftovers from the fishermen.

Then carnival week arrived in Carmen. People in a never-ending variety of masks filled the streets and parks, dancing and living it up, forgetting their cares for a week. Down to the poorest and most humble. Telltale signs of the fever turned up everywhere one looked. Odd, broken strands of pink and purple streamers dragged about in the gutter by a late-afternoon wind. In the evenings, we converged at the large hall in the town centre to dance through till dawn to a big band playing cha-chas and *danzones*. By now I knew many of the townspeople through my father's friends and associates, and I never ran out of dancing partners in step to all those Latin American rhythms.

Here, I was the newly discovered daughter of Don Luis. My father was a well-known personage, the founder of a flourishing fishing industry that had brought employment to many. When he joined me in Carmen he went about the town greeting everyone and chatting to many. He gave the impression of a paternalistic *'patrón'* who looked after the needs of his workers and their families with caring concern. He showed me around the freezing plant, where the prawns were sorted out by a line of young local girls, frozen, packed and transported to the United States, while other sea produce went to Mexican destinations. The atmosphere was friendly and informal and he enjoyed introducing me to everyone. He arranged an outing on one of the fishing boats where we were offered fresh prawn *cebiche* by the crew as we watched the fishermen cast the nets into the sea and later haul them back onto the boat and sort out an extraordinary array of sea creatures. My father was not only eager to introduce me to his work, but also to show me off to his friends and business associates. For my part, I felt flattered and grateful, yet I could not brush off my memory of the long lean years without him: that was too ingrained. He was trying to win me back while my reservations and the distance between us would not let go.

He arranged for a German acquaintance to fly me in his small plane to a place deep in the jungle – inaccessible by road then – where a small isolated community of *Lacandones,* descended from the Maya, lived near the Guatemalan border.

Inside, the aircraft was as cramped as a Volkswagen Beetle. As we flew low over the dense southern Mexican jungle, I could make out the landscape below us in detail and was running a mental calculation of our chances of survival should we fall from the sky into that area, which – if we came out of the crash alive – was said to be full of *tigrillos,* a species of small, wild tiger. And snakes, of course. The swamps which followed might offer a softer landing but were full of crocodiles. I was pleased when we landed instead at our intended destination, a small clearing in the tropical rainforest where the *Lacandones* lived, of which this group of fifty were – I was told – the last survivors. The people who ran to meet us, as we stepped out of the small plane, ranged from small children right across to strong wiry old men, all dressed alike in a poncho-style, folded piece of cotton cloth with a slit cut into the crease to let the head through, and the sides stitched together from the arms down. They laughed and smiled a good deal and made signs at us while they spoke amongst themselves in their own language: their eyes almond-shaped, their heavy cheekbones high and broad, and their hair long and matted apparently to ward off mosquitoes. They liked being photographed and would hold out their hands for payment after each click, rejecting the heavy silver pesos in preference for crumpled paper money. A family of American missionaries who were living with them said they used the money to buy cloth for their dress and guns to protect themselves from the *tigrillos* – they did not hunt, it seems, but lived off the wild fruit of the trees in the surrounding jungle. At one end of the clearing where we landed, were some ancient Maya ruins. Two large stone stelae with carvings, one of a man with an intricate feathered headdress and attire, the other of maybe a masked god, stood under the trees. Nearby was a row of three small rooms, perhaps once part of a temple. Inside, their walls were covered with faint frescoes showing scenes of Maya life: a group of musicians, a battle, a procession of men or priests with high, elaborate headgear and dark profiles, their tapering foreheads level with their aquiline noses – all richly painted in blood red, brown and ochre, with jade and blue in parts, though much faded with time. I later found out this was the site of Bonampak – Maya for 'painted walls' – discovered some sixteen years earlier and a gem example of the classical Maya period of a thousand years ago.

My father took me also to Mérida, in Yucatán, where I saw the Maya pyramids and ball court in nearby Chichen Itza; Uxmal's steep pyramid and large quadrangle with corbelled arches; the carved stone façades in Kabah with row upon row of the sculpted image of Chak, the Rain God. In Palenque's site surrounded by thick jungle, more Maya pyramids, temples and palaces covered with bas-reliefs of ornate figures and hieroglyphs, hilltop shrines, and a small museum. I read whatever books I could find on what was known

*Resting on the Chac Mool while my father reclines on the serpent's head, Chichen Itza*

about that mysterious civilisation, much of it already in ruins and overgrown with the jungle's vegetation by the time the Spanish conquerors set foot here, and – in the name of Christianity – destroyed and burned what was left, including the precious codices in which all the Maya secrets of the universe and their genealogy had been recorded and handed down across countless generations. I read, with awe and curiosity, about the large, Maya network of smooth white roads made from ground seashells which connected their centres and large markets across southeast Mexico and Central America, on which the Maya walked in great numbers with huge loads on their backs held by a strong band of sisal, still cultivated in the area, strung across their foreheads. For they had not discovered the wheel, though they had calculated the movement of the stars and planets and the length of the year down to a decimal point. And I read too about their detailed observation and profound awareness of the natural world around them, and their customary apology to the corn before cutting it and to an animal before killing it out of necessity for food. And that they had a Goddess of The Moment Before Dawn. That timeless moment, hushed and still, when every living thing falls under the spell of the vague lifting darkness – all of nature expectant, glistening with dew, holding its breath at the imminence of the first faint flush of light ...

# Life in Jerusalem

*Ein Karem, 1963.*

BRILLIANT SCARLET shading into vermilion and flaming orange was lighting up the whole western sky through the plate-glass window on the hospital's fifth floor as I was examining a chubby, ebony-skinned, small African prince with an umbilical hernia for the next day's surgical list. This wild fiery display recurred at every day's close, following its monotonously blue sky – unbroken by even the smallest cloud in several months. 'It's the sand that blows across from the desert. It catches the light when the sun goes down and turns the sky red,' I was told with indifference by the hospital's sabra staff.

I always looked forward on my nights on duty to watching the sunset over the terraced hills of rose stone and red earth scattered with silvery olive trees. Way down below the terraces, a small clump of tall cypresses and a white church spire marked the Christian Arab village of Ein Karem, from where the rare sound of church bells pealed across the pink hillside to reach me on my Sundays on call. The Hadassah Medical School Hospital, a tall semicircular building with two side wings, stood alone in the Judean Hills a short distance from Jerusalem where I lived in my one-roomed flat. Every morning, I rose at six to catch the bus and arrive in time to change into my theatre clothes and have the first patient on my list anaesthetised and ready for the surgeon's knife by eight o'clock. More accurately, at six, when my alarm went off, I pulled a string by my bed, the other end of which I had tied to the switch which heated the water for my shower, and then snuggled under the blankets to sleep another half hour before getting up to have a nice hot shower in the small annexed bathroom of green corrugated tin, take a rushed breakfast of coffee and toast, and walk to the bus that took me to Hadassah. Down my short street, Bnei Brit, of large, stone houses and towering trees, along the larger Haneviim Street, and finally across King George V to the bus stop by the Knesset.

*Jerusalem, 1963.*

MY UNCLE FRITZ had encouraged me to come to Israel. I had broken my flight from Mexico to see again my newly discovered cousins in New York. I came off the plane there laden with a collection of indigenous pottery and other handicrafts from Mexican markets and a huge bunch of flowers I was given on my departure at the airport, and thus burdened came across a tall, uniformed gentleman with a peaked cap, bowing right and left calling out my name. In spite of its déjà vu recall of my arrival at the port of New York, some three months earlier, it caught me by surprise

'The limousine is waiting, madam,' he said as he respectfully helped me with my assorted luggage and led me to an enormous white limo parked nearby. He drove off to deliver me to my cousins' house in New Rochelle where Elly was waiting for me.

I also made a brief stopover in Rome to call on Mauro, with whom I had kept a correspondence, and my other cousins, Reni and Renzo.

It was March, 1963, when, as I got off the plane at the end of my journey and stepped onto Israeli soil, I thought of the many Jews who had found a new life here after losing everything from their old: their home, family, friends, roots, bearings, dignity and identity. And of the intensity of their emotions on their first contact with this land and its promise, as they fell to their knees to kiss it. And, at that moment, as my feet touched down, I understood this.

I stayed with my uncle, who had discarded his German name of Fritz Lichtenstein and was now Perez Leshem. Tall, slim and economical in speech, Perez was complemented by his vivacious wife Hava, with her short bob of greying hair and very blue, smiling eyes. Their pleasant apartment was in a row of houses of Jerusalem stone in a leafy street, opposite the octogenarian writer and philosopher Martin Buber, not far from Jerusalem's centre. Soon after my arrival, my uncle spoke with Hadassah's medical director who encouraged me to apply for a post at the hospital. This is called *protectsia*, my uncle explained: a term introduced into Hebrew by the immigrant Russian Jews. In my case, it helped speed up, though not cut out, the bureaucratic procedures that turned out as labyrinthine here as anywhere. I was given an opening in anaesthesia which, apart from being a specialty that interested me, solved the problem of communication with my patients, as I knew no Hebrew. In the course of my work I spoke English, the language of their textbooks, with my medical colleagues; my basic German – from hearing my mother speak it in the background during my childhood – allowed for a dialogue of essentials with the Yiddish-speaking patients; my Spanish likewise with the Ladino-speaking, Sephardic ones; and French worked with those who came from North Africa. The only patients I could not converse with, were those from the eastern Arab countries who spoke only Hebrew and Arabic. Yet I soon learned the most important phrases of my métier, *tinshom amok, liftoach ha pe, tiftechi he enaim, hakol beseder.* Hebrew for take a deep breath, open your mouth, open your eyes, all is well. I could also say perfectly, *Ani lo medaveret Ivrit,* I don't speak Hebrew. Though I did teach myself enough of that revived, ancient language – which my ancestors must have used at prayers – to fill in the anaesthetic forms and sign my name in its characters.

In my room – where I moved when Perez and Hava went to Germany to take up Perez's appointment of first Israeli Consul, as relations between the two countries started to normalise – I set about learning the history of this country, beginning with the Old Testament: a Hebrew edition with an English translation alongside it. I decorated my small room – in which I slept, cooked, ate, received my friends and relaxed – with Mexican rugs, New Zealand seashells and Israeli glasswork. The floor was laid with large slabs of pink Jerusalem stone, and two tall windows gave me a view through their wrought-iron latticework of the street's ancient trees and stone houses. My day at Hadassah was one of concentrated work till mid-afternoon, by which time my

*In Jerusalem, 1963*

operating list was finished and I had seen my next day's patients. When not on night duty, I returned to Jerusalem and sat down to a snack in my room while I listened on the radio to the Arabic music and soaps from Jordan, which was only a few streets away in divided Jerusalem. I especially enjoyed an ongoing saga in which the expressive intonations of the Arabic language mixed with tender sighing, women's wailing, and men's stern talk, enhanced by that language's husky, guttural sounds, made the meaning of the words unnecessary. By late afternoon I went to Café Alaska in Jaffa Street, some five minutes' walk away. The atmosphere here was informal and comradely as I sat among a mixed bunch of people, mostly journalists, around the small tables, sipping coffee and in animated conversation. Most of them were sabras, or native Israelis, for – like the cactus fruit of that name – they were said to be hard and prickly on the outside and soft inside. The sabras I met here were earthy, unsentimental young people, whose prevalent interest and most common subject of study at university seemed to be Arabic: the language, culture, way of life, history, religion, everything – as they seemed intent on learning about and understanding their neighbours in the hope of one day living in peace with them and shedding all the hostility and violence.

'We'll move freely across our borders then, go skiing on Mount Hermon in Syria, and visit the city of Petra in Jordan,' one would dream out loud.

'Petra?' I asked.

'Yes. You haven't heard of it? An ancient city carved into the red rock of the desert. Once the capital of the Nabatean kingdom. I know many Israelis who have risked their lives crossing the border in the Negev, only to see it. They say it is amazing.'

'Lebanon will be the second country to make peace with Israel,' another would say.

'So which will be the first one, then?' I fell into the trap of asking.

'Ah! That's the big question!'

A regular customer of the café, who looked completely out of place among the journalists he sat with, was an English Jew who could have stepped out of *Dad's Army*. He spoke with a plummy accent and had a virulent hatred of Arabs. 'I would like to see *rivers* of Arab blood,' he would spit out, sitting up very straight, his eyes shining. 'That sounds like Hitler ... He could have said that about the Jews ... Have we learned *nothing*?' I whispered, shocked. And one or other of the sabras around the table would quietly nudge and wink at me, 'Don't take any notice of him. He's mad. And quite harmless.'

One day, a tall, hefty young man in shorts and unshaven came into the café with his girlfriend, leaving their heavy rucksacks by the entrance. They turned out to be English travellers who had been backpacking from Turkey, through Lebanon, Syria and Jordan, and had just come through the Mandelbaum Gate to see Israel, which they left till last as traffic across the border was strictly one-way. I asked them about their travels in those countries, which I too would love to visit but couldn't from Israel.

'We had the most extraordinary experience,' the young man said, his expression arched with surprise. 'We got lost while travelling through Syria on our way to Jordan and stopped to ask directions from a man we met on the road. We unfolded our map and asked him to point out where we were and, at the sight of it, his manner changed abruptly. He snatched our biro and scratched Israel out in a frenzy until our map was completely defaced. Then he walked off refusing to speak to us again. You see, we got our map in England. We found out their maps don't have Israel on them.' They had not come in contact with Jews or Arabs before and the implacable hatred of Israel they came across, in all the Arab countries they visited, had astonished them.

I was in my room listening to the BBC World News, one night, while I was dressing to go to a party with one of the journalists I knew from Café Alaska. Suddenly the news bulletin was interrupted by a tense announcement that the President of the United States, John Kennedy, had been shot. The news was confused; it appeared he had been rushed to hospital. While the commentator was trying to ascertain the president's condition, strange screeches and howls rose and dropped in the background of the long-distance transmission, sometimes drowning the snatches of commentary on some new information that had come to light. At this time, Kennedy promised a softening of the cold war and a firm stand against much of his country's injustice and corruption, and this attempt on his life in the full flow of his efforts seemed a tragic blow. I listened to the fitful, disjointed announcements as they competed with the unearthly shrieking and wailing like a blabber of foreboding by a coven of witches intercepting the radio waves. When the journalist arrived to take me to the party, he wasn't the least affected by the news. 'What an inward-looking country,' I thought. 'Not unlike New Zealand in its isolation, though New Zealand's is geographical, while Israel is squeezed between the sea and a ring of deadly enemies.'

At the other end of my short street started the ultra-orthodox Jewish quarter of Mea Shearim. Its large gate marked the entrance into another world. Men with long beards and sidelocks, their remaining hair gathered and tucked under their black hats, walked about slightly stooped in their long black coats, their gaze inverted, while children ran about at play and women, their scarves tied around their shaved heads, were less visible. One late Friday afternoon, the heat of the day unrelieved by the growing shadows, I took a walk through the streets of this quarter with my cousin Micah, son of Perez and Hava and on leave from his compulsory army training. I was wearing a sleeveless cotton dress with a high neck, enjoying the balmy breeze on my bare arms. We walked under a poster stretched across the street and Micah translated the inscription on it, 'Daughters of Israel, go humbly dressed and cover your arms.' A little boy, of barely six years, ran behind us for several blocks until he finally caught up with us. He kept calling out something in Yiddish.

'What's he saying?' I asked my cousin.

'He's calling you a whore.'

Though Mea Shearim has existed in Jerusalem since the nineteenth century – its Jews leading a life of religious orthodoxy distinct from the State of Israel, which they do not recognise until the coming of the Messiah – the Eastern European, Jewish way of life within its walls goes back much further. Or rather, it has not moved forward since the Middle Ages. Was I witnessing here my ancestors' lifestyle in the distant past? I looked about me trying to find some point of reference between these Jews and myself, in vain. They themselves, I was told, wouldn't consider me a Jew; they would ask me to switch on their light on the Sabbath, an unholy task for a goy. Yet my whole life was determined by another group specimen of humanity who would have killed me when I was a child for being Jewish. So, what did it mean? Being 'Jewish'? Here in Israel I could see for myself at first hand the wildly disparate variation within this group of people called Jews. Maybe what pools us together, I thought, is the sense in common of repeated displacement and dispossession, a long history of persecution culminating in the Holocaust, raising questions of identity – individual, racial, national, religious – imposed on us by the society around us. My own sense of Jewishness was inevitably linked to those gas chambers for which I was intended – for if people took so much trouble to put into place a sophisticated machinery for my extermination, and bureaucracy and manpower to track me down, it cannot but have had an effect on how I felt about myself. Since I have no religious claims to being Jewish, what makes me Jewish finally is that I was meant to die for it – when I was even unaware of it, my innocent absence – and its effect on the whole of my subsequent life. And *that* is a common denominator I share with Jews right across the spectrum, from the ultra-orthodox to those who have 'dropped out' and, beyond, even denied their ancestry and adopted Christian or other faiths – for even they were not exempted from their intended fate.

I was at the main post office in Jaffa Street trying to get some information. A tall young man in jeans and sandals, his eyes dark and intense, rather large for his slender face, his hair prematurely thin on top of his head, stopped to help me out. He spoke English and we got into conversation.

'What's your name?'

'Miriam. And yours?'

'Haim.' Hebrew for life.

We started walking down the street together. Jerusalem being a small place, people approached and got to know each other with no formalities or introductions.

'Where do you live in Jerusalem?' he asked me.

'Just up the road. In Rehov Bnei Brit.'

'I'll call on you one day.'

And he did.

Haim had the directness of a sabra, and a curious, singular imagination. He made films, he was also somewhat distracted – he lost a reel once when we were out walking and got really mad about it. He told me snatches of his thoughts and memories.

'I was on guard duty, in the army, one night in the Negev. We were supposed to be looking out for Arab smugglers who crossed the desert in the dark, and we were lying in ambush for them. Suddenly I heard a noise. I looked out and saw a group of them, maybe three or four, walking very quietly. They were very close to us, unaware of our presence. I made a sign to the other guard, and he gave out the signal to shoot. I let out a loud yell. The Arabs jumped, very frightened, and ran for their lives. They got away. The others were very angry with me! But I didn't care. I felt like *God*! I had given them life!'

We started seeing each other now and then. One evening, I thought it would be nice to have a coffee and a chat with him and I walked through the empty streets to his place on the other side of Jerusalem. He didn't answer his bell, so I sat on the steps facing the paved yard at the back of his tenement house, watching the patterns of light and shade in the night. The place was deserted. A great calm descended on me as I listened to the silence, broken only by distant noises from the city and the odd cat meowing nearby. One suddenly appeared, its black-and-white pattern blending with the night's shadows as it started walking rapidly on an adjacent ledge, then stopped and looked back. Another arrived from a different direction and headed towards the first. They stood a short distance apart looking at each other. One meowed again, then the other. The first now slinked away while the second pricked up its ears and, its front paw lifted, listened for a moment, then turned round and disappeared into an alley between the buildings. On the pavement before me, the moon's pearly-white reflection shone uncommonly brightly. At that moment in time, that small terrain was neither the Jews' nor the Arabs': it belonged to the moon and the cats. If only it could be seen that way … I waited a little longer in case Haim turned up, and then returned to my room.

Every Tuesday, I walked across Jerusalem to a musical evening at a young couple's open house. People sat on oriental cushions on the stone floor, surrounded by exotic hangings and furnishings. After the concert, Turkish coffee was served and we mingled and chatted. On my way home, I took in the Jerusalem cityscape of pink stone glistening in the moonlight, and enjoyed the changing imagery on my route across the city. Here, an open view of the glittering town against Mount Zion; beyond it, out-of-bounds Jerusalem with the mysterious Dome of the Rock's gold cupola rising high above the rest. A short cut gave me a more intimate view of a corner of the town. Here my surroundings took over and my senses merged with the images.

*Leafy shadows quivering*
*On paths, stone walls*
*Dappled patterns stirring silently*
*In the drenched*
*Amber brilliance of the moonlight …*

In Hadassah, my daily work was packed with experience. The eight theatres, arranged in a semicircle on the ground floor of the hospital, covered all surgical specialties except cardiac. General; orthopaedic; plastic; ear, nose and throat; eye; obstetric and gynae-cological; urological; paediatric; neurosurgical; and chest. The head of the department was from Bulgaria and the senior members were Scottish, South African and Romanian. The other anaesthet-ists included one young Polish woman and two native Israelis. We were soon joined by a petite, Sephardic Jewess with large blue eyes and fair curly hair, from Turkey, who had a Portuguese passport from her Sephardic ancestors, and studied in Paris. An Australian followed. The surgeons and nurses also came from every corner of the world, the only thing this motley group of people had in common being their 'Jewishness'. Whatever that is. There were also non-Jewish, black trainees from friendly African countries, and, among the patients, I anaesthetised many Muslims from Iran who came to Hadassah for treatment, as well as some Africans, like the small black prince with an umbilical hernia. I revelled in the mix of people. I enjoyed, for instance, talking Spanish with an Argentine nurse and observing her Latin American mannerisms, while I tried to imagine how she might have turned out had her family from Eastern Europe ended up somewhere else instead. The same face and physique with maybe American manners and outlook, or, had they not had to leave in the first place, Ukrainian ones. A hefty theatre porter and a svelte fair theatre sister had numbers tattooed on their arms. I was friendly with the sister and we chattered about everything, but when, one day I asked her about Auschwitz, she answered resolutely, 'Some things one doesn't talk about.'

One night, I was woken by the telephone in the anaesthetists' on-call room in the hospital basement.

'There's a soldier in the emergency room,' I was told abruptly without further elaboration. I slipped on some clothes and ran upstairs. I found a young man the colour of parchment lying stretched out in a cubicle. The surgeon was putting up an intravenous drip, with several bottles of emergency blood next to him waiting to be transfused. The boy was not breathing. I rushed over with my equipment, introduced a tube down his windpipe and started ventilating him with oxygen. By now blood was pouring into him through the administration set and as soon as one bottle emptied, the next was put up. The young man gave off a faintly rancid smell. He lay there naked and unconscious, with not a visible blemish or sign of injury on any part of his healthy physique. No one talked or answered my questions. I saw a small, carefully folded, clean white surgical swab on his upper abdomen, left of centre. I lifted it and there, under the swab, I saw a neat, round, bullet entry wound. And I realised we were pouring blood into and ventilating a dead boy.

'He was on night guard duty, overlooking the border. A Jordanian soldier took a pot shot at him from the other side,' someone finally told me.

Another evening on duty, I was called to the operating theatre. A young man in his twenties was lying there in agony, waiting for surgery. I took care of the anaesthetic while the operation went on for several hours, the surgeon attempting to repair the damage to his stomach, gut, liver, spleen and one kidney from a bullet which had ripped through his abdomen. This patient was Swiss. He was a

Roman Catholic tourist who had come to Jerusalem to visit the religious sites. He strayed too close to the border with his camera, when a shot from the Jordanian side shattered the organs in his abdomen. He survived the operation, and the team of surgeons and anaesthetists attended to him over the next ten days in the recovery ward next to the theatres, which – in 1963 – acted as an intensive care unit. He was uncommonly tall – his feet protruded from the end of the bed – blond and blue-eyed, and had a strong, healthy physique. He had come to Israel as a prelude to his studies: he wanted to become a priest, he told me. And as I followed his care, I watched him, day after day, struggle to stay alive against the deepening complications from his extensive injuries.

'I'm going to die, aren't I,' he began to say to me.

'No …'

I went to see his corpse on his bed in the recovery ward. He lay there, very pale and still, his expression – a mix of pain, exhaustion and fervour for life – gone from his face. His hands had been placed on his chest, the white, bloodless fingers interlocked.

On my weekends on duty, when work was slack, I sometimes went to the hospital synagogue and stood in the middle of the empty room looking at Chagall's stained-glass windows. Crimson, scarlet, ruby-red and vermilion glowed brightly from one transilluminated window in the darkened room. The next shone peacock blue, aquamarine, jade and turquoise as the light blazed through it. Twelve windows, one for each tribe.

Purim announced the arrival of spring. The streets filled with happy children in fancy dress, and the joy and optimism of the moment was experienced to the full as here, in the Middle East, everybody knew it could be shattered from one moment to the next, like the bursting of a bubble.

'There is dancing in the synagogues,' someone told me about a festivity that followed a few weeks later. 'You should go into the orthodox one at the bottom of your street.'

And I did. I sat in the upstairs gallery overlooking the whole bacchanalian scene on the ground floor with the men in their long black jackets and black hats drinking blessed wine and dancing and singing with total abandon and joy, feet stamping, arms raised, sidelocks bouncing, sweat streaming down their ecstatic faces. The women sat bunched together in a row upstairs, their scarves wrapped around their shorn heads, quietly chattering among themselves.

The countryside in the northern fertile valley of Galilee, where I went on some of my free weekends, was bursting with flowers. The fields were full of bright red poppies, white daisies and yellow dandelions. They also sprouted out from every corner, every small patch of earth. They grew on the stony ground near the sea in Ashkelon and on sandy paths by the beach of Caesarea.

On Saturdays, when there were no buses in this country ruled by the laws of the Old Testament, I hitchhiked to get around. Along the coast road, there was a string of Arab towns, the earth colour of their mud-brick houses broken by their brightly coloured doors and windows. On this stretch of road, a van stopped to give me a lift. As I settled down next to the driver and exchanged our first words, I realised – with some disquiet – that he was an Arab from one of the villages. But I was soon at ease again: he was a friendly man with a bright smile, like his small son sitting between us. He spoke some rudimentary English and we managed to converse. He asked me where I was from, while I asked him about his life since the formation of the state of Israel.

'Life – *much* better,' he told me. 'I have *work*. Before, no work, no food, family have nothing. Life *very* bad. Now we eat. Children in school. When children sick: hospital, medicine, all free.' He had learned to speak Hebrew and had merged into life in Israel.

'Would you not rather have a country of your own, though? A Palestinian state?'

'Palestine state yes, I happy,' he said. 'But home, *here*. I stay *here*. I *Israeli*,' he emphasised, to my surprise, '*Israeli Arab*.' Our friendly exchange of information came to an end when he had to turn off the main road. I thanked him for the lift and got off. As I walked along the road again, I thought of the only other Arabs I had known here in Israel: a Druse doctor in Hadassah, a handsome, young, caring physician who was dating one of the Jewish Israeli nurses. They made a delightful couple, yet the nurse had confided in me her great unhappiness with their problems in having their relationship accepted by relatives and friends. I remembered too my encounter with two quite different Arabs in the town of Nazareth, which I was visiting with my namesake – a young Yugoslav journalist I met in Café Alaska. The two Arabs had swept into the café in their long flowing robes and keffiyeh making straight for us sitting in a corner chatting over our coffee, pulled my fair, pretty, blue-eyed friend out of her chair, stood her up, pinched the flesh of her slim arms between thumb and index finger – as a prospective buyer might test a horse – shook their heads in disappointment, and walked out again.

Here, on this northern coastal road, I was not far from my first trip in Israel with some young Israelis. They had invited me to join them on a weekend outing, to get my first taste of Israel outside Jerusalem. Yet, though they all spoke English, they had made no attempt to include me in their conversations in spite of my own efforts to learn my first words – *bokertov, leilatov* – and meet them on their ground. I soon found that the social graces I had become accustomed to in the Anglo Saxon world were not a strong point here, with the sabras. I had also come across many who resented the Jews in the Diaspora, pointing out that while they face the dangers of protecting this piece of land, the others, who live comfortably elsewhere, will reap the benefits should they need someday to run to Israel for cover from a new wave of anti-Semitism. They generally cared little about the rest of the world. But then, I also recognised their all-absorbing concern to survive their ring of hostile neighbours, who were committed – as they so often declared – to pushing them into the sea and erasing the State of Israel. They had to be tough to survive. While Palestinian terrorists, or freedom fighters, crossed the northern border to massacre a busload of schoolchildren, the Israelis prided themselves in managing to destroy a whole fleet of their enemy's planes without the loss of a single human life. That's how it was then.

'We can forgive the Arabs for killing our boys,' I heard them say. 'But we cannot forgive them for turning our boys into killers …'

Which is, of course, what has happened … Going to show that people behave, not according to their history, or lessons learned from it, but much more in response to the circumstances they find themselves in. And if power corrupts, it corrupts universally, unrelated to nationality, culture, religion or race. People are people are people – everywhere in the world. No one group is better or worse than any other, given the same circumstances.

My first impressions of Israel were of a chaotic young country where there were as many opinions as individuals, all of them vociferous and jostling for attention. There was everywhere a somewhat disordered jumble of standards; an absence of, or when present a misguided, hierarchy – yet the standards managed to break through this confusion and reach a par with the best in the world, as though the sheer life energy and ferment of this young country overcame the muddle. My initial disappointment with that uncouth disorder gradually turned into a strong attachment for this land and its people as I was drawn into the heady atmosphere of creating a new country. Out of swamps and deserts. Turning them into fertile land by drying out the one in the north and watering the other in the south. Growing oranges and peaches in the barren, lunar landscape of the Negev, and tomatoes next to the Dead Sea by desalinating its water. There was something very seductive about the frenetic sense of development in every sphere, in the scientific and the artistic, the agricultural, medical, social and demographic. And then, there were the kibbutzim. Building the new out of the old, on a piece of ground rich with history going back to the beginnings of the races now mingling here – tragically at war with each other. I found myself irresistibly drawn to the ambience of so much enthusiasm and construction, a building together, cooperation and optimism. And of the values this fostered, which focused on the human, a large family nation of stubborn individuals who spent their time disagreeing and quarrelling with each other, Ashkenazi against Sephardi, religious against secular, hardliners against peacemakers but, in this year of 1963, pulled together in times of trouble, concentrating the mind on the basic values of life. Here, life had a purpose. And I had no problems about my identity – I merged almost too readily into these surroundings and my name was so common I no longer looked up when I heard it. Though now, here, it was the non-Jew that was at a disadvantage, and to reverse the predicament is not to solve it ...

Yet, at the time, I was experiencing the ease with which the sense of 'belonging' becomes sucked into the gaping vacuum of dispossession, the intense emotions experienced at the notion that a piece of earth is a part of you, one from which you cannot be thrown out, and I could see that the need for such a space on this planet could be so great that one was prepared – paradoxically – to die defending it. I was being drawn to a concept diametrically opposed to my earlier and, again, later convictions. The strength of it, irrational as it might be. And potentially dangerous.

I climbed into a bus and took my seat. It was hot. The passenger in front of me slid open the window to let some air in.

'It's too draughty! Close the window!' another passenger called out from across the aisle.

'No. Leave it open,' demanded one in the back of the bus.

'It's too cold,' a third joined in.

'It's like a furnace,' rebutted a fourth.

Within seconds the whole bus had taken sides on whether the window should be left open or closed, and everybody – except myself, who really didn't care about the window's status – was putting their view forward, talking at once, ending in uproar. And I remembered Eric Geiringer's words.

When I entered a bus, I was likely to head for the seat next to an orthodox Jew, in defiance of his religious conviction of a menstruating woman's unclean, untouchable state. In a collective taxi between Jerusalem and Tel Aviv, I watched a particularly handsome, surely newly wedded, young orthodox couple – he had the face of a prince and a profusion of thick, mahogany ringlets, and she, who wore an elegant wig instead of the usual scarf, had large, doe-like eyes and a warm intimate smile. Though sitting next to each other, they carefully maintained a gap between them and made elaborate gestures to pass each other some papers without touching. Yet, my orthodox male patients in Hadassah submitted to my physical examination of them with gracious dignity, and our exchange was invariably amiable when I took their medical history and they answered in Yiddish my questions in German. The closest I got to this mysterious people. The same who also threw stones at cars on Saturdays, of which our head of department herself was once a victim when she took a shortcut near their quarters to reach Hadassah in an emergency.

Travelling across the country, I saw the lush green fields of Galilee and the lake's pale blue waters, the ruins of King Solomon's palace in Megiddo, the exotic old town of Sfad in the far north. The wild fantastic formations of rock and sand in the Negev; people floating, sitting up, reading a book in the Dead Sea, the busy market in the desert town of Beersheba. The corals and strange tropical fish, each more curious than the last, while snorkelling in the Red Sea at Eilat. On the Mediterranean coast, I swam under the fortress remains of the Crusaders in Caesarea. And back in Jerusalem, I was taken round the ancient ruins on top of Mount Zion, just this side of the border with Jordan, by a friend who had turned the arched chamber of an ancient building into his sculpting studio, next to a room with sunken areas which had once been Turkish or maybe even Roman baths.

One day I woke up with the fresh memory of a vivid dream. I had found myself in the Jordanian section of Jerusalem inside the Dome of the Rock. I was, in fact, floating inside its golden concave ceiling in a diminishing spiral towards its zenith. In my dream I felt at ease in territory that was, in reality, out of my reach. I was climbing to the summit of a most holy Muslim building that stands on the site of the Great Temple of my Israelite ancestors. 'Israel' seemed to stand in my mind for my 'mother', much as 'Europe' – where I began life and was closest to her – also did. By contrast, 'Arab' was to me the other, out of bounds, forbidden area, the 'enemy', rather like my image of my 'father', and, in a sense, Mexico. For as much as Mexico meant to me, it had become my father's territory, and his attempts to win me over from my mother – 'If you stay here, you can have anything you want, all your needs will be taken care of,' he would say to me on a subsequent visit – were doomed to fail, for no matter how great the discord with my mother, I could not but consider myself always on her side. I felt caught and pulled in opposite directions. Father versus mother, Mexico versus Europe, Arabs versus Israel, 'out of bounds' versus 'home'. And while I was still seeking my bearings, trying to fathom my position with this country, and beyond it in this world, and maybe above all with myself, trying to understand where in the end I 'belonged', which are my geographical, cultural, ancestral, and parental 'roots', in the dream I had transcended all. I was circling, buoyantly, unencumbered by gravity, or even national definitions, tribal hostilities or parental competition, freely and naturally, to the top of an astonishingly beautiful golden dome – on the historical site which merged Arab and Jew – transgressing into the mysterious and reaching towards the cosmic heavens.

I had been here fifteen months now and was returning to Europe, but I planned to come back. This was a place I could call *home*, where the very earth welcomed me and made me feel at one with it, and every tree … And if there was another war, I would join the effort to defend this ground – not by killing, but by helping to heal the injured and saving lives. For the first time I had found something I was prepared to risk my life for – such is the heady seduction of 'belonging'. I decided I would leave my things here and take only what I needed for a brief trip to Europe, to meet up with my mother and sister, and to give me a chance to renew my perspective and be sure of my stance.

I wished to come back and dig in Masada. The archaeological team was inviting helpers: I would join it with its work on that historical, desert plateau. I wanted an intimate contact with that earth, to scratch it with my fingers in the search for artefacts buried within it, the excitement of coming across a piece once fashioned, used and held by hands of people long since disappeared. I would share the camaraderie of others who came here with similar minds from a motley pool of nationalities and backgrounds. Days, weeks, maybe months of nothing but sun, earth, simple living and sharing, and the searching and maybe finding of fragments of man-made objects, which piece by piece draw together the threads of continuity of our human existence.

I booked a berth in a ship from Haifa to Piraeus. I wished to see Greece, and then continue through the Corinth Canal and up the Adriatic Sea to Venice and Europe.

Like the Maya in Mexico and the Israelites in the Middle East, the ancient Greeks also intrigued me. Where the Maya were a people engulfed in mystery, magic and mathematics, and the Israelites, wanderers and staunch survivors who relied on their single God, the Greeks appeared an open, discursive people. Here, the tall, mighty, marble columns of the Parthenon alternated with air and light, and the caryatids looked down from their perch on the Acropolis with human grace. I wandered through the hillside remains of Agamemnon's fortress in Mycenae and gazed at the great amphitheatre in Epidaurus. In Delphi, the cool, fresh mountain forests, oracular shrines, temples and amphitheatre were all bathed in an effusion of honeyed light. In the coastal town of Nauplion in the Peloponnese, I left my handbag unattended on the beach while I swam in the sea, such was the sense of trust the people here inspired, and in a small village further down the coast, an old woman all covered in black invited me in my brief bikini into her humble home, more a shack, for a Greek coffee and an exchange of the most basic information about each other through gestures and much laughing. From the beach, I swam with two young Americans to a small distant island. As we approached it after an hour's swimming, a fisherman in his boat came close. 'You're mad, the sea is full of sharks here,' he managed to communicate to us. The island was tiny and uninhabited and we climbed through the undergrowth in our wet bathing suits to reach the small Orthodox chapel on the summit. Inside, its walls were lined with icons and a variety of objects left as offerings – maybe by fishermen. The sharks left us unmolested during our swim back to the mainland.

I took a ferry to the island of Hydra: a profusion of pretty white houses up the steep narrow streets interspersed with bougainvillea, vines, jasmine and other flowering plants, overcrowded with tourists. Mykonos was a symphony of whites. Arches, steps, doorways, paths, ledges and domes – all whitewashed over and over to a snow-like chalkiness, the many layers of lime rounding off their edges giving them an organic look. In the changing lights and shadows I began to see in the whites, tinges of violet, pink, cerulean, lime-green. And again: a dazzling white against a brilliant cobalt sea. The beach out of town, past a barren landscape of olive trees and lacy white dovecotes, each unlike the next, was a long stretch of golden sand with a simple taverna at one end which served delicious fish soup. I joined evenings of Greek dancing in the port town, graceful, repetitive footwork, hands held high, around a circle, to the captivating, windy music which lets one know that the Orient starts here. One young man, who was with a group of friends from Bordeaux, danced with me all night. He was a freshly qualified architect, he told me, and was drawing much of what he saw. St George's Day was celebrated in a town inside the island. The local people sat at a trestle table covered with food and drink that stretched from inside the church to well beyond it, out in the open air. They squeezed tighter together on the bench to make room for me, inviting me to join them. The retsina was light and tangy, and every one talked and laughed and enjoyed the feast and sharing everything without fuss or ceremony, undeterred by the absence of a common language.

I was beginning to sense, here in Greece, that the value is after all one of common humanity. I had, in fact, found more in common with the old Peloponnesian woman in her long black dress who offered me, in my skimpy bikini, her coffee and a chair in her simple dwelling, than with the small boy who chased me in Mea Shearim to call me a whore in my sleeveless dress. The seductive sense of belonging to a nation – now that I had experienced it – was starting to fade. The exuberance of life, bold sensuality, human warmth and – importantly – *inclusivity* here were drawing me to a more universal sense of my identity.

Crete. The little museum in Heraklion. Minoan paintings of acrobats on bulls' backs, of banquets, musicians, dancing figures, women in decorative sophisticated dress: sensuous and vital. The tiny terracotta statuette of a Minoan priestess, her naked breasts boldly protruding out of her dress moulded into her tiny waist and over her curvaceous hips in a series of flounces down to her feet – an unabashed display of feminine power and sexuality, as she stands with a struggling snake in each fist of her outstretched arms. Walking up Heraklion's main street, someone's hands suddenly wrapped over my eyes. I looked round and found my young friend from Bordeaux whom I danced with in Mykonos. Joined by another friend from his group, we decided to travel through the lush fertile centre of the island to Phaestos. Unlike the restored, brightly coloured palace of Knossos in Heraklion, the ruins in Phaestos were a crumbling leftover of this other great palace set in the tranquil surroundings of a green valley. That night we lay on a bed of pine needles in the 'King's Room' under a starry sky and talked quietly in the silence till we were overtaken by sleep. The young man woke me up at dawn.

'Come and see the sun rise!' he said, taking my hand and leading me to the top of the hill.

# The Doctor and the Artist

*London, 1964.*

THE EVENING HAD ALREADY TURNED to night when I was washing my hair and the telephone rang. I was house-sitting for friends in Harrow on the Hill, a pleasant leafy suburb in north London, with my sister. She had finished her music studies in Germany and was settling in England around the time of my arrival in London, while our mother stayed in Göttingen where she had found work as a librarian at its historic university. I picked up the phone and heard Neil Perret's voice at the other end of the line inviting us to his place in Earl's Court, where he now lived. A friend, who was visiting London, had turned up and they were celebrating Guy Fawkes' attempt to blow up parliament, and Goldwater's defeat in the American primary elections: the 5th of November, 1964.

'Yes. We'll come,' I said into the phone, holding the towel over my wet hair with my other hand.

I dried my hair in front of the heater, slipped on a polo-neck, ecru wool dress, and we set off into the drizzly night to the Underground. The front door of Neil's apartment building, in the corner with Brompton Road, was locked for the night and there were no individual flat bells. Not hearing our knocking, we tried to catch Neil's attention through his back window. This time he heard us and let us in. The friend turned out to be Kortokraks, whom Neil knew from Kokoschka's School of Vision: an international summer school in Salzburg which Neil had attended and where Kortokraks taught.

We sat around in Neil's living room chatting about many things. At some point I spoke of my new desire to paint.

'I was travelling around the Greek Islands only a few weeks ago and I was suddenly struck, in Mykonos, by the wealth of colours I could see in the pure white jumble of houses, steps, alleys and churches, all covered and rounded off with thick new layers of fresh whitewash. And here I was picking out greens and pinks, blues

*Kortokraks with Kokoschka, Schule des Sehens, Salzburg, 1962*

and violets, in the *white*! I was amazed. And then, in Mallorca: the magic light of Deyá … And I became aware of my need to *sense* and *take in* the world around me, as against controlling it as you do in medicine.'

Neil's friend, an older man with light blue, watchful eyes and brown hair, was on the other side of him, half reclining against the back of the sofa. He had hardly spoken all evening, but now his face suddenly lit up as though stirred by my words. When we were about to leave, he said, more than once, 'I like looking at you.' Which I didn't understand. The two men had, after all, been knocking back the drink all evening. Even so, looking back on it, it must have been some compliment, coming from a painter …

He heard me talking with my sister about her German piano teacher's recital at the Wigmore Hall the following week, and he was there waiting for us when we arrived. He sat next to me and never took his eyes off my face, which he studied intently in the dark, right through the concert. As we parted, he offered to help me with my painting and arranged a time for my first lesson.

I went to his studio flat in Chelsea and saw his paintings and

*Self-portrait by Kortokraks*

drawings. They struck me as powerful and real, unlike much of what I had been seeing in the then fashionable art scene of op, pop, trash, body, action and minimal. They, instead, breathed *life*. There was also an uneasy tension there. One could sense the complexity of the person caught on the canvas, on paper.

'You lived in Mexico!' he said. 'Then you must surely know a friend of mine, Gustav Regler!'

'Yes! Of course! My mother used to take me on her visits to see him when we first arrived!'

'I knew him in Worpswede – a small town

where I lived after the war in north Germany. He was married to Mieke, one of the Vogeler girls.'

He told me to get a bundle of sheets of brown wrapping paper and some sticks of charcoal.

'Draw the human figure, to start with. Forget what you are drawing or what you think it should look like. Draw what you *see*. Forget about outlines,' he said looking at the life drawings I had done in Paris, where, on my way to London, I had attended evening life classes at the Académie de la Grande Chaumière. 'Only someone who has mastered drawing, like Matisse, knows how to use them. We don't see the world in outlines, we see it in colours. In light and dark. Just look and draw what you see.'

So that was what I did. And I discovered moments in which the flesh before me, its texture, softness, roundness, as it picked up light here and merged into shade there, became one with me and the charcoal and paper and emerging image, all fused into one flow, one focus. And as it was happening I wasn't willing the drawing but it was evolving of itself, and the curve and touch and feel of the flesh came alive in it.

I went back to show him what I had done and he encouraged me to go on.

'Do them quickly, one after another. Don't stop and correct them if it's not going well: throw it away and do another one. Keep working at it.'

He asked if he might draw my face and did several drawings of me. He also started my portrait in oils and worked on it during our following meetings. We spoke about many things, and his sweeping knowledge and insights into everything to do with art, as well as literature, film and music, history and politics, inspired me. He was acutely aware and exhaustively informed of all that went on in the world – including all I had missed during my years in the Antipodes – and our views and tastes matched. Having grown up in Germany, the son of staunch opponents of Hitler's regime, and lived through some bitterly hard times, he understood my background better than I. I also saw how difficult he was, how he could change from all soft-ness and gentleness to great anger and rage – and there was much that made him furious.

I pieced together that he had come to London to attend the aristocratic wedding of one of his students at Kokoschka's school. He had hired a top hat and tails from Moss Bros, arrived at Westminster Abbey on the appointed day to find a crowd of curious American tourists watching the guests file past in their finery from their Rolls Royces into the church, and decided to skip the whole thing. He had recently divorced his young German wife – he showed me photographs of her and their small son, Daniel, whom he missed – and had no home to return to in Germany, so he decided to stay. He *liked* London, he found it *exotic*, he said. Having recently sold several drawings to a wealthy industrialist in Germany, he took a room at Bloomsbury's Imperial Hotel and invited his friends to dine and wine with him in style until the money ran out. Then he slept on a couch at an Irish friend's modest apartment until he moved into his present Chelsea studio flat, within walking distance of friends and acquaintances and their habitual rendezvous: Finch's pub in Fulham Road.

A motley variety of local artists, actors, journalists, bohemians, TV personalities and other characters would stand exchanging jokes and gossip in a loosely knit group at the bar, their faces flushed, their speech relaxed, enveloped in the dim, smoky, alcoholic haze, for hours on end, while the drinks kept flowing. The jovial face and voice of Bill Thomson – a painter, School of Vision co-assistant, friend and sometimes enemy of Kortokraks – was an integral part of the Finch's pub scene, along with others, like the guitarist Julian Bream and BBC presenter Huw Wheldon, maybe one or other of the Goons, and other lesser known but locally recognised celebrities in their own right for their mere unfailing presence and permanent wooziness. Like old Kate who always sat by the door in her frilly hat, and a decrepit elderly gentleman with his dog in the far corner: as essential a fixture of Finch's as the dark brown wooden tables and benches. Behind the counter, the tall cheery Irish publican, Jack Connell, would be dashing about attending to the clientele, his irrepressible dry wit always on hand, with the assistance of his small, good-natured wife, Nancy, and, somewhere in the background, some of their large brood of children.

I would sometimes accompany Kortokraks and watch the scene

from my sober angle, more an observer than a participant. To me they seemed a temporarily, if agreeably, mildly muddled group of people, and I was unable to merge into their blurred sense of togetherness and its fleeting comfort. Maybe the many changes I had recently, and more distantly, experienced prompted me to keep my head clear, or compelled me to keep my hard-come-by sense of my own self distinct and separate. Whatever it was, I would watch and listen, barely sipping my one drink that gave my hands something to do.

In contrast to Kortokraks' alternating states of bluntness and timidity, Bill Thomson was suave and polished. He lived around the corner from Finch's pub in a large house, its attic floor elegantly converted into a spacious studio to which he often invited his friends. When the evening warmed up, Kortokraks might do his one-armed musician sketch, which required a hat, a jacket and a stick. The hat on his head, he wore the jacket over his shoulders with one empty sleeve tucked into the pocket, while through the other his hand emerged holding the stick, which stood for the bow. He would press his chin against the imaginary violin on his shoulder and mime the music he played with the 'bow'. At the end of the piece, he would pass the 'bow' to an index finger which suddenly sprung out through his open fly to hook around it, leaving his hand free to take his hat from his head and pass it round for the odd coin – sending the whole drunken company into stitches.

Around this time, my father came to London on a trip to combine possible business deals with his sea produce – he had recently clinched one with the Japanese – and see his daughters. This was his first time back in thirty years.

'Where are the English gentlemen with their bowler hats and umbrellas?' He would ask with a quizzical smile as he faced in some bewilderment the busy cosmopolitan street scenes before him. He also looked up old friends and acquaintances he had known back in the thirties, when he had felt a strong sympathy for the Spanish anarchist cause – he had produced a documentary, now in the archives of New York's Museum of Modern Art, about the great spirit of Spain and the true face of the civil war as he saw it – and befriended anti-Franco sympathisers in London such as Roland

Penrose and Jenny Lee. Then, at a party at Bill Thomson's, finding himself surrounded by painters, he remarked pensively to one with whom he was conversing, 'I knew a painter once, back in my days in Paris. He was called George … what was it?' and he struggled with his memory, 'Braque! Georges Braque! He was a shy young man. I wonder what became of him?'

My mother also came to London, and we had a Chinese meal in Soho with Kortokraks. She understood and empathised with much about his background and what he stood for, as they shared viewpoints on their country's history. Though she was uneasy about his artist's way of dealing with his insolvency.

Not liking his first name, Rudolf, he was generally addressed as Kraks, which sometimes became Krax, Korto, Kraky … His surname would puzzle people. It sounded so like Kokoschka that some thought he was trying to emulate him and would ask, 'Is that your painter's pseudonym?' to which he would answer, 'No. I use Schmidt for that.' When he was in a patient mood, he would explain the derivation of the name: Cord (a variant of Curt) of Krax – Krax being a smallholding in medieval Westphalia, from where Willelmtokrax, Heindrichtokrax and Johantokrax also emerged. The 'ks' ending was a misspelling by a registrar of births somewhere along the line.

He went back to Germany to get on with the oil portrait of the director of a multinational chemical firm in his home town, Ludwigshafen, to clear his accumulating debts. In the meantime, I lent him money for the rent he owed, cleaned up his studio, packed his things and moved them to an attic flat I found in West Hampstead. I continued to practise my drawing and started looking for an anaesthetic job, planning to go ahead with my postgraduate training. Then his letters started arriving. One after another. Desperate, incoherent letters – things were going badly … he couldn't manage …

I had by now thought that our shared understanding and viewpoints might form a basis for companionship, maybe more. Although I did not feel for him the passionate urgency of past infatuations, it was maybe more important that his world was entwined with mine and my mother's past, that he understood my background and cared for me for what I was. Since leaving Israel, I no longer sought my roots in a piece of land – maybe my sense of belonging there had, paradoxically, dispensed with my need of a 'nation' – but rather within my own past, self and values. Kortokraks fitted these.

But his letters made me think again. Could I really go through all that with him? Was such a commitment not going to be too difficult? And my attention would be caught by one of the many drawings I was storing for him: here, a flute's long, sharp note was brought to life with a few lines – hardly any – that caught the flautist's tensed lips on the shaft of cold silver below the eyes' terse concentration, and the flute and player and sound were all there in the drawing. I would pick up and go through other drawings and works and they would elicit the same core reaction, the same certainty, that sense of worth, an encapsulation in some way of what life is about which words could neither match nor express. The same I had felt in Rome, on my return to Europe, before the small *Madonna and Child* painting that for me had transcended national differences, patriotic fervour, and other shifting conventions around me. The man might be difficult and complicated, but what he stood for was something I could relate to.

My values had found an anchor. And I knew I would stay with him.

∾

*Salzburg, 1965.*
A MAZE OF NARROW STREETS and squares with baroque residences, palaces and churches, their tall spires and turquoise-green domes dominating the skyline, make up the old town, or Altstadt, wedged between the Salsach River and the steep hill with the great stone medieval fortress – past site of Kokoschka's school – on top. Beyond it: a massive mountain range. We would sit in Café Tomaselli, facing the old market square, near the street of Mozart's birth, chatting over cups of aromatic coffee and Austrian *Kuchen* while we watched the fashionably dressed clientele, some nodding a greeting

in Kraks' direction, come and go, and practised uniformed waiters hurried to serve him, respectfully exchanging some pleasantry with their old client. Other days we might sip our coffee in the elegant Café Bazar overlooking the river from the opposite embankment. Or stop at another of Kraks' old haunts, the Welz Gallery – run by the one-time director of the School of Vision, Friedrich Welz – where he would stand at the small bar with other regular visitors to the gallery, artists, business associates and friends, and drink and talk and keep *au courant* of what was going on in town.

He had been very moody and not made much sense when we met again in Mannheim, across the Rhine River from his home town, Ludwigshafen. He couldn't get on with the painting he had come to do, he said. Why not go to Salzburg? He was working on two other portraits there, of a sausage machine magnate and a gallery director.

We were staying in a studio flat within walking distance from the Altstadt. After selling several drawings to the sausage machine man, mainly nudes for his erotic art collection, Kraks bought paints and materials and started work on the portrait, only soon to fall out with him – the 'butcher', as he referred to him when he was angry – and it came to a halt. He then brought out the other portrait, its thickness and uneven surface testifying to the many coats of paint of the much worked over canvas, in which the urgent figure of Welz – his thick glasses distorting eyes that struggled to see – all but rose out of the oils to meet you. He had worked on the painting from memory and some preliminary sketches – one of which is now in the Rupertinum Museum – on and off over several years, and it was now ready for the final touches in the presence of the subject. He wanted to capture, as he would say, the *smell* of the person. Welz agreed to come for a sitting and Kraks started working himself up, the palpable tension and concentration forbidding any talk or disturbance that might interfere with the various processes and calculations going on in his mind – rather like a musician before a solo performance, or an athlete before the final Olympic race. The day arrived, the portrait and painting materials were all prepared and in place, and Kraks, fully braced, waited. The appointment time came and went – and Welz didn't show up. Kraks remained unusually calm and went to the gallery to arrange another appointment with Welz. Then, as the time drew near, he became increasingly tense and nervous, and one day he warned him, 'If you don't turn up this time, I'll paint you the way you really are!' He – Welz – didn't, and their relations deteriorated. The portrait was never sold – though it stands, to this day, a stirring monument of the old art dealer.

These swings in and out of favour with Welz seemed to go back in time. The previous year, the fastidious art dealer had held a one-man, Kortokraks exhibition in his elite gallery. And around the time when the school's future under Kokoschka seemed uncertain, he had discussed with Kraks the idea of making him head of the painting section. But this, in a background of various other ongoing machinations and power struggles, also fell through.

Kraks ran out of money again and we now lived on a daily diet of plain spaghetti with tomato sauce.

We decided to get married.

We chose our wedding rings in exchange for a sketch Kraks did of the Salsach River with the jeweller's shop in the background. Then, the night before the wedding, Kraks went off on his own to spend the evening at the Goldener Hirsch Restaurant in the Altstadt, on the invitation of a former student of the School of Vision, Maria Gabriella di Savoia – Kokoschka having attracted many young people from various branches of the European aristocracy to his school. Her sister Titi, and Prince Michael of Greece, married to another former student, formed part of the group. Kraks would jokingly boast that he had told one of the young princesses that if she wanted to marry him this would be her last chance. They were all discussing Peyrefitte's recent book, *Les Juifs* – in which the author cites various members of the aristocracy and other prominent groups as having Jewish kinship – and who among them was mentioned in it.

The next morning we arrived at Schloss Mirabell, a bishop's palace with landscaped gardens facing the river. A grand marble staircase flanked with angels reclining and sitting astride the balustrades led the way up to the great marble hall, where we waited our turn in that morning's line-up of couples to go into the elegant registry office. I wore a simple, short, silk dress of pale turquoise splashed with aquamarine, violet blue and lime green flowers, a heavy silver Mexican

*Wedding photo*

necklace, my dark hair piled up on my head, my olive eyes outlined with kohl and a glossy, pale pink lipstick. He wore a black suit, his short hair and beard neatly combed, and looked trim and solemn.

My sister had come to Salzburg to be with us on the day, but my mother hadn't managed to get leave at such short notice from her work in Göttingen.

It was a simple civil ceremony in German, the last that morning. Tristram Cary, in Salzburg for the Summer Festival as the composer of the music for Muriel Sparks' play, was our witness. I discovered he had written the music score for the film of his father's book, *The Horse's Mouth*, about a painter in London, played by Alec Guiness.

'Talking of Alec Guiness, did you ever see the delightful film *The Ladykillers*?' I asked him in conversation while we waited.

'He wrote the music for it,' Kraks answered for him.

Sepp Zenzmeyer – who had taught in the School of Vision's sculpture class headed by Manzù – arrived with his wife Anneliese in their Citroen 2 CV as we were coming out of the palace into the front courtyard. He presented me with a lovely sunflower from his garden in the mountains outside Salzburg, and we all posed with the flower for photographs and celebrated.

∼

FLICKERS OF SUNLIGHT filtered through the leafy canopy of alpine vegetation as I strolled up the mountain, my steps slow and meas-ured, following the broad path. The air was fresh with the delicate scents of the trees and wild herbs.

I had set out after breakfast, that morning, from Sepp and Anneliese's cottage at the foot of these mountains. Kraks and I were
recently back from Linz where he had painted a landscape of the
town: the museum director, Walter Kasten, told him the board was
planning to buy a painting. Kraks knew Kasten since the early fifties
when he had lived in Paris on a German grant to further his painting studies, while Kasten's motley career spanned from a cabaret act
with Klaus and Erica Mann in Berlin in the thirties, to his more
recent work with Munich art dealer, Wolfgang Gurlitt. While Kraks
worked on the painting in the museum's studio flat – a single room
in which we also cooked, ate and slept – I had spent our Linz days
walking in the nearby hills. I would pass the hours looking for four-
leaf clovers on the green slopes overlooking the pretty town with the
Danube River meandering through it – much as it was emerging in
the painting – from early morning till late evening when I returned
to our meal of spaghetti with tomato sauce. And, in the end, the
museum board members chose another painting. Still broke, we
stayed a few days in Vienna at a sculptor friend's spacious studio
covered in marble dust – while I sampled the life of that city, once
a hub of culture and vitality, now turned into a cul-de-sac next to a
closed border. We drank coffee at the Café Hawelka where Vienna's
artists and intelligentsia met and talked, and spent congenial evenings in the company of another of Kortokraks' friends, the sculptor
Alfred Hrdlicka – a forceful man with flashing eyes and muscled
arms that chiselled white marble into powerful, twisted, monumen-
tal human shapes – and his pretty young wife, Barbara.

I had made stimulating, new friends here, people who experienced
life with deep passions and no pretensions, who had something to
say and fashioned it with their hands or with colours. I had seen
the intensity of their work and felt the warmth of their friendship.
And their generosity. Yet life with Kraks was exacting its toll too: my
efforts to meet his never-ending needs, the tightrope I trod trying
to guess and anticipate his next mood, expectation, demand, or face
his impatience and wrath, caused me deep hurt and frustration.
Instead of the mutual sharing and trust I sought in a relationship,
I found that, though our basic views about life seemed in concert,
our mutual understanding on a practical, everyday level was fraught

with problems. Kraks now disappeared every morning to catch the early train to Salzburg, with not a hint of his business or return, and I was trying to accustom myself to his unaccounted coming and going. I felt tossed about, from the weight of his demands to feeling alone, abandoned.

One day I needed to escape and be by myself. I heard there was a lake on top of the mountain and I was curious to find it. I looked forward to the sight of the calm smooth surface of a large mass of cool clear mountain water, slate-blue in my mind's eye, on the summit's green peaceful slopes. I needed to put my thoughts in order, here, where tranquillity reigned. And, as it turned out, the mountain's solitude composed me and made me feel whole again.

Morning was giving way to early afternoon when I finally emerged out of the thick shady vegetation into bright sunshine. The summit's wide-open plateau and the rolling hills beyond spread out before me. The ground here was covered with a thick carpet of vibrant green, and the sky soared pristine blue above. I walked along the flat saddle of the mountain taking in every new angle of the unfolding view and the mountain range beyond, all the while searching for the elusive lake I never found. The landscape was stupendous, though, and I enjoyed the wide panoramic view, the tight springy grass under my feet, the golden sunshine, and my complete solitude.

On my return by late afternoon, Kraks was already back from Salzburg, very anxious to find I was not waiting for him and no one knew where I was …

My unexplained absence obviously didn't elicit the same license as his: my freedom and his freedom were distinct concepts. But my own father's role model had led me not to expect 'fairness' in a relationship. I had already decided love and caring and a mutual sense of each other's worth was more important.

∼

*London, 1966.*

TINY SNORTS, SQUEAKS AND GRUNTS emerged from the cot alongside my hospital bed. Then little sucking noises in between silent intervals. I leaned over for another peep. Skin softer than smoothest velvet, eyes more bewildered than sun sparkling on freshly fallen snow, Rebekah lay in a small bundle next to me, her azure eyes oscillating unfocused over shapes and colours around her, her limbs thrashing about uncertainly. Just the two of us in the room. Mother and baby. We were enveloped in silence, and I felt a deep peace and communion with the small creature which only a few hours ago was still hidden inside me. As though we understood each other, perfectly, without words. A magic moment belonging exclusively to the two of us, each separate, yet bound together in primordial rapport. And then, an irrational anxiety came over me, the fear that some danger could overtake the child. I grieved at the thought of what the infant would suffer in this world, and the whole of her life up to her mortality flashed through my mind's eye ... But now Rebekah was hungry, and I picked her up and lay her little body next to mine on the bed and offered her my breast.

My labour had started two days earlier. At two in the morning to be precise. I had spent the day attending to my usual morning and evening surgeries and home visits of my Islington practice. It had already turned dark when I was doing my last call in a run-down corner of Hackney where I found myself struggling up five flights of stairs with my heavy medical bag to reach the council flat of a Cypriot man with chest problems. When I finally reached home, a pleasant apartment in a large Victorian house in a leafy, twisting lane in north London, the place was dark and empty: Kraks would surely be at the pub – I thought – The Old Gatehouse in Highgate to which Jack Connell had moved from Finch's in Chelsea. I ate and waited for him to come home when the pub closed at eleven. 'Time, gentlemen, please! Last drinks!' Jack would call out good-humouredly in his crisp Irish accent. Kraks would be the last one out, though as likely as not Jack would let him stay on after he had cleared the place and locked up, and they would go on drinking and chatting together, maybe till one or two in the morning. Or, if he was too drunk to face the short walk home, he might stay the night in a place I never saw which they referred to as 'Kelly's room' somewhere inside the pub's large, Tudoresque premises – once the village of Highgate's inn where travellers stopped with their horses and rested overnight on their way to London. That night, when he didn't come home after pub closing time, I went to bed. I was not on emergency call and was looking forward to an uninterrupted night's sleep, unlike the previous night when I had been woken by the telephone at three in the morning and, after manoeuvring myself with difficulty, rolling over my large belly to gather the momentum to get to the phone, heard a male patient's voice at the other end requesting a visit to check his stomach ache.

'How long have you had it?'

'About three or four days.'

'And is it worse tonight?'

'No, not really. It's pretty much the same.'

'Should you not have come to the surgery in the daytime?'

'I'm doing night work, doctor, and I sleep during the day,' he explained ...

I heard Kraks come in around midnight with two or three others and head for the living room next to the bedroom. Kraks had turned the spacious, south-facing living room, with its French doors and windows overlooking a pretty Victorian garden, into his studio – though he had not lifted a brush since our return to London. I could hear them talking and laughing with great abandon. After a while, Kraks came into the bedroom.

'Won't you come and join us?' he asked me excitedly.

'I'm too tired.'

He returned to his friends, while I rolled myself over, pulled the blankets up to my chin and tried vainly to sleep through the noise from the next room. Kraks' friends finally left and he was getting into bed when I suddenly noticed I was wet. My waters had broken. He called the ambulance and we went to University College Hospital.

It had been a long and painful labour. I was tense and exhausted from work: I could not afford to take maternity leave, and had not had a chance to think of my pregnancy or prepare for my labour. Having come to the end of my savings, I had done a number of locums across the city on our arrival in London and finally joined an Islington-Highgate medical practice as a full-time junior partner. I was already pregnant when we travelled from Austria back to England and, once in London, I immediately set to work. At the start of my first locum practice, I would arrive home late at night, after a twelve-hour day of surgeries and home visits, to find the table set and a good meal ready, the bed made and the place tidy, with Kraks, all gentleness and attention, waiting for me ... But this soon changed as he started spending more and more time at The Old Gatehouse. My earnings began to disappear as fast as I received them, as I handed them to Kraks to buy our food but instead they found their way into the pub's till and, on top of that, I began to get bills for his drinking on credit. We returned to our diet of spaghetti and tomato sauce. I also worried that the constant fights and arguments, which soon started again and caused me so much anguish, might affect my pregnancy. Would not the hormones of anxiety and distress which flowed in my blood, making my heart pound so, also have an effect on the small developing creature inside me?

After my prolonged and difficult first stage of labour, contributed to by my wornout state, the second stage had instead been easy. I was feeling strong again and managing well. I worried how Kraks at my side was coping, though. I knew what was going on, but for him all this was new.

'Are you alright?' I asked him between contractions, to the amusement of the staff in the delivery room.

Bert Brandt, who had looked after my pregnancy, was delivering the baby. I knew him from New Zealand where he had been the obstetric registrar in Auckland's National Women's Hospital during my final, hospital training year. Now he was Professor of Obstetrics at University College Hospital.

'Will the baby's head come out with the next contraction?' I asked Bert.

'Yes!' he answered, laughing at the accuracy of my clinical assessment in my reversed role as patient.

'It's a Rebekah!' Kraks said excitedly when she emerged. The name we used for the unborn child from the start of my pregnancy. My mother, who was sitting outside the delivery room, rushed in and kissed the newborn infant barely out of my body, as though claiming her for herself before I had even had a chance to hold her, and left again as furtively and unnoticed – except for me – as she came in ... That aside: pristine new Rebekah, still damp and matted, was placed in my arms against my warm naked body and made

*Newborn Rebekah, London, 1966*

her first attempts to suckle me – that evening after seven, on the seventh day of the seventh month of 1966.

A week later, I carried tiny Rebekah out of our protective environment, through the hospital front entrance and down the steps into this big, turbulent world.

# Family Life

*London, 1968.*

SLEEPING PILLS AND ALCOHOL. A combination doctors warn against, but he ignored such details. His paintings, he kept yelling, were no good to anyone. All his life's work, what he stood for, everything he ever lived for, was useless.

'*You* are in the business of doing something worthwhile for mankind! You *cure* people!'

'*Anyone* can learn to do that. If I wasn't doing it, someone else would take my place. But you're the only person who *paints* the way you do. It'll not make much difference when I die: I'll soon be forgotten. While your paintings will still *move* people, after you're gone!'

But he wasn't listening to my clumsy attempts to explain what I felt about his worth. Just as well, he would probably have declared them banal and boring; sentiments fashioned by the limitations of a mind that was too logical, and that tried to tame and harness intuition. He was reeling around in his studio in a rage, screaming that he was going to set fire to everything he ever made.

It was early November. The night was dark and cold. A thick layer of snow covered the garden. He opened the French doors and started to cart his paintings out. He piled them untidily on top of each other on the wet snow. I went up to him and tried to stop him. Talking was useless. My words did not touch the stony, furious look on his face. I tried to hold him back physically, but in spite of the potent sleeping tablets and his huge intake of whisky, beer and cider – his drinks stepped down in price as his daily cash allowance from me ran out – his strength was undiminished. If anything, it had gathered an unnatural boost and there was no stopping him. He wove his way back and forth, from the studio out into the night and back into the studio again, piling his canvases on the snow under the large holm oak in our suburban back garden. They were all useless,

229

he kept yelling, and he was going to set fire to them. Make a great bonfire. Celebrate Guy Fawkes.

It was well past midnight by the time all the paintings were piled on the snow under the tree. Now he was looking for kerosene and matches, which I had hidden away in anticipation. Halfway up the stairs towards the kitchen, he was suddenly overcome by the combination of drink, sleeping tablets, emotional exhaustion and the late hour, and he collapsed into an unconscious heap. I tried to take him upstairs to bed, but he had crumpled into a dead weight now and was beyond rousing. I left him there, returned to the studio and painstakingly started to bring each painting back inside, leaning it separately against the wall in the hope that it might dry and escape damage, until the whole wall space around the room was lined with the canvases. The night was quiet and still and all the world asleep by the time I got to bed.

The next morning he still lay unrousable halfway up the stairs. I dressed and fed Rebekah and dropped her off at playgroup on my way to my surgery in Islington to see my patients and do the medical calls.

Over the next weeks he avoided the door into his studio. The mere mention of it spread a look of terror across his face, looking like a small child asked to enter a room full of monsters. Finally, after I had tidied the canvases, reassured and coaxed him, one day, with a huge effort, his eyes narrowed with fear, he ventured back into the studio to face his paintings again.

This now was our home, in Muswell Hill, to which we had moved when Rebekah was a few months old. It was the second in a row of pretty, early twentieth-century terraced houses in a quiet street. A red-tiled façade encroaching on the first floor sunroom distinguished it from its neighbours. The back reception room was extended with a glass ceiling and surround into the garden, to make a studio for Kraks.

Kraks would say to friends, 'I've never had it so good!' He appeared very happy.

On my birthday, he gave me a pretty mini-dress: a silky jersey tube with a twirly pattern in various soft shades of pink, blue, grey and bits of red that fitted lithely over my body and ended in a roll neckline. It was a great surprise, and all the more precious since our frugal existence had reduced me to wearing my sister's and friends' discarded clothes.

It was a fetching dress, its 'op' design much more suitable to the world of fashion, I thought, than the world of art. This was London's swinging sixties with Mary Quant, mini-skirts and Twiggy, and the Twist giving way to the Beatles.

I was touched.

'How did you manage to get me such a beautiful present?' I asked him.

'I went to Chelsea ... I sold a couple of lithographs ...' he admitted reluctantly.

When the days were crisp and sunny, we might get up early in the morning, and I would drive him to the Billingsgate fish market, in the city, by the Thames, in time to catch the great bustle and activity when it opened at six. We would watch the fishmongers in the enormous hall unpacking and laying out their sea and freshwater produce – every kind of fish, crustacean, mollusc or anything else that lives in water and is edible – on their stands. After walking around and soaking in the atmosphere, Kraks would choose a crayfish to take home and paint. If it was still fresh when he finished with it, he would cook it for our dinner.

Around this time he also went to the Houses of Parliament to sketch the Labour MP, Sydney Silverman, to work on – back in his studio – some drawings and an oil he was painting of the man. Kraks admired him for his dogged stand against capital punishment, which was then still firmly entrenched in British law: it was Silverman who pressed for the bill that finally led to its abolition. Sadly, he died soon afterwards, and on his way to his memorial service in Colne, in the north, Kraks chatted with Betty Boothroyd, sitting opposite him on the train, also on her way to Silverman's memorial, and who would later become the Speaker of the House.

On the other hand, he was less gracious when he received a telephone call from a woman called Yoko.

'We are doing a film about men's bums. Would you be interested to take part?'

'No. I don't think so. Would you mind telling me who gave you my telephone number?' his inflection sarcastic.

'Our film is a social protest.'

'I have nothing to protest about. I'm quite happy, thanks. Where did you get my number?'

Yoko Ono's film of male bums came out a short time afterwards.

I had cut down my work to one surgery and a few home visits a day to allow me more time with Rebekah, though it halved my income. I saw patients from as far afield as affluent, leafy Highgate in the north, to the crowded City in the south, and from underprivileged Hackney neighbourhoods to more middle-class Camden, east to west. The majority were concentrated in Islington, and I became familiar with the problems and poverty in east London – like the Irish family of eight crowded into a single, windowless bedsit, with an old cooker in the narrow entrance corridor for their kitchen. I came to know the varied ethnic groups in the practice, from the predominantly English who attended the Highgate surgery, to the Greek and Turkish Cypriots, Irish, some West Indians and a sprinkling of Italians and Spanish, in what was then Islington.

It was almost certainly from one of the patients that I caught an unusually severe flu-like illness. I was confined to bed, with every muscle in my body hurting – even breathing was painful and difficult – for a week. But most of all, I was distressed at my inability to look after Rebekah. Kraks disappeared to the local pub, while she was crawling from room to room and I unable to get out of bed to take care of her. As soon as I could stand again, I returned to my full roles at both home and surgery – though my muscles continued to ache, and other symptoms I had never before encountered appeared and started fluctuating over the following years, which I misguidedly ignored to carry on as best I could. It would eventually be diagnosed as M.E.

At home I was sucked into an act of emotional acrobatics as I tried to look after the young growing child and keep the household going under the chaotic circumstances that soon returned. From a gentle, quiet mood, even timid, Kraks would switch to an irritable, angry state, at times reaching implacable fury. Then he would spread tomato ketchup or spaghetti Bolognese across bookshelves, walls and ceiling, break china, or empty his desk contents across the room. Rebekah, when she started walking, would go up to him in the middle of these outbursts and stroke him tenderly, trying to console him and calm him down.

He would sometimes disappear for days on end. Haunted by his moments of despair, such as the night he tried to make a bonfire of his paintings, I would worry about his state of mind. But then he would turn up again after an apparently enjoyable binge of drink and freedom with his friends at the French Pub in Soho or Finch's in Chelsea to finish up dead to the world on their living-room sofas or floors. And when I was due at the surgery and he didn't show up to look after the child, I would take her along and leave her with the friendly receptionist while I attended to the patients.

Rebekah was a vivacious child, petite and strong and very pretty with eyes as blue as a lake and her head a mass of golden curls. I would hold her on my lap, the two of us alone in the house, and every time the little creature tilted her face towards me, I hoped she would not understand the wet cheeks and lifeless eyes that met her gaze, or recognise the pain I couldn't hide from her.

My own wish to paint had long fallen by the wayside. Some day, I told myself, he would sell his paintings and I would have an easier time and a chance for my creativity. In the meantime, my life was ruled by the unsparing demands at work and at home, while he instead had no set pattern to his days. And yet, I soon began to rec-ognise a certain recurring rhythm in his life too. Long periods of apparent inactivity in which his days were divided between the pub and his bed, followed by a time of intense activity behind closed doors in his studio, from early morning till late afternoon, with his music and painting. And it began to dawn on me that during his weeks and months of what seemed slothful drinking, socialising and sleeping, he was incubating his next painting. 'Painting is like having a baby,' he would say. And when his 'labour' started, he underwent a transformation. His relaxed, good-humoured manner turned into a tense, brittle state in which any small, apparently innocent remark might enrage him, and he became strictly unapproachable as he dis-appeared into his studio, turned on his music and set to work. First, the delicate harmonious rhythms of Vivaldi might be heard through his closed door; then, it might go on to Bach, eventually progressing to Mozart or maybe a different mood with Sidney Bechet or some old blues. By the time it reached Bartók several hours later, the energy and concentration contained inside the studio spilt over with his powerful hi-fi system at full volume, and I could somehow sense his painting going full force, reaching a high, exalted state.

He sent for his old paintings from Germany. Out of the crates emerged powerful portraits of the French composer Darius Milhaud, the blind Canadian writer Sidney Bigman with his guide dog, interwoven images of events in pre-war Germany, a skinned horse's head he once saw in the south of Italy, a scene at the races, the assassination of Imre Nagy, a portrait of his American girlfriend in earlier years, the black children in Little Rock spat on by their white schoolmates on their first day at a non-segregated school, and many others. Including one, too, of our mutual friend Gustav Regler.

In Kraks' studio in Muswell Hill, the floor was slowly collecting a mountain of screwed-up paper, drawings, empty whisky bottles, cigarette butts, sketches, letters, photographs, a Guinness bottle with its label upside down, clothing, anything and everything that found its way there, until one had to wade knee high through it. Obstacles would stay put, even though walking around them was more complicated than shifting them. And I would try to work out the sense of all that chaos. Might orderliness be, after all, a sign of a boring bourgeois mind? Yet it is present everywhere in nature too, I thought to myself: a bird builds its nest in an orderly pattern and keeps it tidy for its offspring. I found trying to live in all that confusion disturbing. I kept the living room simply and minimally furnished – just a sofa and chairs, a low table, a bookshelf and one or two paintings on the plain white wall – so I might find one uncluttered area to relax in after work. But he turned it into his workshop when he could no longer move in the studio for the accumulated litter, and he used the bathroom and kitchen for his etching.

Yet when he drew and painted he was highly organised. Then, nothing was accidental. Each line traced by the pencil, its position, length, thickness, its relation to the others on the sheet of paper, each smudge the crayon scratched, or his thumb or hand smeared, every brushstroke of oil or tempera he spread on his canvas was carefully calculated with supreme concentration.

'Painting is pure mathematics,' he would say. 'If I want to make this greener,' pointing to a spot in the oil painting, 'I have to add more red there.'

In the course of the next few years, large retrospective exhibitions of his work were mounted in museums in Germany and Austria. In Trier, where the museum director, Dr Schweicher, was a long-time admirer of his work, it was his second show. Then in the north German town of Bremen, the museum's director and art historian, Dr Busch, opened his show with a long scholarly speech about his painting: '... The salt of irony which continually doubts itself, the world, and their vis-à-vis, ensures that the beauty of the craftsmanship, the eminent painterly skill, is never reduced to becoming its own object ...' Another exhibition of his work was hung in the halls of the Secession in Vienna, organised by Georg Eisler and opened by Austria's then chancellor.

*Helmut Kohl and his wife at the Kortokraks exhibition, Trier Museum, 1968*

Pat, my friend from medical school, was staying with us during a stopover in London.

'Why don't you go back to anaesthesia?' she suggested when she saw that, though it was hard work, I was not deriving much satisfaction from my city-based general practice. Unlike the locum country practice I had done in north Auckland before leaving New

*Kortokraks with the Austrian Chancellor, Josef Klaus, Secession Exhibition, Vienna, 1968*

Zealand, where I applied much of what I had learned all those years at medical school and the hospital, here in London it was more like a sorting office for signing certificates, handing out prescriptions and streaming patients to the appropriate hospital departments from one's desk. I missed a more hands-on application of my skills and a closer involvement with patients.

'I need to stay at home at least part of the day to be with Rebekah, and I won't find a part-time position in anaesthesia without my Fellowship.'

'Yes, you will,' Pat replied. 'Some hospitals offer a part-time trainee scheme for women. I've seen them advertised now and then.'

I decided to follow Pat's advice. After three years in the practice, I now resigned and would go back to anaesthesia. In the meantime, my father invited us to Mexico. He would meet us in New York – he wrote – where he had some business to attend to, and we would stay a few days with Elly and Izzy before flying on to Mexico together.

It would be Kraks' first trip to the United States and he felt nervous about it: McCarthyism was still fresh in people's minds. He went to the American Embassy to apply for a visa and, after filling in the form, was summoned to an interview with a senior official.

'You wrote on your form that you once belonged to the Communist Party?'

'Yes. I joined at the end of the war. I was eighteen then. I had lived through the whole Nazi experience and I thought that was the right thing to do at the time. I soon found out my mistake.'

'Don't worry. You're not alone. The cream of the British intelligentsia are up there,' the official said motioning towards the files stacked up to the ceiling on the shelves behind him.

He authorised his visa.

The immigration official at the airport in New York stared into his passport.

'Hey! He's a C!' he called out to his colleague in great excitement.

'It's okay,' the other said, calming him down. And, after scrutinising the stamp in his passport, he turned to Kraks, 'Would you write down a contact address, please?'

Kraks gave him the only one he had on him, which my father

had written him in a letter. It was that of another painter he knew, Vlady Serge, whom he suggested he meet while we were in New York. Kraks had not realised that he was the son of Victor Serge, once a Bolshevik and friend of Trotsky.

My father was waiting for us at the airport. That evening, Izzy invited us all to dinner at the Biltmore Hotel in Manhattan. There we all were, my father, my cousins Izzy and Elly, Kraks and myself – having left Rebekah with a babysitter in the hotel room – sitting around the table with its crisp white tablecloth and sparkling glass and silverware, feasting on an epicurean meal and drinking the best of wines, a quiet hum of voices in the background as the other diners chattered quietly with each other in the large, elegant dining room.

'I'll never forget the times when I was a boy in the Lower East Side,' Izzy started reminiscing, 'and I helped my father with the salt herrings. My arms were covered with eczema from digging into the salt barrels up to my armpits. They were red and sore and my skin kept peeling off in layers. I became a socialist then, and promised myself to put things right one day.' He was getting more and more worked up about the injustice and social ills of the world until, his face reddened with anger, he started pounding the table with his fist, yelling loudly, 'Stalin was right! Stalin was right!'

Kraks, flabbergasted, started looking around the dining room expecting the CIA to pounce on us any moment, while Elly, who was apparently used to these outbursts, was trying to change the subject. 'Let's talk about sex,' she was saying in her rich descant voice, her eyes sparkling good-humouredly, while the other diners continued with their meals and chatter unconcerned.

*Mexico, 1969.*
MY FATHER HAD SWITCHED his old Buick for a Datsun – 'Datsun of a bitch,' he would say in his New York accent with a grin. Joey, my half-brother, was now at university and had discarded the American name his parents had given him for José, and his Euro-American upbringing for a fierce desire to be Mexican: a tall, pale-skinned, ginger-haired Mexican with thick glasses. He would eventually also frustrate his father's wishes that he should take over the fisheries and seafood business, and instead play his guitar and make music.

Susana had become a friendly, bubbly teenager with meltingly blue eyes and reddish blond hair, full of life and dreams.

Kraks immediately found himself in his element in this country of brilliant colours, vitality, music, tequila and pulque. He explored the city and its cantinas where he drank pulque with the local macho population and would describe with fascination their sanitation – from that of the more up-market cantinas in which a continuous stream of running water under the bar counter would wash away the drinkers' waste of which they relieved themselves without interrupting their drinking, to the more modest ones where the water was occasionally flushed through manually and the combined smell of pulque (which according to Kraks tasted of warm beer and vomit) and urine made a heady mix. As he had a flair for languages and already spoke fluently its close relatives, French and Italian, he was soon speaking Spanish. We met the Pecanins sisters who ran an art gallery in the Zona Rosa – an area with a concentration of boutiques, galleries and Mexican craft and jewellery shops, where artists and intellectuals got together at its many cafés and restaurants. The three Pecanins sisters liked his work and made a date for an exhibition.

Rebekah enjoyed the spacious house, three dogs and large garden in Las Lomas. She too, soon learned Spanish – while I made a point of speaking English with her, so she would not forget it – and started going to a kindergarten close by and making friends with other children of her age. She was forever climbing up everything, and Lidia and Amparito, who enjoyed the lively, pretty child, were always calling out in alarm, their hands up in the air, '*Te vas a caer! Te vas a caer!*'

José had outgrown his shock of our first meeting six years earlier, and introduced me affectionately to all his friends as his sister. He took me and Kraks one day to the square in Tlatelolco known as the Plaza de las Tres Culturas for the presence in its centre of the remains of an Aztec pyramid and overlooked by both an early Spanish colonial church and a modern, twentieth-century apartment block. He wanted to show us where the students' massacre had taken place the previous year, in 1968, shortly before the Olympics. He had taken part in what had started as a peaceful demonstration held in protest against the police presence on their campus.

'We were a large crowd of students, some seven or eight thousand, packed into this square. We stood listening quietly to one of our companions who was talking from a balcony in that apartment block over there. He was a wise character; he believed in settling things by peaceful means. Suddenly a helicopter started hovering above us, and the whole square lit up with a green flare. It was weird. Then another flare, and a third ... Next thing we saw several agents in civilian clothes dragging our friend back. He called out to us to keep calm, not to react. It was only a provocation, he said. Those were his last words before they threw him to the ground. Then all hell broke out as we were shot at from all directions. We were surrounded by soldiers and police on the roofs of the buildings, on the ground, everywhere. The soldiers were young natives from the provinces, poor, illiterate souls who were given a uniform and a rifle and led to believe we're evil and it's a great act of patriotism to shoot us. The police were in civilian clothes; they had a white glove on their left hand to recognise each other and a pistol in the other. Everybody ran blindly in every direction – the place was covered with the dead and dying, and you had to pick your way between them.

'I managed to get out of the square and ran up that street over there,' he pointed. 'I couldn't feel my legs or the ground under my feet. I collided with an Indian girl clutching her shawl as though she had a baby in it. I almost fell over her and had my arms around her to steady myself when I suddenly felt her slipping from my hold to the ground. I realised she'd been hit, but there was nothing I could do ... I came across two friends who pulled me into a church where a Mass was going on. Some police came in looking for students, and three humble Indian girls came and sat next to us as though we were together. The police stared at us suspiciously, but saw the girls with us and went away. Eventually, we left through a back door and persuaded someone in a car to drive us out of the area. He said he'd been driving round and round and couldn't get out, what with the chaos and the traffic blocked everywhere. He finally managed to find a way out and led us to safety. I later heard that many students had run into the nearby apartment blocks to hide, and the police had combed through them, forced the doors open and shot everybody indiscriminately. The official number of dead was thirty or forty, but

*Prague Spring*

it seems closer to some 750. The morgues were full, and a great many students were never seen again by their parents …'

The previous year, Kraks had done a collage painting, on which he had stuck among other things one of Rebekah's dolls, in a fit of

Un Lecho de Rosas, *1968*

outrage at the Russian invasion of Prague in the spring of 1968. This time – on our return to London – he worked on the scene José described. He named it *Un Lecho de Rosas* in reference to Cuauhté-moc's famous reply to one of his men who urged him to disclose the location of their gold to the Spanish conquistadors while they were burning his feet with fire. 'Am I, perchance, lying in a bed of roses?'

My father arranged for Kraks, Rebekah and I to be driven to Carmen. On our way, we stopped in Veracruz for a meal of the local fish, *huachinango*, cooked in a rich tomato and chilli sauce in the local tradition, and later that day in Catemaco, a tropical town on the edge of the jungle, for the night.

Carmen, in the tropical humid heat, was a haze of tequila, raw oysters, and shrimp and chilli *cebiches* served in tall glasses in every corner of

*Kortokraks, Ciudad del Carmen, 1969*

the town – for Kraks. As we sat around the large dining table in my father's house, eating once more Viviana's tasty meals, Kraks could hardly lift the fork to his mouth for the tequila inside him – yet he was turning out drawings of the tropical landscape, one after another, as though possessed. We drove to Merida and the ancient Maya sites: Chichen Itza deluged with butterflies, and the Dance of the Rain next to the pyramids interrupted by a sudden drenching downpour. Rebekah feasting on the mangoes from the tree in the garden in Carmen and, one evening, squatting on the veranda's tiled floor, holding forward with her little hands the rag frog she slept with every night, telling it, 'Look! Anover fwoggy!' as she pointed it at a small green croaking frog, the first time she had seen a real one ... Kraks soon came down

*In Ciudad del Carmen, 1969*

with a virulent amoebiasis, whether from the raw oysters or the iguana and crocodile *tamales* wrapped in banana leaves he had eaten in a small joint on the edge of town.

Back in Mexico City, long enthusiastic write-ups in the leading Mexican papers, and the offer of another exhibition in Antonio Souza's elite gallery, followed Kraks' exhibition at the Pecanins Gallery.

On the other hand, relations between Kraks and my father had become increasingly strained. My father was trying hard to be helpful but in return Kraks called him a 'grocer' and suggested he stick to his own merchandise. My father was deeply hurt: he had always wanted to take a greater part in the creative and intellectual world, while Kraks was characteristically 'biting the hand that fed him'. For here in Mexico we were my father's guests. Unknown to me at the time, he took Kraks aside and suggested he go to San Miguel de Allende – a town popular with foreign artists – all expenses paid, to distance him from me. But Kraks declined.

∽

IT WAS PITCH BLACK and raining heavily as we stepped off the old bus straight into a deep puddle of mud and water in the dirt road we couldn't see. The bus took off again leaving us standing there – just the three of us with our overnight bag – vainly poring into the wet dense darkness wondering which way to start walking. After a moment or two, a faint mumble of voices and some moving flickering lights appeared only a few steps from us in what seemed to be a shelter in the corner of the road. The barely discernible forms of a small group could now be made out huddling from the rain. One of the lights began to separate from the rest and move towards us, bobbing up and down in the thick darkness. When it was right up close, the whites of the eyes of the cigarette bearer came into view as he peered at us curiously and moved as though to wrap his poncho closer to his body from the rain while holding something half hidden under it, like a machete.

'Where d'you want to go?' he finally asked us.

'Rincón de Guayabitos …'

'That's way down that road. It's a good walk from here.'

'Is there anywhere round here where we can stay overnight?' I became emboldened enough to ask.

'There's a place over there,' he said, the whites of his eyes motioning towards the dark side road. 'I think they have rooms.'

He led the way along the muddy edge of the dirt road for a short distance until we reached a house, the only one around as far as I could make out. We thanked him, and he silently merged into the night again. We were relieved when someone answered the door and let us in, into some light and out of the rain.

'The bus driver let us out at the crossroads here. We've been travelling since early morning, heading for Rincón de Guayabitos. Would you have a room for us tonight?' I asked the woman of the house.

'Yes. I keep a couple of guest rooms. I'll get one ready for you right away.'

We had come from Guadalajara where Kraks was having a large exhibition of his paintings in its civic hall, La Casa de la Cultura. It had been opened by John Shepherd, the director of Mexico City's Anglo-Mexican Institute. In his speech, he had referred to Kortokraks' '... extraordinary capacity to tackle colour ... his profound humanity ... the (evident) horror that he feels towards any manifestation of totalitarian regimes ...', and Kraks had been fêted by the local dignitaries.

I had also renewed contact with old friends from my childhood who now lived in Guadalajara. I had asked them where, on the Pacific coast, we might spend a few days away from the noise and bustle of the city.

'We've heard Rincón de Guayabitos is a lovely spot,' they told me. 'It lies north of Puerto Vallarta: a small fishing town which became famous with the filming of *The Night of the Iguana*. Richard Burton and Elizabeth Taylor built themselves a house there and it's become quite trendy. But they say that further up the coast is just as beautiful and virtually unknown.'

That turned out to be no exaggeration.

We woke up the next day to a beautiful morning. The sun was shining in a blue sky and the colours of the tropical landscape were bright and clear as we walked down that same road, which had seemed so sinister in the dark the night before, to Rincón de Guayabitos. We finally reached a small collection of primitive dwellings with a single store along a dirt path next to a wide sandy beach with a few straw huts on it. We were assured this was Guayabitos, and the beach huts the only 'rooms' for rent. After spending two nights in one of them – the fine white sand finding its way into our food, clothes, bags and everything, and the beach crabs persistent in entering our abode uninvited – we decided to walk further up the beach to the next village, barely visible from Guayabitos, at a distant point in the glistening white strip of sand which stretched northwards as far as eye could see. In La Peñita de Jaltemba there was a motel by the beach with an abandoned, rarely-used air about it, where we rented a large, basic, but comfortable room facing, along with all the other rooms, onto a square sandy courtyard that led onto the beach. We were the only guests in the motel. In fact, the only strangers in the whole village.

I would pass the hours of day building sandcastles with Rebekah on the wide empty beach. Then up we'd get and run into the shallow edge of the blue Pacific, its transparent waters splashing and cooling, shimmering, teeming with sea life, waves swaying and dancing, gathering force and bulk and rolling over, only to withdraw again leaving a trail of foam and peace.

Kraks used to go out in the early morning to meet the fishermen coming back with their catch, and help them bring it in and sort out the fish. In return, they would give him one or two which he first drew and then cooked over a fire in the motel courtyard for our dinner. He asked them to bring him a crayfish, when they found one, for him to draw. He drank tequila and ate hot, pickled *jalapeño* chillies – they brought back to life his taste buds dulled by alcohol and smoking, he said. He bought the chillies by the kilo from the general store in La Peñita's main street: a mud street lined with adobe houses and, in the morning, two or three vegetable and meat stands, the freshly butchered, dismemebered animals still bloody, their eyes staring from their severed heads.

It was well past lunchtime, one day, when he still hadn't made an appearance since he had gone off early that morning. I finally decided to go and look for him with Rebekah. I combed through the few dirt streets and paths of the village and along the shore asking everybody I came across if they had seen him, but they all shook their heads – until I suddenly came upon him. He was lying stretched out, motionless, on the ground, under the fierce, scorching sun, on the edge of a chalky-white dirt road by the beach, a few steps from the café where the local men were drinking. I squatted down next to him and looked for signs of injury or accident, but there were none. Then I checked for his wallet … but it too was intact, in his pocket. So I set about trying to rouse him, but he was dead to the world.

Then the fishermen came out of the café.

'Throw a bucket of water over him!' they shouted.

'No! He'd be furious when he came to!'

After watching my vain attempts to get a response from him, they disappeared and soon returned again with a jug of cold water, which they emptied over his face with the desired effect.

When he managed to collect his thoughts and talk again, he explained how the fishermen had brought him a crayfish and he had bought them a bottle of tequila and stayed behind to have a few drinks with them ...

It was July, 1969. Neil Armstrong was taking his first steps on the moon and everybody everywhere was glued to the television to witness that momentous event in man's history. We, on the other hand, were spending our days in La Peñita de Jaltemba, where there was not a single radio, let alone television, and the nearest telephone was in another town several miles up the coast. In derision of that event and to demonstrate his indifference to it – as he thought man should turn his attention and capital towards more humane causes than space technology – he made a poster, after Goya's *Giant Sitting on Planet Earth*, of himself shitting on the moon.

∾

*London, 1970.*

I WAS PREGNANT on our return to London. Rebekah being almost four now, and more independent, I had decided I could manage a new baby at home, and it would be company for her.

I scanned the medical journals and came across a part-time, anaesthetic trainee post in a hospital within easy travelling distance. I made further enquiries and was given an appointment to see the chief consultant anaesthetist. Stewart Burns also worked and taught at the larger, university-affiliated, St Thomas' Hospital. At the end of the brief interview, he said, 'When can you start?'

The Royal Northern Hospital had an operating suite of four theatres and separate dental and ophthalmic theatres. I soon regained the skill and rhythm of giving anaesthetics and, at Dr Burns' urging, prepared for the Diploma exam, which I sat and passed.

'Now you'd better start working towards your Fellowship,' he said. Dr Burns was a kind person. He was also full of original ideas and his interests spread far and wide – in addition to his medical degrees and work, he had an MA in history and made a special study of the ancient Greeks. I found his teaching in the operating room a pleasure and appreciated his encouragement, but the Fellowship examinations were notoriously difficult. Their pass rate was less than twenty-five per cent, of which most of the candidates had already had numerous attempts – and I baulked at the idea.

'I'll arrange for you to go to the Day Release Course for the Primary Fellowship,' the first of the two-part examination, 'at St Thomas' Hospital. You'll get a day's leave from work every week, on full pay, so you can attend it,' he told me. It was a three to four months' course.

The idea of having an opportunity of studying in depth the subjects, which not only lay at the heart of anaesthesia, but were in their own right of considerable interest to me, was very appealing. Exams apart, I would enjoy listening to the lectures and going back to academic learning. So I said yes, I would like to attend the course.

Rebekah was now going to playgroup so I found it easier to spend time at work. Indeed, it was a relief to get away from the chaos at home and bury myself in the quiet surroundings of the operating theatre. A place where reason – the kind I more readily understood – reigned. I was glad now not to have followed my original inclination to specialise in psychiatry. Trying to deal with the complications at home was already enough, and it was satisfying to concentrate instead on an unconscious patient. To take care of their breathing and circulation and attend to the machines that supplied the anaesthetic and life-maintaining gases: an exacting mental exercise that required my undivided attention and in which emotions played no part. And here, the focus was on mending defects and disorders, relieving pain, smoothing cares ...

After work, Kraks and I had a steady stream of social engagements including private views at West End galleries and cultural events organised by the German Embassy and Austrian Institute. We attended Brigitte Lohmeyer's, the then German cultural attachée, lively parties at her Belgravia apartment to which she invited all the

English and German artistic intelligentsia of the time in London. We also entertained at home. New friends and acquaintances we made in the course of these events came to dinner, and gallery dealers too, who would look at Kraks' work and say, yes, they could see it was good but it didn't fit their market – and urge, 'Have you tried the Marlborough?' And so he continued to pass his days drinking and socialising at the local Muswell Hill pub.

Those dark oppressive days in that house in Muswell Hill ... Wading through the confusion as through treacle; struggling to patch things up, like trying to fill a bottomless bucket. Then the whispers one night, in the next room, with his friend from the north, the letters, his emerging duplicity, the love in Japan he was planning to join, his growing callous impatience and indifference. My long drives in the middle of the night to escape the havoc and acrimony, as I wandered with my tear-soaked face through London's dark deserted streets glistening with rain, all quiet and still at that hour, trying to collect my thoughts and composure.

He had started bringing home pretty girls from the pub to draw them. He liked painting beautiful women, and I noticed he would briefly fall in love with them. I had learned to accept this as part of his nature, the painter in him, and I found many of the sketches and portraits he turned out, stunning. But I felt hurt and rejected when there were signs of more serious involvement. I had liked the young Japanese woman: she was back in Japan with her English husband by the time I realised their attachment. From me, a European Jewess, consequential and logical, to a dreamy, Zenic Japanese ... Had I then, after all, failed him? As painful as it was, my disillusion became a further challenge to my learning to live with him, at least while we continued together. The one thing I still hoped for in our relation, whether it survived or not, was that it should be honest – for pretence would make a mockery of the bond that I believed had grown between us.

'I can understand it if you fall in love with someone else,' I managed to tell him one evening. 'It is, after all, your capacity to feel things strongly which I admire in you and love you for, and which is part of you as a painter. If you don't want to say anything, that's all right. I respect your silence. The only thing I ask of you is please not to tell me lies.'

He answered with a lie.

And that was the most painful part of all. But I kept silent after that.

It was then too that I began to recognise his complex, multifaceted personality, the contradictory personae that emerged in different company, and I became thoroughly confused as to whom I had married. And when I once asked him, in some despair, 'Who are you?' he waved in the direction of one of his paintings on the wall as though saying, haven't you yet understood?

I also began to realise that my idea to take care of his needs until the day he was in a position to take care of mine, had instead encouraged his untempered abuse, giving way to resentment, anger, maybe even guilt. I could see the appeal of disposing of that image of himself and starting afresh with a new love, untainted by the ugly and painful memories that now existed between us. And this house and household, which he was once proud of and enjoyed, must by now have reeked to him of failure and what he perceived as his own uselessness. I saw that my loyalty and devotion had misfired, that our 'bond' was in essence a mirage – and this new insight would be the beginning of a gradual change inside me. But for the present I thought of Rebekah's and the unborn child's need of a father. Of what I had missed, and didn't wish on my children. To carry on for the meantime, I would gather renewed strength from the worth of his paintings which reflected that part of the man I admired and which embodied my thoughts and values – those the small *Madonna and Child* painting, in the Vatican art collection, had made me realise – beyond his rather less appealing conduct and behaviour.

And so I continued to take care of my work at the hospital, his needs, Rebekah and the household, and to see with him our friends and contacts and attend the various functions he considered necessary, as though nothing had changed. Yet things could go very sour, like the cocktail evening in the Austrian Embassy cut short when he stormed out after I had good-humouredly taken the last glass of whisky on the tray for myself – he had already drunk a large number of them and was beginning to get obstreperous. He flew down the embassy's marble staircase in a rage, rushed home and, his fury unabated, pinned me on the kitchen floor and emptied the rubbish bin over me. Coffee grounds and spaghetti Bolognese spread across my white lacy dress on top of my big pregnant belly, my face smudged black from tears and kohl, like a rag doll. Or a clown.

At the hospital, in addition to my anaesthetic sessions in the operating theatres, I had been asked to draw up the rotas and organise the training of the junior doctors starting in anaesthesia.

The St Thomas' Hospital's Day Release Course for the Primary Fellowship exam covered in exacting and minute detail the subjects of physiology, pharmacology and medical physics. I was learning, down to molecular level, for instance: oxygen's pathway, and every variable which might affect its concentration along its way, from the air, or the oxygen cylinders we used, through the respiratory passages to the lung's microscopic air sacs, its diffusion into the adjoining capillaries' bloodstream, and its transport through the circulation and final delivery to the different tissues, with an emphasis on the life-maintaining organs: heart, liver, kidneys and brain.

As anaesthetists, we were in charge of this whole sequence of events, from anaesthetic machine to the patient's cells – to maintain life. And my responsibility for this oxygen cascade gave me a particular satisfaction: it being the essential requisite for life and the very thing that was cut off by Zyklon B. We were required to be equally knowledgeable and aware of the path of the anaesthetic gases and drugs that kept the patient unconscious, relaxed and pain-free to allow surgical access. Essential to our task was to watch and support respiration, circulation, kidney function and temperature; replace lost blood, fluid, or any other constituent; note the interaction of all drugs we used in relation to each other and to the patient's concurrent pathologies; scrupulously check and monitor our machines and equipment.

Our prime responsibility was to maintain life, whether during surgery in the operating theatre, or in the intensive care unit where the failing life-supporting systems are a result of injury, disease or extensive surgery on ill patients. Our expertise included the relief of pain as an integral part of this whole scheme.

My application to this, my chosen specialty, was all the more resolved and fulfilling in view of the long shadow cast by the Shoah on my life – its focus on the preservation of life and alleviation of pain being that other ideology's very antithesis.

I was at home talking on the telephone one evening, when I felt my waters break. I finished the conversation, hung up, picked up the phone again and called the ambulance. Kraks was cooking some steaks for our dinner.

'I won't be having that,' I told him. 'The baby is on its way.'

I went into Rebekah's room and squatted down to her level taking her little hands in mine.

'I'm going into hospital,' I told her, a big smile on my face. 'Your little brother or sister in my tummy is ready to come out tonight.'

'Does that mean,' Rebekah asked, breathless with excitement, 'that I'll have someone to play with tomorrow?'

The contractions were getting very strong already in the ambulance and, by the time we reached University College Hospital, there was hardly time for the routine preparations before I was wheeled into the delivery room and I was pushing out the baby. A sturdy baby girl with large, dark blue, almond eyes and a head of black hair. I felt so exhilarated at the sight of her, and so strong still, after the short, sharp labour, that I thought I could go through the whole thing over again right there and then.

We called her Anna.

The date of my Primary Fellowship exams was approaching. I would sit bent over stacks of lecture notes and open textbooks spread across the table in front of me, cradling Anna – who wouldn't sleep – on my lap, deep into the night. As was my custom now every day, back home from the hospital, I climbed the stairs to the small attic room – a quiet refuge where I could study, away from the rest of the household – having put Rebekah to bed after the dinner Kraks had prepared for us. He liked cooking. It's like painting, he used to say. In the one you mix paints and colours and spread them on canvas, in the other, spices and herbs that you throw into the cooking pot. But he was too macho for the washing-up or housework. For the present, though, I had decided my exams took priority over dishes – their success would, after all, better arm me for Kraks' demands and the girls' needs. So the pile of dirty dishes got bigger every day, until there were no clean ones left. And then, for the first time since we had been together, Kraks washed the dishes

On the day of the exams, I sat among the other candidates in the long, single rows, not a stray whisper in the large hall, the rustle of turning pages the only intrusion into the silence. I wrote without a break, enjoying the questions and organising them into careful logically structured answers. After the three written exams, the orals began. The last day of orals arrived and I waited with the others to hear the names called out of those who had been successful. As the list reached the surnames beginning with F, I suddenly heard my name. I stood there stunned, blankly repeating, 'Well, well, well ...'

Back at the hospital, Dr Burns walked into the anaesthetic room as I prepared to wheel a patient I had just anaesthetised into the operating theatre.

'I got my Primary!' I told him jubilantly.

'Yes, I know!' he had a big, happy grin in his face. 'Congratulations!' And I was delighted he should see his help and encouragement had not been in vain. Having reached this far, I would now start preparing for the second part, the Final Fellowship, to be taken at the end of four years' full-time anaesthetic experience across all specialties.

Photo: Derry Moore

Meanwhile, Kraks was deteriorating. I had slowly and painfully come to realise my impotence in the face of the human storm that was gathering before me, and stopped trying to prevent him from slipping further into whatever abyss he was surely heading for.

My instinct told me that he would have to crash before he could start picking himself up again and straighten out.

He went off to Germany. He didn't say where, what for, or when he would be back. Then the frantic phone calls started: he'd been on a non-stop drinking binge I was told ... a terrible state ... some kind of breakdown ... wild outburst ... the police ... hospital ... very confused ... kept asking for me ... very frightened ... At the hospital, he was strapped down and heavily sedated until the doctors decided he was over the worst, and then they sent him back to London with a chaperone. As I waited for him at Victoria Station, I caught sight of him stepping off the train, a frail, remote, shrunken figure, hesitant and confused, his eyes recoiling in fear from the bustle around him, his walk slow and uncertain in the midst of the other passengers briskly rushing past him. A squat, beefy German with a Red Cross band around his arm was by his side. On catching sight of me, Kraks' step suddenly quickened towards me, as though to his only refuge. The Red Cross man handed him over and disappeared.

As he recovered, he would timorously refer to some fearful threats he had received when he returned to Ludwigshafen to finish the German magnate's portrait he had been working on when we first met. It appeared he had been careless with his boast that he was forging the map of Auschwitz into the portrait's abstract background – for, he said, the man's firm had made use of the camp's slave labour – and he had been called to his office, ordered to destroy the painting and given a severe warning. He thought someone had slipped LSD in his drink ...

As soon as he was better he returned to Germany. Again, he didn't say what for, but once there he had another crisis. This time he saw Wulf Nachtwey, a friend from their Paris days together in the fifties, when Kraks would comb through that capital's museums and art galleries while Wulf was doing his postgraduate medical work in the Saltpêtrière and a third friend who lived with them, Elmar Tophoven, whose subject was the theatre, lectured at the Sorbonne. Now Wulf was head physician in a large Hamburg hospital.

'You're in a very bad way,' he told him outright. 'If you don't give up drinking, you'll be dead within one year.'

Only Wulf could have persuaded him to do something about it.

I had never dared even suggest it for I knew my word would have made him only more defiant. Others, less wary, had provoked his fury. 'I like drinking, why should I give it up?' or, more sarcastically, 'Are you telling me to stop painting?'

On his return from Germany, he asked me to find a way of drying him out.

Dr Max Glatt came to see him a week later. I had discovered he was the leading expert on alcoholism and ran his own rehabilitation programme. He liked to see his prospective patients in their own home to better assess their situation. Once Dr Glatt satisfied himself that the decision was Kraks', not mine, he agreed to take him on.

The appointed day arrived. Kraks had his last drink like a man about to face his execution, walked out of the house, and climbed into the car next to me. I drove him across London to Southall. On reaching St Bernard's Hospital he quietly walked into the ward, suitcase in hand, ready for his three months' stay.

I used to visit him after work. The first days he was deeply sedated and oblivious of his surroundings; he could barely be roused enough to swallow the food he was fed or be taken to the toilet by the other, already partly rehabilitated patients. Then he started coming to, back into a dry world, having been through the physical ordeal of the abrupt end to his drinking in an insensible state. Now he was timid and docile, even submissive. Max Glatt's ward was largely run by the patients as a self-sufficient and serving community, in which they experienced the satisfaction of helping others similarly afflicted and learned to live responsibly.

'I'm in charge of cleaning the bathrooms and lavatories,' he would tell me proudly. 'I put up a notice on the wall to tell everyone to leave the place clean after they've used it. They make such a mess!'

Each patient also had the task of reflecting and writing down an account of their life and to present it for discussion before the others, patients and staff, towards the end of their stay.

At the end of the three months, he was ready to leave hospital and face the world again in his new sober state.

I was lying in bed, wide awake, in the dark. I had been studying till late from my lecture notes, various textbooks and a stack of anaesthetic journals with the latest research findings, in preparation for my Final Fellowship exams. At the hospital, I had been given the additional task now of looking after a new, four-bed intensive care unit, on top of the daily anaesthetics, organising the rotas and teaching of the juniors. And at home, Anna and Rebekah to look after. I needed some rest before next day's work – it was already three in the morning – but Kraks was wandering around the house with all the lights on and I was trying to make out his whereabouts and activities, as well as listening for any sounds from the children's room in case they were disturbed. He was now fairly quiet, I could hear him in the living room, as though absorbed in something. Now and then: the sound of steps, and things being moved about. Earlier, he had been clattering about with the dishes in the kitchen, and then on the phone making various calls, some of which seemed to be overseas. I dared not fall asleep while he was so active, for he kept talking about the earth being on a direct collision course with the sun, and I worried about what his alarm at such a cataclysmic event might prompt him to do. I got up now and went into the living room. He had arranged all kinds of – to me – unrelated objects on the dining table with the colourful Mexican Tree of Life candelabrum in the middle, and a vivid new sketch next to it of St Anthony's apocalyptic apparition in his temptation. He was standing near the table staring at it with a withdrawn expression.

'Don't move anything on the table,' he told me quietly, pointing out that each object had a special significance and its position on the table was important.

'That's fine – I won't touch any of it,' I assured him. 'It's very late. Aren't you tired? It's time for bed ...'

He had been in this state for some time now. He couldn't wind down and went without sleep, night and day. I had been remembering how, before his admission to St Bernard's Hospital, his heavy drinking bouts would coincide with states of feverish activity when his talking couldn't keep up with his racing thoughts and his painting absorbed him with an unusual intensity. It had now dawned on me that his drinking must have been, at least in part, to subdue himself. Now, with nothing to curb it, his manic state was exposed. And he wove his world of terror and doom into his paintings.

I myself was getting hardly any sleep and reaching a state of exhaustion but, having come this far, I continued to prepare for my Final Fellowship. It would pave the way to a consultant post and fewer working sessions a week to give me more time with the girls. I had always wanted to be close to them, give them my love and attention and share their growth and development, and I had been grieving for the time and peace which our circumstances had stolen from both them and myself.

I came out of the examination hall into Queen Square in the bright sunshine. I had tried to fend off the sudden lapses into unconsciousness that kept stealing up on me during the paper. I was also resisting other tricks – my words kept switching places – from my tired brain. I had hoped for a good rest on my last night before the exams. Instead, Kraks had kept me up almost the whole night with exhausting emotional scenes – as though testing my determination, looking for my breaking point. Now it suddenly came to me that in my marked sleep-deprived confusion I may have written 'coronary' when I meant 'carotid' in my answer on the regulation of the cerebral circulation. I puzzled over what could lie behind such a crass slip: 'Carotid' and 'coronary' have similar sounds, but one supplies the brain and the other the heart! A Freudian might suggest that I was seeking sustenance for my starving heart, instead of the brain. Though the examiner would see it in a different light.

Kraks was finally seen by a psychiatrist at the Maudsley Hospital who put him on lithium, which controlled his excessive activity and fearsome thoughts without interfering with his nature or his painting.

Rebekah was at school and Anna by now going to playgroup.

My mother had left Göttingen and come to London to help look after the girls. This allowed me to work full-time and round off my experience at the hospital. To my surprise, I was presented a prize two years running for having 'contributed over and above my duties to the department', when I had thought I was simply doing my job. And next time I sat my Final Fellowship exams (there was a question in the medical paper on alcoholism, and I doubt the examiner came across a more informed answer than mine) I passed and became a Fellow.

And when Kraks wasn't painting or wandering the streets of Muswell Hill, he wrote letters riddled with nuances, hidden sarcasm, double and triple meanings. Many – often too caustic to publish, though some did reach the printed page – were directed at *The Times*, objecting to a statement by some journalist on a recent world event, or to an art critic's pronouncements on an artist's, for instance, 'anti-art'. He would vigorously resist the general tendency to fall in line with fashion without questioning it, the comfort of conformism: the ultimate expression of which he had observed at first hand as a child in fascist Germany. He would fight with every fibre of his being against the prevalent trend to worship the meaningless artifice and negation of life, that nihilistic element which displaced the awe of creation. The astronomical sums of money spent on gimmicky 'art' angered and frustrated him, and he made his feelings known in abrasive letters that infuriated the Establishment. He acted as the *enfant terrible* of the German art scene, but his outrageous behaviour was in deadly earnest, not another gimmick. And his offence found its mark, and those who decided 'What Is Art' turned against him.

On the other hand, following an exhibition in a Manchester gallery, the English art critic, Merete Bates, wrote in the *Guardian*: '… you feel most for the big news protests. They are crude, exacerbated, even horrible, but for once use photographs and newsprint for their real, not decorative, impact … They make you feel the hope and horror behind the symbols, not deaden them into meaningless pretty patterns which is the dangerous tendency developing among other, unmentioned contemporary artists.'

And when Margaret Fisher, a Viennese art dealer who had emigrated to London, was preparing an exhibition of his work in her Hampstead home, the English art historian and critic Norbert Lynton wrote him the following letter:

*Dear Kortokraks,*
*It's not every day one is asked to write about work one doesn't like. You say … I 'acknowledge it exists but don't like it' … The invitation feels*

*like a challenge. Mrs F. said you should get a friend to write something, and I'm not even your friend. I saw some of your work a few years ago and met you momentarily then. Add two letters, a telegram, some photos received, some not, and that would seem to be the sum total of our acquaintanceship. But I do know you exist, and your art too, and don't mind saying so.*

*Don't I like it? Are you sure you want me to? You could easily please us. In your drawings you come closer to it – not just because they are often of women, and sketchy (we love sketchy things; we call them sincere) – but because of your gift of catching not likeness (how can we tell?) but life. You are unmistakenly good at drawing places too, but to me that matters less because Salzburg or the Place de la Concorde can look after themselves, whereas ... well, making marks on paper so that a person appears before us, not an emblem, but a convincing pattern of humanity, is a sort of miracle ...*

*Your painted portraits have some of the same qualities but, paradoxically, some of these persons strike me as less present, as though the act of painting enshrines them and lifts them out of time and out of space. Is it the colour that does it or the brush marks? Some of your sitters are perceived beyond the paint. My instinct tells me that this indicates a valuing of the subject, a feeling of awe even.*

*'I am not nice,' you say in your letter. A lot of your thematic paintings are not nice either. Do we want to be told about concentration camps and more recent samples of official brutality? We don't, and if we must be, let it be through films and television melodramas with soft-eyed girls and heroic young men so we can personalize both the suffering and them that cause it; it's the ordinariness of human savagery we can't bear to think of, and that is what your painted images insist on grinding into our heads, refusing us all the comforts we still feel we deserve from 'culture'.*

*The other thing you have said insistently is that you don't know anything about art, and don't know how to paint, just keep doing it and often at unhelpful moments like when you can't afford to buy paints. I don't think that is your problem at all, and neither do you: it's your boast. The fact is you know perfectly well how to paint, not because you are a natural painter (whatever that is) but because you know a lot about art. Your association with Kokoschka shows in your work ...*

*but I can also see a hungry absorption of much else, from Daumier and Van Gogh, to cubism and Chagall, Picasso, pop and Breugel. You know art, you know painting, you know what you are painting about. I bet you could charm the birds out of the trees if you wanted to. Perhaps you would prefer that. It's just that there are other things to be done first. You are right.*

*Yours,*
*Norbert Lynton*

Among the people milling around, chattering and looking at his paintings in his crowded private view at Margaret Fisher's, was a quiet, elderly man of European origin who spent the whole two hours quietly peering at the work with great concentration, at the end of which he walked across to Kortokraks and congratulated him. That was Ernst Gombrich.

In the summer of 1976, Kortokraks received a letter from Salzburg inviting him to reopen and head the School of Vision, in homage to Kokoschka on his ninetieth birthday. Here at last, I thought happily, came the recognition he deserved. But I came down with a jolt when he turned down the invitation with an angry reply, referring to various past wrongdoings.

His letters. At the launch of one of his exhibitions, an eminent, local German politician in charge of fine arts had opened his speech, otherwise laudatory of his oeuvre, with, 'I have a chest full of unopened letters from Kortokraks ...' He could not face their caustic contents.

This time round, I set about carefully re-examining our life together so far.

For ten years now I had devoted myself to him and what he stood for. I had learnt to accept he would never trim or moderate his expansive lifestyle, contain his emotions and human entanglements, or be tamed into any kind of domestic life. I had withstood his attacks when he chose to wound and diminish me, while I stretched myself to meet his needs and demands, at times plunging me into such despair that I coldly reflected that my intended fate in

France would have been a merciful relief from all the pain that followed in my life. I had, even so, held on to my belief of better days ahead when his worth would be recognised, his anger diffused and his gentleness resurrected. If instead he turned down this opportunity now, I saw no way out. I added to the equation the likelihood, should he accept the position, of his casting me aside, just when he was beginning to succeed, for some attractive, well-connected, young student. The Summer School setting seemed ideal for such liaisons. Yet, after careful thought, I found that risk infinitely preferable to the certainty of the otherwise unrelenting misery of our life together.

'If you turn down the offer from Salzburg,' I told him firmly and unequivocally, 'I shall divorce you.' And he understood that I meant it.

He wrote to certain people who were in a position to help reverse his refusal. And it worked.

*Salzburg, 1976.*

THAT SUMMER would be the first of five in which he ran the painting section of the International Summer Academy in the old fortress which crowned the hill overlooking Salzburg's Altstadt.

And here, he was in charge. His look firm and focused, his walk assured, purposeful. He held the esteem and respect of vast numbers of students, his assistants, fellow teachers, the Salzburg citizens and functionaries. He threw himself wholeheartedly into his teaching and political manoeuvring on behalf of the school.

We attended the lavish Festival Openings in which leading singers, musicians, actors, playwrights, politicians and Salzburg's society and aristocracy gathered in baroque civic halls overlooking torch-lit processions and dances in the facing square, he in his black tails, I in my long, slim-fitting, red paisley dress, or a crossover silver top and black satin skirt. And we feasted at banquets in outlying castles surrounded by vast landscaped gardens on the edge of lakes and forests. Next to me, in one of these banquets, Karajan's opera stage designer, Günther Schneider Siemssen, was asking me about my husband's art, and I – searching my limited German vocabulary – replying, 'He doesn't think that this,' pointing at my fork, 'is art,' at which he laughed in agreement. Our entrance to a ball in Klessheim Castle frozen in a photograph, I, in my décolleté dress of a heavy, creamy-white satin with a twirling black ribbon appliqué, being welcomed by the Greek millionaire and Mercedes representative who is looking past us at Hjalmar Schacht, once Hitler's enigmatic finance minister, coming up behind us. Complimentary Festival tickets: Vivaldi rippling across the Mozarteum's concert chamber, right up to the sparkling crystal chandeliers; Karajan's *Salome* watched from our box; the medieval Italian opera, *Il Sant'Alessio*, with white angels and black demons flying across the stage to the baroque strings, while the leading lady searches for her lost bridegroom who all the while is living as a monk in the cellar under her home: the irony of our failure to recognise what we look for, even as we stare at it, because it appears in an unexpected guise ...

Rebekah and Anna enjoyed Sepp and Anncliese's household, where they played with their children, dogs, cats and rabbits, surrounded by countryside and high mountains. And the *Leber Knödel* soup and rich *Salzburger Nockerl* dessert served in the restaurants.

We drove across the border into Germany to visit Frau Reck in Poing, near the great lake, Chiemsee. Her fourteenth-century farmhouse, with its original library and private chapel, was once part of the local knight's castle. Kraks had stayed here with his first wife and small son Daniel when he was assisting Kokoschka at his school. He had used the large attic room for his studio. The same room in which Frau Reck's husband, Fritz Reck-Malleczewen – whose *A Diary of a Man in Despair* describes his personal experience of the rise of Hitler and destruction of his country, before he was murdered for his candour – had hidden a friend with his Jewish girlfriend during the war.

Yet, back in London, to his seemingly useless days in the suburbia of Muswell Hill, the chaos in his studio and maybe also his mind in the face of his life here, Kraks' coldness and anger returned. And along with them, our fraught times. When he was feeling lost and forgotten, he would on the one hand want me to be permanently there for him, as though he owned me absolutely, yet at the same time reject me as too intrusive a presence. There was an echo of that possessiveness in my relationship with my mother. Further back in time, I had been pulled hither and thither between my mother and father as they competed for me, and she had won hands down, leaving me blocked and confused.

Kraks once gave my mother a present of one of the many lithographs he had made of me over the years, with the dedicatory words above his signature: 'Here's part of your daughter back. *Meilleurs voeux.*'

෴

I LEANED IN MY THEATRE CLOTHES over the tiny naked creature spread out frog-like on the trolley and wrapped in wadding to keep her warm. I was manoeuvring a fine plastic tube into a vein in the back of her hand in preparation for her anaesthetic, while the surgeons and nurses were getting the theatre ready to correct her congenital defect. The premature infant weighed little more than one kilogram. Here everything was modified and scaled down to fit the special needs of the small patients, and every observation and manipulation carried out with unwavering attention and precision. For the babies, anaesthetic drugs were diluted up to ten or twenty times in the carefully labelled syringes, the volatile gas dial on the machine not even turned but barely lifted, blood loss measured and replaced gram for gram, the nature of every heartbeat listened to with the stethoscope taped on the tiny chest and plugged to one ear, the exact feel of the pulse felt by the finger lightly resting on the small armpit, and the muscle tone continually tested with a gentle arm flexion. Children were referred from across the British Isles, Europe, North Africa and as far as Asia to this, Great Ormond Street Hospital for Sick Children, where I was working as part of my senior registrar rotation – the last step before qualifying for a consultant post. Here I was faced with every kind of specialised children's anaesthesia. On my nights on call, I slept in the hospital to cover the demanding emergencies and look after the cardiac and respiratory intensive care wards. I would find myself, in the early hours of the morning, putting together complicated DIY arrangements of bits of tubing and connections for a baby's specialised management. In this renowned hospital, inadequate funds did not prevent providing what was needed, from such improvised systems to the most advanced and sophisticated care and treatment, those days.

I had started my senior registrar training at the London Hospital: a large teaching hospital, in London's East End, renamed the Royal London by the Queen to mark its 250th anniversary in 1990. I was one of a team of senior registrars whose duties included the supervising and administering of anaesthetics in every specialty, in its long, granite-floored suite of eight surgical theatres. We also prepared and coordinated the daily rotas, looked after the twelve-bed intensive therapy unit (ITU), and assisted with the teaching and training of the junior anaesthetic staff. I was chosen to do a six-month stretch of research, which had just been introduced as part of the rotation, joining Tim Savege, the academic unit's acting director, and Michel Dubois, a senior lecturer, in their work with the Cerebral Function Monitor. This device had been designed to process the brain's electrical waves into a slow, compressed signal, to make for easier interpretation. We were investigating its use to demonstrate depth of anaesthesia with different agents. I enjoyed working with Tim and Michel, as well as the monitor's designer, Douglas Maynard. I was set the task of reviewing the literature on the body's response to stress, as both pain and physical injury, whether from surgery or disease, are powerful stressors. I found that this global response, with all the intricate interplay across the nervous, hormonal, immune and metabolic systems, is set in motion by physical as much as emotional stress factors. The pain from a crushing injury goes through the same pathway and leads to the same ill effects as that from a lost love. Yet we come to the aid of the physical, and tend to ignore the emotional … I presented my review to the department and a group of visiting anaesthetists, and prepared a protocol for our next study. I also organised journal club meetings at each other's homes, providing an opportunity for academic updating, lively discussion and socialising between junior and senior staff.

The patients in the ITU, whether following open heart procedures, or critically ill or injured, were also under our care. Inevitably the fight was sometimes lost, and a Spanish cleaner with whom I exchanged the occasional greeting in Spanish, would say to me, 'I can't understand the English! In Spain, when somebody dies, we cry. Here all they want is a "cuppa tea"!'

After my months in research, I was delighted to see the first publication with my name on it in an anaesthetic journal, and it was soon to be followed by others. Tim Savege initiated me into the academic world by getting me to present a paper on our work at the next Anaesthetic Research Society meeting in Bristol. I was the first speaker in that day's programme and, miscalculating the length of the drive from London, I got there five minutes before I was due to stand before the whole congregation of professors and other academics from all over Great Britain. After a somewhat flustered chairman managed to hook the microphone onto the opening of my blue silk shirt near my bosom, to the audience's subdued amusement, I delivered my paper unaided by notes as demanded. I enjoyed projecting and pointing to the slides with their beautifully consistent, changing patterns of brain electrical activity as anaesthesia deepened with increasing doses of the anaesthetic. I managed to survive the learned audience's inquisitorial questioning which traditionally follows each paper, and Tim Savege, who was there for background support, nodded his approval in my direction from his seat in the audience – to my considerable reassurance – when I finished.

Although the work was demanding I found it satisfying, and I found myself for the first time since my marriage almost grateful for its long hours, which kept me from home. The girls were both at school now, and although I would have much preferred to have been there for them when they came home, I didn't miss the complications with Kraks. Up until that time, home, Kraks and the children had always been foremost in my mind, yet now I found myself separating home and work as though leading two separate lives. Except on one occasion, when there had been another of those terrible night scenes at home when he would pick a fight and keep it up until there was little left of the night for sleeping. That morning in the hospital, while we were sitting down to a cup of coffee at the end of the ITU ward round, I suddenly burst into a fit of uncontrollable crying, hiding myself in embarrassment. Like the time in Mexico when my books fell down as I was getting off the school bus – except this time there had not even been a trigger.

I was giving an anaesthetic to a small child in the ENT theatre at Great Ormond Street Hospital when a nurse came in and said there was an outside phone call for me.

'Would you take a message, please? I can't take it right now.'

She came back, 'It's Dr Savege from the London Hopsital. He asked if you would please phone him back when you're free.'

Michel Dubois' job was being advertised, he told me. Would I be interested in it?

'I haven't finished my rotation yet.'

'You've done most of it. We can probably work something out.'

So I sent in my application and, on the appointed day, after a series of searching questions from the appointment's board – composed of the dean, our newly appointed Professor Payne, Tim Savege and others – facing me across the large polished table in the boardroom at the London Hospital Medical College, I was appointed senior lecturer in anaesthesia. What had started years back at the Royal Northern Hospital as friendly encouragement from Dr Burns had ended up in an academic career.

∾

AND AS KRAKS STARTED DISTANCING me from his life in Salzburg too, I would leave him there with his school, his students, his outings and social engagements, his manoeuvrings, his flirtations and romantic involvements, and I would take off with the girls, drive to Venice, get a ferry to Greece and visit the islands. Sitting together over an evening meal on the terrace of a taverna watching the sun's huge orange globe slowly sink into the darkening sea; the heavy fragrance of jasmine on the veranda where we slept facing a mountain with a solitary white monastery; the dazzling white beaches and crystalline sea; the day we wandered about the Acropolis in Athens. The magical double image of Venice lit up at night reflected on the still waters of the canal as we sailed into it.

A dream kept recurring over the years. Though the landscape, events and images were different every time, the theme was the same. I would be travelling south along the eastern coastline of some country, the surroundings gentle and appealing and the water stretched out smooth and limpid, while all the while I was trying to remember my way to a particular place somewhere along there, where I had once been and now almost forgotten, the beauty and tranquillity of which I wanted to recapture. In my dream I never quite got there, but the search and anticipation were delightful in themselves. Around this time, quite a different version appeared to me one night. This time I was travelling north along a western coastline. The sea to my left was becoming more restless and threatening every moment until the waves, by now gigantic, were advancing over the shoreline, the water murky and littered with rubbish. As it threatened to engulf me, I ran into a telephone booth which I found in my path and with great difficulty managed to close its door against the rising water, but its force had become so great by now that the glass panel started cracking from floor to ceiling …

I was sitting at the table having breakfast one morning in our house in Muswell Hill, while Kraks stood by the kitchen bench, twisting words and meanings, intent on hurting and insulting me. I was trying to ignore him and continue with my breakfast – but he wouldn't stop and I suddenly had enough. I was hit by the idea of giving him a taste of his own behaviour to shut him up. I looked around the table and saw the marmalade jar. I lifted it in the air and smashed it onto the kitchen floor, enjoying the lovely crashing sound of the glass against the tiles. The sugar in a dispensable jam-jar followed. The Welsh quarry tiles of varying shades from red to brown which covered our new kitchen floor were now overlaid with a sticky mixture of jam, sugar and broken glass, to which I added some cups and plates – which were anyhow already chipped – while taking care not to disturb the beautiful ceramic teapot: a present from my cousin Elly in New York, handmade by her daughter, Judy. Kraks just stood there, frozen, absolutely amazed, jolted into silence at last. It had worked.

But this latest strategy soon backfired. A neighbour called round a few days later, looked at me strangely and, seeing I was my usual old self, told me Kraks was going around saying that I was out of control and out of my mind. I began to hear the same from others who became concerned on my behalf.

'You really should take care. He sounds very convincing, and somebody who doesn't know you might believe him. He could do you some real harm,' my cousin Peter, who was visiting us, warned me.

Around this time, Dr C-B at the Maudsley Hospital asked if I would agree to be seen jointly with him: Dr C-B was concerned about a new development. He was visibly confused when I gave my version of our problems, and I began to realise he had formed a picture of Kraks as the responsible husband, father and provider of the family who was having to deal with a mad uncontrollable wife. Faced with our persistently contradictory statements, and in his desire to be 'loyal' to his patient, C-B determined to believe him rather than me, with the consequence that Kraks now basked in this authority-backed, new image of himself, giving him a sense of right-eousness and vindication on top of his unchanged behaviour. The psychiatrist, instead of helping his patient to face his problems, was sanctioning his avoidance tactics – which eventually wore off for Kraks was too intelligent to continue believing in his own charade.

Meanwhile, Kraks would suddenly disappear and not return for weeks. Once he went away the day after his son Daniel arrived from Germany, after he had agreed with Jutta, his ex-wife, that he should stay with us while she went on holiday – and he did not return during the rest of Daniel's stay. The boy was miserable and lonely spending the days all alone in the house – as I couldn't take time off from the hospital at such sudden notice, and the girls were at school. Another time I found Kraks gone when I returned from work. There was a ticket on the table from a pawnshop, where he had exchanged the few items of jewellery a cousin had given me from our dispersed family, in order to buy his fare. I eventually pieced together that he was seeing a new girlfriend in Salzburg, one of his young students.

I went to see John Steiner, my old friend from New Zealand. He had become prominent in the field of psychoanalysis, and I asked his advice. He suggested Kraks and I see one of his colleagues in the Tavistock Clinic who dealt with marital problems.

Here, I was told that I was responsible for everything negative in my life. My moves when I was a child, my parents' break up, had happened because I had willed it that way. I had married Kraks because he was like my father and I wished to be unhappy: the painter in him had nothing to do with it.

'You mean, a mountaineer who wants to climb Everest does so for the pain and discomfort? The exhilarating panorama, his intimacy with the mountain, the excitement of coming to grips with it, none of these play a part? And if he falls down a crevasse, it's never from freak weather conditions, but because he wishes to die?'

'Yes,' said Dr L.

And about my problems with Kraks: 'You want him not to succeed. You want him to remain dependant on you. To maintain your power over him.'

'Why then did I give him a clear ultimatum that if he refused to head the School of Vision in Salzburg I would divorce him? And then have such a happy time when he was teaching so brilliantly, and at last in charge?'

Dr L. had suddenly gone deaf.

On the other hand, everything good that happened was because we were attending him. One day I mentioned happily that I had just been informed I had been granted a Merit Award at work.

'Ah! That's because you come to see me!' he said, without realising that my professor had recommended me for the award and started the process long before I had even heard of him.

The result of all this was that Kraks could behave as he liked with impunity.

'You *want* me to behave like this. Dr L. says so,' he would say smugly.

And I saw what a destructive tool psychiatry could be when it relied on dogmatic misinterpretation.

I remember his attempt at an oil portrait of me.

I sat in the diffuse, grey, English daylight facing him and his easel on which rested the painting he was working at, amid all the clutter in the glass extension of his Muswell Hill studio. Tight and nervous, he moved from paint to canvas. His face tensed, his eyes now screwed up, now arched widely as he also opened his mouth as

FAMILY LIFE

though trying to imbibe what he wanted to capture in the painting.
He leaned across to his palette – a broken piece of glass encrusted
with a thick, uneven spread of paints in various stages of mixing –
and then turned again to face the painting, his body, arm and brush
all one, as though driven by an independent energy, as he daubed
some freshly constituted hue here, scratched another there, rubbed
that area with his thumb or the side of his fist, now stood back to
peer at it through half-closed eyes, a sudden movement to add what
he saw missing in that corner, and then he turned to look at me
again, as though *I* wasn't there, rather a projected stead, *his* vision of
me, in which he was totally immersed.

Over the years, he had turned out sketches, drawings, etchings
and lithographs, one after another, of my head and body, and caught
in them every nuance that he saw flitting through me. But this had
been his first attempt to translate his knowledge of me into a carefully calculated spread and mix of oil pigments since the portrait he
had painted of me, when we first met, in his Chelsea attic studio. On
*that* one, he had worked intensively over a matter of weeks. I had
seen layer after layer disappear under new paint, pointing out in the
end that there were several astonishing portraits buried under the
final one ('It's part of the process,' he had replied unconcerned) of a
well defined, young woman with a dark soft open look.

*This* painting was different. A woman with a contorted face, which
he was struggling with, or maybe against. And in the image that was
evolving, I began to perceive all I had experienced in my life with
him in the intervening years – between those two portraits – that
he had so coldly disregarded in our everyday life, as though facing
a canvas now with a brush in his hand and tubes of paint by his side
had suddenly shed his callous stance. I had then understood that he
*knew* what I felt, and he could *paint* it – even if he didn't act on it
in our relationship – as though only in painting could he express it.

He had continued to work on the portrait over several months,
until he finally gave up. He never finished it. For, he would say, the
face is the whole person, everything experienced, all one is, it can
all be seen there. And the difficulty of painting our life together –
which he was looking at every time he peered into my face – may
have proved in the end too great.

And as I watched his all-consuming preoccupation with his métier, I had also made more sense of his reluctance to share anything of himself, and his abhorrence of dialogue or discussion. He seemed to be guarding jealously his all-involving communion with the world, as he absorbed, digested, and worked it into colours and brushstrokes: any exchange or 'togetherness' must have been a distraction, an interference. All his observation, insight and intelligence seemed to be channelled through the brush onto the canvas, making all that which he did not, or could not, express in his everyday human contact, emerge instead in his finished work. There, perhaps, lay the answer … And, if his raison d'être was putting paint on canvas or smudges on paper, would not any other commitment – such as human loyalty – become an irrelevance? And would not his wife be reduced, in the final analysis, to another means to those, his, ends? Was that, then, what he meant every time he had screamed at me angrily, 'You're not fit to be a painter's wife!'?

I was beginning to break away. Sometimes I went to Regent's Park. One of the junior anaesthetists training in my hospital had mentioned he liked going there with his books when he was tired of studying indoors. I had first really noticed him one day when, lost in conversation, talking animatedly to someone sitting next to me in the coffee room, I glanced up and caught him looking at me from across the other side of the table. His black eyes soft and shining, his dark hair falling about untidily. And he had quickly withdrawn his gaze. I had seen him stealing the odd glance at me before, but the unguarded depth of his look this time stirred me, and I began to be more aware of him. When we worked together, he would stand behind me, very close, almost touching but not quite. I realised it one day, when I fell over him as I stepped back. After that, I knew he was there. And it felt as though our minds were one, with no need to talk, or touch, or even look at each other. And here, at Regent's Park, I felt close to him.

I imagined him sitting carelessly on the grass, the sun glinting on his raven hair, his books spread before him. Maybe his girlfriend would be there with him also, the two laughing and carefree. Today I started walking along the paths; now I was on the grass. The elder trees where I entered the park were laden with clusters of tiny white flowers and I inhaled their heavy pungent male scent. Other trees scattered in the park were tall and spreading, their angular branches splaying their lacy green load. By now, the sun had come down very low and its light cut across the park at a shallow almost horizontal slant, lengthening shadows and bathing everything in a soft honeyed radiance. Distant voices floated across disjointedly from young men playing with a ball. From further still, the faint sound of traffic. But here, where I was, there were only the trees, the grass, the silence and myself. I sat on the grass and closed my eyes, the better to sense the light warm breeze. It blew softly on my cheeks, my forehead. It brushed against my neck and my bare arms. And my tension suddenly lifted away and calm took its place. My intense longing for him had given way to an overwhelming sensation of his closeness. He was in the warm caress of the sinking sun, in the breeze blowing on my face, in the air I breathed in and out. And an exquisite peace descended on me …

Whatever small, subliminal signs might have passed between us during our work, they were left unspoken and unexpressed.

'I shall miss you,' he had said, as we sat facing each other somewhat stiffly at a safe distance, the one and only time we ever spoke about any of this, when I was about to leave that hospital. And I had hung on these words, savoured them, wrapped them up and placed them in a secret corner of my being. But I said nothing and he dared venture further: 'Yes,' and, carefully emphasising each word, 'I shall miss you very much.' And the world had suddenly stood still.

On my last day, we had come across each other in the unit's sideroom. I felt taut, like the string of a bow, while outwardly I carried on with our normal conversation. Then I had noticed the ashtray. It was empty when we walked in. By the time he left, it was filled to the brim with cigarette butts. Some fourteen or fifteen of them. In the space of a few minutes. They had all been smoked right to the end and tightly squashed. That was the last we saw of each other.

I rose from the grass and started walking again. Dusk was settling in now.

When I arrived home, Kraks looked at me pointedly.

'Someone called, but when I answered the phone they hung up.'

We had now lived in the Muswell Hill house for fourteen years. The longest I had ever lived in any one place before that was two years, and often less. But the house was not right any more. Kraks had outgrown the studio and spread his work into the remaining rooms. He used the living room to frame his pictures and the bathroom and kitchen for his etching. Moreover, the long hours I spent in heavy traffic every day to and from the hospital, I could spend with the girls instead.

And things could no longer go on as they were. Our common ground was not enough in the face of our differences. My need to be consequential, while he lived in the present with no thought of its aftermath. I tried to be consistent, he – on the contrary – was proud to be perpetually changing his mind. 'Proves I've got one,' he would say defiantly. In his dimension, only his painting mattered and the rest paled into insignificance. His was a lonely preoccupation; I had wanted to be at his side, to assist him, but maybe that had been my mistake: nobody could enter his world, by its very nature. I had seen his soft blue eyes, child-like and gentle, in an instant turn cold and callous, or twist into a defiant stare full of mistrust. And I had felt my impotence. Our different bearings had made our daily communication a hit-and-miss, mostly miss, operation. I could no longer deal with his pull-me-push-me act. And what is more, for some time now I sensed I had been switched to the 'enemy' camp of his sharply divided world.

He had referred sometimes to the dilemma of art's worth against the humane. If one had a Rembrandt canvas and a man were dying of cold, should one sacrifice the canvas to wrap the man in it? Of course one should, he said. But he did not practise it.

One of the many variables in all this was our life in suburbia. He was wasting away in that environment. A bigger studio where he could paint and teach, even start a school here too, nearer the heart of London and the art world, might restore his self-worth and help him come out of this impasse …

Islington, which I knew well from my general practice days, seemed right. There was a lively mixture of different races and nationalities, old markets and leafy squares, it was on the edge of the City, near the West End, and ten minutes' drive from the London

Hospital. Parts of it were becoming rather fashionable, yet a large house here at this time was the price of a one-roomed apartment in Chelsea and just within my reach. I would look for a place with the space for a large studio where he could work and teach and exhibit his work. If this failed, we would go our separate ways.

It would be the fifth and last summer of Kraks' teaching in Salzburg. The school's director was being replaced and it was taking a new direction.

We were staying back with the Zenzmayers at the foot of the mountains outside Salzburg. Rebekah and Anna were happy in their country surroundings and in the company of Sepp and Anneliese's children and all their animals, and for the first time in my fifteen years of marriage, I decided to take a weekend off on my own without explanation. I set the alarm for six in the morning, and woke up exactly at six to find the alarm clock had been switched off. Kraks, sleeping next to me, had been trying to dissuade me from going. I set off on the long drive. I had arranged to meet Mauro, whom I hadn't seen or heard from in many years. He had responded full of delight and charm to a scribbled postcard I had sent him when I passed through Rome the previous summer with the girls on our way back from Greece to London. And we agreed to meet in Venice, halfway between Salzburg and Rome. The day was hot and sunny, and arriving in the outskirts of Venice with time getting short – there had been an interminable queue at the border with a line of trucks waiting in the overwhelming midday heat, and I still had to leave the car in the multi-storey car park outside the city and take the vaporetto to the centre – I got a puncture. This calmed me down as I reflected, whatever happens, there is always a possibility of worse to come. Then I tried to put on some make-up, and the eye pencil smudged impossibly in the heat.

He was standing in Piazza San Marco, at four o'clock as agreed, in his jeans, and little changed over the years. I picked him out from the large crowd of people and pigeons milling around in the square. He too recognised me instantly. We left behind the fashionable sidewalk cafés in the piazza and walked around in the small back streets looking for a simple one where we could sit and talk. I showed him my hands: they were black from changing the tyre and I wanted to wash them.

'*Ma sono belle le mani sporche!*' he said, and we laughed. Eighteen years were suddenly obliterated, and a delightful weekend spread before us. My first: after fifteen faithful years of marriage on my part, and any number of infidelities from Kraks' side.

I was easing myself out – giving only the slimmest of chances, now, to the possible rescue of our marriage in a new, more appropriate home in London.

Back in London, the girls and I were sleeping together on the top floor, when I heard a lot of loud knocking. It was our first night in our new house and the front door didn't have a bell. Kraks was not back yet from his teaching, and I had packed everything in our Muswell Hill house and organised the move. I had managed to secure this house after taking a large bridging loan – though I am no gambler by nature, in this instance I put all my stakes in this plan: we would either end up in this large, Islington, four-storey Regency house, with two enormous open floors as studios for Kraks, or in a bedsit. It had worked, though I wasn't sure yet how we would pay off the mortgage. I looked at my watch. It was five o'clock. The knocking went on, so I went down the two long flights of stairs to open the door. A uniformed man jerked forward his identification card.

'CID.' he said. Still half asleep, but waking up rapidly now, I tried to think what I had done to alert the CID.

'A man was shot dead in his car on the other side of the park, in Colebrook Row, about an hour ago. We are checking every house to see if anyone heard or saw anything. Do you remember anything?'

'No … I've been fast asleep.'

'Did you hear any shooting?'

'No,' I said stupefied. 'What happened?'

'He came out of a club, and he was found dead in his car a short while ago.'

'Oh!'

'If you come across any information please let us know.'

He thanked me and left.

I returned upstairs and walked across the chaos of our partly

unpacked household on the top landing and in our room, where
Anna and Rebekah were still asleep, and looked out of the window
onto the Victorian park below, with its oval rosebeds and tall linden
trees, which separates Duncan Terrace from Colebrook Row. In the
faint, grey, predawn light, the park was crawling with uniformed
policemen combing every corner, checking under bushes, around
trees and along the ground. It seemed a weird spectacle to welcome
us into our new home.

# A School in Italy

*Italy, on the road to Tuscania, 1981.*

DRIVING IN THE DARK, I was following the country road twisting this way and that, denser shapes by the side of the road now and then emerging in the beams of the car's headlights. Bushes and trees, I imagined. Then all dark again. Since leaving the *Firenze-Roma* motorway at Orvieto, I had driven through the odd cluster of houses or maybe towns. One of these, Montefiascone, was by the lake according to the map. I caught the occasional glimpse of a sheer drop into black nothingness – might that be the lake? – as I drove through the town's winding and confusing streets. Another stretch of unseen countryside and we reached Viterbo. The road here suddenly widened and a row of trees towered above us like twisted giants against a tall medieval wall: a spectral scene in the dim lights of the town. Then back again on the dark country road.

Anna was fast asleep by my side. Rebekah had chosen to stay in London.

After maybe another half hour, we finally entered the town of Tuscania. I drove through the first gate into the walled historic centre, and – out of the darkness – a rare magical scene suddenly appeared before me. The soft, flat, ochre façades, arched stone doorways and tall shuttered windows that lined the ancient cobbled streets were awash in a suffusion of pink gold from the glowing brass lanterns dotted all over the town.

'Look, Anna! Wake up! We're here!'

I turned left into the short Via del Gallo, then right again, and stopped. We were right next to La Casa del Prete. We had arrived. As I stepped out of the car and stretched my legs, the silence of the town zoomed in my ears. Above soared a starry clear sky, inky black. The night air was fresh. Anna was standing next to me, still sleepy, and we went through the doorway into a short passageway that opened into an inner courtyard.

'Kraks,' I called out quietly, hoping to rouse him without disturbing anyone else.

I could not make out the layout of the building and gave up trying to find him. Back in the passageway inside the entrance, I found a side door that led into what seemed to be a room. I now noticed a pile of mattresses in the passageway, presumably for the students we were expecting. I moved two mattresses across the floor, unloaded the car and we went to sleep.

We woke in the morning in a large empty room. The walls were freshly whitewashed and a window looked out onto the narrow cobbled street outside. I dressed and started exploring our surroundings. A flight of stairs in the courtyard led to a balcony and entrance on the first floor. There I found Kraks with some students in the kitchen making coffee.

The recently renovated Casa del Prete – once a convent attached to the *duomo* in the central piazza – was to be the living quarters of the twenty students who had applied to come to the school's six-week course that summer, which we had organised at the last moment with the help of Mauro who introduced us to the town. I had taken my full, four weeks' annual leave from the hospital to assist with the school's administrative and any other needs.

Following the end of Kraks' teaching in Salzburg, I had come with him to Rome that Easter, in 1981, as Mauro had received a favourable reply from the town council in Tuscania about forming a school there for Kraks. Mauro had been working on the restoration of Tuscania's historical sites following an earthquake ten years earlier that had left thirty-five people dead and much of the town destroyed, and he knew the town and its councillors well.

On the morning after our arrival in Rome, we heard a loud explosion from the lobby of our small hotel near Campo di Fiori. Everyone had flattened themselves on the floor and behind the reception counter. A block away in Via Vittorio Emanuele, we came across a bus enveloped in flames. It was barricaded by two other buses which had been emptied of their passengers, and a crowd of people, standing well back from the fierce heat, stood and watched. The event turned out to be the Red Brigades' commemoration of the anniversary of Aldo Moro's murder.

We rented a car and went to Tuscania for the day. We walked down the short main street, Via Roma, and came upon a square overlooking a green valley and the Romanesque basilica of San Pietro in the distance. We lunched in the square with the locals at Alfreda's homely eating place, ending our meal with the strong pecorino cheese and raw broad beans that were left on the tables according to seasonal local custom. The town was busy with its yearly agricultural fair that day, and was teeming with men and here and there some horses as farmers milled around inspecting and discussing tractors and other farming machinery outside the town's walls. Mauro's friend, the councillor for tourism, seemed to be at the centre of all this activity, and we explored the town until he was free to speak with us.

The councillor, a short, sturdy man with black hair, rosy cheeks and beady brown eyes, readily agreed the arrangements for the school: he would request from the bishopric the use of a deconsecrated church, San Silvestro, for its site and La Casa del Prete for the students' quarters that summer. While he talked to us, he was also overseeing the preparations for the horse show that afternoon: the most important event of the fair. He snatched a few minutes from the fair to take us to San Silvestro, just inside the north wall of the town. It was a simple Romanesque church with an empty, ample rectangular interior and some ancient frescoes on its walls. Kraks was happy with it; it would be fine for the school. Then back to the horses and riders who were about to start their show in the stadium on the way to Madonna del'Olivo – a church on the crest of the hill next to some Etruscan tombs.

We spent the rest of the afternoon walking around the town that would become the new seat of Kraks' school. Inside the medieval wall, it was a rich play of earth colours: ochre, rust, mauve, sepia. The doorways, arched or rectangular, were framed by a broad surround of grey stone, some with a medieval coat of arms carved into the stone to represent maybe a noble household or some public building. Overhanging balconies dripped with plants from their stone balustrades or metal grilles. The narrow cobbled streets wove up and down the town opening into small piazzas with often a fountain emerging out of a wall: the head of a lion worn by time, a round face with fat cheeks spitting into a scalloped basin, a pair of women's heads with ornamental headdress. The churches were Romanesque and showed the changes over the centuries where arches were filled in or more wall added. Many houses still lay empty and in need of repair from the earthquake, and the roads on the edge of the town were overgrown with weeds. Behind the Hotel Gallo, a bridge led to an arch between tall houses in rich ochre. Splashes of red and pink from flower-laden balconies; a wall of green ivy; a cluster of bushes with an orange tree and two palms below. Swallows soaring and swooping against the blue sky.

∾

THE MODEL, her black hair pinned on top of her head, stood naked in the middle of the church enveloped in a shaft of light from the high window. She moved around where she stood, relaxed and not self-conscious, while students lost in concentration shifted their eyes from model to paper – clipped to a board on their easels before them – picking and changing colour pastels from one hand to the other and scratching them over their drawing, then discarding it and starting afresh. In the twilight atmosphere inside the church, quiet voices rose above the silence that was otherwise interrupted only by the rustling of paper or a student's footsteps

*At work in San Silvestro*

moving to a new place. The teacher, Kortokraks, his dominant presence felt by all, stood quietly to one side or walked about from one to the other looking at their work intently and without comment. Maybe a gesture, or a few economical movements with his hands. The atmosphere was charged, everyone's attention entirely immersed in capturing the colours, their relations and movement, form, depth and vitality, and translating them onto the sheet of paper in front of them.

Occasionally Don Lidano, tall, thin and a little stooped, in his long black habit, his hands clasped in front of him like a figure in an Italian opera, appeared at the door of his church. The students, their easels before them and their materials on the floor nearby, were spread around in the soft natural light inside the church facing the naked model in the middle. And Don Lidano would take a timid peep at the whole scene. I need not have worried, after all, about how the priest and townspeople would react to the presence of a naked woman inside their church. This was Italy: the land of Da Vinci and Michelangelo.

At lunchtime we all sat around a large table under a tree in Alfreda's square, eating her home-made tagliatelle, while she moved or waddled in her apron, back and forth, between her steamy kitchen and the school sitting outside. Making sure everyone got what they wanted.

*The school at lunch at Alfreda's*

In the afternoon the students were free to paint in the town or countryside – to gather again in the evening at six at San Silvestro where Kraks looked at their work and discussed it, using the odd word here, an indicative movement there, that the student might feel it more and 'think' less.

During their free time, I would fill the Renault 4 with students and take them to the nearby lake or sea. Most of them were from north

Germany and had attended Kortokraks' course in Salzburg in previous years or heard about him from his reputation at that school.

In the evenings, we often organised parties inside the church to which the townspeople were invited. Food the students helped to prepare would be served, and we all danced to the music from a local group of musicians. The townspeople in turn invited the school to warm evenings seated at long tables out in the open to sample the various local pizzas baked on the spot in a clay oven. Other times we were driven through small country roads to feasts out in the countryside – the food and wine, all their own produce – sitting around a large table under the stars.

Angelo and Serafino ran the main bar in town, which was next to the first gate, Prima Porta, of the town wall. Everyone congregated there – it was open from four in the morning when the local men went hunting, until one the following morning. The school had no telephone, and all messages were relayed through Angelo. He had lived in England and spoke English well, and his wife, Gina, with whom I had spoken my somewhat patchy Italian the whole of that first summer of the school, turned out to be Jean from Manchester. Angelo would get on his *motorino* and drive to San Silvestro or look for us elsewhere in the small town – he always found us – with the latest telephone message. His brother, Serafino, not only did not speak a word of English, but his Italian was pure local dialect and hard to follow – except for Kraks who had a flair for picking up the most idiosyncratic idioms in any language. Serafino looked after Kraks, the students, Anna and myself with a paternal interest – Anna became *Annarella* and he would invite her to come to his side of the counter and help him serve – to the point that, in the later years of the school, he would refuse to serve Kraks his fifth or sixth *doppio*, or double expresso, for breakfast, telling him firmly that he had had enough, having seen the excessive highs it tipped him into.

The whole town, including the mayor and his councillors, came to the school's exhibitions of the students' work held at San Silvestro or at a walled park nearby. They would turn the event into an official function and open it with a speech by the councillor for culture. Though Kraks' intention was to show the town what the school was about and the evolution of the students' work from the first clumsy efforts to the inspired studies seen within a short week, many works were bought by the people and hung in their homes. They had captured the beauty of their town, of which they were proud.

While Kortokraks taught, I dealt with the various needs of the school and students, liaising with the town's councillors when necessary: more beds for new students arriving, more materials for the school to be fetched from Viterbo or Rome, frames and easels to be shifted for an exhibition, food and wine for a party, the care of a student who became ill.

The female students elicited the attention of the male population. Like the young policeman, standing in full uniform in the middle of the road, totally lost in his contemplation of a pretty Nordic blonde who was sketching a view of the town, and completely impervious to the minor traffic jam he was causing.

During the third year of the school, Champa – married to Douglas, the designer of the Cerebral Function Monitor I had been researching at the London Hospital – came and danced for the students.

Champa was slim and wiry, her long hair black and straight, her dark eyes a narrow almond shape. She danced in ancient Indian costumes, some brightly coloured and stiff, others soft and diaphanous, her ankles jingling with bells, her feet bare. The powerful atavistic character of the dances, the highly controlled, mimetic movements and expressions of eyes and face, arms and fingers, ankles and feet, fused the present with a dim, remote past. And the students had the difficult task of capturing her in motion with their pastels on paper.

She agreed to put on a performance of the ancient Hindu dances for the town.

'Would it be all right to hold it in San Silvestro?' I asked Don Lidano.

'Well … I'm not really sure … Is her belly covered?'

'Oh, yes! The dances are religious and very respectable,' I said, immediately regretting it. Hindu dances in a Christian church?

'I think it should be all right,' said Don Lidano, somewhat uncertainly. And then, leaning across to Kraks, he whispered, 'In a way, I wish it *were* belly dancing!'

The first summer the school was held in Tuscania was everything I had ever dared hope for. I remember many moments which, after all the difficulties of the previous years, were like manna from heaven. I had watched Kraks, relaxed yet fully focused, create a kind of miracle with the students and the town. Inside San Silvestro, the atmosphere had been spell-like. The experience of being. The concerted struggles to reach that particular moment, empathy, fusion, at which the vision before you would flow through eyes and being down to the fingertips and onto the paper. And in different ways, this had permeated throughout the town. There had been many meeting points, a warmth and friendship, between the local Tuscanese and the group of strangers that had invaded their town. A sharing and getting together of very different people. Town life and the school were one. The townspeople would stop Kraks in the street and discuss their problems with him and expect his advice. He became 'il nostro professore' in its widest sense, and I was 'la moglie del professore', an interesting change from 'the doctor' in London. During the town's feast days, the local people would make room for us to sit at their tables in the streets, share their food with us, and mix and dance in the open to the town band till the early hours of the morning. All these students had come to paint their town, to appreciate and enjoy its beauty, to take part in their celebrations. Our neighbours at La Casa del Prete had offered their help at every opportunity: 'We learned the importance of sticking together and helping one another during the earthquake. And that spirit has remained with us,' one of them said. Though there were moments of tension and disagreement too, in the end it was the greater sense of harmony that had so skilfully been created and held together by Kortokraks that prevailed.

Back in London, letters from students who had attended the course would describe its extraordinary effect on them. Pages and pages of them. The students had gone through a process of discarding their outer layers full of preconceptions, peeling them off like an onion till they were face to face with themselves. They had had to forget scaled distances and measurements, and relearn instead to see, as a child does, with the impact and wonder of the first time. Creativity linked with caring, or – the word Kraks chose

– responsibility, as opposed to alienation and decadence which are closer to destructivity. Though it didn't come easily. I remember watching how he would leave a new student to struggle on his own for days on end: the odd one who couldn't handle it would drop out. He would quietly but intently observe them at work till he came to understand their difficulties, and then he would find the right word, the well-aimed sign or gesture to reach them, to get them to relax and be fully receptive. In one week, a student's stiff, self-conscious drawing would be transformed into a lively flowing image – as they found their courage and confidence to realise it. First hand.

In the second summer in Tuscania, the students more than doubled and the school continued to stir and excite. That year we rented a small apartment and, for the first time in our eighteen years of marriage, he was being loving and attentive, all the time, day after day. I had never had such a relaxed and happy time with him. Maybe he had decided to make our marriage work after all – though I am only guessing as he never said what was on his mind. We had, in fact, had a bad time again in London after the first summer in Tuscania. That was the year when I had found a buyer for our Muswell Hill house, completed the sale on my return to London, and packed and moved all our belongings to Islington while working full-time at the hospital. Yet, when he rejoined me at the end of his school two weeks later, he had been angrier, less communicative and more savage in his verbal attacks than ever. He appeared determined not to like the new place, though he had two enormous floors to himself, each a large, spacious studio with a smaller back room projecting into the walled garden, practically in central London. The exorbitant telephone bills that started coming in, which I had to meet as with everything else, and the strange calls when I came home earlier than usual, suggested he was once again involved in another relationship: maybe the new place didn't fit his plans. And now, back in Tuscania, he was in control of the school, his students, his marriage. Although there were difficult moments again towards the end. I remember helping with an exhibition of the school's work at which he was barking his demands at everyone, and nothing anyone did satisfied him. The tension was sky high, and the young student Britta, who had come to the school the first summer and had become a kind of junior assistant by then, was trying her best to please him, and suddenly burst into tears at the impossibility of it. I was angry with him for upsetting her.

At the end of my annual leave from the hospital, I returned to London. Kraks stayed behind for the remaining days of the school and a few more after that. One or two of the female students also extended their time in Tuscania.

I met Enrico La Penna the following, third year of the school. He was an Italian architect from Rome with connections in the Vatican who had come to assist with the school. He had turned up the previous summer after the course to talk with Kraks about his interest in the school.

'I was sorry not to meet you last summer when I came to Tuscania. You were asleep when I arrived at your apartment. Kortokraks said you were very tired, so we sat and chatted in the garden not to disturb you.'

In fact, it was not me. I had long left Tuscania when Kraks met Enrico.

Some years later, I came across a letter from Britta to Kraks. She referred to her continuing search for a home for the two of them in north Germany. It was clear from her writing that the relationship had been going on for some time. Perhaps since that summer?

In the third year of the school, the students more than doubled again. Over a hundred came in staggered groups across the duration of the course. They ranged from young to old, from beginners to postgraduates in fine art. They came from Germany, Austria, Holland, France, England, Spain, Italy, Scandinavia and the United States. Halfway through the course, five national Italian newspapers wrote lengthy articles about the school, and students started arriving – sometimes after a telephone call, others unannounced – from Torino down to Sicily, to attend the school. Some just packed a few things and got on a train, and took a bus or hitched a lift with a local farmer the last strip to Tuscania. An assistant came from the United States, and a potter from California to take a pottery class, for which the local ceramics factory offered space for a students' workshop and the use of their kiln and glazing facilities. The town provided a recently restored, large public building in the main piazza for the students' accommodation, as well as a second church, San Baggio, for an additional class. Kraks started losing his focus of the first years. He would send the students he didn't want in his class to San Baggio or to the pottery class, and then complain because they didn't attend his classes. Yet he would not attend to his own group of students in San Silvestro for days on end. Sometimes he would go off, to maybe Florence or some other place, just as new students arrived and expected to see him.

Relations with the town's governing body also became increasingly strained, and Kraks became obsessed with the emergence of two camps: those for his school, and those against it. These last included a fringe group of Tuscanese who befriended some students and smoked the odd joint together. Kraks feared it would destroy the town's image of the school and their relations, as well as his own work with the students. Yet he was more likely to be wandering around the streets of the town angrily remonstrating about the lack of support he was getting, than to be in San Silvestro teaching. The students became disturbed, while at the same time continued to appreciate the snatches of his charismatic teaching. He seemed to use his penetrating insight to both create and destroy, to make or unmake. He could elate a student by leading them to new heights in their work, or bring them to desperation and tears. I was once told by a gifted young sculptor and art school graduate: 'Kraks' teaching is unequalled. I've never come across anything like it. He's given me insights I would never have reached otherwise. But his disruptive influence is too much, and I'm not coming back next year.'

During the following summer course, a group of influential men in Tuscania got together to try and rescue the school and ensure its future. They saw its awesome potential as a great international centre for teaching various branches of art with Kraks at its head. A skilled etcher who taught at the Salzburg Academy had already declared his interest to take part, and a sculpture class was also in the planning. They were looking at the possibility of transforming a great *palazzo* in the middle of Tuscania's historic centre into the seat of the school. It contained large halls ideal for classes, smaller ones for workrooms and offices, and many rooms that could be turned into the students' quarters. Support for the project also came from Germany, from people both close to and within political circles. A meeting was arranged with a powerful prospective backer, but Kraks didn't turn up. I received distressed telephone calls from the politician who had organised it asking where Kraks could be contacted. I didn't know. Then, one day, Kraks phoned from a German railway station sounding very frightened and saying he was coming straight back home. He would worry increasingly about what he perceived as jealous competitors planning to take over the school and turn it into something very different from what he had in mind.

And the whole thing became impossible and slowly collapsed.

∽

SINCE THEN TIME has moved forward. All the damage left behind by the violent convulsions of the earthquake has been repaired. The upturned dirt roads we came upon on our first visit to Tuscania – all those years ago – have now been recobbled in the centuries-old pattern, and the empty houses inside the walled town are all restored and lived in. Through open doorways, women are seen preparing the evening meal for their men, while they in turn sit lazily chattering away in knots and groups outside the cafés. Outside Alfreda's previously unmarked eating place, an ornate signboard now hangs announcing *Osteria Da Alfreda ~ Vino e Cucina* and, on the other side of her square, the wild piece of ground which was said to be snake-infested is now a fenced park with a neat lawn, a tall circular fountain and a small amphitheatre facing the fertile valley and hill with San Pietro beyond. The Hotel Gallo is still the only hotel in town but has been completely refurbished; the new reception room displays Etruscan pottery under an arch cut into the wall, and two elegantly framed Kortokraks School of Vision posters hang on the wall. The summer *Feste*, in which tables and chairs were brought out into the streets and local dishes served to one and all followed by dancing, don't take place anymore. The Easter fair is no longer an agricultural show for farmers from the neighbouring countryside; instead Tuscania fills with visitors and tourists who crowd the streets as they mingle with the local Tuscanese and meander past the many stands of handicrafts including items from Peru and Guatemala, mammals and birds from as far as the Amazon and Patagonia, and here and there a small Japanese man selling his bonsai trees. The horse show is still a feature, and the men still strut in their boots and leather leggings, brown waistcoats, and Sevillian-type hats next to their splendid horses. But now the town might bring an equestrian event from Paris, to add to its own.

Outside the town, below San Pietro, is one of the many towers that rise over Tuscania. It stands on a large piece of ground with rows of peach and pear trees. At its gate, Kraks has attached a notice: Scuola di Visione. In the garden around the tower he has planted rose bushes, chrysanthemums and peonies, while at the back he has built a large pergola with a vine growing over it. In the tower, the ground floor serves as a dining-kitchen-living room, the next floor is his bedroom and in the third he does his painting. From here one can climb onto the flat roof and look at the valley below with the River Marta winding through it, San Pietro on top of the hill, and the walled town beyond. The tower is now Kraks' living studio, and paintings at various stages of work, drawings and materials are mixed with his everyday needs. He has also rigged up a hi-fi system with powerful speakers, and lined his walls with cassettes from jazz and flamenco to Mozart passions and Bach cantatas, among much else. When the occasional private student comes to Tuscania to study with him, the tower serves also as his school.

He drives around town in his old *motorino*, and some of the townspeople will nod their heads in greeting, *'Buon giorno, professore,'* as he goes past. But mostly, he buries himself in his tower with his painting and music. And reading. He was always an avid reader. Close to his bed, he keeps the *I Ching* and the Old and New Testaments, which he himself bound in raw linen.

When he is not in his tower in Tuscania, he is likely to be in Germany or in Salzburg. He might be invited to stay a few days at his new friend Anya's castle near Frankfurt – the countess came to Tuscania to get private tuition from Kortokraks. In Salzburg, a permanent room is kept for him at the Maria Plain Hotel, which sits high on a hill with a large garden restaurant overlooking the town spread on the plain below and the great range of mountains beyond.

The walls of the hotel are covered with Kortokraks' paintings, and he has become a friend of the management. He has the occasional exhibition in the town and has maintained some contact with the art world there. Then, back to his tower in Tuscania, perhaps a trip to Sicily, to one of his old students, or to Tunisia to savour a more exotic landscape and paint some more.

I myself acquired a small house which looks out onto the valley and San Pietro from Tuscania's *centro storico*. It backs onto the town hall, whose ochre wall, with four large windows, overlooks my small, enclosed garden. On warm evenings, I can listen in on the town councillors' lively discussion on the affairs of Tuscania emanating from the top two windows while I relax in my patio under the vine. The lower windows look down onto Tuscania's yellowing archives in the town hall's basement. In the middle of the garden, a stone bird bath is surrounded by purple lilies and blood-red and orange Indian shot flowers.

In front of the house, to the left, two acacia trees and several tall umbrella pines frame the Romanesque ruin of San Francesco, in which St Francis of Assisi is said to have stayed. Further over is the little church of Santa Maria della Pace with a monastery above, from which pealing bells ring out at certain times of day. The hill with San Pietro rises to the right. In the evening, as the sun lowers, its apse is drenched with a rosy glow as the shadows creep along the valley below. The continuous twitter and chirruping of birds outside my window never cease to delight me, and the dogs bark their dialogues in the distance.

I bought this place when the school ended and our marriage broke down. Though not before I had thought hard about whether my love for Tuscania could overcome my unhappy associations with it, should I return ...

During the last year of the school, Kraks had rented the tower. We had stayed together uneasily that summer. He was almost unusually friendly, but I didn't trust it. He had been away from London a great deal the previous year, staying only two or three days when he turned up, and then mostly packing his belongings to take with him on the Felixstowe-Hamburg ferry. I noticed he didn't bring them back. He appeared to be moving out, piecemeal, I knew neither where to, nor with whom. In Tuscania, the school had dwindled. Then I came across the house for sale in Largo della Pace. It was the loveliest and quietest spot in Tuscania. I decided I could, after all, enjoy being there, quietly and in my own right. I bought the house. After my return to London, he rang a few weeks later to say he was coming back. I told him it was best he didn't.

'Why don't you go to Emma's? She has always invited you, and it should be lovely in Sicily now.' Emma was one of the older students who had come to Tuscania. She lived in Catania with her husband, a doctor, and they had a holiday house by the sea in Augusta. She had frequently invited us.

'All right, perhaps I will,' he said. And he did.

And that was the end of our life together.

The following summer, during my annual leave from the hospital, I started settling in the house in Largo della Pace. Kraks was not around. I met a long-standing student of the school in town. He said Kraks had told him to come and bring other students with him, that there would be a course that summer, but nobody knew anything about it or where he was. A young girl had come from Holland too. I was shown the open letter she had left behind: in view of the positive response she had received to her queries about there being a place for her in the school, she had used up all her savings to attend the course. She had heard marvellous things about it and had been excited and very much looking forward to taking part in it. Instead, she had come and found nothing. She was bitterly disappointed. And angry. All she could do in the circumstances was to turn round and return to Holland.

A new café has opened in the piazza opposite the town hall. The odd morning, when I feel like celebrating the bright sunshine and the melodious chirping of the birds, I saunter round to the piazza and sit outside the café sipping my cappuccino and eating a fresh *cornetto* while I read the local paper, facing the row of reclining stone figures draped in the loose folds of their robes – once the lids of Etruscan sarcophagi from local tombs – on top of the wall overlooking the square. Patches of yellow and orange lichen on their surface match the ochre of the town hall.

Occasionally someone comes up to me and greets me. Sometimes they will turn to a friend by their side and say quietly, as in explanation, 'È la moglie del professore.'

The last two summers at the school had been very difficult. Over that time, Kraks had distanced me more and more from the school and his work. He would at the same time command and resent my assistance, send me on various errands and then demand angrily, 'Whose school is it, yours or mine?' And he would say his painting was 'none of my business' – at which point I started rethinking my twenty years of dedicated support for it.

Maybe my commitment to his art and what it stood for had been the greater for my lack of a sense of nationality, some roots, or even a cohesive family. I had searched for something that would embody the values I had gathered during my life experience of exile and moves and the disintegration of my family, close and far. The small *Madonna and Child* I had stood in front of, at the Vatican Museum, when I first arrived in Europe from New Zealand, imparted something of what I had been looking for, much as Kraks' art did too. I realised even then that my reliance on him and his art for those answers was, in a way, a kind of laziness on my part. My own profession dealt with those same core values of human worth in a practical way, while Kraks enshrined them (as the art critic Norbert Lynton had written) in what should turn out as a lasting oeuvre. And I had chosen to help him, as well as I could, with his pursuit. I had imagined that some day, when his work would be more widely recognised, we might be rewarded with happier times. That fantasy had kept me going. And now, when such a thing seemed in sight with the magic and promise of the school in its early stages, he was shutting me out. I felt profoundly let down – his sweeping disloyalty, as I saw it, was much more shattering than the sum of all his sexual infidelities.

I saw now that 'our' struggles on behalf of his art had turned instead into too much intrusion on my part, and dependence, resentment and acrimony on his. Rather than drawing us closer together, they had torn us apart. There was nothing, any longer, to stay together for.

I had seen a letter the previous year, back in Duncan Terrace.

He had left a few days earlier without saying where he was going, as was his custom, and I was emptying the waste bin in his studio when I noticed a torn-up letter. I stuck it together to see if it threw some light onto what was going on. It was in German, to his friend Wulf, in Hamburg, whom he knew from their Paris days together in the fifties. In the letter he was telling Wulf that I was 'finished' and he was deciding to leave me as there was still a great deal ahead for him: '… rotten for her, but I have to take care of myself.' He hadn't sent it; maybe it was only a jotting down of his innermost thoughts, the kind we all have. Even so …

My mother had died recently, and her loss had left me sad and bereft. I felt infinite regret at our lack of communication for most of my life. I remembered saying to her once, when already in my forties, working, lecturing and researching at the hospital, 'I would like us to be friends,' and she had replied an unarguable, 'That's impossible. I shall always be your mother. I have twenty-eight years more experience than you and I shall always feel obliged to guide and advise you.' And now I felt the loss of all she and I could have shared. As friends. A few days before her death I had asked her: 'Tell me about yourself when you were young. Tell me about France,' and she replied: 'I was just a silly young girl then.' And that was all. She had insistently asked for Kraks during her last days. But he was away and I had no idea where to contact him. I shall never know what she wanted to see him about. I wondered whether, her maternal role strong to the end, she wanted to ask him to take care of me. If so, it was as well he didn't turn up, for death is not a time for false promises. There was a vast amount for me to think about and digest during those days. I continued to go about my work at the hospital every day and to busy myself with all that was demanded of me, but – yes – at home I was very low, trying to find my bearings again through a haze of uncertainties, regrets, confusion and great sadness. His letter now made me feel utterly abandoned. Like an empty eggshell after the contents have been sucked out, or a carcass gnawed clean.

But he was wrong: I was not finished. I was only starting.

That letter turned out to be very helpful. It shook me out of my seemingly downward spiralling state. Slowly but surely, it started me off on my upward path. That letter became my springboard.

One of the students of the school – in that last year – was due to play some music in the church of San Marco. I had arrived early and a service was still going on. I sat in the back pew and surveyed the scene around me. The diffuse half-light inside the church was broken only by the gentle glow around the burning votive candles. The congregation consisted of a few local women scattered in the pews in front of me. They all wore simple cotton dresses of different patterns, but always black. The women's faces and stances were lost in devotion; they seemed transported, at peace. And as I watched them, I suddenly envied their faith, their capacity to slip so readily into that abandoned state of acceptance, of being at one with the subdued lighting, soft resonating prayer, gentle smell of incense, and the priest's utterances and gestures in his colourful vestments. Such consolation ... And I realised the absence in my life of some shared communal experience, and the high price of attempting to maintain my independence of mind.

I had often stood for hours trying to get through to London on the telephone at Angelo's bar or the Hotel Gallo. To speak with my mother and see how she was. That was in the school's third summer. It was also through a telephone call that I first discovered that all was not well with her. I had been to San Francisco presenting a paper at an international congress and I phoned her on my return to London. As we spoke I could hear a thin whistle with every breath she drew, as though something was partly blocking her breathing.

'What's the trouble with your chest? Are you not well?' I had asked her.

'I've had bronchitis for the last three months and the GP has given me several courses of antibiotics, but it still hasn't cleared. I've got another appointment with him tomorrow.'

'Has he sent you to have a chest X-ray?'

'No.'

'Or listened to your chest?'

'Not really. He just gives me more antibiotics every time.'

'Ask him to arrange for an urgent chest X-ray when you see him tomorrow. If you have any problems, ring me from his surgery and I shall speak to him.'

And sure enough, there was a sinister shadow in the film that proved to be malignant.

She was treated in the Brompton Chest Hospital and had a course of radiotherapy. Then, although very weak, she had gone to stay a few days with her brother Hans in Holland, and even spent a week in her beloved Deyá – '*my* Deyá', as she always referred to it: the site of happy sunny times with her friend Seppel and her pregnancy with me. Her farewell to the place she remembered more fondly than any other – in her difficult, displaced life.

෴

THEY HAD BOTH TRIED to rule me, in their different ways, Kraks and my mother – while I had tried to break free and face my separate worth.

Now I recognised another way. Maybe, in the same way as the struggling beginners I had watched at Kraks' school had had to deal with the moving model in front of them and the pastels in their hand without help, or as a Zen master's disciple is left to work out the sound of one hand clapping to break through our well-trodden mould of thinking and reach a deeper insight, so too I had had to go through all of that for my own illumination. Like a jet breaking through the sound barrier: its nose bursting through the huge bank of air that builds up in front of it as it reaches the speed of sound to suddenly free-fly through the skies. It was my koan.

෴

PUMPKIN SHELLS GRINNED sardonically in the dark from window ledges and from on top of the medieval town wall: their hollow eyes and mouth spitting the light from the candle inside them into the night. Glowing Chinese lanterns swayed from higher windows, and a profusion of white streamers stretched across the streets lined with burning torches. People dressed for the *Festa* crowded the medieval quarter inside Tuscania's first gate. They strolled in the narrow streets and stood in groups in the small piazza, while youngsters stole up behind them to stick burrs on their hair and women entered the tiny chapel, La Chiesetta della Neve, in tribute to a summer's miraculous snowfall. They knelt and prayed and wept openly with emotion before the faded fresco of the Virgin, La Madona della Neve, a large bunch of flowers at her feet next to a tray covered with money to which people continually added more notes, intent on leaving their offerings. The Madonna sat draped in a red gown, her gold-rimmed blue dress peeking out of it where it parted to reveal her bared breast presented to baby Jesus who sat on her lap, a gold turban on his head, holding its nipple between his lips.

The emotions mother and child elicit ... Here distilled and lifted to divine status.

∽

WE CELEBRATED HER SEVENTY-SEVENTH – and last – birthday at Duncan Terrace. I invited all her friends, and a trio of my sister's flute and two strings played music. She sat the whole evening: a small, thin, frail figure in her white and grey chiffon dress, her snow-white hair freshly dressed, almost lost in the middle of the plush chair. She was looking as radiantly happy as her weakness allowed, surrounded as she was by so many friends, listening to the music and, now and then, even though she no longer had a taste for it, picking a small snippet from the platters of savouries we had prepared.

Soon afterwards, she was readmitted to the Brompton Hospital with a recurrence of her cancer.

∽

WHEN I ONCE COMPLAINED of his lack of responsibility, Kraks yelled angrily, 'I *teach* responsibility.' Meaning responsibility for one's beliefs and actions in the wider context of humanity.

Different meanings. Different understandings. I was talking about one's behaviour towards others. He, about one's integrity towards oneself. I felt the pains of others in my attempt to lessen them, while he let others work things out for themselves. We were using different systems in our appraisal of the world.

———

My cousin Peter recalled our grandmother Clara – when her friend pointed out my mother's beauty as she cycled past – replying, 'Yes, but so irresponsible!' Irresponsible to the rules of the bourgeois society Clara knew and valued. Yet my mother had her own sense of responsibility in her stance towards humanity, as when she helped the effort in Spain against fascism, and later the refugees in Collioure.

And *she* had accused *me*, *her* daughter, of irresponsibility – yet I took care of people's lives, which were literally in my hands, every day.

What lies in a word …

Another was *trust*. The utter unquestioning trust I felt for my mother when we had been thrown so close together, mother and child, against the dangers we faced and in our constant moves in Europe and our early time in Mexico. And the shattering, splitting asunder of that trust when we started growing apart and misconstruing each other's ways and thought processes.

Kraks accused me of not trusting. Back in Muswell Hill, when I returned home from a demanding, full day's medical work, he would ask me for some cash to buy potatoes for our supper – having spent all I had left him in the morning, for our meal, on drink.

'Here it is, Kraks. But *please*, I am tired and hungry. The girls too. Please get the potatoes and come home this time.'

'Of course! What do you take me for! You should learn to *trust*.'

Four hours later he was still drinking at the pub – and we had finally eaten, what little I could find in the house, without him.

'You must trust me,' he rebuked me, indicating the fault lay with me.

Maybe he was asking for unconditional love, come what may, unidirectional, from me to him. Different interpretations of the word 'trust'.

It was his practice to lean on me, full-weight, with all his needs and demands, while at the same time he did his utmost to undermine everything I did – rather like cutting down the tree you are sitting on. My own reliance on his recognition of me, at a deeper level, had made me put up with such a state of affairs. I had kept my sights on the man beyond his behavior, his particular vision and grasp of the world, expressed in his painting, which resonated with me to the extent that it had been – maybe unbelievably – a source of consolation in a world which had often appeared alien to me.

But I was emerging from that need and insecurity.

I would no longer rely on him or his art, but on *my* art and myself.

∾

KRAKS ENJOYED ENTERTAINING VISITORS at his tower in Tuscania. He once prepared a meal for a group of archaeologists working in the valley and it turned into a lively party.

His son Daniel, whom he hardly ever saw, came to stay on one occasion with his girlfriend. It was the first time he had visited his father here. Kraks now wished to involve him in his life and seemed eager to gain his affection and regard. Intent on pleasing him, he invited a large group of people from the town, including the musicians – as in the days of the school – and rushed out to buy food and wine and then spent the rest of the afternoon cooking a huge amount of spaghetti and making several bowls of salad. He hung Chinese lanterns all along his pergola behind the tower, and laid many places on the long trestle table beneath it. And then we waited.

After some time one old drunk arrived, and a little later a man who was out of Kraks' favour. As time went by – the drunkard steeped in incoherent talk and the unwelcome visitor trying to make polite conversation – it became evident that no one else was turning up. Kraks served the food and the small group, which included myself and our daughter Anna, sat quietly and ate. His eyes were screwed with disappointment and, for an unguarded moment, his image revealed his lonesomeness and isolation.

∾

AS I SIT AND WRITE at my window in Largo della Pace, the profusion of greens in the valley – from the fields' patchwork of lime, sage and chartreuse to the darker greens and mulberries of the wooded slopes – is forever changing with the sun's trajectory. I watch the blues in the sky progress from palest to deepest, and drifting fleecy clouds now and then give way to an ominous dark mass looming over the hills beyond. I have seen both skies at once with a large rainbow arched across the valley flushed gold from the oblique sunlight. At night, the scene changes again with the moon's waxing and waning, while San Pietro and San Francesco stand out from the darkness enveloped in the soft glow of Tuscania's lanterns. And the birds in the acacias and pines across the street never cease their melodious symphony of song.

As Easter approaches, dark-haired youths gather with large chains in the street below my window. They struggle for some time attaching the chains around their ankles and, when finally in place, stand up and start dragging them up and down to try them out. The chains are said to weigh up to 300 kilos. The young men are practising for the Easter procession.

They are bringing out the *Vergine Addolorata* from the church of San Giovanni inside the walled town. A group of strong young men struggle with her weight until they finally lift her high. The painted wooden figure is clothed in a black dress embroidered with gold, a burning heart pierced by seven swords on her chest, as she sits on a platform flanked by angels. Her eyes turn in abject pain and supplication towards Heaven while her hanging, outstretched hands, palms facing forward, point to her dead son lying across her feet: the Jewish rabbi persecuted for preaching compassion and sharing in a world torn by greed, power and intolerance. The crowd, which has waited for hours for this moment, part to let her pass. People line the streets and fill balconies and windows all along the route. And finally, as night falls on this Easter Friday, the *Addolorata* – Our Lady of Sorrows – is ready. The penitent youths in their peaked white hoods and long white robes, four abreast with arms entwined to help each other heave, start dragging their long, heavy chains from their naked ankles – the loud, drawn out, metallic scraping against the cobbled streets, ringing out in the night. Their bare feet pull each step forward while they peer through two small holes in their hoods to follow their course. The low chant of women's prayers starts to mix with the regular tautophony of the dragging chains, and two single files of women dressed in black appear. Black veils hide their faces and each holds a tall, white, burning candle in her hand. Two long lines of flickering flames move slowly past as the eerie monotonous chanting prayer takes over and disperses into the night. After the women, a lone, bare-footed priest in a brown habit struggles forth with a large wooden cross, followed by the rest of the clerics who proceed comfortably in full ceremonial dress. Loud exclamations from the excited crowd announce the appearance of the *Addolorata*, as the procession now reaches its climax. The richly decorated wooden figure moves slowly forward under the laborious efforts of her sixteen weight-bearers, not a flicker in her painted, upturned eyes as the people pour out their veneration and intense emotion around her. Then come the mayor and councillors of the town leading the multitude behind them. And in this powerfully hypnotic atmosphere, the palpable mass fervour of the Middle Ages spills over into the night dissolving centuries of time at Tuscania's Easter procession.

Of a mother's grief for her dead son.

∽

MEANWHILE, MY WORK IN LONDON was also centering on motherhood. In the course of my clinical and academic work, I was conducting studies which aimed at safer anaesthetic methods and improved pain relief in obstetrics. In another hospital, I was invited to manage the unusual anaesthetic service to patients submerged in a bath of water for the non-invasive fragmentation of their kidney stones, until a simpler method was developed. I went on to embrace obstetric anaesthesia and analgesia as my

*Anaesthesia in a bath of water for the non-invasive fragmentation of kidney stones*

sub-specialty, the expertise of which not only strove towards a successful outcome in the face of maternal and infant complications, but also made possible the first bonding between mother and child when an abnormal labour would have prevented it.

I was now in charge of the anaesthetic service of an obstetric hospital in east London in addition to my work at the London Hospital. I supervised the anaesthetic requirements specific to the mother and child, both in its unborn and newborn states, when complications of pregnancy or labour required surgical intervention. I was following the development of increasingly refined techniques, which allowed the mother to be conscious and pain free during a Caesarean section with her husband or partner by her side. An epidural required the introduction of a needle blindly, by feel, into a space – maybe no more than a millimetre deep – inside the vertebral canal, threading into it a fine plastic tube, judging the necessary dose and volume of local anaesthetic that will block the targeted nerves crossing that space, and effectively numbing the surgical area without causing a drop in blood pressure or other adverse effects which might endanger the mother and unborn child. Then to watch the surgery progress unhindered and place the newborn child in the mother's arms, and look on at the radiant and tender family group at my end of the operating table while the surgeon continued with his work to stitch back together all the layers he had cut open and close the abdomen – always gave me a sense of satisfaction.

I remember my follow-up visit to a young mother who had undergone a difficult breech delivery under an epidural. I asked if she had been comfortable during all the manoeuvring by the obstetricians for her baby's delivery.

DR. MIRIAM FRANK, the writer of this week's Personal View, is a consultant at The London Hospital and Newham Maternity Hospital.

'Yes, doctor. The epidural worked well and I didn't feel any pain. But what I'll remember you most for, and shall never forget, is the way you stayed by my side and held my hand and explained to me everything that was going on.'

More than the pain relief afforded by my expertise, that had allowed her conscious participation in the complicated delivery of her child, I had also cut through the isolating divide between people and accompanied her in her loneliness and fear. I was maybe trying to give her that closeness I had once experienced, and then lost, with my mother. But, more than that, it represented the antithesis of human indifference, the final path of which led to the Holocaust and every other act of savagery committed in the world to this day. And, for me, that was what it was all about.

I attended international congresses where I read papers and met and exchanged ideas with other anaesthetists across the world. San Francisco, Manila, Paris, Rome, Washington, Rotterdam, China. I was also invited to lecture in Mexico and Argentina. At a meeting in Cardiff on consciousness and anaesthesia, I was invited to join a small international group in the presentation of papers and discussions on the nature of unconsciousness and its measurement. At the Association of Obstetric Anaesthetists meetings, I read papers on my research and surveys, and spoke with pioneers of our specialty. Gertie Marx, from New York, had fled as a young woman from Hitler's Germany to Switzerland and emigrated to the United States, where she led the earliest developments in obstetric anaesthesia and still worked and taught well into her seventies. I invited her to be guest speaker at a scientific conference I organised at the London Hospital, to which 250 anaesthetists came from all over the UK and overseas, winding up with an elegant banquet at the fourteenth-century Apothecaries Hall near Blackfriars Bridge. I was juggling my expanding professional life with my more disturbing personal one – each drawing their disparate demands from me.

∽

I REMEMBER MY MOTHER once telling me, her expression wooden and her voice bitter, 'You have betrayed me.' The words stuck in my mind.

My cousin Peter, halfway between us in age, had been close to both of us. While she lived, he always remained discreet. But, after her death, he allowed himself to make certain observations.

'It used to pain me to hear your mother speak about you. Occasionally I would point out to her that she had also rebelled against her parents, and she would not respond. She kept a stony silence at the challenge. As though she hadn't heard it,' he had said. I could see her face, the hard impenetrable expression that would glaze over it in her determination not to give way, if one touched on something sensitive.

My mother's liberal ideas and way of life as a young girl must have surely caused her more conservative mother, Clara, considerable grief. During Clara's final illness my mother was in Barcelona and unable to be at her side. To comfort her. Or to come to terms with each other. Not even in the face of death. My mother couldn't return to Germany, given her stand against her country's political and racist policies. Added to that, her advanced state of pregnancy and my imminent birth at the time.

My mother always kept her lovingly framed photograph of Clara on her bedside table or her desk. She told my daughter Anna that when she received the letter with the news of Clara's death, she had locked herself in her room in La Floresta and cried all day. I was one month old then.

Was she seeing in me her own regretted behaviour towards her mother that seemed to burden her for the rest of her life? Reminding her maybe of her own independent spirit, and – remorseful of its effect on her mother – punishing me for it? Unlike the deep division in principles between Clara and herself, our views were essentially in agreement, yet her odd show of pride in me and my achievements was overshadowed by her disapproval of my independent behaviour in simple everyday things. Might her excessive anger against me have been an overspill of her own sense of guilt? She had betrayed her mother much more profoundly – yet it had been inevitable if she was to be true to herself, given the situation in the world around her then.

Or maybe she interpreted my behaviour as disloyal when it did not conform with her ideas. And then again, she sometimes saw my father in me, which was not complimentary. Perhaps too, after all we had lived and experienced together in my early life, and our close-ness in those difficult and dangerous times, she thought I had for-gotten it. Or maybe her love for me then had given her the strength to save us both, she may have relied on me as I did on her, and my growing up and apart made her feel exposed and alone …

So many possible sources telescoped together into one feeling.

Once, as we were driving down Finchley Road in London, I turned to my mother during an argument and heard myself saying, 'You taught me to hate myself!' My sister in the back of the car was hys-terically trying to shut me up. My mother, though, had suddenly become silent. She said quietly but emphatically, 'No. Let her talk. I want to understand.'

I also remembered how, back in New Zealand, my mother had woken from a nightmare once in the middle of the night and cried out: 'I hate myself!'

I never understood the source of this self-deprecation. Could it have sprung from the inherent insecurity of a permanent refugee? Of a family disintegrated and friends and homes constantly lost and renewed … Maybe some vestige of centuries of irrational hatred and rejection, which had reached its climax in our own lifetime, leaving its mark? The image we carry in some deep hidden corner within ourselves, as an object of collective hatred, and passed on from mother to child.

I have before me my mother's handbag of soft black leather that I gave her in her last months before she became bedridden. I also bought some new clothes for her in my attempt to make her look ahead and not give in.

She had kept her handbag by her bedside during the last month.

Inside it, I found the old photograph of her mother that she had always kept near her during her lifetime. The frame's delicate black stain is worn away in some sections, exposing its beautiful wood grain, and its gilded inner rim is finely crenellated. It is clearly worked by hand and looks old enough for me to think that she must have acquired it in Barcelona. Maybe when Clara died? Clara sits before the camera with her hands gently folded one over the other

*Clara's photograph*

on her lap. She is wearing a starched, high, white collar, its lapels tucked under a soft black dress, and white matching cuffs. Her white hair seems to be caught in a fine net in gentle waves. She is smiling and looks very kindly.

There are also two recent photographs of Chemnitz, possibly sent to her by one of her brothers. On the back, written in German, it says: 'July, 1967. Villa Klara in Augustusburg.' It is still there, now a children's home for the Party. The other is of a large, rather severe building with a baroque clock tower. Scenes from her childhood, when things were orderly, before the chaos which ruled the rest of her life.

Then: two very fine, white linen handkerchiefs, hand-embroidered, also in white, with a most delicate pattern on one, and, on the other, a large 'K' set in a white floral motif. Other contents include a small pillbox with a porcelain lid and two pills inside; an ivory comb, lipstick and face powder; her last cheque book, all neatly filled in, and a note in shaky handwriting about some food and toiletries she must have needed; a photograph of daffodils in the garden; a *Süddeutsche Zeitung* article about a book on the Holocaust; a list of books scribbled on a bit of paper: Naipaul's *Among the Believers*, Fanon's *The Wretched of the Earth* and Lore Wolf's *Resisting Adolf*; her steroid treatment card; a few last bills; a present for her consultant at the Brompton Hospital; bank cards, travel permit, library and Film Institute membership cards. A blue purse which inside out becomes a carrier bag: she liked practical things like that.

Finally: a pair of American twenty-cent stamps cut from an envelope, with the word 'LOVE' repeated vertically five times, the V in the shape of a heart in five colours. I wondered what it was doing in her handbag. Maybe it reminded her of that which – in spite of her many great friendships throughout her lifetime and in different parts of the world – had, in the end, eluded her.

Maybe both of us.

The old Spanish song my mother used to sing to me in Marseilles came back to me like an old refrain: *Donde estás corazón?*

*Where are you my heart?*
*I can't hear your beat.*
*My pain is so great*
*That I cannot weep.*
*I would like to cry*
*And have no more tears …*

∽

SHE DIED IN LONDON, in April, 1984.

From her bed, my mother could look out through the glass door and windows of her room onto the pretty, north London, garden.

'It will soon be springtime and all the daffodils will be out. It will be lovely to see them from your bed,' I was telling her. But she looked away, the enthusiasm gone from her face.

She once came to stay a few days at my home in Duncan Terrace, and I arranged a bed for her in my study and tried to make her comfortable.

'Is there anything you would like? Maybe some music?'

'I'd like to hear the Sardanas,' she said.

So I played the Sardanas, with their fresh lilting sounds and plaintive repetitive phrases from the ancient instruments still used in Catalonia. This music seemed to transport her back to happier times in Barcelona – when every Sunday, in Barcelona's central square, a group of musicians played the Sardanas and people danced in large circles holding hands and tripping a light, complicated step – before the start of the war and her permanent exile.

'You never wrote your memoirs, as so many people have often urged you to …'

'No. I don't know how to write them,' she said weakly. '*You* might do it some day,' and she turned her head and closed her eyes.

In the last days, she often clutched in her hand that photograph of Villa Klara in Augustusburg. Now and then, she would gaze at it silently for long periods at a time: a large house surrounded with fir trees where her mother Clara used to sometimes take her – just the two of them there together. Once, while I was sitting by her bedside, my mother came to from her dozing. She looked at me for a few moments and a loving expression flooded her face. 'Pretty,' she whispered, and closed her eyes and dozed off again.

I was sitting with her in her room in north London a few hours before she died. She was very weak, too weak even to talk. Her hair very white and her eyes intensely green, their pupils small from the heroin she was receiving for her pain.

'Is there anything you want to tell me?' I asked her.

And she whispered weakly, with great effort, 'I have understood.'

And that was one of the last things she said. She died in the early hours of the morning, with me by her side. I closed her wide-open eyes.

# A Writer in the Andes

After my mother's passing, and closure with Kraks, I went through a period of intense mourning, questioning and re-examination. Time moved on and work continued ... A congress in Washington led to a meeting with an Argentine author and his writing which opened up momentous new insights in my search for answers.

*Washington, 1988.*
A cocktail party in Woodrow Wilson's house.

Small groups of anaesthetists stood around chatting to one another while drinks were passed around in this famous home turned museum. At this get-together of researchers presenting papers at the World Congress of Anesthesiologists in the American capital, I was talking with one from Argentina whom I had just met.

'I've never been to Argentina, though I know Mexico well,' I was telling Eduardo whose tall figure stood before me, attentive and slightly stooped, a glass of wine in his hand, as we conversed in Woodrow Wilson's elegantly furnished living room. Following our exchange on our clinical interests and research work, he suggested I give some lectures at the forthcoming meeting in Buenos Aires, of which he was one of the organisers. 'I've always thought of Argentina as very European, unlike Mexico where much of its own culture has survived in spite of the Spanish colonisation and its proximity to the United States. Can one find anything of the original civilisations there?'

'Certainly! The area in the northwest,' he told me excitedly, 'has a rich local culture of its own. There's one particular village there, Purmamarca, which attracts many painters for its beauty. The little town of white houses is surrounded by hills of amazing colours. I dream of retiring there one day!'

'Oh? Maybe I'll get to see it sometime. After this congress in Washington, I've taken some leave to go to San Cristóbal de las Casas in the south of Mexico near the Guatemalan border. It is Maya country. It is also the place where Traven, a writer who has always intrigued me, is said to have lived.'

'Ah, yes?' Eduardo looked curious.

I told Eduardo what I knew about that mysterious writer who never revealed his name, was said by some to be the Kaiser's illegitimate son, and by others to have Scandinavian origins. His book, *The Death Ship*, about the fate of a stateless man, implied he had been closely involved with events in Europe between the two wars, and had given me further insights into our own predicament in Vichy France. Maybe his political activities had led him to hide his identity and escape to Mexico. He was well known for his *Treasure of the Sierra Madre* which was made into a film with Humphrey Bogart. He also wrote *The Rebellion of the Hanged* on the mistreatment of the natives who collected rubber in the Mexican jungle during the time of Porfirio Díaz: the great-grandfather of Conchita's friend Kitty.

'When he first went to live in San Cristóbal, you could only reach it by mule! I believe there's a road now. I'm looking forward to seeing it!'

The following year in Buenos Aires, at the end of the Latin American Congress of Anesthesiologists, where I was invited to give three lectures, I set off to visit the area in the northwest that Eduardo had told me about, where remnants of Argentina's pre-conquest cultures had survived and the landscape had a flavour of its own.

Back in London, I couldn't shake off the impression left from that brief visit. I called the Graham-Yoolls – Andrew and Michaela had moved to London when the military junta took over in Argentina. They had mentioned a writer they knew in that area.

'I loved Jujuy!' I said to Michaela on the phone. 'Would you have any books about it, maybe by your friend, that I could borrow?'

'Yes,' she answered.

I had stood in the study of the Graham-Yoolls' north London home, surrounded by shelves full of books on Argentina and Latin America – the subject of Andrew's journalism and writing – when Michaela thrust the slim paperback volume of *Fuego en Casabindo* in my hand. I turned to the first page and read:

*Aquí la tierra es dura y estéril; el cielo está más cerca que en ninguna otra parte y es azul y vacío. No llueve, pero cuando el cielo ruge su voz es aterradora, implacable, colérica ...*

The words stirred me. I tried to keep my hands steady as I glanced through the pages.

I took the book home and settled down to read it but soon came across many unfamiliar expressions from the archaic Spanish still spoken in that cut-off corner of the Andes, along with occasional Quechua words. I was struggling with the text when the idea struck me that, were I to translate it into my now more familiar English language, the very process would help me grasp its meaning more clearly. I sat with the book in front of me and surrounded myself with dictionaries – an old Spanish Larousse, Cassell's Spanish-English, the Oxford English, Roget's Thesaurus – and painstakingly started translating every phrase. I soon began to feel the need to capture, not only the meaning, but the rhythms and nuances, the stark, economical language, its poetry, freshness and surprise, the evocative sounds and smells, the beauty, subtleties and savagery depicted in the Argentine text.

I dialled international directory enquiries.
'Which country?'
'Argentina, Jujuy.'
'What name?'
'Héctor Tizón,' and I gave the address of his law offices, which Michaela had told me.
Three hours later, international directory enquiries called me back with the number, and I dialled it.
'*Hola?*' a man's voice replied.
'May I speak with Señor Tizón?' I asked in Spanish.
'*De parte de quien?*' Who shall I say is asking for him?'
I firmly gave my name with my title, hoping to persuade the person at the other end of the line to put the call through to Tizón, in what might be a busy law practice.
'*Soy yo,*' I am he, he said simply.
'*Señor* Tizón? Am I speaking with Señor Tizón?'
'*Si.*'

I introduced myself and told him I was reading his book *Fuego en Casabindo*.

'I'll send you others, if you wish.'

'I like it very much. Does it exist in English?'

'No. But a French translation of another of my books was published last year.'

'May I translate it? And look for a publisher?'

'Yes.' He had a rich, expressive voice.

The conversation was the start of a regular, lengthy correspondence.

I went back to my translation with increased application. I worked at it every evening after I got home from the hospital, far into the night – unravelling each sentence, digesting it, feeling its life and rhythms, recreating it in English. And as I watched myself reaching out towards the imagery emerging out of the words on the pages, the tenuous concepts lifting out from the misty boundaries of my mind to become clear scenes of Latin American village life, and then again saw myself transforming them back into words and sentences, English this time, I appeared to be stirring some out of reach, half-forgotten corner of my being still smarting like an unhealed wound, and digging out the bits of myself that were torn asunder during my translocation from Acapantzingo to Christchurch. A break in my life that went hand in hand with my break with the Spanish language and adoption of English. In my endeavour now to express in English the colours, music, smell and taste of life in the Andean *puna*, I was bridging that break between my lives in Acapantzingo and Christchurch and, along with it, between the two languages. I was overcoming my loss of what Mexico had stood for in my life, which was in Spanish, and my difficult readjustment to life in New Zealand, linked to English. English had been my language of a life gone dull and grey, of my sense of alienation, of supression of my passion. Telling Tizón's world in English was healing my resentments and resolving those long-buried frustrations. Marrying those two worlds inside me and making them into one whole. I was making friends with the English language, getting to like it, delighting in my manipulation of its words to pass on a wealth of sensations and ideas. To love it. And it shook me up …

I had gone in search of Traven in San Cristóbal de las Casas, and found Tizón in San Salvador de Jujuy.

∾

THE 'HOUNSLOW CENTRAL' sign flashed past as the train slowed down and stopped. It was cold and overcast: a fine mist hung in the air and everything merged into a shadowless grey. The buskers stopped singing their rowdy country songs, scooped the coins from the more sympathetic passengers out of their hat and left the carriage. We pulled out from the station on the last stretch to Heathrow. I would soon be comfortably seated in the jumbo jet as it climbed into the skies and headed out, high over the Atlantic.

*Jujuy, Northwest Argentina, 1990.*
HERE THE SKY was a brilliant blue, broken only by small clusters of luminous white clouds straddling the distant hills that bordered the wide expanse of flat scrubland. This was the *puna*. We were 4,000 metres above sea level, the air was light and transparent, and breathing short with undue effort. Westwards, at the edge of these plains, rose the tall chain of snowy peaks that formed the cordillera of the Andes on this side of Chile. The sun was fierce, it burned where it touched, and the colours vibrant, clear and sharp, while the shade was etched out, very dark and ice-cold.

I had come here to soak in the atmosphere of the flat *puna* landscape, the changing skies, violent thunder and lightning storms, the wind that invariably blows after midday lifting dust and buffeting iciness. I hoped to see the descendants of these peoples, once ruled by the Incas, and the villages with their adobe houses and small white churches in their central squares. Of these, the one I most wished to visit was Casabindo. It lay at the end of a rough, stony track and across riverbeds swollen with fast-running waters from recent rains. I had spent many long hours working my way through vivid passages in *Fuego en Casabindo* that gave an insight into life on this Andean plateau. It touched on all that converges on man here to make him what he is: the land, his history, his superstitions and age-old habits, his struggles, the skies, the storms, his animals.

South of the *puna* at a lower altitude, at a point between mountains covered in lush vegetation where two rivers join, is the small village of Yala – a cluster of houses, a few unpaved roads, two or three general stores, a railway station, and one telephone – where I found Héctor Tizón's house. I had come at his invitation to meet him and spend some days at his home. Sitting on the veranda overlooking the luxuriant garden, Tizón spoke of his childhood in Yala, of his first writings, of his time as a diplomat in Mexico and later in Milan, of his years of exile in Spain during the colonels' rule in Argentina, and his life now back in Yala with his law practice in Jujuy, where he can be himself among the things he knows and in the land and with the people he can write about. And in the early morning, when the rest of the household still slept, I lay in bed in the guest room listening to the riot of exotic calls from the native birds outside my window, the occasional dog bark in the distance, a dialogue between roosters, and the silence of the mountains here in the lower reaches of the Andes.

We set off to the north in a small truck – Tizón, his wife and I – for the unusually late rains that year had made even the main road difficult to negotiate. We drove across riverbeds with huge boulders dragged down by the torrential currents, and past rocky mountains stratified into layers of violet, rust, pink and ochre from their rich mineral content. Before the Spanish conquest, Tizón told me, gold and silver also abounded. As we gradually climbed higher, the skies became clearer and bluer, and the clouds brighter and more luminous. Paved roads and towns were left behind and long stretches of lonely bare hills and a great silence appeared, and then finally the flat *puna* landscape with here and there a herd of llamas, sheep, goats or the occasional vicuna. We finally reached Abra Pampa. There the Tizóns bought half a sheep which they found next to the llama meat in the local market and, after a lunch of a thick soup of maize, vegetables, meat and chilli, we took the road to Casabindo. As we drove through the *puna*, a lonely adobe farmstead with its goats or llamas would appear every now and then dotted in the bleak, empty landscape. Finally, the village of Casabindo came into view: a small cluster of adobe houses nestling at the foot of gentle hills at one end of the flat tableland, the sparkling white twin steeple of the church

*Abra Pampa in the Andes, Argentina*

rising high above the rest. It was early afternoon when we arrived, and the place was deserted apart from two young children who sud-denly appeared from nowhere and produced a set of very large noisy keys, with which they proceeded to open the gates into the churchyard and the church door itself to let us in. Inside the simple bare interior of the church, Tizón, his voice lowered, talked to me about the stories of the wooden saints, their layers of paint and gold now wearing thin with age, which stood in the shadows. And his quiet whispers resonated and were multiplied in the empty church.

In the streets, the eerie, silent emptiness contrasted with the crowded scenes I had translated

*With Héctor Tizón in Casabindo*

313

*On tour with Tizón on the publication of his books in English, St Andrews University, Scotland, 1993*

from *Fuego en Casabindo*, based on local events in the second half of the nineteenth century.

We returned to Abra Pampa and the Tizóns took the road back to Yala – while I made my base there, from which to travel and see more of the *puna* and other villages.

*Orus, the French Pyrenees, 1991.*
WE SAT AROUND the dinner table on the roof terrace under a night sky crowded with stars, helping ourselves to *spaghetti alla carbonara* and passing around the wine. Snippets of conversation in French, Spanish, English and Italian were flying back and forth across the table between Françoise's family and myself. One of her daughters was describing her life with her architect husband in Casablanca, the other her work researching viruses in Central Africa, while the third talked of the specialised editions of nineteenth-century art books she published in Paris.

'Was it your own work which fired your daughter's interest in publishing?' I asked Françoise who was sitting next to me.

'Maybe … Who knows what is involved in such decisions.'

Françoise had been telling me of her work in publishing. Our common interest, which had first drawn us together, was in our translation of Tizón: Françoise Campo-Timal was his French translator.

On my arrival to meet her in her mountain house, where she spent her time when she was not in her Paris apartment, Françoise had shown me the recent work on the stable – once the main part of her narrow village house – now converted into additional rooms and bathrooms for family and friends. On the top floor of the steep staircase the landing contained her work area with her computer, papers and books, and a door led into her bedroom, its walls freshly whitened, a white wool carpet on the floor, a thick white cotton cover on the bed and a large white cushion on the floor, with a breathtaking view of the mountains through the window. Another door led to the roof terrace, which was bordered with potted flowering plants and overlooked the back of the village as it climbed up the mountain.

Françoise used her entirely white room for her daily meditation in her resolve to improve her health, through both orthodox and alternative means, for her advanced illness.

The next day we took a walk together, Françoise and I, past the last village houses of local stone and along a path through the outlying woods. Here we looked out onto the valley below, which dropped steeply down the side of the mountain I had driven up the previous day, winding my way on a track barely wide enough for my small car. Another chain of mountains rose on the other side of the valley, its peaks enveloped in a blue haze.

'Orus was built at the turn of the last century, after another older village further up the mountain was destroyed by fire,' Françoise was telling me. 'This valley is full of history. There are many caves in the area, some with prehistoric drawings. There are also many great old castles. You must have seen some on your way.'

'Yes! They seemed to belong to fairy stories!'

Orus lay off the main route between Tarascon and Andorra. I had driven through the medieval town of Tarascon and seen its large ancient clock on top of the hill and the river running through its centre.

'Of course, this has nothing to do with the Andes, yet ... there is something between them. I think all the mountains in the world have something in common. And the mountain people too. They are very shy, very closed, but when they give you their friendship, it's forever. I lived in Orus for two years when the children were small, and I got to know all my neighbours. They are a great people.'

Françoise took off her wig. She had just undergone her second course of chemotherapy and all her hair had fallen out.

'You don't mind, do you?' I didn't. I felt privileged that after our short meeting, Françoise should reveal herself to me, vulnerable as she was with her illness, with no artifice. 'I'm feeling too hot,' she added simply. Her shocking baldness could not detract from her beauty. Her eyes were like two intense blue crystals, and they shone with a mixture of wisdom and a great warmth.

'Maybe in the mountains, the harsh life, the need to deal directly with the elements and the forces of nature, concentrates people's minds and efforts on survival, on the essential,' I suggested to Françoise. 'There is no room for the trivial, for anything superfluous or phoney. Friendships are important in such conditions.' I was, without realising it, reflecting on the sense of values I too was surrounded with as a child, grown from the hardships inflicted by man then.

We stopped for a moment to gaze at the changing view before us and to allow Françoise a brief rest. Although she did not complain, she was surely in pain.

'I grew up in Indochina,' Françoise told me. 'We moved there from France when I was three months old. My father was an engineer and he was posted there to supervise the building of roads, including a very long one all the way from the south of Indochina to Laos in the north. It was during the war. I was looked after by an Indochinese nurse as we moved around the countryside with my father's work. My mother stayed in the more civilised town – she liked to play cards and poker with her French friends. I spoke Vietnamese with my nanny: Vietnamese was my first language. I didn't speak any French then.'

'So you grew up in two very distinct cultures too. How fascinating to find these parallels in our lives!' I suggested. 'I think we must have been born within two or three years of each other.'

'I was born in 1938,' Françoise said. 'I returned to France from Indochina when I was nine, and I had to learn to speak French. And to write. It was a big shock. I felt trapped, very closed in, in the strict, formal atmosphere of a French boarding school after my wild, free life in the Indochinese countryside, which I had loved. I think that's why I became so interested in foreign languages. Now I *love* French, I *love* my language. I love all languages.'

'Maybe our translation is related, in some way, to an attempt to bridge the various cultures we have experienced, maybe even a search for our roots. You know, I once heard Salman Rushdie say in an interview, "Modern man has no roots." I was very intrigued by that statement, its paradox – how can a man not have roots? And yet many of us fit into that statement. Half of humankind seems to be moved, displaced, ending up as refugees. It's a pretty universal state. And Tizón has a special way of writing about it and looking into it.'

'Tizón *has* roots,' Françoise pointed out. 'We don't, but *his* roots are very deep. And he writes about them, he doesn't want to forget them. In his notes about his last journey through the *puna* before his exile to Spain, he writes about his wish to record his landscape, memorise every intimate detail, to always remember his roots.'

'We are searching for roots we don't have – or at least are muddled and confused – and Tizón, who has them but was torn from them at one stage, is exploring their meaning in depth.'

'When Van Gogh does a painting of his own chair … his chair, that's all … it's universal!' Françoise asserted. 'And that's what Tizón is doing.'

We followed the track a little further surrounded by the straggly trees and vegetation of the Alps, and a silence broken only by our voices and the songs of birds, and then started on our way back.

'That's right,' I agreed. 'I have found that when the exotic and unfamiliar layers of Tizón's characters are peeled off, I can see aspects of myself in them.'

'I too.'

*Back to Jujuy, 1990.*
FROM ABRA PAMPA I took a bus to La Quiaca on the Bolivian border, and walked across the bridge to the Bolivian town of Villazón along the path known as El Camino de las Hormigas, the ants' track – a fitting description of the large human traffic ferrying a variety of goods back and forth between Argentina and Bolivia at that point. Back in La Quiaca, I climbed onto the back of a small open truck with some eighteen *Coyas* – four of these, small children who took up little space but made up with their din – bound for the village of Yavi. It was Easter Friday and there would be a special Mass in Yavi's seventeenth-century church. I found the small white church, off the main street, against a background of tall yellowing poplars. Inside the church, its baroque interior entirely covered in gold sparkled

dimly in the muted light that filtered through the onyx windows. As the sun went down, groups of women congregated to take part in the singing of the *doctrinas*. They walked in file through the streets of Yavi in the black icy night, their hands cupped around candle-lit, paper lanterns which glowed in the dark and illuminated their faces, as they sang their strange, three-toned Easter chant. Above the collective singing, a clear descant warbling would ring out in the chilled night air. Each group came from a different village and would collect in turn in the small church to sing their own variant of the chant, pray with the priest, and then set out once again to walk through the streets of Yavi, all through the night until sunrise. Then they all climbed to the cross at the top of a hill and chanted around it as the light of day started breaking and a cold wind blew. Later that morning, people from the surrounding countryside were busy arranging their goods on open ground – basket work, dead sheep, earthenware and tin pots, a variety of cloth and wool – and cooking various foods over small wood fires in preparation for the Easter Fair.

To venture into other worlds, abandon ourselves to their wonder. Open up new visions, enrich ourselves with the fruits of cultures not our own. And, in turn, to delve back into our own world with a new light, see it through different lenses.

The multiple, fragmented worlds of those who have been moved across countries and cultures, each inner world interlocked with its language. And within one language, still more worlds. Like the Castilian and Mexican Spanish of my childhood – the Castilian that to our Spanish refugee friends stood for their lost Spain, and to the Mexicans, the language of their past oppressors. My switch from one to the other as a mark of respect for the two peoples, each of which was trying to protect its own identity. Earlier, in France, I had had to replace my Spanish, just as I mastered talking at the age of two, with French, unaware until much later about the dangers of speaking the 'wrong' language in Vichy France. And again, I had reached complete fluency in French by the time we were obliged to leave France for Mexico and face a new switch of languages, back to Spanish. And a few years later, abandon it once more, this time for English. With every change, my brain would have to deal afresh with the coordination between my thoughts and the new sounds I had to produce to relate to the new people around me – and each change would interfere a little more with the normal fusion between language, thought and expression, between language and identity. And beyond, with the easy flow between people who share a common background. Yet each change too, helped to enhance insights, broaden dimensions, increase choices. A wider view perhaps, for the price of greater isolation.

German was my mother's tongue. Back in my infancy, it had percolated into my fuzzy awareness from background conversations between my mother and her friends, its soft timbre inextricable from my mother's voice – a comforting sound which took me back to my beginnings when my identity was still blurred with hers. I never spoke it – it was just there, a warm, familiar, intimate sound. When I stepped on German soil for the first time on my return to Europe, I surprised myself suddenly speaking it. The sentences simply turned up, readymade, in my mind. If I could not think of a word or phrase, I would call up my mother in my imagination and I would hear her speak it. And as I became aware of the events in Europe during my absence, I began to also hear the shrill German commands rounding up Jews, shooting them into mass graves, squeezing them into cattle trains bound for the extermination camps, and I slowly began to hate German until my insides curdled at its sound. The beautiful, tender language of my mother had turned into the language of unimaginable horror. To change again and blend with my image of today's Germany. Language does that to you. You respond to it as to a human being. And transcend the ghosts one language raises, by saying in it what you feel in another, closer to the heart. Translating.

It was during my translation of Tizón's work that I experienced the part language plays in our sense of self. I began to understand how, with each change of language, I had undergone a whole new system of thinking, a new view of the world experienced through different sounds and associations, another grammar and vocabulary, so that the image of who I am in one language is distinct from my self image in another. It seemed as though each language had its own, particular, separate, nervous network, or circuitry of associations, in my brain, making up a whole inner world in my mind that was *I* in that language, and these different networks in parallel were being bridged every time I moved from one language to another, as in translating. Perhaps, the more established and numerous these neuronal bridges become between such networks in a multicultured person, the more integrated their identity. My confused sense of self, rescued and integrated. Maybe, I thought, the relationship we develop in our early life between the world we come to know and the language we use to express it, goes hand in hand with the emerging self we call identity, binding language with identity. Then too, any changes and shifts in language during childhood along with changes and shifts in surroundings, customs and behaviour, may cast off the strong associations which give us our 'group' or 'national' identity. And out of the diversity and wealth of experience, a distillation of the self might emerge. A firm, clearly defined self, less dependent on the group character with its own different richness. I now appreciated that I am plainly and simply the sum of all I have lived and experienced, that I don't need to fit into a classification, a stereotype. And it felt comfortable to be me.

On my return to Yala, Héctor Tizón read out some passages from his diary written during his trips through the *puna* :

> *Here, when shadows begin to fall, everything starts. Young goats, an animal renowned for its lust and lunacy, will be served for dinner, and the wine will be on the house. At the feast, no one will retrieve any bit that falls on the floor, because that slip shall be a favourable sign, a sensuous wink from everlasting life. Afterwards, the canticles and coplas will start, and the beating of drums. There will be one, two hundred singers. Rhythm, harmony, measure: there is no place for these here. Nor are these fiestas for youths and young girls only. Old women and men past their prime are not set apart. Everyone becomes equal by a levelling that is formal and absolute. All have the same worth starting from that uncertain moment when consciousness starts to mist. Then is the chance for the stranger, he who is not from these lands, to exercise humility. To drink and surrender himself as befits him and his body demands. And to sing, but without the shouting or mannerisms*

*of a false enthusiasm, rather to the rhythm of this monotonous sound marked by the hopeless movements of those who adopt it like a joy that appears rigid, ritualistic and wretched. Civilisation is killing the gods, and the gods are withdrawing to the countryside, the pastoral. Here there are no fiestas other than the religious, and they are observed with drink and song. Every celebration relates to the earth, to death, to fate; and the temple of their gods is their way of life.*

The breaking down of barriers while safeguarding distinctiveness and diversity, pooling the universal without undermining the particular. Transmitting through translation insights and ideas not only across cultures but also time. A window into another world long since disappeared. To express the inexpressible, translate a culture's unique concepts into another's language that lacks the words to describe them. Yet such is the nature of words, so infinite the possible combinations and arrangements in their rainbow subtlety of meanings and associations, and such the basic common denominator of humankind, that there is always a way. The art is in seeking it out, in its discovery.

The process of transforming idea, sensation, experience into words. Reaching towards the nebulous edge of awareness where shadowy, half formed concepts hover, dissolve and reappear, until they are entrapped, clarified, defined and transformed into language. Abstract sounds and scribbles which conjure up thoughts and memories in a rich web of shifting meanings and associations. Their allusive, ephemeral quality, yet their peculiar power. Their spell. Their capacity to arouse emotions, effect profound change, cause lasting effects. All this I saw while I struggled with the words, squeezing them out like a baby from the womb. I found myself piercing through the meaning of the words in my attempt to reach beyond them to the very essence of the sense they suggested – like treading on quicksand reaching for an anchor. I had never imagined words could be so devastating.

Not long after my visit to Orus, I received an envelope addressed to me in Françoise's handwriting. Inside there was a solitary poem with the date of her death ...

*S'il est vrai que plus tard*
*s'il est vrai que peut-être*
*alors laisse que ton oeil*
*se ferme*

If it's true that beyond
if it's true that maybe
then allow your eye
to close.

Beyond the rainbow-coloured mountains to the west of Pur-mamarca lies a salt lake described in *Fuego en Casabindo*, Salinas Grandes, which I have a burning desire to see some day, that I might lose myself in the vast whiteness, the silence, the great calm. And – like Françoise in her white room of meditation – come face to face with the universe within myself, and the awesome diversity around me.

*The salt flats, like the face of a mirror, reflected the moon and reflected, like a shapeless stain, the belly, the body of the horse that was gallop-ing that evening; the horse that carried encrusted on its back a man without a soul. The horse was flying over the salt flats to which the moonlight was at that moment returning their ancient nature of the sea ...*

# Mightier Than Fate

MY NEBULOUS IMPRESSIONS, as a child, of my mother's and her friends' pressing questions and dilemmas that seemed to besiege us, needed elucidating. People I remembered from my childhood whom I met again in later years helped to bring into sharper focus the immediate political circumstances and personal troubles that determined our lives and helped shape me.

In my search to understand more about those times at the start of my life, I sought Seppel, my mother's great friend in her youth. I had been given her address and telephone number, many years previously, by Kraks' long-standing friend, Elmar Tophoven. We had gone from Tuscania to spend an afternoon with him and his wife on the outskirts of Rome, where they were staying that summer.

'So your mother was in Barcelona during the Spanish Civil War!' Elmar had repeated with interest, leaning forward attentively, a disarmingly warm smile on his face, a mop of prematurely snow-white hair flopping over it. We were having coffee on the balcony of their rented apartment where Elmar was translating Samuel Beckett's works into German.

'She might have known a good friend of mine who was also there: Seppel von Ranke!'

'Ah, yes! Seppel was my mother's closest friend!' I declared, somewhat astonished. 'But since my mother's return to Europe after the war, Seppel has refused to see her. She appears to have fallen out with my mother over something to do with her husband's activities during the Spanish war.'

'Hm ... I knew old Hubert well ... There *was* something disturbing them ...' Elmar remarked thoughtfully, speaking fondly about his friend, yet with a teasing twinkle in his eyes. He then added, 'I have Seppel's address and telephone number in Munich, would you like to take them down?'

'Yes! Certainly!'

I had kept Seppel's details in my address book ever since that meeting. I had used them only once before, when my mother lay dying and kept asking for Seppel; there seemed to be something she wanted to talk to her about before it was too late. I wrote Seppel a letter telling her of my mother's impending death and wish to see her. She never replied.

Some years had gone by when I was trying to piece together those days of my mother's life in Spain, and I decided to ring the Munich telephone number Elmar had given me. If Seppel was still there, the worst that could happen – I told myself – would be that she'd hang up the phone if she didn't wish to speak with me. I took courage and dialled the number.

'Hello,' a woman's voice answered.

'Hello! I would like to speak to Seppel von Ranke, please. Does she still live there?' I asked in my best German.

'Yes. It is I,' came a curt, distant reply.

Then I told her, simply, my first name, adding, now in Spanish, 'I am Käte's daughter.'

There was complete silence. Finally Seppel's voice returned, this time tremulously full of emotion and surprise, 'This is astonishing! I was just thinking of you! I was sitting on my balcony, this very moment, looking at old photographs, and I came across yours in Barcelona!'

We spoke to each other, somewhat shaken and incoherent, for the first time since Seppel held me as a baby on her lap during those eventful times in Barcelona when she and my mother had been so close. She invited me to come and stay in her flat in a leafy suburb in Munich. And one day, I went. We spent hours sitting on her flower-laden balcony looking at the many photo albums I had brought with me that my mother had kept from those early years. Seppel was warm and affectionate, the

*Seppel, myself and Käte in Spain, 1936*

special tie still there, and I felt myself stretching back across time to my mother's life when mine was just starting.

Seppel would say it was my speaking to her in Spanish on the telephone that made her give way. After that, we kept in touch.

At that first meeting in Munich, Seppel spoke of her friendship with my mother from the time they were seventeen or eighteen.

'She was very important for me. She had been living in Berlin and had already experienced and learned a great deal and met many people. She had an interesting and sophisticated view of the world. I had come straight from my home town, near Frankfurt. My father was a doctor, very kind and upright and liberal in his views – he couldn't stand Hitler – but even so, I was trying to break away from that narrow lifestyle. Käte introduced me to a much wider world. In those days, we worked very hard. But we also had some good times together!' she – now in her eighties, petite and hesitant, with those opal blue eyes which I somehow seemed to remember – added with her girlish laugh.

My mother followed her to London, where Seppel had befriended and was minding the small son of the Penrose family in their flat in Russell Square. Ilse Lüneman, a friend of Seppel from her school days, also joined them. Then – the situation in their native Germany worsening and Hitler's power mounting – the three of them decided to move to Barcelona.

She described their first meeting with her first husband, Rafael Campalans.

'One day we were invited to a fancy dress party, Ilse, Käte and me, and we went as Mexican revolutionaries: in narrow trousers and big sombreros. Quite natural, no make-up. We didn't need it: we were slim and svelte and good-looking then! Rafael Campalans was there. He asked who we were, and someone told him, "They are three idealistic, young, German communist girls." He was very intrigued and wanted to meet us.'

Campalans was a much loved and admired Spanish politician, deeply committed to finding a fair and peaceful solution to the problems that were shaking up Spain then, Seppel explained. She got up and went to fetch a number of books written by him, and by others about him. She opened one, and quoted at random: 'To be different does not imply to be enemies. At heart, the solution to the peninsular problems consists of finding a way for the collaboration and friendship between the various peoples, within a context of mutual respect, and with every one's freedom in view.'

Words which impressed me, being as relevant to the problems of the world today, as to Spain then in the early thirties.

'Rafael became a good friend. He would often invite Käte and me for a meal and we spent many hours together conversing and exchanging ideas. Eventually Käte said he must crystallise his feelings and decide between us! He chose me – though he liked Käte very much too – and we got married. He was older than me. He'd been married before. His wife died in childbirth. His daughter and son came to live with us.'

We were sitting in Seppel's living room as she told her story. It was fitted with antique furniture from the von Ranke family, and the wall was covered with books and old paintings. An abundance of beige and brown cushions covered the sofa, and mushroom velvet curtains framed the windows and French doors that opened onto her balcony full of flowers.

'Rafael took a summerhouse by the beach in Torredembarra where I stayed with the children while he commuted to Barcelona. It was heavenly! We often had marvellous dinner parties with his friends. One day, we were expecting a large number of people that evening, and he brought heaps of good food and wine and lots of colourful lampions which he hung everywhere in our beach house. Lunch was ready, but he insisted on having a short swim first, so we went into the sea. Rafael, the children and myself. I was feeling cold and I got out before the others. I was drying myself when I suddenly heard the children yelling. "*Socorro! Socorro!*" I ran back … Rafael was floating in the water, dragged around by the waves. The sea was getting rough and I called Pedro, a fisherman who lived nearby. He found it difficult to reach him on his boat with the growing waves, but he finally pulled him out. I was desperate. We called a doctor, but he was already dead. His head had been knocked against the rocks and he had an injury to his temple. Your mother was in New York – a wealthy family from Barcelona had taken her with them to look after their child – and as soon as she heard, she returned to be with me. We used to sleep together in the big bed in Rafael's Barcelona apartment. I was devastated. Käte was very comforting. She helped me a lot.'

Seppel also told me of her first meeting with Hubert von Ranke.

'I was given a lift by a young man, from my home town in Germany, who was travelling to Paris from Barcelona. When we arrived, he phoned a German baron he had met in Canada: he had invited him to call on him if he ever came to Paris. The baron was very pleased to hear from him and asked him to drop round with his friend – that was me. We arrived at a very grand villa with a large garden in an exclusive suburb outside Paris, and he invited us inside. He was one of those tall, blond Germans, with very blue eyes. Absolutely charming. *Gnädige Frau, Küss die Hand*, and so on, the lot. He fussed around me and asked me to sit down on the large sofa in his elegant drawing room, and – as I looked up – I suddenly realised I was sitting under an enormous, life-size portrait of Hitler! I was horrified! At the first opportunity, I made some excuse to leave. I said I had an appointment with someone. The charming baron absolutely insisted on accompanying me, so I ended up being driven in his Mercedes to the poorest quarter of Paris where Gertrude Düby, another friend of ours had her apartment. Her street was called Rue du Paradis!' Seppel gave her little-girl laugh again, and she continued: 'I asked the baron to let me out about a block before Trudy's place and pretended to go into another house until he left, and then I walked the rest of the way, and up the narrow stairs to her apartment. There I found Trudy and Hubert, whom I was meeting for the first time. Trudy was the leader of the Comité des Femmes Antifascistes de France. She always had to be the leader of something or other! I told them my story, and Hubert got very excited and said I must go back to the baron's place! Apparently he'd been trying to infiltrate his circle for a long time: he was the head, or something, of the Gestapo in Paris! But I absolutely refused. I wasn't going back there again!'

Seppel later married Hubert. He was a German, first cousin of Robert Graves, and she was amused to recall her first sighting of Graves some years before in the *cala* in Deyá, in Mallorca, sitting in his red pyjamas under a large straw hat against the rock on which my mother and she had been sunbathing.

After that first meeting in Munich we kept in touch by phone and letter. We met again in Paris three years later. She had a tiny flat in Rue du Dragon, in St-Germain-des-Prés, from the time when it had been her and Hubert's sole living quarters in the late 1930s. The concierge had kept it for them during the German occupation, and they returned to it after liberation.

As I walked down Rue du Dragon, I read plaques saying that Jean Giono and Victor Hugo had also lived there. I reached Seppel's building and climbed the seven floors to her place at the top of the building. This small room, she told me, served as living, working, eating and sleeping room for the two of them; they cooked in the cupboard-sized kitchen with the water they collected from a bucket kept on the landing. Here they wrote articles for the cultural section of the new German newspapers of the time, starting with the *Neue Zeitung*, with the aim of re-educating the German nation after the Nazi indoctrination it had suffered in the preceding years. In this room, too, Seppel pointed out, she nursed Hubert for six weeks after he had a heart attack and refused to go to hospital. She would settle herself on the small settee for the night, so that Hubert might rest more easily on the sofa. Hubert survived another sixteen years.

'We had a very difficult life, in this room,' Seppel went on in her timid, vulnerable voice. 'I was often tempted to climb on the roof and jump off,' she added simply and unaffectedly. We were sitting on the lush burgundy rug on her sofa looking out through the window onto the roofs and chimneys of Paris. From a recess in the wall next to us, a life-size image of Jeremiah looked languidly at us, his eyes expressing an exquisite peace, a mass of trailing locks and beard floating down from his sculpted medieval head in the black-and-white photograph.

'I lie on the sofa when I'm tired and nervous and look at him,' Seppel almost whispered, 'and it calms me down.'

After the start of the civil war in Spain, my mother and Seppel had started seeing less of each other. My mother was working at Barcelona's main post office censoring German mail supportive of Franco's campaign. She was also beginning to feel disillusioned with the programmes and instructions from Moscow that were being discussed at Communist Party meetings she attended. This finally led to her resignation from the Party – a party whose ideals she had thought so much more humane an option to Hitler and his rising Nazi party, when she had joined it back in Berlin. Hubert, on the other hand, led Barcelona's hardline, Russian-backed, communist faction, which began to carry out purges of allies of the sort Stalin had started in Russia.

As the Republican defeat became imminent, Seppel and Hubert went to Savoia where he joined the French Resistance at the outbreak of World War Two. At the end of this war they moved to Paris, to their small frugal apartment. Seppel and my mother had written to each other when it became possible again – until the day Hubert and Seppel met some friends from Barcelona, in the *Café Dôme* in Montparnasse, who said that my mother had revealed Hubert's code name.

'That had placed him in danger for his life,' Seppel told me, an edge in her voice. 'Käte was the only person I had confided this information to …'

'She never said anything to me about that. She always spoke of Campalans with huge affection and admiration, but on the rare occasions she mentioned Hubert, it was with strong disapproval. He followed Stalin's instructions, she said …'

'That's not true,' Seppel had precipitously dismissed.

In the international community in Barcelona, what had started as a shared commitment against the growth of fascism and a passionate belief in the fight for a world free from social injustice – a dream for which so many men and women were ready to die in a foreign country – had, after the initial burst of enthusiasm and euphoria, cooperation and comradeship, turned into argument and disagreement followed by a web of manipulation, disinformation, betrayal and murder. In the anti-fascist camp, made up as it was of republicans, anarchists, socialists and communists, with various further subdivisions within those groups, many whose loyalties didn't follow Stalin's vision were tortured and 'eliminated', leading to divisions and betrayals between comrades and friends. In the end victory was grasped by the united enemy, followed by forty years of an oppressive regime and social, cultural and economic regression for the Spanish people.

Much of what happened in those dark days was now dead and buried, probably for ever. My mother and Seppel's close friendship was one more casualty.

Before leaving, Seppel gave me a recent article which appeared in a German newspaper about my mother's love, Alexander Granach, in Berlin and beyond – they had continued to correspond till his untimely death in New York – with a striking photograph of him as a young man, reporting the revival of his old films. We climbed down the seven storeys into Rue du Dragon and emerged into St-Germain-des-Prés, past the Café de Flore and through a narrow street behind the church to a quiet square bordered by classical buildings. Its pervading sense of grace and peace made Place Furstenberg Seppel's favourite haunt.

*Alexander Granach*

A few birds pirouetted from the square's tall leafy trees into the misty, grey sky.

'Would you put some flowers on Käte's grave for me?' Seppel asked as we parted.

My mother's loss had opened so many questions and uncertainties.

Before she died, I had tried to retrieve something of our early life together of which I only had snatches of memories, a child's view of a complicated world. But apart from her account of her capture by the German military police when she went to fetch me from Biarritz, she had never talked of our life during those years. Now, when she was about to depart for ever, her only reply had been, 'I was a silly young girl then'.

I needed to try and cobble together the fragments of our life during that period, to seek some resolution and peace from our conflicts and their aftermath.

I had gathered that much: the historical events around my mother had changed her from a free, idealistic young woman who rejoiced in what life held out for her, to a fugitive scraping her last resources to avoid capture, detention and death for the two of us. It must have been in Foëcy and Marseilles where the dangers and her desperation reached their peak.

My mother's letters to Lotte, which I read after her death, helped to conjure up something of those critical times. As did too my visits to the Grandjean family in Foëcy who gave us refuge in Vichy France. I stopped off to see Jeanne on several occasions on my drive back from Tuscania.

Sitting in that same room, half a century later, I had tried to recapture my memories. I couldn't remember the trip there in my father's old Ford. Nor have I ever understood why we went there. Maybe my mother, as a refugee from Franco's Spain, was unsafe in Collioure, our first home in France over the Pyrenees: many others had been placed by the French authorities into the camp in nearby Argeles. Or maybe my father decided to stop renting our little cottage there, their relations seemingly at their worst. Or perhaps the reason for finding ourselves in Foëcy in 1939 was something else I shall never know.

This room – where I was undressed and put into a large bed, in that corner – I remembered. The furniture had changed, and the front room – where the family had shared that first meal with us on our arrival that night – now communicated through a large new opening with the back one, where I was sitting this evening with Jeanne. She, a sprightly eighty-four now, was watching the large television set which dominated the room, bringing into it a world of shiny, noisy advertisements, dubbed German and American police dramas and soaps, and all the rest of the busy, snazzy paraphernalia of the 1990s. Gone was the old, silent, darkened room in which the only sounds were those of the family chattering amongst themselves, the dogs barking and chickens cackling in the yard, and, at regular intervals, the loud bell followed by the thundering clatter of the train next to the house.

'There was a large bed in that corner,' I suggested.

'That's right,' Jeanne confirmed. 'It was Yaya's bed. It was always there until she died. Now Claude's daughter has it in her flat outside Paris.'

I tried to visualise my arrival to this new place, which would temporarily become our home in the midst of an uncertain Europe shortly to be at war. I looked through the window at the same back-yard I remembered – silent now: the rabbits, chickens and dogs all gone. On the other side of the empty animals' hutch, I could still see the outdoor loo, though its use had long ceased. Beyond it, in the distance, a tree was silhouetted against a sombre luminous sky, the dense blanket of cloud slowly turning darker and more leaden while a pink tinge towards the horizon was becoming duskier and more intense. The same kind of sky I must have seen while playing outside in the evenings with Jeanne's children, Claude and Michelle. I was turning time back to re-experience myself then, trying to recover my viewpoint, my sense of the world at that moment in history.

Many years had passed since my first visit with my mother to the Grandjean family in Foëcy on our return to Europe, and then again later when, one day, I was driving nearby and decided to make a detour and see them again. I had found the house with difficulty on that occasion, and Jeanne had looked at me gloweringly and impa-tiently when she came to the door, until I said '*Je suis Miriam*', at which her scowl suddenly turned into a big warm smile and she rushed over to open the gate and embrace me and kiss me twice on both cheeks and usher me into the house. It was full of people that time: Claude and her family had come from Paris to visit Jeanne. They had all welcomed me with great fuss and surprise and sat me at the table to share their evening meal and, as all the beds were already taken, I slept with Jeanne in her large bed – as on that first night, a lifetime ago – the darkness of the night punctuated regularly by the chimes of the old clock.

This time, Jeanne was on her own. She moved and talked with her usual simplicity as she busied herself around the house and garden. Her eyes, set widely apart under her broad forehead, had the same clear, candid look I remembered. A look which seemed to say, 'I live according to my instinct of what is right, as I've always done – even in the most difficult of times. While others were frightened and ambivalent, and compromised themselves, I never vacillated about what to do. Here I am. This is I.'

'The village policeman denounced Käte as a spy to the Germans as soon as they entered Foëcy,' Jeanne reminisced the following morning at breakfast. 'She was a foreigner and had a typewriter, he told them. They immediately went to look for her.' My mother had already left – she had hurriedly climbed out of the window with me and a few possessions, avoiding the door in case the Germans were already there for her, and we were hurrying across the fields to the next village to continue by bus. Our bus journeys: a slice of which I remember.

Yayo had been less fortunate: he was taken away by the Gestapo following the release of two communists in the village who turned collaborators. 'They denounced him falsely. He had never joined their group – in fact, he was not affiliated to any party as he had grown disgusted with all politics. They named him to save their own skins,' Jeanne was saying, her voice barely hiding her scorn and disgust. 'We went to visit him a few days later. His fingers were bandaged, and their ends were bleeding through the bandages. They had obviously tortured him, but he never complained. Though they had nothing on him, they took him to the camp in Compiègne, and then to Germany, to a work camp for French prisoners. Dora. He died two months before liberation. His body was thrown into a pit and burned along with all the others.'

Jeanne got up and fetched a letter. It had been written by another French prisoner of war from Dora, several pages long, in very neat handwriting. He wrote about their life in the camp and his admiration for Yayo. Though he was Catholic and Yayo didn't follow his faith, his kindness to everyone in the camp had been greater than that of many self-professed Catholics, his 'exemplary love, caring, self-effacing sacrifice, and devotion to others …' Jeanne read the letter matter-of-factly, with no emotion other than her simple, direct warmth.

I was beginning to build a picture of this man: the head of the family that had received me and my mother into their fold in early 1939. Yayo appeared to have been one of those men of the land who have a mind and strength of their own. He had renounced all forms of politics and, Jeanne explains, though he had given up his fore-fathers' religion, he believed and practised doing unto others as he would have them do unto him with a greater commitment than many of his Christian neighbours. But his independent thought had made him unpopular with some of the villagers. And he was taken from the family he loved, tortured, made to work in pitiable conditions and finally thrown into a mass grave – on the false testimony of neighbours who walked free.

In the village cemetery, his name was inked *in absentia* next to Yaya's on her tombstone, and one of the village streets was now named after him.

'My husband was conscripted at the beginning of the war. With Yayo gone too, there were no men left in the family and we had to do their jobs as well as ours,' Jeanne went on. 'I used to smuggle letters between prisoners and their families across the River Cher. We were occupied this side of the river and the free zone started on the other side. Vierzon, a few kilometres from here, was a very important strategic site: it is right in the centre of France and its railway station was a busy, crucial junction. I also helped people across the river. Jews who were trying to escape. I did it for nothing: I was glad to be able to do it. Once I took a desperate young woman across to join her newly wedded husband – she was shaking so uncontrollably that I thought she'd give us away. There were German guards on this side of the Cher, and French on the other. I got to know the 'good' Germans from the 'bad' ones – *les bons et les mauvais*. There was one who would always let me through. 'Let her pass,' he would tell the others when he saw me, and he never searched me. He was nice, tall and strong, looked like Curt Jürgens. We used to meet sometimes, and when he was posted elsewhere, we wrote to each other – I even got myself a book to learn German and struggled with the Gothic writing. Then his letters stopped. He probably went and got himself killed on the Russian front, the poor sod. There was another guard who was a nasty piece of work and very strict. I didn't go across when he was on. I got to know their guard duties, so I would choose when to go. There were also some women from the German military who would frisk me and feel under my skirt. I didn't wear any knickers so I wouldn't have the bother of taking them off and I'd be through more quickly. I used to go on my bicycle and say I was going to work in the vineyards, to pick grapes, and they would look at my hands. They'd see my fingers weren't stained, they weren't stupid, but they'd let me through anyway. Once – I had the letters in a false compartment of my handbag which I'd fastened with a safety pin – they'd already taken the handlebars off the bicycle to check down the tube and examined the other bag I'd left on the bike, and they asked to look at the one I was carrying that had the letters. I opened it wide and showed them my lipstick and other odd bits a woman carries in a handbag: 'There you are,' I said to them, and they were satisfied and let me through. On the other side I would deliver the letters and then cycle along the Cher to get back across the next bridge five kilometres further on, smuggling back a good sausage, or some bread or fruit which we couldn't get on our side. When the war was over, some of the French people in the village took me into the woods and treated me worse than the Germans had, accusing me of befriending the German guards. Yet the same people had been pleased to get my help while the war was going on.'

A large frame with family photographs stood on the sideboard facing the small table in the kitchen where we were having our breakfast. There was one of Yayo sitting rather stiffly in a suit, looking very serious and straight at the camera, and another of the top half of Yaya – I now saw Jeanne's resemblance to her mother – and some of Claude and Michelle and *their* children and grandchildren. Standing apart, on its own, was a larger, close-up photograph of a youngish man, curly-haired and smiling, with a dry leaf inside the frame. Jeanne's husband. It was taken after he returned from the war. He died some years later in an accident in the village.

'*Il était beau, huh?*' Jeanne pointed out fondly.

Jeanne got up from the table, cleared away our breakfast things and started preparing food for the birds: a grain mixture that she had spent some time sorting out the previous evening after our dinner of rabbit and wine stew. She added to it some bread and other leftovers she had left soaking in water overnight, and carefully distributed it into several dishes that she took out and left in various places in the garden. By the afternoon they were empty again. All the birds from the surrounding countryside appeared to converge in Jeanne's garden to have their regular feast, and twitter and sing for her.

When we first sought the Grandjean family, my mother and I, on our return to Europe, we had also found Yaya's other daughter Margot, in Perpignan. My mother and Margot had spoken at length – it was evident they had formed a strong friendship and knew much about each other. André was there too, at that meeting. André who had washed my bleeding heel in the River Cher when it was caught in his bicycle wheel. That, I never forgot. The pain that made me howl had long left my memory, even André's features were almost lost in its haze, but I still carried clearly within me his care and tenderness. And there I was facing an unfamiliar, solidly built, middle-aged man, as though for the first time – yet he was the same slender young boy who had cupped me in his lap and bathed my hurting foot in the river's cool flowing water.

From our time in Marseilles, I would always remember Harry and Willi. They were there, like our brothers, a source of comfort, protection and strength. Harry stood for that solidarity between friends that dominated my early background and has stayed with me since.

I sought him out when I first returned to Mexico. I asked everybody about Harry, but no one knew where he was or what had happened to him: '... nobody's seen him, not in years. I wouldn't look for him if I were you ...'; '... he's gone downhill, you know. A life of dissipation ...'; '... he's taken to drinking ...'

Until I asked Jorge, whom I had known when we were both children, from our circle of refugee friends.

'I know where he lives,' he said.

He drove us far out to the outskirts of the capital, finally ending in a dirt road surrounded by Mexican slum shacks. He stopped the car outside one of these, and knocked on the door. Harry opened it. He was greatly surprised when he recognised Jorge, whom he had clearly not seen in a long time, and invited us into his room. He stood there before us, somewhat flustered at the unexpected visit to his humble surroundings, looking at me and waiting to be introduced.

'Don't you know who this is?' Jorge asked him smiling broadly.

Harry looked at me harder without a flicker of recognition on his face.

So Jorge told him.

Harry almost leapt as he started walking towards me, his arms lifted to embrace me, but stopped as suddenly again as he faced me now, a grown woman, a stranger maybe ... And I myself was too slow and overcome to make a move. A moment lost, forever regretted.

We talked for a while, standing in the middle of the small, dark room, its sole furniture a rickety old bed just inside the door.

'It's very rough around here,' Harry was saying. 'They're pretty trigger happy. Only the other night someone fired some shots through my window.' And he pointed to the bullet holes on the wall above his bed. He lived there on his own. He had a Mexican wife somewhere near Veracruz, and a young daughter whom he saw occasionally ...

As we left, Jorge invited him to have dinner with us.

Harry arrived on the appointed day. He had somehow managed to get a suit and had dressed immaculately, though his badly frayed white shirt cuffs could not disguise their wear; his hair was carefully combed back and his worn shoes had been highly polished. He seemed to be trying desperately to hide his fall from social grace. I should have told him that, to me, he was still the same Harry from our boxing contests in Marseilles; the same Harry who had carried me on his shoulders to go down to the port to collect oranges from the boats, and rejoiced in picking the best and juiciest for me; the same Harry who used to give me a lump of sugar dipped in his coffee every time we sat at the café with his friends – and that our different worlds now should not create this gulf between us or make us strangers. But the words didn't come out.

*Our friends' farewell, with Harry far right, at the station in Mexico in 1945*

Harry mentioned some kind of basic allowance he was receiving from Germany – a meagre *Wieder-gutmachung* – which Willy Brandt had arranged for him. It seems they had once been pals, fought side by side in Spain for the same things ... but that was long past. In the meantime, Brandt had become the socialist chancellor in Germany, and Harry a slum dweller in Mexico.

I never saw Harry again. He died a few years later.

I have a photograph of our friends who came to see us off on our departure from Mexico on our way to New Zealand in early 1948. We are all standing in a group, some fifteen people, on the platform in front of the train. Harry towers above everybody. He is wearing his suit and hat, standing with his feet apart, very straight, arms by his sides, looking at the camera from under the brim of his trilby pulled well down, in a stance and with an expression that would do the detective proud in a Mickey Spillane movie.

Throughout my childhood, as far back as I can remember, my mother would engage in long heated discussions with all these friends, the meanings of which only hazily reached me. Surrounded as they were by the dire events brought on by the ideologies and governments of those days, in time I started grasping the political nature of these discussions. And this too was part of my background and what shaped me. There had been a special bond between friends that grows from sharing the hardships and dangers of the time and helping each other out. In Mexico, we saw much of Mollie and Senya, with whom we travelled on the *Serpa Pinto*. In their last years, they had moved to Cuernavaca and lived in a small apartment overlooking a ravine near the entrance to the town. Gone were the days of Senya's renowned studio photography in Mexico City. His black-and-white studies – actors in dramatic poses, patterns of human bodies in dance, ripples of light and shade – had all been packed away.

'They will end up stored in some photographic archive,' Mollie said, disillusioned. We were conversing around the table that filled the small sun porch, surrounded by the upper branches of the tall eucalyptus trees in the ravine, while we sipped her Russian tea.

Mollie talked of their dream of a world in which people would live in peace, where greed and mistrust would be replaced by love and joint effort, a society run on the basis of humane values. They still believed it was possible.

'That sounds too idyllic,' I suggested, more sceptically. 'Human nature, being what it is …'

'Human nature is capable of warmth and love. And good,' Mollie said with her characteristic unshakeable faith. 'Children would find that way of life quite natural if they grew up in such an atmosphere. There would be no need for hierarchy and everyone would assume responsibility for their own behaviour.'

Mollie was speaking for the two of them, as she had always done – while Senya sat quietly near her, his look drawn and wistful, with a weary smile on his face, as if the world had been after all too much for him.

'I have always believed in individual freedom, in its full sense,' she was saying. 'And in everyone's right to develop their potential. I believe the day will come when, instead of the present division into nations which fight and compete with each other, we shall all extend our hands to one another, everywhere, in fraternal love.'

Her words – spoken with the same gentleness and melodious Russian 'L's – were rebounding like echoes from my past. Words floating across the table, talking with my mother, while sipping Mollie's Russian lemon tea in the small kitchen area in Senya's studio. And though I may not have reached their meaning then – when I was six and seven – some stirrings of the spirit in which they were said had remained with me.

'I was imprisoned for my beliefs in both America and Russia,' Mollie went on. 'I remember my disappointment when we arrived to that wonderful promised land of the United States of America, still in my teens, after emigrating with my family from Russia to leave behind the pogroms and harsh life. We became very excited, a few years later, at the prospect of a free Russia when we heard the Tsar had been removed, but our enthusiasm was short-lived as we watched President Woodrow Wilson sending American troops against the Russian people. I had seen and experienced the terrible conditions of life in rural Russia, the indescribable misery and oppression of the people. A group of us set out to fight for man's dignity and freedom through peaceful means. I helped with the publication and distribution of a journal we named *The Storm*. But our words bothered the authorities and I was sentenced to fifteen years in an American jail. The famous American lawyer, Harry Weinberger, obtained my freedom after three, but with the condition that I leave the United States and never set foot in it again.'

I was trying to imagine Mollie as a young girl: full of vitality, with her soft, wistful eyes and a head of black curls, radiating her passionate commitment to an idyllic vision of the world. I came across a book about her, written some years later after her death, where she was remembered by an American friend and writer, Emma Goldman, as 'a small, enchanting girl with oriental looks, very firm ideas, an iron will and great tenderness'. The book also described how, when her jail sentence was passed, along with that of three of her companions (the fourth died from the injuries he received when they were beaten up at their arrest), two American judges strongly disagreed with the Supreme Court's decision. They pointed out that the accused had aimed at helping their own country, Russia, rather than at impeding the war effort. One of them, Oliver Wendell Holmes, wrote: 'In this case, I believe that the twenty-year prison sentences' – the term received by the men – 'are unjust for the publication of two pamphlets which, in my opinion, the accused had as much right to publish as the government has to publish the Constitution of the United States of America, that which now has been vainly invoked in their defence.'

One of those others so sentenced was Jacob Abrams, whom I also remembered well, and with fondness, from my childhood in Mexico. The *Abrams' Case*, as it came to be known, would be cited as the first important trial of its kind and one of the most flagrant violations against constitutional rights during the period of the 'red menace' which followed the First World War. During the hearing, Abrams had drawn attention to the fact that his beliefs, for which he was being tried, were the same as those of Christ, but he was sharply reminded that it was *he* who was on trial, not Jesus Christ.

In Mollie's biographical publication, there was also reference to her quotation – in a letter to her lawyer from her prison cell – of a poem by Edward Cooke:

*You cannot salt the eagle's tail,*
*Nor limit thought's dominion;*
*You cannot put ideas in jail,*
*You can't deport opinion.*

At their small apartment, overlooking one of Cuernavaca's wild, gaping ravines, Mollie continued: 'When I was freed, I returned to my beloved Russia full of hope and enthusiasm, only to be disappointed once again when I found the new proletarian dictatorship. I met Senya then, and we both fought together and with our companions against the new despotism which was replacing the old. We used the written word, we didn't believe in violence, but again we were arrested and put in prison. Several times. The conditions were terrible. Long interrogations. Small, dark, damp rooms crawling with bugs and lice and with malaria mosquitoes, the only furniture a hard wooden bench, and the only window – the size of a cigarette packet – opened onto a corridor as stuffy as the cell. I could hardly breathe. We went on hunger strike on several occasions in protest against the conditions. In the end, our freedom was secured with the help of Maxim Gorky's partner and others. This time, on the condition that we leave Russia for ever.'

We had moved to their modest but comfortable living room.

'Senya started his photographic career in Paris and then he worked with Sasha Stone in Berlin, but we never rested from doing all we could to help our companions who were still suffering in Russian jails. We always remembered them. Then we were faced with Hitler and *his* fascism and we had to leave Berlin. Back in France, I was put into a concentration camp during the occupation, while Senya found his way to the free zone. I managed to escape and find him, and we headed south to Marseilles.'

I was looking at Mollie as she sat there, her black hair turned snow-white now, though her eyes' warmth and vivacity remained undimmed, her arms and feet crossed in a pose of self-containment as she talked, and I marvelled at how this tiny woman who spoke fluently six languages, had devoted her life to Senya and her ideals, and had been obliged from the age of fifteen to leave one place after another – hounded out, if not for her political beliefs, for her Semitic origins – could have retained her unshakeable optimism through all she had experienced.

'We had some wonderful friends in Paris. We also met your father, Lou, there. We had no idea then, that he had a wife and child. In all the years we had known him, he never mentioned Käte! When we met you and your mother in Marseilles while waiting to board the ship to Mexico, we were very shocked. She was in a terrible state. Poorly dressed and very thin and undernourished. She had obviously been having a hard time, while Lou led a comfortable life. He knew everyone and was always travelling and lived well. He was very wealthy. We never forgave him for the way he treated your mother.'

As I left, Mollie gave me a book about Raúl with an introduction by Viadiu, that kindly-looking man with a wild crop of white hair with whom my mother used to talk in the passageway by his small bookshop when we first arrived in Mexico. It described Raúl's early life in a small Ukrainian village, his apprenticeship, at the age of ten, to a locksmith and his daily work of fourteen hours in the industrial city of Yekaterinoslav. At the end of the day, he slept under the table in his master's dining room and listened to the discussions, long into the night, of the locksmith's daughter and her student friends, sitting around the table above him, about a movement that was growing among the people with new notions of peasants' and workers' rights and political freedom for all. The small boy became determined to help create that better world he heard them talk about. After a severe injury from the Cossacks at the age of fourteen, and periods of hospitalisation and imprisonment, he started a walkout in his factory, which escalated to a general strike, in protest against the famous massacre in St Petersburg in 1906. Now sought by the police, he escaped to Argentina and joined the anarchist movement which had a large following there at the turn of the century. During a peaceful demonstration, the head of police, Colonel Ramón Falcón, ordered his troops to open fire into the crowd with several deaths. Falcón's brutality reminded him of his experiences in Russia, and in his desperation he decided to make a bomb and kill Falcón and then himself. Which he did, except that in the chaos that followed he only managed to wound himself. He was sentenced to twenty-one years in the infamous prison of Ushuaia in Tierra del Fuego, and endured long stretches of solitary confinement in a freezing subterranean cell, too small to stand in or sleep stretched out. Yet people said he never complained, and a legend grew around him that he was so gentle, generous and self-effacing that even the most hardened criminals admired and respected him. He became known as The

Martyr of Ushuaia and was finally released through international pressure and wide public support.

Federica Montseny, a Catalan anarchist, wrote of meeting him when he came to fight in the Spanish Civil War after his release from Ushuaia. She described him as 'a modest, silent man with clear, luminous eyes which expressed an extraordinary kindness' and spent his time listening and giving his full attention to others, himself speaking only in response to a question, when he would demonstrate a penetrating grasp of complex problems gained from his own experience and observation rather than from books.

So that was the story of the timid man I used to see moving like a shadow in the background in Senya's studio. And his name was not Raúl, it was Simón Radowitzky.

Peter, Lotte's eldest son and fifteen years older than me, had a host of memories that predated me. We travelled in Italy and broke our journey in Venice.

We took a vaporetto on the Grand Canal.

'I was in Venice with our grandfather. It was October, 1937. I clearly remember the occasion. He came to see us in Florence and at the end of his visit he asked me if I would accompany him to Venice on his way back to Chemnitz. He was on his own. Clara had died the previous year shortly after you were born – though she lived to receive your mother's letter announcing your arrival.'

We were gliding past an old palace, its walls plummeted straight into the canal. We glimpsed the decaying, grandiose interior through its great open portal. Outside it, a sculpted horse stood life-size on the water.

'He had never been to Venice before, but he'd heard a great deal about it and he wanted to see it. I knew it well – I'd been here many times – and I showed him around.'

'How old were you then?'

'I was sixteen.'

Two gondolas made their way slowly down the canal – the gondoliers in their identical straw hats with identical trailing red ribbons.

'And Oscar?'

'He must have been in his early seventies.'

'The same as you, now.'

'Yes, I suppose so,' Peter admitted – somewhat reluctantly – in his deliberate, slow, Cambridge accent.

He had, in fact, the appearance of a much younger man: quite trim and neat, his tanned face framed by a head of white hair waving in the breeze and glinting silver in the sun. His eyes appeared to be laughing at the world with a good-natured insolence from behind his spectacles, and the pleasing, asymmetric curl of his lip I remembered from our much younger days – I in my early teens, he in his late twenties – was still there. He was leaning against the vaporetto rail in his short-sleeved black cotton shirt and light beige trousers.

'What was he like, our grandfather?'

'He was a quiet man. He never said much. At home – when I was a boy, still in Chemnitz – he was given to fits of anger and Clara would bear these outbursts meekly and uncomplainingly. Women in those days were supposed to suffer in silence. She always wore a slightly pained expression on her face, almost with a kind of sa-tis-fac-tion,' Peter was saying mischievously.

A palazzo's grand doorway here led to a short jetty and a wide platform with a motor launch standing by.

'I took Oscar into many of the churches here. I don't think he had ever been inside a church before. I'll never forget his reaction. There was a service going on inside one of them, and he suddenly sat down. He appeared mesmerised. He was staring at the grand ornate interior of the Venetian Catholic church and listening to the Mass. He wouldn't budge when I wanted to leave. I went away and left him there for a while, and when I came back, he was still sitting in the same position.'

Long, narrow windows curved gracefully into peaked, oriental arches – their glass panes divided into domed segments that sparkled in the sunshine.

'You see, he was a very unaffected person. At home, the family didn't observe any Jewish traditions or go to synagogue. Though their social life was Jewish: their friends and business acquaintances all came from the same Jewish background. But they were completely assimilated into the German way of life, and he blindly believed in the Kaiser and that Germany could do no wrong.'

In the welter of greys, golds and pinks of the Venetian palazzos, a green garden suddenly appeared. A cluster of trees and bushes with one tall palm rose above its enclosure along the water's edge.

'My mother, Lotte, told me how once Oscar announced to the household that Hugo Haase – a cousin or nephew of his – was in Chemnitz and was going to visit them. He said it with a distinct dislike: he was one of those "social democrats" – he was, in fact, a Member of Parliament. But as he was a relative, he had no choice but to receive him in his house. My mother was very young at the time, and she didn't know what social democrats were. During dinner, she leaned down to pick up something from the floor and she noticed that a bit of the seam of Hugo Haase's trouser leg was undone and his long woollen sock showed through it. She thought, "Aha! That must be what social democrats are: people who go round in slovenly clothes."' Peter paused and gazed into the water. 'He was later murdered on the steps of the German Parliament in Berlin. Like so many others.'

A small house with a little side garden appeared unexpectedly along the bank of the canal. It was dwarfed by the towering palaces on either side.

'You see, people were brought up in Germany in line with the ideas of a Dr Schreber – Germany's nineteenth-century equivalent of Dr Spock. According to him, the purpose of education is to break a child's will so completely that – if "successful" – he should have no will left of his own by the age of twelve. You should read Zuckmayer's play, *Der Hauptmann von Köpenick*, to help you understand our grandfather and the times he lived in. In the play, a man pretending to be a captain blasts, "An order is to be obeyed, not questioned!" And when an officer says to another, "How do we know that this man is genuine? Ask him why he is issuing those orders," the other replies, "Don't be stupid, he himself is just following orders."'

We were sailing past a palace turned into a lavish hotel. Between two rows of tall windows, its name in large gold letters glinted in the sun across its russet velvet façade.

'When we were in Venice, Oscar asked me to go back with him to Chemnitz to take over his factory. He knew I didn't have much of a future in Italy and he thought his firm would provide me with a secure position. You must understand that he had devoted his whole life to his textile business. He had expected Fritz, the eldest son, to be his successor but he had gone to Palestine, and Hans was occupied with his music and lived in Holland. His daughters' husbands had also turned out unsuitable.'

The redbrick bell tower and dome of a church cut into the blue sky. The smell of the still waters of the canal mingled with a faint trace of the vaporetto's engine.

'He was still thinking of the continuity of his business in the family when every one else was leaving Germany.'

'What would he have thought of it all when he was dying in Theresienstadt?'

'We'll never know …'

A grey decaying wall rose out of the canal's waters. The plaster had broken off in many places exposing the crumbly surface beneath.

'He sent a note to Hans, towards the end.'

The sun was beating down. A single bird fluttered overhead.

'What did he say in it?'

'I haven't read it. I would find it too upsetting. But your mother saw it. She once told me that it showed he wasn't the remote figure they had imagined. He turned out to have been very caring.'

Shortly after that meeting with Peter, I went to Bad Sooden in northern Germany to join my uncle Fritz on his yearly visit to Europe. He was about to turn ninety-one and we would celebrate his birthday together. As he approached to greet me, I found him little changed: tall and thin, very upright in his bearing, his walk slow and wooden, his eyes smiled with suppressed delight while his face kept the characteristic deadpan expression which – I had learned – hid his strong emotions. Several years had passed since we had last met, and we embraced warmly.

Bad Sooden is a *Kurzentrum* – a leafy corner near Kassel, where salt waters are pumped out of the ground and trickled down a high vertical stack of twigs for elderly people to breathe in the curative, damp, salty air. There are many clinics, hotels and quaint houses with narrow overhanging roofs, conical turrets, wooden beams across their walls, and flower-laden balconies.

As we walked through the gardens surrounded by tall poplars, spreading oaks, drooping cedars, glistening silver birches and bright green acacias – the path widened to accommodate a fountain in the middle and we sat on a facing bench. Five tall jets of water reaching different heights arced to converge over a bronze stork in the centre, wings outspread in alighting, bearing the full impact of the force of water crashing down over it as it balanced on its spindly legs.

'I saw my father for the last time in *Bahnhof Friedrichstrasse*, Berlin's railway station, at the end of August, 1939. It was just before the outbreak of the war. I was passing through from Denmark on my way to a congress in Geneva, and he had come from Chemnitz to meet me. We stood together on the station platform for ten minutes. He handed me a special gold ring set with diamonds and asked me to give it to Käte who was in France with you. He knew she was having a hard time and was badly off,' Fritz recounted in his quiet, matter of fact manner. 'A few minutes later, he asked me to return the ring to him. He said he had already registered all his valuables with the German authorities in Chemnitz: should they discover that something was missing from their list, he would get into difficulties. Then he reconsidered, and gave it back to me. He said, "Käte needs it". And then, at the last moment, as the train was pulling out, he asked me to give it back to him again.'

I remained silent as I thought of my grandfather's last brief meeting with his eldest son. And of his agonising, moving concern for my mother and me.

'He was a good father,' Fritz went on, his voice disclosing a gentle affection. 'He always took care to look after his family's material needs. I remember, during the Winter of Hunger in 1915, when food was severely rationed, he would send us *graue Erbsen mit Speck* from Königsberg, whenever he went on his business travels. It is a specialty from there which he was particularly fond of and the family also enjoyed.'

'Did you ever hear anything about his last years?' I asked.

'Yes. He left the family apartment, which had only been rented, and moved into a smaller one for himself. Then he was shifted to a ghetto for the Jews in Chemnitz, and finally he was put onto a train, the XV-1-785, which started its journey in Kassel and stopped to collect Jews in designated stations, including Chemnitz, for deportation to Theresienstadt. He arrived there on the 9th of September 1942, and died three weeks later. The official cause of his death is pneumonia. It was on the 2nd of October 1942.' His recall was unmisted, even at ninety-one.

Oscar had been in touch by letter with Hans who was in Holland, and with Lotte who arrived in New Zealand at the end of 1939, Fritz told me. He could not communicate with *him* as he was travelling a great deal, involved as he was in organising the escape and transport of Jews to Palestine, nor could he have reached my mother in occupied France. He mentioned a letter he received from Lotte, shortly before her death and already in her nineties. 'In one of his last letters,' she had written to Fritz, 'our father said, "*Wenn es etwas gibt gewaltiger als das Schicksal, so ist's der Mut, der's unerschuettert traegt.*" Who would have thought it of him!'

If there is anything mightier than fate, it's the fortitude to endure it unflinchingly, he had written.

Here, a few kilometres from Kassel, from where the XV-1-785 started the journey that took Oscar on his last trip, all was now peaceful. We were surrounded by a profusion of greenery and bright flowers, and the bronze stork before us still held its precarious equilibrium against the powerful jets of water crashing down on its wings stretched out full span at a graceful angle.

'Did you know Hugo Haase?' I asked my uncle.

'Yes. He was married to a cousin of my father. He became the leader of the Social Democratic Party in 1911 – after August Bebel, one of its founders – and he tried to prevent the outbreak of the 1914–18 war. I sympathised with his views: he was a socialist, but he believed in following the majority decision even if he didn't agree with it. He was a real democrat. He was a very fair man and had vision. I believe he was the only one who could have got us out of the mess Germany was getting into. But he was murdered in August 1919 by a leather worker. The head of his faction also worked in leather, and I believe – though it is my personal opinion as there's no evidence for it – that he ordered the killing.'

I also asked Fritz about his own early activities when, shortly after the First World War, he gave up his promising apprenticeship at the

Goeritz textile firm, and what appeared at the time a comfortable and secure future, for the primitive working conditions and communal life in the swampy marshes of northern Palestine.

'I began to notice in my work at the factory that I had nothing in common with the others there. It soon became clear to me that Jews would always be kept outside main society in Germany. Although my family had been assimilated into the German way of life – like other German Jews, they were born Jewish and accepted it, but they didn't care for it, while the Eastern Jews were actively involved in their Judaism – even so, the gentiles did not mix with us. At school we were kept separate from them and we were not accepted into their social circles. I didn't wish to live like that. I saw the solution in the Zionist movement, and I joined it. Palestine had become a British Mandate when the Ottoman Empire broke up at the end of the First World War: it was taken from the Turks by the British under the jurisdiction of the League of Nations. It was part of Greater Syria then. Weizmann was in dialogue with King Faisal, who was King of Syria and close to the Palestinians, and later with King Abdullah, the grandfather of the present King of Jordan, and a peaceful agreement to live side by side with the local Arabs was expected. There were ten or twelve Jewish agricultural communities at the time I arrived in the winter of 1925–26. I started working in a place called Yaasor, which later became Yagur. The land for these kibbutzim had been bought from wealthy Arab landowners who lived in Beirut or in Paris – Beirut was then under French Mandate and was the main fashionable centre, south of Anatolia. The well-to-do Arabs considered the land in Palestine too poor to live in. North of the smallish township of what was then Jerusalem, it was swampy and full of malaria mosquitoes, while south of it was the desert. Arab and Jewish communities had existed in the area in continuity over the last two thousand years. Then came the events that led to the Second World War and Hitler's programme of genocide, and we started operating routes of escape for the European Jews and to organise their settlement in Palestine. After the war, back in Yagur, I had a severe accident with a tractor which almost severed my foot and I had to give up my life in the kibbutz. That was when I started my work in the Diplomatic Service.'

We got up and started walking again. We reached a corner of the park where there was an open-air café facing a bandstand, in which a large brass band was preparing for a morning of schmaltzy German music.

'If we sit on that side, we'll have to drink coffee and if we sit on this side, we'll have to listen to the band,' I observed. Fritz broke into a gentle laugh, his face filling with sunshine for a brief moment, and we decided to move on.

His bearing still echoed the good looks of his youth. When he was a young diplomat in London as First Secretary of the newly opened Israeli Embassy, under his adopted Israeli name, Perez Leshem, he was mistaken on several occasions for the actor Leslie Howard. Even now, he had an air of quiet dignity, observation and restraint.

'As you know, not all the family agreed with my convictions. Lotte once wrote to me, "I am a citizen of the world, not a Jew".'

Recalling Lotte's attitude to my Mexican dress and American idiom on my arrival in New Zealand, I wondered whether her 'world' didn't end at the borders with Europe and New Zealand.

Fritz's eldest son, my cousin Guideon, who was born in Yaasor and lived all his life in Israel, told me recently, 'Our fathers, when they came to this land, had no idea what they were getting us into ...'

And: 'You know, when Moses died, he instructed that his grave should be left unmarked – so that the ideas he left behind with the nation of Israel should not be identified with a site, but rather live on in the minds of the people.'

Fritz's grandson, Noam, in contrast with his grandfather's life-work and ideals, has left Israel to start a new life in England.

What started off as an attempt to give a home and country to a homeless, stateless people, has ended up with another group of people's misery and displacement.

A few days after my meeting with Fritz, Hans died in Holland.

Hans had become increasingly depressed over several years. A young doctor who attended him said this was a common problem among people who had experienced difficult survival conditions during the war and were now growing old. The stresses of their earlier life seemed to come back to haunt them. His characteristic liveliness and good humour had deserted him, and he became weepy and irritable and would often insist he no longer wished to live. He broke his leg, refused to cooperate in his rehabilitation and died tired and peacefully holding Rita's hand. She never left his side.

He had met Rita during his years in hiding in Holland. He had been constantly on the move from one household of Dutch friends to another, in The Hague and around Haarlem, to escape from the Gestapo and their race-purifying activities in occupied Holland. At the first home which offered him refuge, the wife of the friend who was hiding him fell madly in love with him making his situation impossible and obliging him to move. He was later protected by his friend, Mari Andriessen, a sculptor whose bronze figure of a docker stands in a square in front of an old Sephardic synagogue in Amsterdam, in commemoration of the dockworkers' strike in protest against the first trainload of Dutch Jews sent to the concentration camps. As a result of the strike, German supplies were held up and many dockers executed. Occasionally, German patrols would come and search Hans's place of hiding, alerted by some neighbour. Once, while such an operation was in progress, as he lay narrowly stretched on top of a wooden beam in the ceiling scarcely daring to breathe, one of the German soldiers combing the rooms for him glanced up. Their eyes met and froze for a few moments, then the soldier lowered his gaze again and silently continued his search with the others.

It was during his stay with Andriessen that Hans met his niece Rita. They were married at the end of the war, to her Catholic parents' strong disapproval.

Hans returned to his music, but soon came across the jealousies and in-fighting between the Dutch Catholic and Protestant music circles – from which Jews were excluded altogether. He taught singing in the Rotterdam Conservatory and became an occasional guest conductor of the Dutch Concertgebouw. He never fully recovered from the interruption of his promising musical career in Germany and his enforced exile. Even so, music was his life and his two daughters inherited his love of music and his red hair: Sabijn took up singing and taught history of music, while Babette became a cellist. Though Hans spoke fluent German, Dutch and French, his Italian never went beyond the musical. Once, in the back of a taxi in Rome and in a great hurry, he leaned across to the driver and said, *'Presto!'* As the taxi started weaving madly, Italian-style, through the traffic, Hans promptly added with some trepidation, *'Ma non troppo!'*

*Fritz, Käte and Hans reunited on my mother's return to Europe from New Zealand*

After he died, at the age of eighty-nine, Rita came across a bundle of letters and postcards from his father, from the time the family had been dispersed and Oscar alone remained in Chemnitz. The war had broken out and he was waiting 'to be taken on a trip', as he wrote. Hans had hidden his father's letters and his armband with the Star of David all those years, and had never shown or shared them with anyone.

I was beginning to build a picture of my mother's life and my childhood from our friends and family, a flash of my elusive roots, however incomplete.

María Rioja had been another Spanish friend – a handsome young woman with light regular features and dark earthy eyes, in the photograph my mother kept of her – and the wife of Ortega, whom my mother had dragged across the fields to freedom from the concentration camp near Collioure. I once visited her in Troyes where she was living.

'I shall never forget that day when your mother walked up the path to my room escorted on either side by two heavily armed Germans,' María reminisced as we sat and sipped coffee in her modest living room. 'I was very alarmed ... I immediately realised the danger she was in. She said she had come to fetch you ...' and she proceeded to tell the story, identical in every detail to my mother's description of it over the years.

When I first met Kraks, he introduced me in Paris to his friend Nina, from the Vogeler family in Worpswede, a long-time mistress of Giacometti, and written about by Sartre. She had looked after the young Kraks when he first came to Paris on a grant to further his art studies. Nina turned out to have been the friend who had procured the *laissez-passer* in Marseilles for my mother that had landed her in the hands of the German military police, at the border with the occupied zone, on her way to fetch me in Biarritz in 1940.

My father, though, had his own view of that episode.

'Do you remember the time my mother nearly fell into the hands of the Germans, when she came to fetch me in Biarritz?' I asked him during one of my last visits to Mexico before he died, at the age of ninety.

My mother had always declared her profound gratitude to him for handing me over without fuss, which would have given her away, at a time when their relations were at their grimmest.

'Your mother was on best terms with both the communists and the Nazis. She recruited her German Nazi friends to force me to hand you back to her,' he had said bitterly – adding: 'She was a double agent.'

I was dumbfounded; lost for words. And only then did I begin to get a glimpse of the magnitude of the unbridgeable chasm and misunderstanding between them.

On another occasion, I mentioned our last meeting in Marseilles.

'Remember our last night in Marseilles before I went to Mexico? You came to say goodbye to me!'

'No,' he replied without hesitation. 'I wasn't in Marseilles when you left. You must be mistaken.'

'You don't remember?' I asked disbelievingly. How could he forget? My own memory of that night is so vivid. 'We stayed in a small hotel in a street by the port!'

'No. I wasn't there. I would remember.'

'You gave me your binoculars and sat on the bed, while I stood at the window looking through them at the ships in the port and the houses on the opposite side of the street!'

A wave of surprise suddenly flashed through his face. 'I *did* have a pair of binoculars ...'

The *binoculars* seemed important. More memorable, apparently, than seeing off his small daughter in the middle of the war, whom – considering all the uncertainties of the time – he might never see again. Those binoculars suddenly acquired a greater significance than my child's fascination at their powerful optical effects. I now began to wonder: what was he using them for, in Marseilles, in 1941? By the power of their magnification, which I remember so well, they were no ordinary binoculars. In the autobiographical notes he compiled, he wrote of his counterintelligence activities in the First World War. And in the Second World War: his constant comings and goings in France, his trips to North Africa, his prosperity ... And then, when America joined the war, his internment in Baden Baden's Brenner Park Hotel, which was reserved for prestigious and 'important' prisoners. Add to that, his staunch dislike of communists and communism – his sympathies in Spain had been firmly on the side of the anarchists – and, though he had chosen to live elsewhere after the war, an underlying loyalty to the country in which he had grown up would emerge when he was hosting or conversing with his American friends. Maybe his astounding notions that my mother was a 'double agent' sprang from the suspicious mindset prompted by his own activities ...

There was so much that would never be known about him. Maybe it all started in that disused railway carriage and the park by the Hudson River, where he drank the urine his schoolmates forced onto him, to prove himself worthy of their friendship.

After his death, a young Mexican director made a film based on his life having researched it in detail. Marcela Arteaga, the creator of this film, contacted me – some twenty years had passed since my father's death by now – when she was approached by a woman in her sixties from Alsace in search of her father. Thus it was that I met my new sister. Edith was born in 1942, a year after our departure from Marseilles to Mexico. My mother knew of my father's love affair in France and the resulting child. I remember her sympathy for the mother: 'Little does she know your father,' she used to say with bitterness, back in our Acapantzingo days. My father visited the mother and newborn infant at the hospital, but they lost contact after that. I invited Edith to my home in London and spoke of our father and showed

With Edith, *my newly discovered sister*

her his photographs, and she introduced me to her family in Alsace. I also met her mother, then in a nursing home, aged ninety-two. It was a memorable meeting. Denise was visibly moved when she realised who I was. She reminisced about her work at another of the Quakers' children's home where she had worked and met my father – in his role as inspector of these children's homes for the Quakers – and of the Jewish and Spanish refugee children in her charge who had been separated from their parents, and all the anguish she witnessed. A strong-minded, sweet and gentle woman.

*Sibling reunion in Mexico, José, Susana, Edith and myself, 2008*

A few months after meeting this new sister, I was searching the internet for the facts about our sailing on the *Serpa Pinto* to Mexico in 1941 and came across a group of boys who knew my father in France during the war. They were Spanish children refugees in the home Denise worked in, and my father had obtained passages for them to the United States where they were fostered in American homes. One of them sent me the only photograph he has of my father standing with the whole group before leaving Marseilles. All these children, now advanced in years, wrote enthusiastically about their great admiration and affection for him and their eternal gratitude for his help in getting them to safe shores.

Yet my mother had to struggle on her own to save us, and might even not have made it …

In my search to learn more about the Portuguese steamship, *Serpa Pinto*, that had delivered us to safety, I approached the naval attaché of the Portuguese Embassy in London requesting information about the ship's transportation of refugees during the war. A courteous reply assured me of his assistance: he would pass on my queries to the officer in charge of the naval archives in Lisbon. After several months and further reminders, I was finally invited back to the Portuguese Embassy in Belgrave Square and handed several shiny brochures advertising the *Serpa Pinto* as a luxury liner …

For my mother and me, the vessel had been our bridge to life. Our deliverance from hunted to free. It had also led to my break of cultures, from all I had experienced in Europe, to the new in Mexico. The nebulous maze of impressions punctuated with the odd, sharply recalled experience which belonged to my pre-*Serpa Pinto* existence: a vague sense of a carefree time in a large, happy house full of people and a world I was free to explore almost lost in the twilight of my memory, with glimpses of far-off homes and gardens with other family members sharpened into still scenes in my album photographs; a small cottage by the sea where my earliest clear memories are frozen in time, the long columns of refugees, the immense star-studded sky; a village surrounded by fields and the River Cher and more friends and playmates; long, inexplicable bus journeys and moves, fleeting meetings, shifting back and forth between my father in the children's home and my mother; a small, dark hotel room in Marseilles, strange worries, fear of the police, outings with Harry and Willi, lengthy discussions in German between my mother and friends, preoccupied and portentous in tone. And post-*Serpa Pinto* Mexico with sun, thunder and earthquakes, vibrant colours and sweet pungent smells, markets full of fruit, beans, pottery and rugs, a blending of indigenous American with Spanish colonial and a thread of continuity with our European life in our ties and friendships with the Spanish who had fled Franco and the German and Austrian who had fled Hitler. The continuum of change had not been broken but here in Mexico it aimed at recreating our lives, settling down, in place of the struggle to escape life-threatening forces which I gradually came to recognise. Our ocean-crossing also stood for the transition from the Old World's violent clashes between long-established orders and new emerging ideologies, and the brighter but impassive ambience in the 'New', in which life and death through disease and a more impulsive violence was an endemic part of that land's culture. The endless discussions all around me in search for answers to the convulsive events which were turning our worlds upside down, and the strong sense of sharing and solidarity between friends: all this, I had been taking in, imperceptibly but surely, as in a process of osmosis, and it had become ingrained into me, incorporated in the heart of my being.

Back beyond the beginnings of my conscious memory, I had met my grandfather once. A photograph has caught the stilled image of Oscar sitting with me, a baby, on his knees, at a family meeting in Malveno, in 1936. His hands, one wrapped

*With my grandfather, Oscar, in Malveno, Italy, 1936*

around my chubby thigh and the other spread across my chest, are holding me firmly, if a bit shyly, and with great tenderness. 'Oscar doted on Käte, she was his favourite,' Fritz had told me, and though my mother had chosen to follow the opposite views from her fastidiously patriotic, Prussian Jewish father – in the end, the strength to stand up for what they believed in and the courage to look fate straight in the eye, had prevailed.

Yet dig under this inbred stoicism and all the censored, unacknowledged conflicts and pains, ambivalence and contradictions will emerge jostling with each other, unable to find admission or expression. Turned inwards against oneself. One's vulnerabilities denied, when they can be the most warming and forthcoming qualities. Maybe *that* played its part in holding others at bay: my father from my mother, each of us from the other and from others.

I now remembered my mother, while she lay very ill in bed in her last days of life, holding on to the photograph of Villa Klara in Augustusburg: the one place where she had received her mother's undivided attention. I remembered too how she had once told me that the most precious moment of the day for her, as a child, was when her mother came to kiss her goodnight, having already been put into bed and tucked in by her nanny. Maybe *there* lay the answer. I can now see her as a little girl longing for a greater closeness with her mother, at a time and place when bonding was not deemed important. Maybe her attachment to her dolls, followed by the infants she looked after in her nurse training days, her own children and finally grandchildren, filled that void. Might it even explain her stolen kiss to newborn Rebekah? Here was another baby to hold close to her, that which she had longed from her mother …

The closeness in time between my birth and her mother's death surely must have had a profound effect on her. She had become a mother and motherless at the same time: her overwhelming new maternal joy and love mixed with the pain and sorrow at the loss of her own mother, further complicated by her sense of guilt for all the grief her unconventional life had caused her demure mother. She had become a proud new mother and been plunged into mourning, both at the same time, her roles of mother and daughter confused

– maybe her burning need for solace, love and support now concentrated on that one tiny baby she held in her arms with such a fierce passion ... to become ever stronger in the uncertain climate of war, continuous moves, and immediate danger we were enveloped in over the next years. Then the break: the realisation that I – her little girl – was growing up and no longer fulfilled that role she must have so needed.

Maybe she herself was in the end a lonely little girl seeking approval and motherly warmth herself ... If only I could have seen it that way while she was still alive ...

*My mother with me, newly born, in the hospital in Barcelona*

'I have understood,' she said a few hours before her final departure, and just maybe, while she was struggling with her approaching death, somewhere inside that restless nightmare she seemed to be going through, she sensed my closeness, heard my voice holding on and fighting with her. Though she couldn't surface enough to tell me so, it is just possible that she was understanding that I had never abandoned her or stopped loving her. I was, in the end, the only one facing her death there with her, close to her, much the same as we had been when we confronted all the dangers, mother and child, together in France.

# The Constant Enduring Centre

Frozen moments, images, fragments of memory. Instants strung together to fashion a life's impression. Multiple strands woven across a spectrum of wars, moves, friendships, loss and reconstruction. Families dispersed and disintegrated. Spread across a blink in time. Impressions dug out from the past, akin to unearthed shards painstakingly pieced together to reveal an incomplete pot. But the form is captured, its gist. The sense of who we are: from the sum of all those moments we have lived through and experienced, and the roots we sprang from.

'Where are you from?' people often ask.

'From New Zealand.'

'Yes but … originally?'

And then, 'But what do you *feel*? Which country do you think of as *home*?'

I would have turned out a full-fledged Catalan had it not been for Franco's war, or French had we not had to flee Vichy France, or even Mexican had my parents' marriage lasted. Maybe a gypsy – had I not been found when I vanished in a gypsy caravan from La Floresta. Had my mother not reached Biarritz when the Germans caught her on her way to fetch me, I would have been re-homed, maybe in Belgium or the United States, as many Spanish refugee children were, and lost all track of my origins. Or been caught up with and turned into a fistful of ashes in a camp's oven – which would have made me Jewish. Had my father sent me to a boarding school in the United States, as he wished, I would be as American as any American today. By the time I reached New Zealand, the country which paradoxically provided me with a nationality, I had become too much of a hybrid to blend into its homogeneous population.

'Yes, but … where are your *roots*?'

The one common denominator through all the changes in my life might be my Jewishness. Though I was eight before I was told I was a 'Jew' – yet my whole life had been determined by it. *That* I shared with a large number of people spread around the world. The frequent moves, a life of exile; perhaps too my quickening heart while trying to simulate indifference when the word 'Jews' comes up: *do you like them – I mean us – or hate them?* But maybe what I shared most with other Jews – and minorities of every kind – was the sense of having been hounded for being what I was.

In Israel I finally felt like a grain of sand in a beach. Though degrees of belongingness emerged there too, for someone from the Diaspora does not belong as much as a sabra ... Even so, I felt so thoroughly accepted and integrated that I could have easily become Israeli. Though it felt flawed in the face of another people's displacement, and anyway this sense of 'belonging' started to wear thin back in the big world again. Perhaps, and paradoxically, my experience in Israel of at last 'belonging' had given me the strength to not need it, the courage to be myself without an attachment to a piece of land. And this 'being Jewish', this belonging to such a diverse people – right across the board from tall, blond, pale-skinned, blue-eyed, thoroughly European individuals to the blackest African desert communities; from Spanish, Roman Catholic *conversos* to the Indian Bnei Brit and Chinese Jews; from scientists, bankers and artists, through unremarkable, middle-class families to hoodlums and criminals; from the most tolerant and liberal to the most unswervingly orthodox religious – this 'being Jewish' was narrowed down in my own experience to the fate I had escaped, which had shaped my life and my self. Yet a sharing of this 'near-miss' did not necessarily lead to a common bond between people either – as I reflected every time I passed in the corridors of the London Hospital a European Jewish professor, who, after fifteen years of this almost daily encounter, still did not nod even faintly in my direction or hold open the door through which he had just passed when I was a few steps behind, demonstrating the alienation even between persons who might have stood side by side in their last moments in a Nazi gas chamber.

'Do you have a crisis of identity?' people have asked, thoroughly puzzled.

'On the contrary,' I felt now, having discovered that the absence of a fixed background's cumulative baggage could give me a clearer definition of myself – much as the keel of a moving boat is free from the barnacles which collect and encrust on a stationary one.

I was recognising that the many changes in my life helped me distinguish more readily the relative in us and to dispense with the inessential. It had also helped to arm me with the courage to face new problems and adjustments with dare and resolution, which must be part of a survivor's kit. But it had taken time to reach this state, and its toll too in uncertainty, hurt and insecurity … My vain effort in New Zealand to blend with my peers. And in Israel, where I did so with ease – to find that belonging to one group encouraged the rejection of others and the exclusion criteria of opposing groups are much the same in reverse.

I came to understand that my roots, in the end, were not located in some geographical site outside myself, but enmeshed in my own nature, incorporated within me, all the way from my start in life, and within my genes beyond; and my identity, a culmination of all my memories and experiences, the richer for their spread across cultures, continents and languages.

There is a central part of me that has always been stirred by the haunting majesty of mountains, a tranquil lake, a surging sea, the riotous colours of a setting sun or the captivating delicacy of a flower, the pure rhythms of Bach and tempestuous fervour of Beethoven, the beauty of line and proportion of an Etruscan porch or a Maya temple. They all reach and touch off something powerful and real inside me, regardless of time, current fashions or the predominant culture around me. And here is the constant, enduring centre of my being, my root, from which sprouts all that which makes me who I am: a flux and flow of memories, feelings, thoughts and reactions, which dissolve and return and renew, from moment to moment, interweaving the steadfast with the ephemeral of myself.

Moments, too, of reconciliation.

The table in the middle of the room is set with plates of a blue and white onion design and fluted wine glasses over a clean checked tablecloth. Three wrought-iron chandeliers, each of a different design, hang low from the high ceiling. The soft, flickering light from their tall candles intermingles with that of the terracotta oil lamps against the tower's bare stone walls on which strange criss-cross patterns of askew lights and shadows are playing. A stone stairway follows two side walls to a balcony level with the chandeliers, its railing overhung with flowerpots and framed with a pair of old faded peach brocade curtains draped like a stage backdrop overlooking the room with the set table below. Kraks has made a special effort to tidy up the worst of his usual melange and is putting the finishing touches to the gourmet meal he has invited me to, in his medieval tower in Tuscania.

He is now a respected, elderly personage; a stout, bearded figure often seen flitting around the town's cobbled streets on his dilapidated *motorino* in his cord or drill trousers, distinguished jacket and colourful silk cravat, plastic bags full of shopping swinging precariously from the handlebars. If he is not in Tuscania, he is likely to be in Salzburg. In that old city with which he has had a love-hate relationship all the way back to his teaching days in Kokoschka's school at the hilltop fortress in the Altstadt, people are now likely to come up to him and ask for his autograph as he sits sipping coffee in the Café Bazar. The *enfant terrible* of the sixties and seventies has reached something of the status of a living legend. Or other times ignored.

We are friends now. We can talk. Of people we know, memories, our daughters, our lives, problems, the funny side of things, the world. We manage the communication which had eluded us in all our twenty years of life together.

One day, I am feeling thoroughly discouraged.

'I don't know whether what I'm writing is any good. I seem to be describing only the surface of things,' I say to him.

And he answers, 'I only paint what I see, what's there.'

The next day he disagrees with himself.

'I don't paint things the way they are, because how could I ever know how they are. I paint them the way they come out of the brush.'

And, after some thought, he added, 'I paint what it looks like, what it looks like always, without the transient. The archetype. When Delbanco in his Cork Street gallery saw my little portrait of Charlotte, he said, "I have seen that somewhere." And I said of course you have seen it, a good painting has always existed.'

And he would refer to the Latin credo in the Catholic Mass, *Genitum non factum.*

Moments marking the passing of time.

On a shelf on my desk in front of me are a handful of delicate, iridescent shells. Pearly pink, frosted violet, palest buff, lucent gold. They resurrect the fresh smell of sea air, the sun's warmth on my skin, the luminous light. A small piece of La Peñita de Jaltemba in Mexico's Pacific coast. Some smooth oval stones – reddish, purple, grey – bring back to me the *cala* in Deyá. Some shimmery pieces of slate recall bright magenta cactus flowers against an emerald sea in Sardinia's Stintino.

A shell, a pebble, pieces of my life.

An old Mexican melody – and I am ten again walking past the corner cantina in Acapantzingo. A Gershwin song or Dixieland rhythm – and I am a student in Dunedin.

The thick, hand-spun, woolly Maya blanket reminds me of my quest for the writer Traven in San Cristóbal de las Casas, while the golden brown llama bedcover, still embedded with tiny twigs, of the puna in Tizón's country.

A striped mohair top knitted by Barbara Hrdlicka for little Rebekah. A tiny, yellowing vest, crocheted by my mother, that once covered Anna's chest and belly.

Outgrown clothes. An old tune. A familiar smell. A piece of the past brought vividly back to the present – its struggles, hopes, cares.

The fabric of memories. Each experience stamped into our nervous circuitry, making minute, measurable changes in the biochemistry of our brain, each sensation, observation and response engraved in anatomically re-formed and biochemically facilitated neural circuits, shaping the I which we become, yet each moment also a unit of experience, the now, both distinct from and continuous with all other moments and containing the whole of our existence within it.

Life, the self, is a string of moments. And as I stand back and watch my memories across the years flash by, so all these 'I's flit back and forth, now one, now the other, becoming interchangeable. Not only myself at every moment of my life with today's me, but also with unaccounted others in a century of human displacement and across the ages of movement and migration ... A singular life merges into the collective.

The sense of life.

That raw sense that wells up and inflames us at the full, rich, minor chords of a choral Mass, the syncopated counterpoint of a jazz musicians' jam session, the zapateo of a flamenco dance, to reach the core of our senses and human experience, devoid of artifice, that profound, timeless, quintessential sense which cuts into the quick of life, its palpitating rhythm, dignity, primeval wonder, its ultimate sense of harmony.

The way it flows out of the brush.

That which we feel so clearly and surely that there is no need to search or affirm an 'identity'. Moments in which we know who we are and sense the larger order which we are all part of.

The sea's powerful surge and fade against the rocks, the massive swell and roar, then the ease. On and on. From long before we were here to hear it, till long after we will have ceased to exist. And here the self evaporates and the mind fuses with infinity.

Globalisation and muticulturalism in the third millennium.

On a clear, starlit night, walking along the embankment by the Festival Hall in the South Bank, I come across people from every country and culture and fragments of conversation in every language. The lights from the boats and buildings opposite are replicated in their dancing reflections on the Thames River, and Waterloo Bridge and the dome of St Paul's cathedral rise above the skyline beyond – while I too am reflecting on all I have learnt on this island and from the English. Their comical sense of the absurd, a pithy satire, liberal thought, a special subtlety in our exchanges. I enjoy too the more empirical approach which goes with the English language construction. I have come to treasure these differences in my life in this city: the London of today, which also reflects the trans-racial person of tomorrow.

And I love and enjoy each place I find myself in, without missing the others, as I learn to come to terms with myself and find contentment within.

One moment at a time ...